The Springboard in the Pond

Graham Foundation / MIT Press Series in Contemporary Architectural Discourse

Graham Foundation for Advanced Studies in the Fine Arts   Chicago, Illinois

The MIT Press   Cambridge, Massachusetts   London, England

An Intimate History of the Swimming Pool

The Springboard in the Pond

edited by Helen Searing

Thomas A. P. van Leeuwen

Every reasonable effort has been made to clear the copyrights of the pictures used in this book. Any mistakes or omissions brought to the attention of the author will be rectified in subsequent printings.

 Publication of this book has been supported by a grant from the Graham Foundation for Advanced Studies in the Fine Arts.

This book was set in Caecilia by Graphic Composition, Inc. and was printed and bound in the United States of America.

Library of Congress Cataloging-in-Publication Data
Leeuwen, Thomas A. P. van.
   The springboard in the pond : an intimate history of the swimming pool / Thomas A. P.
van Leeuwen ; edited by Helen Searing.
     p.   cm. — (Graham Foundation/MIT Press series in contemporary architectural discourse)
   Includes bibliographical references and index.
   ISBN 0-262-22059-8 (hc : alk. paper)
   1. Water and architecture. 2. Swimming pools—History I. Searing, Helen. II. Title. III. Series.
NA2542.8.L44 1998
725′.74—dc21   98-8461
                                                     CIP

This book happened by itself. The idea came almost without announcement and the writing took place under the brightest of circumstances which, apart from the natural brilliance of the subject of the swimming pool, occurred thanks to the assistance of many enthusiastic supporters. The project was begun in the summer of 1989, first simply as a suggestive and amusing exercise, later as the starting point for more serious explorations. During the course of 1990, I began to feel somewhat uneasy: there was sufficient documentation on swimming but hardly anything on swimming pools. Taking it as a given that there were more pools in the United States than in the rest of the world, and that there were more (private) pools in southern California than in the rest of America, I decided to pitch my tent first in Los Angeles.

My stay in southern California was made possible by a grant from the Fulbright Foundation, by the hospitality offered by the University of Southern California at Los Angeles, and by a leave from the University of Leyden. Greater Los Angeles proved excellent hunting grounds. Digging through hedges, climbing fences, and dodging guns, dogs, and patrol cars was a welcome change from the stifling quiet of the reading rooms which, it was quite clear from the beginning, never had the intention of collecting texts on swimming pools. A heady sense of liberation came with the inevitable realization that only oneself could solve such puzzles as, for example, the identity of the first swimming pool. The affinity with Indiana Jones became so marked that eventually outward appearance and certain patterns of behavior had become similar, a not unusual circumstance in movieland. Foremost among the positive voices was Virginia Szeeman Drabbe, who mobilized a large contingent of advisors, of whom special mention should be made of Joseph and Brig Troy, Richard Colburn, Kathleen Thorne-Thompson, Ann Child, Anita and Julie Zelman, Betty Freeman, and Anthony Eckleberry. Generous assistance was provided by Mark Pentz, Fay Coupe of the *Pool and Spa News,* Charles Lockwood, and Marc Wanamaker of the Bison Archives.

Preface

During the quest others joined forces. Ken Brecher, Rebecca Rickman, and Helen Jessup alerted their far-flung agents, including Michael Webb, Ann Kerr, Thomas S. Hines, Thomas G. Smith, Ilona Von Ronay, and Doreen Nelson, who deserve my everlasting gratitude. Barbara Higgs took care of European-American relations and constantly updated my supply of Austro-German publications.

From the West Coast I worked my way through the central states to the East Coast and to the old-money estates of Long Island, where paths were cleared by Barbara Lister, Michael Somers-Abbott, and many others. And although the book happened by itself, it could only become a real book with the help of others: Roger Conover, Hubert Damisch, and Teri Damisch, who took her turn in the editing process, together with Helen Jessup, Virginia Drabbe, and Barbara Ghyczy. To Helen Searing I am indebted forever, because without her imaginative editing, inspiring criticism, and relentless energy, nothing would have gone to the printing press. As far as adventure goes, thanks have to go to my faithful companion Hudi and the big old Cadillac that steered me safely from one water hole to another.

The Springboard in the Pond

La matière est l'inconscient de la forme. Bachelard

Payne Martyn voiced the expression of the universal desire when he said of the swimming pool: "It is a walling in of a portion of an elemental thing, and owning the tenth of an acre of the deep sea and all rights and privileges thereto." Phoebe Westcott Humphreys

The Springboard in the Pond is a reflective history of the origin and the evolution of the private swimming pool as a building type. My purpose in this volume is to explore the material philosophy of water, to investigate—concentrating on the ambiguities of function—the social, religious, artistic, and technical ramifications of man's relationships with water, and, finally, to deal with the problem of form.

The pool's form is straightforward and simple, determined by its main *modus usandi*—swimming and playing. The pool is the architectural outcome of man's desire to become one with the element of water,

Introduction

privately and free of danger. A swim in the pool is a complex and curious activity, one that oscillates between joy and fear, between domination and submission, for the swimmer delivers himself with controlled abandonment to the forces of gravity, resulting in sensations of weight- and timelessness.

To secure such a high degree of individuality and control, a privately owned piece of water is a prime requisite, yet where such is not available, segments of natural bodies of water may be isolated and identified by the eloquent paraphernalia of the craft of swimming—springboards and ladders, often attached to rafts. A pond, a lake, a river may be changed into a swimming hole by the simple introduction of a springboard, which transforms any kind of water—natural, sacred, or ceremonial—into athletic water.

As a test, take a well-known piece of ceremonial water, the reflecting pool of the Washington Monument, which connects the obelisk with the Lincoln Memorial (fig. I.1), the term "reflecting pool" referring to its double function—to reflect and to inspire to reflect. Now put a springboard at one end (fig. I.2). Instantly visual perception yields to sensations of smell and touch. This almost chemical shift is but one of many manifestations of the materiality that water communicates to our senses.

Springboards have been introduced into the domain of swimming to enhance feelings of abandonment and weightlessness and as launching pads for the swimmer's eternal game with death. The swimmer is, as Gaston Bachelard worded it, "un être en vertige. Il meurt à chaque minute."[1] The embrace of water is an erotic one, yet at the same time its cool fingers presage the immediacy of mortality. Eros and Thanatos occupy the two antithetical components of the complex sensation that we call swimming, with diving as its most radical extension, for whereas the swimmer merely challenges fate, the diver insults and bullies it.

I.1.   Washington, D.C.: reflecting pool of
        Washington Monument. (Postcard.)
I.2.   Reflecting pool, with springboard.

The idea that swimming essentially is a game played by man, Eros, and Thanatos has always been found irresistible. In preceding centuries, when swimming was the sport of romantics like Byron, Swinburne, and Shelley, the art of staying afloat was not known to all, and certainly not to Shelley, who drowned miserably while beating the waves of the Mediterranean. As Charles Sprawson, swimming historian par excellence, noted, "when Shelley drowned off Viareggio, a volume of Sophocles clutched in one hand, it was the culmination of a love affair with water that influenced him to sink rather than swim. 'Arms at his side he fell submissive through the waves.' It was as though the act of swimming somehow disturbed and diluted his 'fornication avec l'onde.'"[2]

By fitting this study into my much larger projected tetralogy of the architecture of the elements, I can examine in greater range and depth the primitive force of water, its tactile quality and its powers of metamorphosis.[3] Bachelard, in a groundbreaking work on the four elements in which he explores the poetic imagination of matter, distinguishes two kinds of "forces imaginantes." The first, the "imagination formelle"—attracted to novelty, variety, and the unexpected—is interested in the external form. The second, the "imagination matérielle," concentrates on the constant, the *primitif*, and the eternal, and explores the internal shape "où la forme est interne." In further extending his distinction to the epistemology of form, attributing to vision the nominative force and to touch the cognitive one—"La vue les nomme, mais la main les connaît"—Bachelard pries open the long-closed argument that "man doesn't think matter" by inviting us to cover our eyes and try to "feel matter" again.[4] For the knowledge and perception of architecture this is a most enticing invitation; for our present investigation of the synthesis of architecture and water, it offers invaluable clues.

Epigraphs: Gaston Bachelard, *L'eau et les rêves* (1942; Paris: José Corti, 1989), 70; Phoebe Westcott Humphreys, *The Practical Book of Garden Architecture* (Philadelphia: Lippincott, 1914), 76. Who Payne Martyn is, alas, I do not know.
1. Bachelard, *L'eau et les rêves,* 218. And what Bachelard called "le complexe de Swinburne."
2. Charles Sprawson, *Haunts of the Black Masseur: The Swimmer as Hero* (London: Jonathan Cape, 1992), 76–77.
3. See my *The Skyward Trend of Thought* (Cambridge: MIT Press, 1988), on air; in preparation is my third volume, on fire: *Columns of Fire.*
4. Bachelard, *L'eau et les rêves,* 1–2. Before Bachelard, perhaps the only exception to this dictum was the sensitive John Ruskin, who claimed that he could feel the hand of the craftsman in the worked surfaces of traditional architecture, and used that quality of "feeling matter" to mark the distinction between "mere building" and architecture.

5. Dorothy Lefevre, "Geographic Aspects of the Private Swimming Pool Industry in Los Angeles" (M.A. thesis, UCLA, 1961), 9. Since literature on private pools is rare and since field studies, especially in southern California with its proverbial paranoia about security, are a hazardous business, much of my research there had to be conducted on the highest levels, literally—reconnaisance flights and aerial photography. At times this resulted in breathtaking discoveries, sometimes in mere glimpses of the real thing plus a residue of hearsay. More often, regrettably, I found that important monuments of swimming history had been updated (for hygienic reasons) so much as to be unrecognizable, or had been simply destroyed.

6. To such a degree that even recently Kelly Klein, wife of the fashion designer, felt compelled to air a long-held concern about this matter in the promotion of her glitzy, well-stocked photo album, *Pools* (New York: Knopf, 1992): "After looking for a book ... that might inspire me and help me to decide what kind of pool to build, I realized there weren't any books on pools." There are, however, catalogues, do-it-yourself manuals, and practical guides such as the $7.95 *Sunset Swimming Pools,* and a variety of pool manufacturers' magazines. With the exception of the works of Thomas D. Church, such as *Your Private World: A Study of Intimate Gardens* (San Francisco: McGraw-Hill, 1969), books on swimming pools are rare indeed and, where they appear at all, deal chiefly with public pools. The best American study on the pool-building industry, concentrating on the West Coast and including a fair number of private pools, is Fay Coupe, "Pool History: A History of the Pool and Spa Industry," *Pool and Spa News,* fifteen installments numbered I–XV (November 17, 1986–October 23, 1989). In London, The Architectural Press has published several handbooks on the design and planning of public swimming pools, among which are John Dawes, *Design and Planning of Swimming Pools* (1979), and Anthony Wilson, *Aquatecture: Architecture and Water* (1986). In France, Editions le Moniteur published *Piscines; équipements nautiques,* by Sophie Roché-Soulié and Sophie Roulet (1992), dealing exclusively with recent public pools. In the Netherlands, the photographic essay by Daria Scagliola and Peter Nijhoff, *Zweminrichtingen* (1991), provided some long-needed documentation on the country's many public pools. The German-speaking part of the world is much better represented in both the historical and the practical field, yet the two most complete studies on swimming pool history and design are already almost a century old: Felix Genzmer,

This Modest Hole in the Ground This study commenced as an architectural one, and attention is primarily focused upon the outdoor swimming pool as a building type, one that is most rewarding in its simplicity of form, its economy of materials, and in the irresistible vulgarity of its use. No other building type compares, in the purity of its mathematics and the modesty of its phenomenal appearance, to this unpretentious hole in the ground. Even garages and parking lots offer more in terms of complexity and sublimity, but they lack the pool's ceaseless power to inspire interpretation, analysis, fantasy, or just straightforward narration. The pool urges us to make excursions into the mysterious realms of mythology, the soothing depths of psychology, the adventurous heights of social biology, and the powerful history of religions and ideas (fig. I.3). But this modest hole in the ground also demands that we remain as close as possible to its original point of departure; its simple form excludes endless structural or stylistic ramifications.

So the focus is directed toward the private pool, and most of its history is traced in the country of its widest and most imaginative development, the United States. The fashion of owning a swimming pool initially appeared on the East Coast, moving later to California and more particularly to Los Angeles. Mirroring the glamour of Hollywood, Los Angeles quickly became the "swimming pool capital of the world,"[5] and that city ultimately supplies most of the reference material.

However, although in this volume the private outdoor pool plays the main part, no history could take off without attending to the early beginnings of swimming instruction and the pools that were built around it. The public floating pools of the late eighteenth and early nineteenth centuries—the first public floating baths were those in Paris, 1761, Frankfurt, 1774, and Vienna, 1781; the first floating swimming pool was installed in Vienna in 1812—offer provocative insights not only into the teaching of swimming but also into the rationale of the unique architectural form that resulted from the activity it was supposed to accommodate. Thus before we leave Europe for America and launch ourselves into the private pool, we must touch on the history of swimming, the floating pool, and some remarkable landbound public pools.

The domestication of water itself requires brief investigation as well. Consider the importance of this topic in the formation of the bourgeoisie. While continuing many feudal customs and traditions, the new rich sought to improve on the hygienic habits of their illustrious predecessors, introducing hot and cold running water and the separate bathroom or water closet, manifesting thereby not only bourgeois technical advances but a serious new attitude toward hygiene. And just as hygienic hydraulica gained ground, so did athletic. The bourgeois desire to transform bathing into swimming, to make the pool the extension of the bathroom, resulted in a revolution in the use and design of domestic water. Backyard swimming pools established themselves as decorative and practical additions to the house and the garden in a way that not even such an important building type as the private garage could match.

Yet in terms of written publicity, the swimming pool, oddly enough, has attracted scant attention, and what little there is deals predominantly with bathhouses, spas, and the act of bathing—classical, therapeutic, and so forth.[6] Moreover, the history of the swimming pool, which in more than one aspect is bifurcated into opposites, serves the other half of the term—swimming—equally badly. Although the present book is not the place to tackle such an enormous topic, I have tried to formulate a few essential questions that merit some long overdue answers: Why do people swim? Do they do so for pleasure or do they swim for survival? Are humans well equipped for swimming, or are they born drowners? If so, what drove them to build swimming pools? How do these pools follow their owners' intentions, and what, finally, do the owners do with their swimming pools?

Frogs, Swans, Penguins   The argument of this book is centered on man's attitude toward swimming, ambivalent as this may be. While almost everything evokes a two-sidedness, surely this is nowhere more manifest than with water. On the one hand there is its destructive power in the form of rainstorms, floods, and the arch-destroyer, the deluge; on the other, its life-bringing springs. Water acts as both "Naturspender" and "Erotikon," as Horst Bredekamp has so aptly written.[7]

There are three basic attitudes toward water: the hydrophilic, the hydrophobic, and the hydro-opportunistic. Hydrophilia is a direct, uncompromising longing for the wet. Surrounded by water, the wet body is "in its element"; only when resting does it seek the comfort of the dry. This is the way of the amphibian (fig. I.4). Still hydrophilic, yet less directly committed and with certain conditions and reservations, is the way of the hydro-neutral,

Bade- und Schwimmanstalten, in Josef Durm et al., eds., *Handbuch der Architektur*, 4:5:3 (Stuttgart: Arnold Bergsträsser Verlagsbuchhandlung, 1899); and W. Schleyer, *Bäder und Badeanstalten* (Leipzig: Carol Scholtze, 1909). The best modern studies on the history of the architecture of bathing and swimming are Austrian initiatives: Herbert Lachmayer, Sylvia Mattl-Wurm, and Christian Gargerle, eds., *Das Bad; eine Geschichte der Badekultur im 19. und 20. Jahrhundert* (Salzburg: Residenz Verlag, 1991), and Sylvia Mattl-Wurm and Ursula Storch, eds., *Das Bad; Körperkultur und Hygiene im 19. und 20. Jahhundert*, ex. cat. (Vienna: Eigenverlag der Museen der Stadt Wien, 1991).

More strongly represented were, and still are, the historical studies of the baths and swimming pools in hydrotherapeutical establishments and spas. With a certain regularity exhibitions are staged, with or without accompanying catalogues, and luxuriously appointed books find their way to the bookshop. Alev Lytle Croutier's *Taking the Waters* (New York: Abbeville, 1992), and the three books by Ulrika Kiby—*Bad und Badevergnügen von der Antike bis zur Gegenwart* (1993), *Badewonnen; Gestern, Heute, Morgen* (1993), and *Bäder und Badekultur in Orient und Okzident, Antike bis Spätbarock* (1995), all published by DuMont of Cologne—are the most recent. The best, however is Lise Grenier, ed., *Villes d'eaux en France* (Paris: Institut français de l'architecture, 1985). For a more extensive listing of studies on the subject, refer to the bibliography. All in all, Kelly Klein's remark was quite justified,

I.4.   Amphibians, longing for the wet. (A. J. Rösel von Rosenhof, *Historia naturalis*, 1758.)

hydro-opportunistic creature who prefers a life on land, with occasional excursions into the wet as necessary. Finally there is hydrophobia, defined in the present context as the melancholic condition of the dry body, afflicted by strong reservations about water that often are aggravated into aversion, but feeling socially, morally, or medically obligated to take to the pool with due regard to mitigating circumstances.

Hydrophilic man uses a pool for swimming, and frequently gets access by means of a diving board. Hydrophobic man employs the pool for anything except swimming, often organizing parties around it, having musicians play amid it, or floating upon it himself via inflatable beasts and small vessels that keep it from touching him directly.[8] Hydro-opportunistic man uses water only when he wants to achieve specific, water-related goals; lacking the irresistible longing of hydrophilic man, he needs other incentives—all sorts of playful, profitable, even hazardous challenges—for entering the water. For him the pool is not the end but the voyage, the cushion for a fast ride on the aquachute.

In the text these three types are metaphorically illustrated by three animals: the frog who lives in, the swan on, and the penguin next to, the water. They symbolize, respectively, the hydrophilic, the hydrophobic, and the hydro-opportunistic spirits; whether loving, hating, or just using water, they share a very great attraction to it. This includes the type who, for the sake of clarity, has here been indicated as hydrophobic but in actuality might be called "mildly hydrophilic with strong resisting tendencies."

The Sacred, The pool is very much a challenge when it comes to interpretation. Although
the Profane, it may be small in size, the range of its references and the scope and profun-
and the Vulgar dity of its meanings are overwhelming. That indeed is the beauty of this
subject. Fascinating fields such as the culture, engineering, politics, religion,
and philosophy (here mainly understood as the history of ideas) of water, as well as the history
of swimming, diving, the outdoors, and related fields of modern recreation, are brought
within reach.[9]

While the pool allows, even invites, intellectual wanderings, at the same time
it prevents the wanderer from losing his way. However far his excursions may take him, the
simplicity of the architectural object enables him to pick up the thread where he left it, leaving
no room for confusion, bombast, or contrivedness. The architectural part—the artifact—is,
from the outset, easy to define, whereas its contents—the natural part—are highly complex.
The container encloses but also retains, holds together, and keeps from spilling. While stirring
the imagination, it also prevents it from rambling; the container both kindles and quenches.
Without this paradoxical mechanism, working with the history and the philosophy of water
would simply be impossible. For the history of water per se, which incorporates the history of
life, of the world, of just about everything, threatens to become its own deluge. With the introduction of the swimming pool as focal point, however, the deluge can be evaded.

This does not mean that complexity and confusion have been altogether ban-
ished. Take, for example, the first book that caught my attention, on the basis of its fitting title,
The Treatise of the Pool. Contrary to expectations, this small volume was a theological treatise
on the sacredness of water in the thirteenth century, by Obadiah Maimonides (1228–1265).[10]
The word "pool" had nothing to do with the modern meaning but was used exclusively to
denote cistern, a collector of drinking water, which the owner had to keep flawlessly clean.
The cleanliness of the pool and the purity of the water led to a series of religious meditations
on the ways to God.

Although not what I had hoped, the book unwittingly suggested an urgent
avenue of interpretation—that water could be in different states of sanctity. Whether contained
in formally identical containers or insignificant ones—swimming pools, ponds, puddles, deep
spots in a river—water commands various states of respect, even awe. The systematics of this
transformation may be illustrated by the traditional French term for swimming pool: *piscine.*

Piscine *Piscine* (Latin *piscina*) originally meant fishpond. Quatremère de Quincy, in his
contribution to the *Encyclopédie méthodique* (1825 edition), distinguished two
sorts of *piscines:* the fishpond, designed to keep fish for commercial and domestic consumption,
later a decorative feature in the gardens of wealthy Romans such as the famed Lucullus, and
the cistern, a reservoir for drinking water.[11] But during the Christian period—something Qua-

and as far as comprehensive picture books are concerned there is no equivalent of her own *Pools.*

7. Horst Bredekamp elaborated on this theme in his contribution "Wasserangst und Wasserfreude in Renaissance und Manierismus," in Hartmuth Böhme, ed., *Kulturgeschichte des Wassers* (Frankfurt: Suhrkamp, 1988), 145–189.

8. Robert Burton, in *The Anatomy of Melancholy* (1621; London: Dent, 1972), characterizes the fear of (drinking) water as a condition in which the hydrophobic imagines various animals (dogs, asses) in the water. "Hydrophobia is a kind of madness, well known in every village, which comes by the biting of a mad dog . . . and is incident to many other creatures as well as men, so called because the parties affected cannot endure the sight of water, or any liquor, supposing still they see a mad dog in it. . . . The common cure in the country (for such at least as dwell near the sea-side) is to duck them over head and ears in sea-water."

9. The most recent publications on the cultural history of water include Böhme, ed., *Kulturgeschichte des Wassers,* and Pierre Goubert, *The Conquest of Water: The Advent of Health in the Industrial Age* (Oxford: Polity Press, 1989; originally *La conquête d'eau,* 1986). On the politics of water see Karl Witfogel, *Oriental Despotism* (New Haven: Yale University Press, 1957), and H. W. Gaebert, *Der Kampf um das Wasser* (Munich, 1973).

10. Obadiah Maimonides, *The Treatise of the Pool* (London: Octagon Press, 1981).

11. A.-C. Quatremère de Quincy, "Dictionnaire d'Architecture," in *Encyclopédie méthodique* (Paris: Panckoucke, 1788–1825), 3:132.

12. E.-E. Viollet-le-Duc, *Dictionnaire raisonné de l'architecture française du XIe au XVIe siècle* (Paris, 1854–1868), 7:187ff. "Cuvettes pratiquées ordinairement à la gauche de l'autel, dans lesquelles le célébrant faisait ses ablutions après la communion."

13. Ernest Bosc, *Dictionnaire raisonné d'architecture et des sciences et arts qui s'y rattachent,* 4 vols. (Paris, 1884), 3:511. Like most other writers on classical bathing, Bosc assumed that the Romans had used the larger pools in their bathing establishments to swim in: "Les piscines des thermes antiques atteignaient des proportions telles qu'on pouvait se livrer à la natation."

14. Léonce Reynaud, *Traité d'architecture,* 4 vols. (Paris, 1858), 2:453. The internal distribution of a modern thermal bath-spa "consiste souvent en une longue galerie, donnant entrée à l'autre dans les cabinets de bains ou de douches. Une piscine ou bassin commun, avec vestiaires, est parfois annexée aux cabinets."

15. Roché-Soulié and Roulet, *Piscines; équipements nautiques,* 4.

16. Bachelard, *L'eau et les rêves;* Böhme, *Kulturgeschichte des Wassers;* Ivan Illich, *H₂O and the Waters of Forgetfulness* (London: Boyars, 1986); Mircea Eliade, *Mythes, rêves et mystères* (Paris: Gallimard, 1957).

17. This contemporization was first proposed in the excellent series of the *Sunday Times Magazine:* "Eureka: History of Inventions," 1971.

18. The blessings of hydro-vulgarity are well known. Water has become a mere commodity that leaves the tap in two varieties, hot and cold. Toilets, dishwashers, carwashes, etc., waste enormous quantities every minute as excellent drinking water is used to flush away our excrement, clean our streets, and wash our cars. Worse, we scorn our pure drinking water for bottled sources. Swimming pools are even more insidious, not only wasting more water than the sum total of household appliances, but evaporating it in such massive quantities that entire environments are changing. The desert community of Palm Springs brings so much vapor into the air through swimming pool evaporation and sprinkler systems that not only are underground water reserves rapidly being depleted but a completely different climate is in the making.

19. Hans Surén, *Mensch und Sonne: Arisch-Olympischer Geist* (Berlin, 1924). German naturalism developed in a straight line, with only slight variations, from post–World War I health-seeking into National Socialist paramilitary combat simulations in the nude. By 1941, Surén's book was in its twelfth printing, totaling 235,000 copies. Through exercis-

tremère had no desire to discuss—the *piscine* became better known as the baptismal font, a holy-water vessel found at the entrance to a Catholic church. Viollet-le-Duc included "Piscine" in the *Dictionnaire raisonné* exclusively as a liturgical vessel, hinting neither at its profane history nor its vulgar future.[12]

As late as 1885, Ernest Bosc in his *Dictionnaire raisonné* could do no more than refer to a *piscine* in classical times as "a vessel large and deep enough to allow one or more persons to lower themselves into the water it contains," and to a *piscine* in the other meaning of the term as "a *'crédence'* [table] of natural stone that we find in churches."[13] Even Léonce Reynaud, considered by several present-day writers as a "progressive" theoretician, did little more than mention the modern variant of the Roman *thermae* in which one could occasionally find "a *piscine* or common bath."[14] It is difficult to say precisely when *piscine* became identical with swimming pool. The compilers of the most recent portfolio, *Piscines; équipements nautiques* (1991), deduced, from the fact that the *Grande encyclopédie* of 1890 still defined *piscine* exclusively as a development of the Roman *thermae* and as a liturgical vessel, that the term in the modern sense only came into use in the early twentieth century.[15]

As the meaning of the contents of the pool changed from secular to religious and back to secular—an inversion of its original interpretation—the physical composition altered as well. Like the water in Plato's theory of emanation, which gradually loses its purity on its way to civilization, the natural, life-bringing *eau vive* is set aside to make way for what is now understood as clean water free from germs. In fact, however, the water that is now considered to be fit for the *piscine* is clinically dead.

Until the advent of modern times, man's attitude toward water had been inspired by reverence and respect. Water was seen as the element of life and of death, and as such it was sacred in all respects.[16] And although water continued to be treated with respect, the general attitude changed from a religious to a philosophical and from a philosophical to a practical and aesthetic one, thus from sacred to profane to vulgar.

About the same time that the Picturesque movement carried the aesthetic attitude to its meaningfully associative limits, water also began to gain importance as a means of industrial production and as a simple, if costly, commodity with which the streets of the cosmopolis could be washed and the newly invented water closets could be flushed. Arguably, modern culture begins with the invention of the water closet, the valve closet of Alexander Cummings being patented in 1775 while Joseph Bramah logged in his improved version in 1778. The famed Thomas Crapper lent his name to a major part of our hygienic exercises, not unlike le Docteur Poubelle, whose name has become synonymous with the garbage can, and Monsieur Robinet, who has become homonymous with the water faucet he patented.[17]

The vulgarization of water, the introduction of universal hygiene, and the democratization of power were products of enlightened thinking that eventually led to the foundation of the first modern and distinctly hydro-vulgar society, that of the United States.

Surely it is no coincidence that in the years between Cummings's and Bramah's respective patents, the thirteen original colonies declared themselves independent. And although the (re)-invention of swimming was largely a product of continental enlightenment, the ideology of individualism, the increasing employment of private water, and the vast dissemination of private pools has made the United States the main hunting ground for this study.[18]

Of a different nature and of a more recent origin was another constituent of the swimming culture: the interest in physical health and athleticism. In fact, the history of swimming instruction coincides with the beginning of organized physical education in the military and the improvement of the athletic constitution by the *Turnverein*. Two military superpowers of the early nineteenth century, Austria-Hungary and Prussia, organized swimming instruction in enclosed rectangular spaces following the choreographies of military drill. Natural irregularity and freedom were deemed inimical to the development of the martial spirit.

Pools for Ponds The narrative that follows examines the origin of the man-made pool in the pond of nature, the product of a paradoxical play of nature and artifice where man relived his evolutionary past as an aquatic ape in the company of frogs and fish. At first, man, like the baby that leaves the womb, swam instinctively, without fear; then, at a certain point in his evolutionary life, he developed hydrophobic anxieties. Swimming stopped being automatic and the art of swimming had to be taught.

The history of swimming became the history of the instruction of swimming. Pools began to resemble parade grounds or classrooms as insouciant paddling was replaced by drill and exercise—breaststroke, sidestroke, backstroke, crawl—and the pool became a center for survival strategies. The springboard acted as a therapeutic means to cure the swimmer's original fear of unfathomable depths. High boards and diving towers first cultivated, then helped him to overcome, his angst. The excitement of the free fall, of ultimate weightlessness, became an addiction. At that moment the nervous balance between controlled hydrophobia and restrained hydrophilia tilted in favor of reckless hydro-ecstatica. This was the period of Leni Riefenstahl's flying divers and the "Aktkultur" naturalists of Hans Surén, who gave free rein to their "Aryan-Olympic Spirit" in the water-rich territories of northern Germany.[19]

In America, the hydrophilic period manifests its most radical efflorescence in and around Hollywood. Instead of exposing their skin to the pallid sun of the Baltic, Americans delivered their bodies to the sun-beaten pools of southern California, either in physical reality or virtually, on the tinsel screen, which reflected the high point of American swimming. In the neo-bourgeois period after the Second World War, a strong tendency toward coziness, family togetherness, neo-puritanism, and all the other war-related regressions replaced Eros and Thanatos with family-oriented socializing. The swimming pool and its hydro-opportunistic attractions became the center of family life. Activities—cookouts on Sundays, fully dressed

ing, swimming, and camping in the nude, modern Germans looked back to the original Germanic tribes, when men and women alike were famed for their ability to swim. See also Sprawson, *Haunts of the Black Masseur,* 218–219.

—9

20. *New York Times*, Home Section, June 27, 1991, C1.

sunbathing and uninspired swimming in Bermuda shorts, floating on rubber mattresses, playing volleyball in pools that become shallower every day—developed not so much in as on or around the pool.

Then spreading litigation further diluted the experience; aquachutes arrived and the diving board was expelled. The relentless march of litigation, combined with an increasingly all-consuming, apocalyptic fear of, and for, the environment, led to the gradual drying up of most private as well as public swimming waters. We are left with a growing number of indoor aqua-amusement parks, where the open air has been exchanged for the stifling temperatures of the digitally controlled hothouse and swimming is replaced by hydro-opportunistic voyages in serpentine tubes.

An entire history of sanctity and sacrilege, of sacredness and profanity, may be found within these developments. Yet at the end, the story has reversed itself. If the pond became pool, now—as we can read in the media of our times—the pool has reverted to the pond: "You don't see many diving boards in pools these days," the *New York Times* informed its readers. "They want pools to pass for ponds."[20] This is where the book ends.

one

Dreams, Tactics, and the Floating Swimming Pool

Fleeing and Flying

1.1. Robert Tait McKenzie, *Le Plongeur/The Diver*, 1923. (Montreal, Musée des Beaux-Arts/ Museum of Fine Arts.)

A fundamental principle of synchronized swimming is that what you are keeping afloat is not really your body, but the illusion that water is not different from land or air. JEANNE RUDOLPH

Tom was now quite amphibious. You do not know what that means? You had better, then, ask the nearest Government pupil-teacher, who may possibly answer you smartly enough, thus: "Amphibious. Adjective, derived from two Greek words, amphi, a fish, and bios, a beast. . . ." CHARLES KINGSLEY

The history of human swimming has been written following the lines of its two basic rationales: the voluntary and the involuntary. It has been suggested that the problem of human swimming could just as easily be approached as the problem of human drowning.[1] The point is that swimming does not come naturally to man; it has to be taught. Without having been taught to swim, man is bound to drown. Everything he undertakes to overcome this condition could be explained as the continuous battle against what by nature he does best: sink.

Olphar Hamst (Ralph Thomas), the witty compiler of publications on swimming written before 1876, observed that "Diderot et d'Alembert's *Encyclopaedie* [sic; 1765] contains a short general article, and mentions Winman [Wynman], Digby and Thévenot as having written on the subject, and that if the latter had read Borelli's *De Motu Animalium* he would never have made such a mistake as to assert that men could swim naturally."[2] Compared to all other swimming fellow creatures, man performs miserably. Even Olympic gold medalist Aleksandr Popov (Barcelona, 1992, and Atlanta, 1996) could not exceed an average of c. 7.5 kilometers per hour over a mere 100 meters, hardly better than somebody taking a brisk, but not too brisk, walk. Frantically flapping his arms and legs, Popov squandered energy on almost anything but gaining distance. Only one animal that swims at all is less efficient at it: the mink. Man's technique of swimming is mechanical, and certainly not natural.[3] Yet there are reasons to suppose that this has not always been the case.

For a very short period, from birth to about four months of age, swimming *does* come naturally to man.[4] The current thinking, based on Ernst Haeckel's formulation of 1866 that "each individual, during his development, 'recapitulates' the evolutionary history of the species," is to link this phenomenon with the idea that man originally had gone through an aquatic phase of evolution. This theory of the aquatic ape was first developed in 1929 by marine biologist Alister Hardy.[5]

The Aquatic The aquatic ape theory is based on the assumption that man, unlike the
Ape other primates, underwent an aquatic phase of evolution. The theory has gained in popularity since the 1960s and has recently been presented to a wider audience by Elaine Morgan.[6] The outcome of the crossing of two disciplines, marine biology and evolutionary human biology, the aquatic ape theory has gained substantial support but still must confront a multitude of critical questions. Nevertheless, for historians of swimming it is indispensable.

Without an aquatic past, swimming and diving were bound to have stayed outside the grasp of human development. The Aquatic Ape Conference of 1987 concluded: "As a result, we humans today have the ability to learn to swim without too much difficulty, to dive and to enjoy occasional recourse to water."[7] But this attractive explanation is based on circumstantial rather than hard or fossil evidence and cannot reconstruct the missing links between man and species such as sea mammals, links suggested by man's upright posture—inevitable for a creature spending much time wading—his streamlined silhouette, the absence of body hair, the subcutaneous deposits of fat, and the occasional webbings between fingers and toes.

Oceanic Notwithstanding its shortcomings, the aquatic ape theory still offers promis-
Feeling ing perspectives on the problem of swimming. If we fuse Haeckel's Law of evolutionary recapitulation with the hydrophilic babies described by obstetrician Michel Odent (see note 4), we will arrive at the speculative theory that in newborn infants a genetic memory is activated by which the aquatic episode of mankind is reenacted. The unconscious hydrophilia of the baby could be seen as a residual "marker," a rudimentary gene that has been with us for the last five million years, to be superseded by a series of hydrophobic impulses of an increasingly stronger composition. It is entirely possible, however, that hydrophilic-genetic memory is activated in the fetal period, during which the infant is kept in a state of hydraulically controlled weightlessness in the amniotic water of the womb.

Epigraphs: Jeanne Rudolph, *Psychoanalysis and Synchronized Swimming and Other Writings on Art* (Toronto: YYZ, 1991), 5. This remarkable book was brought to my attention by a synchronic source. Charles Kingsley, *The Water-Babies: A Fairy Tale for a Land-Baby* (1863; London: Macmillan, 1889), 84.

1. Jan Wind, "The Non-Aquatic Ape: The Aquatic Ape Theory and the Evolution of Human Drowning and Swimming," in Machteld Roede et al., eds., *The Aquatic Ape: Fact or Fiction?* (London: Souvenir Press, 1991), 263–264.

2. Olphar Hamst, *A List of Works on Swimming from the Invention of Printing to the Present Time Bound Together with R. Harrington, A Few Words on Swimming* (London, 1876), 1. (Thanks to Jacob Voorthuis, Kingston, Jamaica.)

3. Dick Wittenberg, "Mens is geboren verdrinker," *NRC/Algemeen Handelsblad*, July 27, 1993.

4. French gynecologist and obstetrician Michel Odent, in a series of experiments originally directed toward delivery of babies in lukewarm water, a zero-gravity environment that guarantees a seamless transition that benefits both mother and child, discovered as a corollary that human infants were able to move freely in water for the first few months of their lives, only to lose that ability immediately afterward. *Bien naître; la naissance sans violence en pratique* (Paris: Seuil, 1976); *Genèse de l'homme écologique; l'instinct retrouvé* (Paris: EPI, 1981).

Desmond Morris noted that "human babies can swim when only a few weeks old. If placed in water they do not struggle but make reflex swimming movements, which actually propel them forward. They show breathing control, inhibiting their respiration when submerged. Young apes tested in this way failed to show these reactions." Could this be, Morris speculated, "the awakening of some primeval response from man's ancient past?" *Manwatching: A Field Guide to Human Behavior* (New York: Abrams, 1982), 296–297.

5. Roede et al., eds., *The Aquatic Ape*, passim.

6. Elaine Morgan, *The Scars of Evolution: What Our Bodies Tell Us about Human Origins* (London: Pelican Books, 1991). Originally published by Souvenir Press, 1990.

7. Roede et al., eds., *The Aquatic Ape*.

8. Michael Balint, *Thrills and Regressions* (New York: International Universities Press 1959), 73. Jeannot Simmen of Berlin directed my attention to this important study.

9. Ibid., 75–76. The concept of regression and the feeling of being separated from a former blissful state of existence have become popular again in our times, as all sorts of angst scenarios have been cooked up by a panicking mankind afraid to lose control over the earth's resources, in particular when faced by the declining quality of air and water.

10. Salvador Dalí, *The Secret Life of Salvador Dalí* (1942; London: Vision Press, 1968), 27–29. Prompted by memories from his intrauterine existence, the great vertiginous ecstatic wrote: "Surely most of my readers have experienced that violent sensation of feeling themselves suddenly fall into the void just at the moment of falling asleep, awakening with a start.... You may be sure that this is a case of brutal and crude recall of birth, reconstituting thus the dazed sensation of the very moment of expulsion and of falling outside.... But after this moment of pre-sleep anxiety, sleep—'this most delightful and exceptionally longed for and refreshing sleep'—has set in, 'dreams of flight' provide the sleeper with feelings of erotic well-being, also called 'the conquest of paradise.' The 'dream of flight' is nothing but a memory of the state of weightlessness, which the unborn has undergone in-utero."

11. Dalí illustrated his image of the uterine paradise with the assistance of Jean-Auguste-Dominique Ingres's *Le bain turc* juxtaposed to a picture of Dalí himself curled up in an eggshell. (See fig. 2.6.)

12. See Jeannot Simmen's captivating analysis of the theme of weightlessness in *Vertigo: Schwindel in der modernen Kunst* (Munich: Klinkhardt & Biermann, 1990). Ernst Gombrich, explaining Poussin's painting *Orion Shot by Diana*, showed the humiliated hunter in anxious confrontation with a visibly wadable stream. Chased by Diana, the unfortunate giant could only escape her arrows and the snake (one of her amazingly modern remote-controlled weapons) by crossing a river in a hasty and confused mixture of wading and swimming. ("Poussin's Orion," *Burlington Magazine* 84 [1944], 38.) Similar in intention is the gruesome story of the hunter Actaeon, during a quasi-accidental erotic encounter with—again—a bathing Diana. The vengeful deity punishes him by transforming him into the phenomenal guise of his own prey: a stag. Naturally his own dogs turn against him, and in an effort to escape them he has to swim away from the scene of his mischief. After crossing the stream he takes to the mountains:

Presumed aquatic phases of early mankind are often traceable in legends and myths as well as in the tales of religions in their archaic phases. In both the "collective unconscious" of Jung and the psychoanalytic work of Freud, indications of "oceanic" residues are present. Sigmund Freud described the sensation of weightlessness as a feeling of "eternity," of something limitless, unbounded, "oceanic."[8] Psychologist Sándor Ferenczy elaborated on the idea of floating sensations and the attraction to water in an article in 1924 called "Thalassa," in which he combined Freud's suggestion of memories of being rocked in the mother's arms with his own idea of reminiscences of the stay in the mother's womb. Over the years Ferenczy's elaborations on the *Flugtraum* theme, such as his concept of the symbolic identity of baby and penis and his phylogenetic theory of coitus producing a somewhat exalted feeling of oneness with the environment, have accentuated some interesting aspects of the joy of swimming. The *Flugträume* and the oceanic feeling are to be regarded, Michael Balint explained, "as the repetition either of the very early mother-child relationship or of the still earlier intra-uterine existence, during which we were really one with our universe and were really floating in the amniotic fluid with practically no weight to carry." The regressive tendency is to be explained as the "wish fulfilling memories of all these states," and thus, concluded Balint, "conversely, these states activate a strong attraction for regression."[9]

The Joy of Swimming The regressional tendency, whereby we long to return to the former blissful state of intrauterine experience, definitively represents the voluntary or joyful rationale for swimming. Salvador Dalí, who made it his lifelong mission to challenge the concept of mental sanity, developed a theory of salutary weightlessness and thus contributed to the concept of joyful swimming. Apart from diving from springboards, racing down steep stairways, or hiding under tables, Dalí claimed that sensations of flying and floating could nowhere be better experienced than in the mother's womb.[10]

Flying and falling can be transposed into swimming and diving. By diving the swimmer retraces the expulsion from paradise, brought about by birth, in the certainty that his fall will be broken by water. The water of the pool acts as shock absorber for a gradual reentry into paradise. Once in the water, a state of weightlessness envelops the diver, who becomes swimmer the moment he loses his postnatal anxiety and returns to the womb, where he regains his original state of intense well-being. In that sense diving and swimming belong to the same order of existential experience, just as Jonah and the Whale belong to each other: the dangerous journey ends in the ultimate safety of the "whomb."[11]

Involuntary Swimming In contrast to voluntary or hedonistic swimming, involuntary or forced swimming belongs, from the very beginning, to the much larger complex of heroic epics and the art of warfare. It is interesting to note that heroic acts of water-crossing by means of wading, swimming, or "swimming with ground contact" (historians are still not very much in agreement on what archaic swimming actually was like) were more likely performed as part of evasive than of aggressive actions. Fear of water was overcome by fear of a more frightening menace. Indeed in many classical sagas the dream of flying changes into the nightmare of fleeing—ferocious manhunts often resulted in heroic attempts at swimming. Since the gist of these stories is obviously generated by subconscious fears of drowning, such acts point more toward an instinctive *horror aquae* than to a relatively balanced attitude toward the element.[12]

De arte natandi It is hardly surprising that the strategic and tactical use of swimming became of paramount importance to those tribes and nations that were dependent for their very existence on success in battle. The Germans and the Romans were well aware of this. Military historian Vegetius (c. 400 A.D.) wrote in his *De re militaria*: "Recruits have to be taught swimming and its employment in warfare in summer. Rivers and bridges are not always negotiable and, especially during a forced retreat or while fleeing, the army has to resort to swimming. During periods of abundant precipitation rivers will overflow their banks and those who cannot swim will either perish by drowning or by the hands of the enemy."[13]

The institutionalization of military swimming in Rome led to the creation of the first swimming school in history. According to Vegetius, "Therefore the ancient Romans, who had fought so many battles and who had to endure so many dangers, had learned much about all this and so they built their swimming school near the Campus Martius in the river Tiber."[14] Piranesi, who in 1762 published his "scenographic" urbanistic reconstruction of the Campus Martius, faithfully added two military (?) swimming schools, *natationes*, designed as circular and triangular inlets of the river Tiber.

From here on, the history of swimming may best be pieced together from the history of its own instruction; what occurred before that time remains uncertain. Swimming in the Greco-Roman period has been adequately documented, but the references are generally restricted to gods, heroes, deified emperors, and other mythical beings.[15] For the rest, particularly with regard to Roman *thermae*, swimming is often confused with adventurous bathing. Most *frigidaria* (the German *Bewegungsbad* comes closest to their original meaning) were hardly deeper than 1.0–1.1 meters, encouraging a swimming style that children tend to practice when they are not yet able to go into the deep—"swimming with ground contact."

By walls of rock, on daunting trails or none,
He fled where often he'd followed in pursuit.

(Ovid, *Metamorphoses*, trans. A. D. Melville [Oxford, 1986], 57.)
But by the very trick he had taught his dogs, they outmaneuver and kill him. In the Actaeon story all the ingredients of the *Angsttraum* have been conjured up: unsuccessful flight, swimming, and vertiginous pursuit.

The exploit of Horatius Cocles, the Roman hero, is somewhat similar, but turns out well. The giant of a soldier has orders to keep the Etruscans at bay while his own troops break down a bridge to prevent the enemy crossing a river. Ultimately forced to withdraw, the only way left to him is to jump in the river and swim, notwithstanding that he was in full armor. See Erwin Mehl, *Antike Schwimmkunst* (Munich, 1927), 65, and S. Reinach, *Revue archéologique* 1 (1915), 155. The subconscious fear of drowning has been effectively woven into the story by mention of the armor weighing down the already heavy and exhausted body of the soldier, who has to invoke the help of Tiber, the river god, to keep him from drowning and enable him to swim to his own side.

The Horatius Cocles story is often used to illustrate the alleged ability of the fighting heroes of antiquity to swim. Julius Caesar, Scipio Africanus, and Sertorius, scourage of the Teutonic tribes, all accomplished swimmers, were also specifically mentioned by historians and mythographers, not simply because they could swim but because they could do it under dire and uncanny circumstances (Mehl, *Antike Schwimmkunst*, 62 [Caesar], 72 [Scipio], 75 [Sertorius]). It is hardly accidental that they were wearing unsuitable outfits for swimming: on the run, escaping more pressing catastrophes, they hardly had time to change. Or take the tale of Cloelia. In Livy's version, the virgin daughter of a noble Roman is, with her handmaidens, given as hostage to the Etruscan king, Porsena. Led by Cloelia, the girls escape from Porsena's camp through enemy lines and into the Tiber. They undress, bind their clothes on their heads, and swim through a barrage of arrows back to their own lines. But the poor maidens had no knowledge of the diplomatic dealing that had been going on and, upon their safe arrival, are sent back to the Etruscans. Porsena is so overwhelmed by Cloelia's bravery that he grants her freedom. (Ibid., 67.) Livy does not tell us whether after she had regained her freedom she had to get into the river for a third time. An interesting discussion of

1.2. Jan ten Compe (1713–1761), attributed to,
Bathers in the Boerenwetering, Amsterdam,
detail. (Amsterdam, Historisch Museum;
reprinted from Carasso-Kok, *Amsterdam
Historisch,* 1975.)

Only two avenues can lead to a realistic picture of the state of swimming: a bibliographic survey of texts on swimming and the historiography of its systematic instruction. Several works on swimming from the late nineteenth century give a clear picture of the spasmodic survival of Nicolaus Wynman's and Everard Digby's sixteenth-century treatise, *De arte natandi*. As late as 1876, Olphar Hamst, in his invaluable bibliographic study *A List of Works on Swimming from the Invention of Printing to the Present Time,* saw little advancement in the art of swimming since Digby's treatise.[16]

With the fall of the Roman Empire the art of swimming faded from memory. It was only in the wake of the new educational spirit of the Enlightenment, and after the development of the great professional armies during the time of the Napoleonic wars, that it was seriously reinvented. So, with a break of about 1,500 years, the history of swimming could be taken up in the second half of the eighteenth century.

Although corporeal hygiene, bathing, and swimming were strictly out of bounds to the general public in the Middle Ages and during those periods when Christian prudery ruled politics, this did not necessarily apply to the higher echelons of society or to those communities where clerical control could be ignored. In the Netherlands during the seventeenth century, the more rustic social strata still could find some innocent fun in nude bathing in lakes and ditches (fig. 1.2), and painters like Henrick ten Oever and Nicholaes Maes have recorded several scenes of al fresco swimming in the Dutch countryside. The art of swimming, as opposed to mere bucolic frolicking, was the coveted pastime, and very special secret, of kings and princes, millionaires and military leaders.

Education and Swimming in the Age of Light During the Enlightenment interest in the therapeutic and athletic uses of water received new stimuli,[17] yet it took time and much revolutionary rhetoric before these were accepted as an indispensable part of the educational curriculum. Even among the very wealthy, swimming was not particularly favored because it was not considered to be sufficiently prestigious. Young gentlemen of the better circles of society were taught to ride on horseback but not to swim. "Yet," Rousseau stated in his challenging *Emile, ou de l'éducation* (1762), "nobody has ever been forced at the risk of losing one's life to mount a horse, whereas the risk of drowning frequently occurs to everyone. Emile must be as agile in the water as on the land. If only he could live in all elements! If he could learn to fly I would make him an eagle, and if he could harden himself in the fire I would make him a salamander."[18]

A dramatic change in attitudes toward the physical and the natural took place in the mid-eighteenth century. The principles of education inspired fierce debate, in which *Emile,* dealing with a more "natural" and therefore less doctrinal rural state, was probably the most popular work in the western part of Europe. Johann Bernard Basedow's *Elementarwerk* or

Rubens's representation of the story is provided by Hessel Miedema, "De Tiber en de zwemmende maagden: een afknapper," *Nederlands Kunsthistorisch Jaarboek* 19 (1968), 133–155.

The Horatius Cocles and Cloelia sagas belong to a larger body of escape stories that are predominantly of a military character. For more, see the tales of Turnus, the opponent of Aeneas, and of Metabus and Camilla in Mehl, *Antike Schwimmkunst,* 63–65.

13. Ibid., 69. Soldiers were supposed to be able to swim, and so were their leaders. This must have been the case in even the most ancient military histories. Of Egyptian swimming, for example, what little is known of it usually applies to some important battle: "Descriptions of swimming figures are found only in accounts of the Battle of Qadesh, when Rameses II faced a strong coalition of princes and tribes on the Orontes in the 5th year of his reign." A. D. Touny and Dr. Stefan Wenig, *Sport in Ancient Egypt* (Leipzig: Edition Leipzig, 1969), 27.

14. Mehl, *Antike Schwimmkunst,* 69.

15. Mehl's study from 1927, however, is still the most complete source.

16. For Hamst, see note 2 of this chapter. Wynman's *Colymbetes, sive de arte natandi; dialogus & festivus & iucundus lectu* (Ingolstadt, 1538) is a distinct rarity. More accessible is Everard Digby's version of the amusing dialogue between Geronicus and Nugenus, *De arte natandi* (London, 1587). Although the text is in Latin, the contents bear no relation to classical knowledge of swimming. Olphar Hamst's witty remarks on the books he catalogued are still very useful. On Digby: "On the whole, the instructions are good, though not sufficient to make a perfect swimmer, as its author expected; and taking into consideration its early date it is the best book that has been written on the subject. The grandfather of Sir Kenelm Digby must have been an expert and true lover of the art, and from his work it appears that little progress has been made since he wrote" (1). It is true that the bulk of treatises on swimming do not deal with the technique of swimming, but rather with machines to facilitate a stay in the water. The most complete bibliography up till 1903 is by Archibald Sinclair, *Swimming* (1893; London, 1903).

17. The first serious study on ancient swimming was prepared in 1777 by Ameilhon, "Recherches sur l'exercice du nageur chez les anciens," *Histoire de l'Académie des Inscriptions* (Paris, 1777), 38:11–28. Monsieur d'Aumont, who contributed the article "Natation" to the *Encyclopédie* (Geneva, 1778), worded his doubts about the ancients' ability to swim:

"On observera ici, qu'il ne faut pas confondre la *natation,* qui est l'action de nager, avec une sorte de *natation,* qui, dans le sens des anciens, etait une manière de se baigner dans un vase beaucoup plus grand que les baignoires ordinaires."

18. Here Rousseau refers to the popular belief that the salamander could survive in fire. Jean-Jacques Rousseau, *Emile ou de l'éducation* (1762; Paris: Edition La renaissance du livre, n.d.), tome premier, livre second, 141–142: "Une éducation exclusive … préfère toujours les instructions le plus coûteuses aux plus communes.... Ainsi les jeunes gens élevés avec soin apprennent tous à monter à cheval, parce qu'il en coûte beaucoup pour cela; mais presque aucun d'eux n'apprend à nager parce qu'il n'en coûte rien, et qu'un artisan peut savoir nager aussi bien que qui que soit … mais dans l'eau, si l'on ne nage on se noie, et l'on ne nage point sans l'avoir appris.... Emile sera dans l'eau comme sur la terre. Que ne peut-il vivre dans tous les éléments! Si l'on pouvait apprendre à voler dans les airs, j'en ferais un aigle!"

19. It was Sigfried Giedion who introduced Basedow into the history of swimming-as-regeneration, as "one of the first to incorporate swimming, fencing, riding and outdoor life in education." "The Mechanization of the Bath," in *Mechanization Takes Command* (1948; New York: Oxford University Press, 1969), 653, fig. 454. An abbreviated version, translated into German, appeared in *Werk* 44, no. 9 (1957), 295–297. Later than Basedow, but highly important as the first institutionalizer of physical education, was Theodor Chr. Fr. Guts Muths (or Guthsmuths or Gutsmuths), author of *Spiele zur Uebung und Erhohlung des Körpers und Geistes, für die Jugend, ihre Erzieher und alle Freunde unschuldiger Jugendfreuden* (Schnepfenthal, 1796), as well as of *Lehrbuch der Schwimmkunst* (Weimar, 1798).

20. Giedion, enthusiastic advocate of modernist hygienism, manifested an early interest in the technicalities and architecture of pre-twentieth-century bathing and swimming. (*Das Bad im Kulturganzen,* 1935; "The Mechanization of the Bath" in *Mechanization Takes Command.*) The most recent source for the Parisian river baths is *Deux siècles d'architecture sportive à Paris; piscines, gymnases …* (Paris: Délégation à l'action artistique de la ville de Paris, Mairie du XXe arrondissement, 1984). The boat of Docteur Poitevin accommodated hot and cold baths, steam baths, and a barber and wigmaker's shop. The baths were opened to the public in 1761.

21. Giedion, *Mechanization Takes Command,* 654–655. See also Hans Kraemer, ed., "Der Mensch und das Wasser," in *Der*

"Elements of Education" of 1774, a study of the role of physical training as a part of elementary education, was more influential in the eastern regions, but both Rousseau and Basedow shared a practical philosophy aimed at "hardening" mind and body.[19]

In *Emile,* for example, Rousseau suggested that various degrees of "hardening" could be achieved if babies could be bathed in water that was gradually decreased in temperature. The important role that aquatic hygiene would begin to play may be illustrated by the advance of a new type of amphibious architecture: the floating bath and the floating pool.

Floating Baths Just as the *natatio* of the Campus Martius was no more than a simple broadening of the river, so the early eighteenth-century floating baths and pools were but part of river life. Floating baths, *bains flottants* or *Flussbäder,* first made an appearance in Paris, Frankfurt, and Vienna in the 1760s, at about the time of the publication of *Emile.* The first documented floating bath on the Seine was that of Docteur Poitevin. Sigfried Giedion highlighted the role of the good doctor who, in deference to the dictate that bathing was acceptable chiefly for its medicinal benefits, could only open his public bath by invoking the endorsement of the "Doyens et Docteurs Regens" of the faculty of medicine.[20]

In 1760 Poitevin began to accommodate his warm baths and showers on a specially constructed barge that was anchored in the river Seine.[21] Plans of the Poitevin barge were published in the *Encyclopédie* in the same year as *Emile,* 1762.[22] Maxime Du Camp, chronicler of Second Empire Paris, confirmed that the first floating hot baths were indeed those of Poitevin, whose widow, "the moment he died, married his bathing manager Vigier, who was responsible for making the bathing trade into a vastly expanding and highly respectable business."[23] The Vigier baths remained popular up to the time when most households were beginning to be connected to the city's main water supply, in the mid-nineteenth century.

In his seminal study *Bäder und Badeanstalten* (1909), Wilhelm Schleyer identifies Frankfurt as the first city to have a public floating swimming bath, in the river Main; it opened the same year as Basedow's *Elementarwerk* was published—1774—to be followed in 1800 by a *Badeschiff,* a bathing barge.[24] Vienna was a close runner-up, with a floating bathhouse in the Danube near the Augarten, designed by the municipal and judicial physician Pascal (or Pasqual) Joseph Ferro in 1781 (fig. 1.3). With exquisite timing, Ferro launched his bathing barge in the same year that he published its pictures in his pioneering study *Vom Gebrauche der kalten Bäder,* in which he advocated the medical use of free, natural, cold water as superior to the temperature-controlled water of the bathhouses. The Ferro bath consisted simply of two rows of changing cabins girded together on a floating platform. Access to the river was through a hole in each cabin, where a generously permeable wooden barrel was hung. The bather was just to sit there exposed to the cold and dark water of the river; if he could hardly be expected to derive any enjoyment from it, he might safely experience beneficial medicinal effects.[25] This

1.3. Vienna: design for Ferro baths, 1781.
(Lachmayer, Mattl-Warm, and Gargerle, eds.,
Das Bad, 1991.)

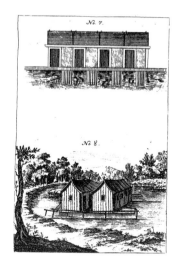

kind of bathing was definitively different from swimming; on the whole a sedentary affair, it belonged in the medico-social realm.[26]

Floating Pools Floating pools, and the swimming schools they often accomodated, appeared some thirty years after floating baths. The first "floating" swimming school, later destroyed by ice, was founded in 1786 by a swimming instructor called Barthélémy Turquin.[27] Before he was able to establish his *école de natation*, Turquin was forced to endure several years of litigation with Poitevin, who claimed exclusive title to the privilege of exploiting a bathing barge on the river. But Turquin prevailed, even upgrading his school to *école royale de natation*. Installed in 1796 on the Seine off the Quai d'Orsay, Turquin's establishment subsequently became even better known as the royal swimming school of his son-in-law, Deligny.

The popularity of swimming was considerably enhanced by the circumstance that France was involved in building the largest army ever raised, an army in perpetual need of swimmers, swimming instructors, and teaching establishments.[28] So when Deligny wanted to build a *bain flottant* for his swimming school, he derived its plan and arrangement from an engraving in Docteur Le Roux's 1782 supplement to one of many variations on Thévenot's *L'art de nager*, originally published in 1696, perhaps because that also had been directed toward a public of young soldiers and—a novelty—navy men. ("Ouvrage utile à tout le monde, et destiné particulièrement à l'éducation des jeunes militaires du Corps Royal de la Marine.")[29] Deligny came up with a barge measuring 106 by 30 meters, which was not freely floating but partly supported on wooden pilings. Around a central rectangle, left open for the water of the river

Mensch und die Erde (Leipzig: Deutsches Verlagshaus, 1912), 9:81.

22. Kraemer, ed., "Der Mensch und das Wasser," 82–83. An unusual personality during French Revolutionary times must have been the multitalented techno-philosopher and proto-aviator Jean-François Pilâtre de Rozier, famed for his experimental flights with Montgolfière-type balloons, who presented himself as "maître de natation." Simon Schama tells us that "a certain Pilâtre, inventor and swim instructor, offered demonstrations of a drysuit in or about the month of February, 1782. Over seven hundred subscribers signed on from all ranks and conditions and heard Pilâtre himself lecture on the art of swimming as well as demonstrate a watertight robe by emerging dry from a bath filled to a depth of six feet." (Schama, *Citizens: A Chronicle of the French Revolution* [New York: Knopf, 1989], 126–127, and note on 885.)

23. Maxime Du Camp, *Paris, ses organes etc.* (Paris, 1875), chap. 5, 327 (1993 reprint, 112–113): "lorsqu'il mourut, épousa son garçon baigneur, Vigier, qui devait donner à ce genre d'industrie une célébrité et une extension considérables."

24. W. Schleyer, *Bäder und Badeanstalten* (Leipzig: Carol Scholtze, 1909), 273.

25. Dr. Pascal Joseph Ferro, *Vom Gebrauche der kalten Bäder* (Vienna, 1781). Illustrated in Sylvia Mattl-Wurm and Ursula Storch, eds., *Das Bad; Körperkultur und Hygiene im 19. und 20. Jahrhundert*, ex. cat. (Vienna: Eigenverlag der Museen der Stadt Wien, 1991), 30. Ferro's example

was followed all over Europe. In Holland, where Germanic mores tended to leave a deeper impression than French ones, a Ferro-type barge called "Bade Anstalt" was docked in the river Amstel, at the Oude Turfmarkt, Amsterdam (1844–1912; see below).

26. Ferro's main concern, however, was to take bathing out of the bathhouse into free nature. That neither nature nor society was ready for taking the waters al fresco was a small obstacle that Ferro thought could be overcome by installing mesh casks below and cabins all around to keep onlookers out. Ferro's spirit must have been congenial to Theodor Guts Muths (1759–1839; see note 19), who established a so-called "philanthropic" or reform school (*Erziehungsanstalt*) in Schnepfenthal, for physical, moral, and practical education. Guts Muths's example was followed by Friedrich Wilhelm Jahn (1780–1852; see below). Influential also was the Swiss educator Johann Heinrich Pestalozzi (1746–1827) with his article "Über Körperbildung," *Wochenschrift für Menschenbildung* (Aarau, 1807).

Exposure of the body to fresh air and especially water was the specialty of the "water doctor" (*Wasserdoktor*) Vinzenz Priessnitz (1799–1851), founder of a center for hydrotherapy in Gräfenberg, Schlezien, which became a popular spa (*Kurort*) from 1830. Priessnitz's method had an impressive following in the Anglo-American world, as at Dr. Richard Barter's spa, "the Irish Gräfenberg," in Saint Ann's, of 1856. See Giedion, *Mechanization Takes Command*, 670–671.

Other famous hydrotherapists were Pfarrer Sebastian Kneipp (1821–1897), M. Platen, *Die neue Heilmethode* (Berlin and Leipzig, 1899), and F. E. Bilz, *Die neue Naturheilmethode* (c. 1900). In America, Bernarr Macfadden, *MacFadden's Encyclopaedia of Physical Culture* (1911, 10th ed., New York, 1928), ruthlessly applied Teutonic methods of rigorous fasting and swimming in subfreezing temperatures to harden his spoiled countrymen.

27. Barthélémy Turquin, *Avis au public sur l'établissement d'une école de natation* (Paris, 1786; copy in the Bibliothèque Nationale); see *Deux siècles d'architecture sportive à Paris*, 39. Originally most "swimming instructors" were quasi-professional lifesavers, frequently Bretons who had earned their livelihood saving shipwrecked mariners. Only a few made it to the elevated level of the Parisian *écoles de natation*.

28. Already in the seventeenth and early eighteenth centuries spas were established expressly for the rehabilitation of the wounded—in Saint-Amand (1698), Bourbonne (1718), and Amélie. Mattl-Wurm and Storch, eds., *Das Bad*, 200.

Seine, four wooden pontoons were interconnected and covered with decks on which a variety of structures were erected: "340 changing cabins, distributed over two floors, six private salons, seven common rooms. . . ." There was an "appartement" reserved for members of the royal family, with an "antichambre," a waiting room, a salon, and a private exit. In addition to the "rotonde" or "amphithéâtre" with a café, a restaurant, and a club room, there was an instruction room where swimming was taught "dry," a first aid post with a bed, a barbershop, a pedicure salon, and rooms for the chief instructor and the bath attendants.[30] The school's clientele was very distinguished. Among the many high-ranking officers and aristocrats, the most elevated pupils were Charles X, king of France from 1824 to 1830, and his successor, Louis Philippe, who reigned from 1830 to 1848.

To attract such prestigious patrons, it was necessary to maintain the baths in as luxurious a state as possible. This was incredibly expensive, and in 1840 Deligny was forced to sell his establishment to the ambitious brothers Burgh. It had fallen into such a deplorable state that the barge had to be rebuilt from scratch; only various ornamental pieces from the roof were recycled for the new floating pool. A recurring theme in the reports on the rebuilding is that the *bateau-cénotaphe* that had transported Napoleon's ashes from St. Helena was utilized in the operation.[31]

This time the fuselage consisted of fourteen hulls, five on each side and two at each end. The bottom of the pool, made of planks, gradually inclined from 0.6 to 2 meters, finally reaching 4.5 meters at the bottom of the river. The area was surrounded by nets to keep wayward swimmers in and unwanted matter out. At the deep end a diving tower, terrifying in its dimensions, had been assembled from elements of a spiral staircase and a ship's mast. Designed by the architects Philastre and Cambon, the rebuilt baths had cost the princely sum of 250,000 francs, thanks chiefly to the lavish decoration in a Turco-Arabic style. On August 6, 1899, the Deligny pool hosted the very first swimming championships held in France.

In 1937 the original system of overall permeability was replaced; now river water was pumped up, filtered, and then conducted into a watertight basin in a closed system where water floated on water separated by a steel wall. In 1953 the management caught up with the postwar fashion of sunbathing and had large sun decks installed. After a fire in 1953, a complete modernization took place that gave the Bains Deligny its subsequent and final look (figs. 1.4, 1.5), a floating unit measuring 115 by 25 meters, with a pool of 50 by 15 meters ranging in depth from 0.8 to 2 meters.[32] Strongly articulated by the dark background of the houses on the Quai Anatole France (former Quai d'Orsay) was the silhouette, which resembled that of an aircraft carrier.

The Bains Deligny became a popular hangout for a fashionable crowd that included heiresses like Barbara Hutton and movie stars like Audrey Hepburn, Michele Morgan, and of course Esther Williams. It also served as meeting place, pick-up joint, and display "beach" for those of various sexual proclivities.[33] On July 8, 1993, Les Bains Deligny were de-

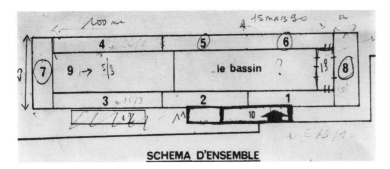

1.4. *Below:* Paris: Bains Deligny, plan. (Archives of the Bains Deligny: survey, March 15, 1990.)

1.5. Paris: Bains Deligny after reconstruction of 1953. *Also plate 1.*

SCHEMA D'ENSEMBLE

stroyed by an explosion of unidentified origin. The wooden superstructure was devoured by flames, the pontoons sank, and the pool caisson filled with muddy Seine water. During the summer of 1994 most of the various components were salvaged and cleaned; "la plage de Paris" is expected to be restored to its former glory.

By the mid-nineteenth century, bathing and swimming barges had become a familiar, if not unavoidable, sight along the Seine, especially when looking toward the Pont Neuf and the Île de la Cité. A splendid fin-de-siècle photograph (fig. 1.6) shows all of them except the Deligny, which had moved to its present location near the Gare (now Musée) d'Orsay. Taken from the Quai du Louvre toward the Place Dauphine and the Pont Neuf, it reveals three large floating pools (*bains froids* or *bains de Seine*). Closest to the Louvre are the Bains des Fleurs (*pour dames*) and the Bains Leneru-Hugo. The pool near the Pont Neuf that resembles a Mississippi river boat—with palm trees, not funnels, emerging from the roof!—is Les Bains Chauds de la Samaritaine.

The same photo shows Les Bains Henri IV, docked at the pointed end of the Square du Vert Galant with its monument to Henri IV, whence the bath's name. Tucked in between the Bains Henri IV and the Square du Vert Galant were the old Bains Poitevin-Vigier, which had expanded from one boat in 1761 to a fleet of four in 1800. The most luxurious of these became the object of passionate descriptions: "It was there that the peaceful bourgeois could sweetly luxuriate in the depths of his tub, quietly soaking, his favorite playthings—watch, thermometer, handkerchief, snuffbox—at hand, his spectacles firmly planted on his nose and, under his eyes, his favorite reading. That is what he likes the best—filling and refilling his tub, artfully regulating the temperature, proudly watching his big belly floating on the surface [fig.

Saint-Amand was specifically designed as a thermal hospital for the military by the fortifications engineer Vauban.

29. Thévenot, *L'art de nager, démonstré par figures, avec des avis pour se baigner utilement* (Paris: T. Moette, 1696); *Supplement*, 1782.

30. *Deux siècles d'architecture sportive à Paris*, 26–27.

31. Ibid., 24. Primary sources are Eugène Briffault, *Paris dans l'eau* (Paris, 1844), and Eugène Briffault, "Une journée à l'école de natation," in *Le diable à Paris*, 2 vols. (Paris: J. Hetzel, 1845), 2:124–146.

32. Data were taken from the following sources: "Les origines de la Piscine Deligny," *Ponts de Paris, 1986, Procès verbal de visite; commission de surveillance; bateaux recevant du public en stationnement, 20 fevrier 1988*, Archives of the Bains Deligny, and the help of Frédéric Tell.

33. See for example the *à la mode* novel *L'archimandrite* by Gabriel Matzneff (1966), which dealt generously with daily visits to the Deligny. (Thanks to Brigitte Forger, Brussels.) Also, Bruno van der Weerdt, "Les bains Deligny; Saint Tropez op de Seine," *De Gay Krant*, no. 186 (September 7, 1991), 23. For a charming picture of the pool in the years around World War II, see Henri Cartier-Bresson, *A propos Paris* (London: Thames and Hudson, 1994).

34. Briffault, *Paris dans l'eau*, 128: "C'est la que le paisible bourgeois s'enfonce douillettement dans les profondeurs de la baignoire; il se trempe à l'heure; il a su s'entourer de toutes les sensualités qui lui sont chères; sa montre, son thermomètre, le mouchoir, la tabatière, les besicles bien affirmés sur le nez, et, sous ses yeux, son livre bien aimé: voilà ses joies. Il fait et refait son bain, le gradue avec art, voit avec orgueil flotter sur l'eau le ballon de son abdomen. Au bain, le bourgeois de Paris rêve l'Orient, ses délices, ses voluptés, ses parfums et ses odalisques, l'opium et ses extases, et prend une croûte au pot." For the Bains Henri IV see Felix Genzmer, *Bade- und Schwimmanstalt*, in Josef Durm et al., eds., *Handbuch der Architektur*, 4:3:5 (Stuttgart: Arnold Bergsträsser Verlagsbuchhandlung, 1899), 129–130.
35. Briffault, *Paris dans l'eau*, 130: "en attendant que les côtelettes soient cuites; on entend quelques explosions de bouteilles de vin de Champagne; le café, le *gloria* et le punch parfument l'atmosphère; le cigare fume partout."
36. Ibid.
37. Contemporary photographs by Soulier (1865) and Dontenville (1867) show a vast establishment extended over two barges moored off the pointed end of the Île de la Cité. See Mike Weaver, ed., *The Art of Photography, 1839–1989* (Houston: Museum of Fine Arts, 1989), fig. 80, *The Pont Neuf, Paris 1865*, Soulier, and François Loyer, *Paris: Nineteenth Century* (New York: Abbeville Press, 1988), 120, fig. 1.

1.7]. In his bath, the Parisian bourgeois dreams of the Orient, of its sensual delights, its scents, the voluptuous beauties of the seraglio, of opium and its ecstasies, while at the same time he could simply take a bite to eat."[34]

Yes, a bite to eat and a smoke were among the simple pleasures of the hydrophilic Parisian around 1845. At lunch time, baths and pools were generally deserted, although one or two enthusiasts might be observed standing ankle deep in the water. Patrons were more likely to be in the restaurant, "waiting for the lamb chops to be cooked, [where] several explosions of champagne bottles being uncorked could be heard while coffee, often fortified with rum [*le gloria*], and punch scented the air. Cigars went up in smoke all over the place."[35] It was the time of the *cigar*, an exotic new smoke that added high fashion to the pleasures of bathing. The swimming school even smelled like the most chic restaurant of the day: "Sommes-nous chez Véfour ou à l'école de natation?"[36]

Neither cigars nor opium nor voluptuous *houris* were to be had at the Bains Henri IV, a pool 77.7 meters long and 14.8 meters wide, designed for swimming, not lounging (fig. 1.8). The wooden pool floor slanted from a depth of 0.5 to 1.9 meters; the pool was closed off from the river by a mesh fence. Its dependence on the Viennese swimming school of 1813 is clearly visible in the general layout of decks, cabins, and the footbridge that crosses the pool midway, separating the shallow pool (Bassin 1 in the plan) from the deep one (Bassin 2).[37]

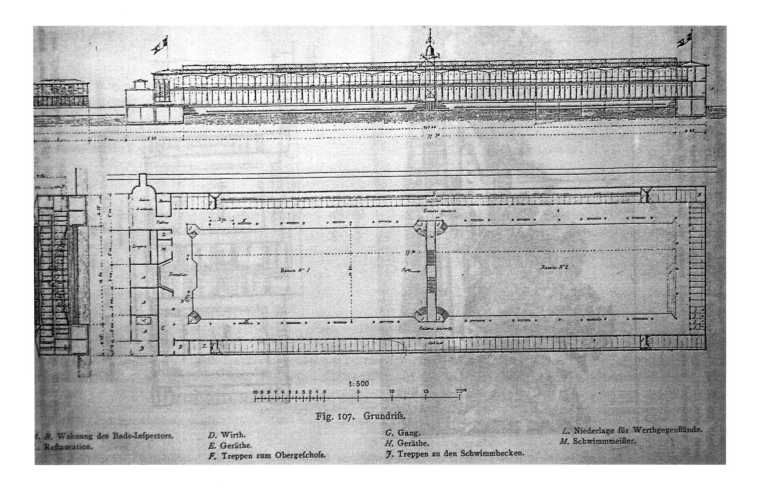

Fig. 107. Grundriſs.

A. B. Wohnung des Bade-Inſpectors.   D. Wirth.   G. Gang.   L. Niederlage für Werthgegenſtände.
   Reſtauration.   E. Geräthe.   H. Geräthe.   M. Schwimmmeiſter.
                                        F. Treppen zum Obergeſchoſs.   J. Treppen zu den Schwimmbecken.

1.6. *Opposite, left:* Paris: bathing establishments
     along the Seine at the fin-de-siècle. (Loyer,
     Paris: Nineteenth Century, 1988.)

1.7. *Opposite, right:* Etching by Gavarni, in Eugène
     Briffault, "Une journée à l'école de natation," *Le
     diable à Paris,* 1845.

1.8. *Above:* Paris, Bains Henri IV, plan. (Genzmer,
     Bade- und Schwimmanstalt, 1899.)

38. *Deux siècles d'architecture sportive à Paris,* 19. For the Seine and its stifling effects on the Parisians, see Alain Corbin, *Le miasme et la jonquille; l'odorat et l'imaginaire social, XVIII–XIXe siècles* (Paris: Aubier Montaigne, 1982).
39. Charles Meryon, *Le Pont-au-Change,* etching and drypoint, 1854, Rijksprentenkabinet, Rijksmuseum Amsterdam. See Irene M. Groot, *Charles Meryon,* exh. cat. (Amsterdam: Rijksmuseum, 1991), 60–61. Meryon drew the prints both from fantasy and from actuality.
40. Ibid., 60.

Bathing in the Styx The popularity of the floating baths in the Seine increased in part because free bathing and swimming had been forbidden by decree in 1783, but doubtless their mesh substructures, which kept out the horrible thick soup of cadavers and excrement that composed the Seine water most of the year and is compellingly described by Alain Corbin, played an important role.[38] Nevertheless, documents suggest that despite the attractions offered by the floating pools, the great majority of the Parisians simply could not afford them and had to make do with an illegal bath in the Styx. Pictures from the first half of the nineteenth century show men diving off and swimming around rowboats.

Two states (figs. 1.9, 1.10) of the etching *Le Pont-au-Change* by Charles Meryon (1854), of a scene near that Parisian bridge, provide gripping evidence. Meryon had made a series of poetic, freely interpreted views of buildings and city scenes around the Île de la Cité and his attention in particular had been caught by the infamous Morgue. The gruesome juxtaposition of the bathhouse and the morgue, discharging its lethal effluent into the Seine (ironically, this highly unsavory and dangerously infective institution would in 1864 merely be moved a little further upstream, east of the island, so that it could now infect not only one but two arms of the river, and bring all bathing barges within reach of its deadly waste), was the subject of this particular river scene.[39] A rowing boat pulls away from a person in the water—under the circumstance "swimming" would be an overstatement—who is waving for attention. Anchored in front of the bridge, two hulks are visible, the nearer a laundry barge, a *bateau-lavoir,* the farther possibly a bathing barge.

What makes Meryon's prints so poignant is the constant presence of death. Whereas the barges, and perhaps even the man in the water, might suggest regeneration, the presence of a funeral procession on the bridge, on its way to or from the Morgue, and the fact that the unhappy swimmer looks on the verge of giving up on life, strongly point in the opposite direction. Several states of the print (fig. 1.9) show a balloon, inscribed with the word "Speranza" (hope; but perhaps an allusion to canto 3 of Dante's *Inferno*), wafting over the bridge, suggesting hope for those who despair. But for the hapless swimmer, that hope seems beyond reach, since the nearby boatsmen have eyes only for the balloon. In later states (fig. 1.10) Meryon replaced the balloon with vast flights of ghastly black birds—ducks and albatrosses. Together with the macabre cavalcade on the bridge, the powers of destruction are very much in command.[40]

The scene has a curious similarity to Pieter Bruegel's *Fall of Icarus* in the Brussels Museum of Fine Arts, which depicts the doomed son of Daedalus a split second after his body has struck the waves. Splashes mark the place of impact, yet not one of the people within reach of vision pays any attention. The man in the water appears to be suffering from a disease so frightfully contagious that even the sight of it can cause great physical harm. Indeed, in a time when virtually everybody who hit the water was certain to drown, the sight alone reminded man of his fragile existence, his existential solitude, and the possibility of individual

1.9. Charles Meryon, *Le Pont-au-Change,* 1854.
(Amsterdam, Rijksmuseum-Stichting, Inv. nr.
RP-P-1987-13, D 34 V.)

1.10. Charles Meryon, *Le Pont-au-Change,* 1854.
(Amsterdam, Rijksmuseum-Stichting, Inv. nr.
RP-P-1956-17, D 34 IX.)

salvation. Like Bruegel, Meryon captured all this in a single scene. Although the man in the water is about to succumb, all eyes are fixed on the balloon carrying the message "Speranza." Hope is for all, death is for the single drowner.

It is interesting to remark that to prepare many of his views, Meryon circled the Île de la Cité and captured it in the process of decomposition, since many of the monuments he drew in clear outlines and in great detail were about to be removed or had been destroyed already. The Morgue seems to have been his pivot. Death and the Morgue seem omnipresent in fact and symbol, whether or not literally appearing in the scene. Looking sluggish and syrupy, heavy with waste and debris, the water of the Seine could be that of the Styx, the river of death and forgetfulness. The bathers in the river are lifeless, unseen beings who find themselves in the same phase of transition as the despairing swimmer by the Pont-au-Change. Nevertheless, even in Meryon's time, bathing and swimming were not yet identical.

Military Swimming France's many swimming pools contributed to the Gallic lead in swimming and may have been a factor in French hegemony on the battlefield. After numerous military defeats, authorities in Austria and Prussia evidently learned their lesson. Thus Friedrich Ludwig Jahn's Turnverein of 1811 in Berlin-Haseheide, and the publication of his book *Die deutsche Turnkunst* in 1816, were the direct result of the Prussian debacle at Jena in 1806, which would lead to the competition for a physically superior army. Likewise swimming was rediscovered not only as an excellent method of physical exercise but as a means of keeping the army maneuverable at all times, as it had been in the time of Vegetius.

1.11. Jacob Alt, watercolor of the Kaiserliche und
Königliche Militärschwimmschule in Vienna in
1815. (Vienna, Museum der Stadt Wien, Inv.
63.435.) *Also plate 2.*

It should come as no surprise that the Austrians, too, after a succession of losses, should decide to embark on serious training. On June 6, 1813, the Kaiserliche und Königliche Militärschwimmschule was founded in Vienna, on an arm of the Danube in Prater Park (not far from Ferro's cold-water baths), by Feldmarschallleutnant Franz von Schulzig and Oberst Graf Bentheim-Steinfurth, with the help of private funding. Jacob Alt represented the pool in full use two years later in 1815 (fig. 1.11), faithfully delineating the teaching poles balanced on the railings.[41]

Following roughly the configuration of the baths on the Seine, the pool consisted of four platforms resting on a pair of five linked pontoons that left an elongated rectangle of Danube water in their midst. Alt produced at least three delightful if somewhat clumsily drawn treetop observations of the pool, the softly contoured surrounding landscape set in vivid contrast to the angularity of the pool.[42] The elevated vantage point allows a good view of the configuration of the pool and the various activities taking place in and around it. Two long rows of changing cabins are placed on beams or trusses that rest on skifflike pontoons, which comically look like Turkish slippers under an old-fashioned four-poster bed. The topmost and lower ends, covered by hipped roofs, accommodated exercise rooms and possibly also storage space. Normally, in a floating pool like this one, the bottom consisted of wooden or iron mesh. Possibly to enhance the elongated character of the pool, the artist has flattened the sides dramatically, exaggerating the narrowness of the changing cabins and adjoining platforms. To allow participants to cross the pool halfway, but more importantly to give the frame some rigidity, an elegantly curved footbridge was constructed.

Following the success of the Militärschwimmschule in the Danube, which remained at its original site until 1874, similar pools of the floating and the semi-floating type (anchored by poles driven into the river bed) were erected in the rivers of northern Europe. In 1817 the Berliner Militär-Schwimmanstalt was built in the river Spree by General von Pfuel, followed by facilities in Potsdam, Amsterdam, Hamburg,[43] as well as in the Elbe river near Magdeburg, initiated by another military reformer, Major von Neindorf.[44] General von Pfuel, an influential advocate of sport, advised on the construction and layout of swimming pools and had published—anonymously—several books on swimming. One of 1817 was instantly translated into English as *Pfuel's Celebrated Treatise* (1817 and 1828).[45]

A well-preserved military swimming school is the K.u.K. Militärschwimmschule at the spa in Baden bei Wien, originally built in 1831 (fig. 1.12). A dual open-air pool (for women and men) with apsidal endings on both sides, the two halves separated by a walkway, it is not floating but has been excavated over a sulfurous artesian well. Overlooked by most authors on the subject, it must be, together with the Damenschwimmanstalt in Vienna, one of the earliest open-air swimming pools of the western world. It survives today in a virtually unchanged state as the Mineralschwimmbad.[46] The elegant dimensions of the pool are accentuated by surrounding buildings that accommodate changing cabins and the centrally located

41. Wilhelm Seledec, Helmut Kretschmer, and Herbert Lauscha, eds., *Baden und Bäder in Wien* (Vienna: Europa Verlag, 1987), 22. I am grateful to Barbara Higgs, who provided valuable information. The pool was used by the military during certain hours of the day; beyond that it was open to civilians, including women, who were allowed on certain days to watch the men swim. Within the said limits, the pool was open to anyone "welcher einen Schwimm-Unterricht zu erhalten wünscht, sich bei der Schwimmanstalt zu melden. Die Unterrichtsstunden für das Zivil sind täglich von 10 bis 1 Uhr mittags und von 5 bis 8 Uhr abends." The 1903 *Brockhaus Konversationslexikon* clearly exposed the homonymity of the term *Schwimmen*, explaining that it could be used in the passive or active voice. "Von diesem passiven Schwimmen unterscheidet man das auf der Gegenwirkung beruhende, durch Bewegung bewirkte aktive Schwimmen." (In German, *schwimmen* means "to float" as well as "to swim.")
42. The one shown here figured at the exhibition "Das Bad" (1991) in the Hermesvilla in Vienna, cat. no. 2.22. The second is taken at closer range and shows the diver at the point of taking off; illustrated in Herbert Lachmayer, Sylvia Mattl-Wurm, and Christian Gargerle, eds., *Das Bad; eine Geschichte der Badekultur im 19. und 20. Jahrhundert* (Salzburg: Residenz Verlag, 1991), 158. The third, a view of the short side showing the five pontoons, is illustrated in Seledec, Kretschmer, and Lauscha, eds., *Baden und Bäder,* 25.
43. Genzmer, *Bade- und Schwimmanstalt,* 125ff., "Flussbäder."
44. Schleyer, *Bäder und Badeanstalten,* 273. See also Genzmer, *Bade- und Schwimmanstalt,* 49. Germany counted a relatively large number of *Flussbäder.* Just to mention a few: Alte Militär-Schwimmanstalt, Angermünde (on poles); Alsterlust, Hamburg; Frauenbad and Männerbad in the Hunte, Oldenburg, 1879 (two separate pools); Städtische Flussbadeanstalt an der Oberspree, Berlin (floating plus poles); Thiebesche Flussbadeanstalt, Bonn (floating). From Schleyer, *Bäder und Badeanstalten,* 705ff. An important milestone in the development of swimming pools for women was the fixed Danube river pool in the Viennese Augarten, the so-called Damenschwimmschule of 1831. It was destroyed by fire in 1848. See Mattl-Wurm and Storch, eds., *Das Bad,* 267. In England, the only floating bath that I know of is the one in the river Thames, at Charing Cross, illustrated in *The Illustrated London News,* 1875. See John Dawes, *Design and Planning of Swimming Pools* (London: Architectural Press, 1979), 3, and Mattl-Wurm and Storch, eds., *Das Bad.*

1.12. *Above:* Baden bei Wien: former K.u.K.
Militärschwimmschule, 1831; view in 1990.
Also plate 3.

1.13. Graz, Austria: Militärschwimmschule, 1839,
with pool for women, plan. (Genzmer, *Bade-
und Schwimmanstalt,* 1899.)

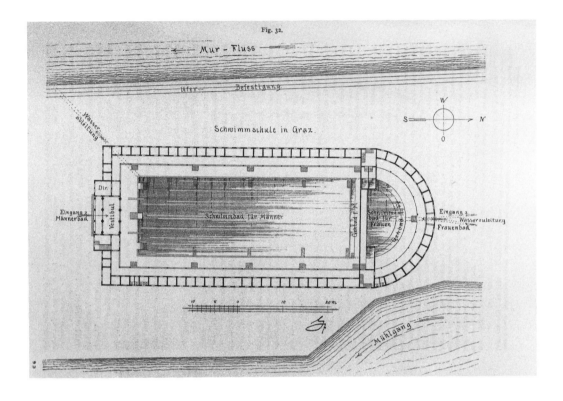

entry and administration building. The reason for its persistent success is its continuous supply of healthy, decent-smelling, sulfuric water.

These army training schools were in some cases open to civilians, occasionally even to women, and quite often to horses. This makes sense. Crossing rivers by swimming was what the army and the engineer corps had to do when there were no fords or bridges; this was no less the case for the cavalry, the mounted artillery, and all the other units in which horses were used as means of transportation. Horses can swim naturally, by instinct, but they get into problems when carrying heavy loads and need instruction for this. Frédéric Bachstrom's treatise on swimming, *L'art de nager* of 1741, was subtitled *ou invention à l'aide de laquelle on peut toujours se sauver de naufrage, et en cas de besoin faire passer les larges rivières à des Armées entières,* and an anonymously penned *Instruction für das Schwimmunterricht der russischen Cavallerie* (Vienna, 1894) was written to teach riders and horses alike to swim.[47] The Militärschwimmbad in Graz (fig. 1.13), built by and for the army in a fork of the river Mur in 1839, was designed for the instruction of men, women, and horses.[48] It would not be surprising if the instructional pools for horses actually preceded those for humans.

45. Other books based on von Pfuel's method were *A Treatise of Swimming as Taught at Berlin in the Military College,* by C.W.S. (from a German manuscript, 1846), and *Instruction für den militärischen Schwimmunterricht nach der Pfuel'schen Methode* (1861), which may be identical to *Instruction für den militärischen Schwimmunterricht nach der Pfuel'schen Methode, Bearbeitet von K. von Thümen Premier Lieutenant im 3ten Pommerschen Infanterie Regiment* (Berlin, 1861). Cited from Sinclair, *Swimming,* bibliography.
46. There are, however, uncertainties about its present location, and whether it changed position when the present complex was established. Wallner and Hubmann, *Baden bei Wien* (St. Pölten, 1987), 37.
47. See Sinclair, *Swimming,* 439–440.
48. Genzmer, *Bade- und Schwimmanstalt,* 49–51.

49. Sinclair, *Swimming*, 45.
50. Thanks to Professor Frits Happel, Amsterdam, for his professional advice.
51. Charles Sprawson, *Haunts of the Black Masseur: The Swimmer as Hero* (London: Jonathan Cape, 1992), 24.

Tools of When we now return to the Jacob Alt drawing, two features are especially
Instruction provocative, the teacher's poles and the diving board or diving tower. Poles, resembling hefty fishing rods, are held at one end by the teacher and are connected at the other, via a simple leather strap or harness, to the pupil (compare fig. 1.14). Archibald Sinclair, "honorary secretary of the Life Saving Society," explained in 1893 the workings of this device: "A favourite implement is the teacher's pole, which is about seven feet long and a half to two inches in diameter, mounted at one end with a ring, through which a cord made into a loop is passed. On this a belt of webbing is strung, the webbing being fitted at each end with a ring, so as to enable the looped cord to slide through it. The instructor holds the pole, and then passes the belt to his pupil, who places it round the body, and then leans forward on his breast to take the lesson, the instructor keeping on the side of the bath and giving the tuition therefrom."[49] This early form of remote-controlled tuition has never gone out of fashion and is still practiced today.

Diving could be practiced dry, the victim (fully clothed) suspended by webbing over a sand pit. In a 1930 demonstration in the courtyard of the Heiligeweg Bad, Amsterdam (fig. 1.15), swimming pool director Mijnheer Kuiper balances his assistant Gerard, wearing dancing shoes, no less, in fetal position before releasing (?) him.[50] Considerably more sophistication was demonstrated in the gamut of diving positions that legendary swimmer/diver Annette Kellerman excelled in and which were illustrated as instruction material in Bernarr Macfadden's manual for a healthier lifestyle, the *Encyclopedia of Physical Culture* (fig. 1.16). The "Nautilus," for example (lower left in the picture), became a routine figure in synchronized swimming, practiced by, among others, Kellerman-impersonator Esther Williams, who looked her very best wearing the original Kellerman "one piece bathing suit" in the "gorgeous aquatic marvel," *Million Dollar Mermaid,* 1952 (fig. 1.17).

Most instruction manuals, however, promoted the use of swimming machines of various degrees of impracticability that could be used in the water as life-saving devices, or on shore as dry-swimming instruction apparatus. Of the latter, the majority consisted of contraptions based on the technique of the frog. The leg action was often imitated by pupils lying on their bellies on a table or chair at the same time that they watched pictures of frogs, or the live frogs themselves kept in a jar or a tub. A hilarious scene in Shadwell's *Virtuoso* (1676) adumbrates the later practices. The eccentric Lord Nicholas Gimcrack is dry-training in his study and his wife reports what she sees (I follow Charles Sprawson's brilliant retelling): "'He has a frog in a bowl of water, tied with a pack-thread by the loins, which pack-thread Sir Nicholas holds in his teeth, lying upon his belly on a table; and as the frog strikes, he strikes, and his swimming master stands by him, to tell him when he does well or ill.' When asked if he had ever tried out the stroke in the water, Sir Nicholas replies: 'No Sir, but I swim most exquisitely on land. I content myself with the Speculative part of swimming, I care not for the Practick. I seldom bring anything to use, 'tis not my way.'"[51]

1.14. Jacob Olie, photograph of the Westerdoksdijk
swimming pool. (*Jacob Olie: Amsterdam
Gefotografeerd, 1860–1905,* 1974.)
1.15. *Below:* Mijnheer Kuiper and his assistant
Gerard, demonstrating diving at the Heiligeweg
Bad, Amsterdam, 1930. (Amsterdam,
Gemeentelijke Archiefdienst.)

1.16. *Left:* Annette Kellerman diving and swimming.
(*Macfadden's Encyclopedia of Physical Culture*,
1928.)

1.17. Esther Williams in *Million Dollar Mermaid*,
1952. Publicity still.

1.19. *Right:* Dry training techniques, from *Outing* magazine, 1902. (Lencek and Bosker, *Making Waves,* 1989.)

1.20. Trying out for Billy Rose's 1940 Aquacade. (Lencek and Bosker, *Making Waves,* 1989.)

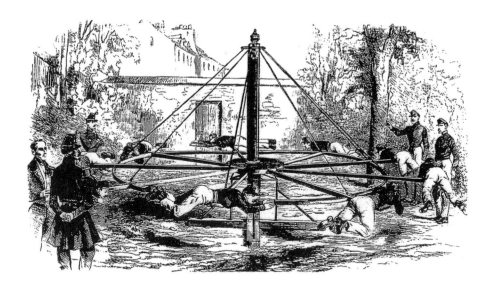

52. Engraving in *L'Illustration*, June 25, 1895, reproduced in *Deux siècles d'architecture sportive à Paris, 8.*

Breaststroke was the technique most widely taught. Although the leg action was derived from the frog's, the arm movement had to be invented (probably mirroring the movement of the legs), since frogs hardly use their forelimbs in swimming. The breaststroke was popular with the military because it was a symmetrical, well-balanced action that allowed both the head and the marching kit and rifle, strapped high on the back, to stay above the water. The "Natateur-le-Chevalier" (1859) was an ingeniously recycled merry-go-round (fig. 1.18), designed to teach French army men the breaststroke with an efficiency that Frederick Taylor would have envied.[52]

Yet dry training techniques have never been able to avoid an air of distinct silliness. The actions illustrated in *Outing* magazine, 1902, intended as instructions to "put a woman through the surf," resemble more a violent dance than a frolic on the beach (fig. 1.19), while a photograph that documents one of the apparently many sessions staged by Billy Rose to select swimmers for his 1940 Aquacade exudes an air of domesticity (fig. 1.20).

Diving and the Springboard Jacob Alt's picture will serve as illustration once again, this time to show a diving stand of the fixed tower type. More sophisticated—and prescient— was the structure in the 1831 Damenschwimmschule in Vienna, where something resembling an actual diving tower with integrated ladder was constructed (fig. 1.21). Springboards had become the marvel of the moment, having been specially designed for military instruction by no one less than Friedrich Wilhelm Jahn.

1.18. *Opposite:* "Natateur-le-Chevalier," 1859. (*Deux siècles d'architecture sportive,* 1986.)

1.21. *Above:* Vienna: Damenschwimmschule, 1831, with diving tower. (Mattl-Wurm and Storch, eds., *Das Bad,* 1991.)

53. Giedion, *Mechanization Takes Command*, 658. Giedion referred to Carl Euler, *Encyclopaedisches Handbuch des Turnwesens* (Vienna, 1894).

54. Archibald Sinclair, *Life Saving Society's Handbook* (1891, with many revised editions). See also Capt. W. D. Andrews, *Swimming and Lifesaving* (1889).

55. *The Oxford Companion to World Sports and Games* (London: Oxford University Press, 1975).

56. Hans Luber, *Der Schwimmsport* (Leipzig and Zurich, n.d.), 113–114.

57. Sprawson, *Haunts of the Black Masseur*, 195.

58. Rudolf Ortner, *Sportbauten* (Munich, 1953), 229–231. The most elegant solution was reached in the pool at the Foro Italico, Rome, 1932, with its hydraulically operated telescopic springboard. The board could be put in a position directly proportional to the chutzpah of the diver.

59. *The Physician and Sports Medicine* 16, no. 3 (March 1988), 72. Archival sources: Olympic diver Wessel Zimmermann, Zoetermeer.

60. Doctor Arntzenius, *De Zwemschool en Bad-Inrigting te Amsterdam* (Amsterdam, 1846), 4: "Eindelijk heeft men in navolging van hetgeen de Generaal von Pfuel in Pruissen heeft tot stand gebragt, onze armee in het zwemmen geoefend. Hier blijkt weder de meerdere zorg die door het gouvernement voor de gezondheid onzer militairen, dan voor de burgerklasse wordt gedragen.... Het ware voorzeker meer doeltreffend onze Nederlandsche jeugd in het algemeen in deze weldaad te doen deelen."

In *Die deutsche Turnkunst,* Jahn had presented his training methods and the matching machinery he had invented specifically for the first of the many *Turnvereine* he had founded after the disaster encountered by the Prussian army in 1806. For gymnastics Jahn's training methods may have become obsolete, but his equipment—the wooden horse, the parallel bars, and the springboard—has survived virtually unchanged. Also swimming and the patterns of swimming still relate very much to the martial concept of exercise ("Körperübungen, Leibesübungen, Turnübungen, etc."). If there was one thing Jahn despised more than anything it was "freie Uebungen." "Every exercise must have an object," he wrote. "Let us take fencing as an example: cutting and lunging at the air can amount to nothing more than mirror-play."[53]

Swimming for fun, in unpremeditated figures with no particular goal, was equally out of the question. It was precisely at this moment that swimming was restructured according to the rules of the exercise field: marching in straight lines and turning in sharp angles. Prussian frustration over military reverses still reverberates in the swimming pools of today; the swimmer is restricted to straight laps, and turns are executed with the same crispness as the about-faces of the marching drill. Accordingly the ground plan of the swimming pool has been fixed as the standard 1:2 rectangle, with no other use possible than as an aquatic parade ground. A telling example is the Militärschwimmschule in the river Mur near Graz, Austria, of 1839, particularly in the contrast between the semicircular addition of the Schwimmschule für Frauen and the extended rectangular plan of the men's pool (see fig. 1.13).

Civilian practice was influenced also by Jahn's springboard. A totally logical application was found in 1837 when the National Swimming Society, which had established six swimming pools in London, fitted them all with springboards that served, it was claimed, "to simulate the dive from a ship into the ocean, in order to salvage shipwrecked mariners."[54]

Based on a varied mixture of unidentified sources, *The Oxford Companion to World Sports and Games* (1975) offered its reconstruction of the origin of diving: "Diving, meaning basically to plunge into water, is used generally to describe any method of descending beneath the surface of the water. At the beginning of the nineteenth century a new form of diving was developed in Europe, mainly in Germany and Sweden. During the summer months, gymnastic apparatus was transferred to the beach. The flying rings, the trapeze and the springboard were erected and used from high platforms to enable gymnastics to be performed over the water. This was the beginning of fancy diving."[55] Hans Luber, in *Der Schwimmsport,* favored a Germanocentric history of diving, giving the palm to the Berliner Schwimmverein, but the date he assigned to the invention—1878—put the Prussians hopelessly out of competition.[56] Following the more orthodox version of diving history, Charles Sprawson highlighted the superiority of Swedish diving around 1900: "The Swedes introduced the art of diving to England at the turn of the century. Their impact was enormous. The crowds were amazed at their daring and graceful evolutions, as they watched one diver after another hurled into space from a pagoda platform sixty feet high, with such force and spring that their bodies were carried about thirty feet away from the diving tower, the head thrown backwards, the back sharply hollowed, arms flung out to form a horizontal line through the shoulders like the spread wings of a bird, a position maintained until about six feet from the water."[57]

After springboard and platform diving became part of the Olympics in 1904, the structure and composition of the boards propelled divers still further away from the water. Diving boards were positioned at dizzying heights, distancing the sport more and more from the original rationale of entering the water in a crisp and efficient manner. Diving towers developed into menacing structures often accommodating four or five satellite platforms. The basin below, smaller and deeper than a swimming pool, merely acted as a safety net. With the quadruple towers of Zurich's Letzigraben, the quintuple Olympic tower at Helsinki with platforms at 1, 3, 5, 7.5, and 10 meters, and the quadruple space-wheel tower with two flanking boards at Castel Fusano, Rome, diving entered the space age.[58]

It seems hardly surprising that to the less accomplished, these altitudes aroused sensations of horror and anxiety. Furthermore, diving could inflict serious back injuries, ranking "after car accidents, falls or jumps, and gunshot wounds as the fourth highest cause of such injuries [to the spinal cord]."[59] Is it any wonder that from the late 1950s, springboards became the target of collective litigation? In America, where product liability clauses and the subsequent lawsuits belong to the national folklore, an anti-springboard mood developed in public and private sectors alike.

Floating in the Low Countries   The Low Countries, renowned both for the struggle against a boundless supply of water as well as for the many modes of enjoying it, offer a varied history of swimming. The Netherlands Society to Prevent Drowning (Nederlandse Maatschappij tot het Redden van Drenkelingen) was founded as early as 1767, preceding the introduction of military swimming by almost a century. The military stimulus reached Holland from neighboring Germany, evinced by the introduction of several river-based swimming pools and full-floating pools derived from the model of the Berliner Militär-Schwimmanstalt, whose founder, General von Pfuel, had achieved some celebrity in the Netherlands.

In 1845 the Dane C. W. Ploenius, or Plönius, a follower of von Pfuel originally from the Gymnastic Institute in Copenhagen and later attached to the Royal Military Academy in Breda, built a pool in the IJ, the vast inlet of the Zuiderzee that served as Amsterdam's harbor. Doctor Arntzenius, a local advocate of sports and swimming, wrote on the occasion of the pool's dedication in 1846: "In imitation of the work General von Pfuel achieved in Prussia, our army has finally taken up the teaching of swimming. However, this demonstrates that our government shows more interest in the well-being of our military than in that of our civilians. . . . It certainly would have been more effective if our Dutch youth could have shared in this beneficial initiative."[60]

61. Jos van den Bongaardt, *Elke week een goed bad! Geschiedenis en architectuur van de badhuizen van Amsterdam* (Amsterdam, 1990), 10.

62. Genzmer, *Bade- und Schwimman-stalt*, 78.

63. Amsterdam, *Historisch Topografische Atlas*. See also D. van Vugt, "Baden en Zwemmen in Amsterdam," *Ons Amsterdam* 2 (January 1950), 5–9.

64. Ibid., 11, fig. 3; *Algemeen Handels-blad*, November 4, 1957. See also Juliette Roding, *Schoon en Net* (The Hague, 1986), 57. The caption to van Vlugt's illustration reads: "Zwemschool aan de Westerdoks-dijk in Amsterdam." Like most other European swimming academies, this one was related to a military establishment.

65. Genzmer, *Bade- und Schwimman-stalt*, 78. It was designed and built by the respected firm of G. B. Salm & A. Salm, Amsterdam.

In fact, the Germanic fashion had been introduced two years earlier, in 1844, when the first bathing barge in the Netherlands opened, anchored in the river Amstel at the Rokin by the central Dam square, from which the city derives its name. Built on a former regular service barge, it boasted a superstructure that was distinctly reminiscent of its Austro-Germanic forerunners, as was its name, Bade-Anstalt. It was demolished in 1914.[61]

In contrast, the pool Ploenius was to build at Westerdoksdijk between 1845 and 1846 was of the semiamphibious type, its main buildings anchored to the bank and its four (!) swimming docks projecting into the harbor (fig. 1.22). An ambitiously conceived structure with an overall length of 70 meters, erected over a foundation of pilings like almost all of Amsterdam's buildings, it comprised a service wing attached to the dike and two semifloating basins, 2.5 meters at their deepest, jutting out into the inlet. Predictably the structure was thoroughly permeable, allowing the waters of the IJ and the Amstel to follow their course unhindered. Instruction was accomplished from rowboats provided with a superstructure to which lines were attached; four pupils could be served simultaneously (fig. 1.23).

In keeping with its dominant ratio of water to land, Holland is distinguished by its large number of river and harbor pools. The *Handbuch der Architektur* for 1899 noted that "of the other European states only Holland is worth mentioning. Whereas the Italians mainly concentrate their swimming pools in the coastal areas, the Dutch make use also of their inland waters. Even in the smallest places one finds well-developed floating baths, as long as water conditions permit."[62]

Amsterdam was probably the best place to look. Besides those cited above, there had been at least two floating swimming pools in the river Amstel. The earliest was the Bad- en Zweminrichting in the Buiten-Amstel, built in 1856 but demolished in 1862. It measured 89.5 by 34 meters and had two pools, one for beginners and one, with a springboard, for advanced swimmers. The establishment included a billiard room, a lounge, and seven bathtubs (fig. 1.24). Its successor (fig. 1.25) opened to the public in July 1881 (it had to be restored in May 1887). This one was anchored in the middle of the river, the better to scoop out water of the best available quality, and consequently could be reached only by private boats or small ferries. A large platform was created at one end to accommodate an elegant café (Cafe de Amstel) and a jetty that received customers and their means of transportation.[63]

Possibly the largest floating pool of its time was the Bad- en Zweminrichting Th. Van Heemstede Obelt, named after its owner-director. With an English degree in sanitary engineering, Theo van Heemstede Obelt had founded a business in porcelain water closets and bathtubs; he subsequently utilized his goods in his own bathing establishment, constructed in 1881 in the south-central part of the Amsterdam harbor at the De Ruyterkade (fig. 1.26). This was near the site of the future Central Station, and the advent of that colossus required the displacement of the pool to the opposite bank, where it could be reached by a special six-cent "swimming-pool ferry."[64] Reputed to be "one of the largest, if not the largest of its kind,"[65] the

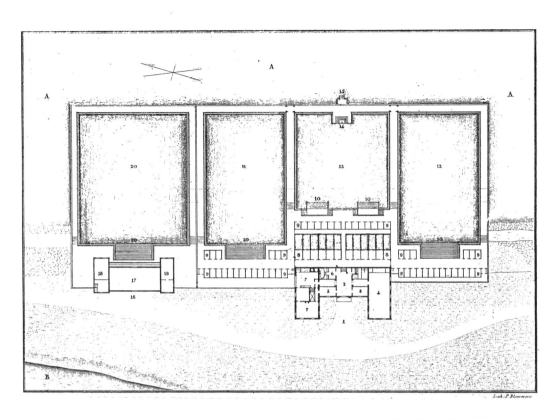

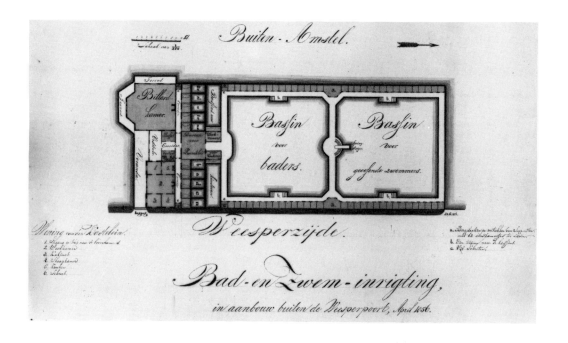

1.22. *Page 41, top:* Amsterdam: Ploenius's floating swimming pool, Westerdoksdijk, 1845–1846, plan. (Amsterdam, Gemeentelijke Archiefdienst.)

1.23. *Page 41, bottom:* Instruction at the Ploenius swimming school. (Amsterdam, Gemeentelijke Archiefdienst.)

1.24. *Opposite, top:* Amsterdam: Bad- en Zweminrichting, Buiten-Amstel, 1856, plan. (Amsterdam, Gemeentelijke Archiefdienst.)

1.25. *Opposite, bottom:* Amsterdam: Bad- en Zweminrichting with Cafe de Amstel. (Amsterdam, Gemeentelijke Archiefdienst.)

1.26. Amsterdam: Bad- en Zweminrichting De Ruyterkade, built by G. B. Salm and A. Salm. (Amsterdam, Gemeentelijke Archiefdienst.)

harbor pool at De Ruyterkade comprised three swimming pools for men, women, and children, respectively, with 250 changing cabins for men and 60 for women. In addition there were service rooms, hot baths and showers, and a restaurant.[66]

Below the surface, cages of mesh and planks fenced in the swimming area, keeping out debris and the larger impurities while ensuring a constant flow of water. The underside consisted of a sloping, solid wood floor that was covered with white sand to give the impression of an unspoiled Polynesian beach (!); the depth increased from 0.6 to 3.5 meters, and to 5 meters in the diving area. The diving tower was an impressive steel structure that blended picturesquely with the surrounding tall ships and steamers in the harbor. The sheer magnitude of the complex may be grasped by noting the presence of a hospital room, with a doctor and an array of machinery to assist in cases of drowning and sudden indisposition, and a steam-driven laundry. Swimming pools of the size and prestige of the Van Heemstede Obelt establishment, with its permanent staff of forty, were expected to provide a full line of traditional services that included steam baths and showers.[67]

Floating at Sea It took a while before river pollution aroused serious concern, but by the 1890s the downstream reaches of most rivers—such as those in Bremen, Hamburg, Amsterdam, and Paris—had become so unfit for bathing that swimmers either went to the fixed outdoor and indoor pools or to the seaside. The search for cleaner water had already resulted in the colossal floating bath, Bagno Maria, in the Bay of Trieste. Built in 1858 for two Italian entrepreneurs, Chiozza and Ferrari, by the German firm of Gebrüder Strudthof

66. The first swimming club for women was A[msterdamsche]. Z[wemclub], founded in 1870, followed by Hollandsche Dames Zwemclub, 1886, both resident in the Van Heemstede Obelt establishment. *De Volkskrant,* October 26, 1957. The first swimming club for men was possibly the one in Uppsala, Sweden, founded in 1796.
67. Genzmer, *Bade- und Schwimmanstalt,* 78. Other features included a restaurant and a terrace overlooking the men's pool and, charming detail, the house of the director placed exactly in the middle, so as to separate the men's pool from that of the ladies.

68. Genzmer, *Bade- und Schwimman-stalt,* 146; see also Schleyer, *Bäder und Badeanstalten,* 717–718. Schleyer gives 161.2 m for the total length.

69. The Frauenbad is now firmly fixed on poles driven into the bottom of the river Limmat. In 1993 Japanese artist Tadashi Kawamata made ironic-artistic replicas of the Frauenbad for the Zurich museum Helmhaus accross the river. (Thanks to Iri von Moos and Marie Louise Lienhard.)

70. *Heute* (Gewerbemuseum Basel), June 2–July 7, 1935, 16.

71. The English situation is somewhat confusing. Dawes mentions a series of "bath-houses," meaning "washing facilities," beginning with "a floating bath barque named 'Waterloo' [no doubt inspired by the same envious Napoleonism as the Prussians and Austrians nourished] moored on the Thames in 1819. The first public municipal bath was opened in Liverpool in 1828, and was looked upon with the same disdain as the workhouse. There were six baths in London by 1837, and an Act of Parliament in 1846 granted local authorities official leadership for public baths and wash houses.... In the 1880s, floating bagnios might have been made popular on the Seine, but an attempt to reintroduce one commercially on the Thames failed dismally." (Dawes, *Design and Planning of Swimming Pools,* 3.) Stefan Muthesius, "The Sanitary Revolution'—Englische Badekultur als Vorbild im 19. Jahrhundert," in Lachmayer, Mattl-Wurm, and Gargerle, eds., *Das Bad,* 122–135, provides some interesting, but undocumented, data. As a rule of thumb, however, one could state that in England, before the Reform Bill (1832) and the Cholera (1833) and Public Health acts (1848), no important innovations had occurred. Liverpool takes pride of place here: "To Liverpool must be given the credit of having the first modern public bath. The corporation established in that city, in 1794, a public swimming pool which from the start proved successful. This modest beginning was followed by another and larger type of river bath (the St. George Bath), since remodeled and in use to-day and known as the Pierhead Baths." (Harold Werner and August P. Windolph, "The Public Bath," *The Brickbuilder* 17 [1908], 28.) But the authors do not seem to have had any knowledge of the continental initiative, which makes their claim a frail one. The most reliable source and the most detailed description of the Liverpool bath is in Genzmer, *Bade- und Schwimmanstalt,* 51–52.

72. See Sinclair, *Swimming.*

73. The early development of the European and American public bathhouses and indoor swimming pools is best documented by Werner and Windolph, "The Public Bath." The year 1850 is given as

(figs. 1.27, 1.28), it was 190 meters long and 110 meters wide. Bagno Maria resembled a blunt-nosed raft carrying a Roman castrum, with defensible towers on the corners and a basilica in the middle.

The description reads: "This unusual floating building was located in one of the cleanest and deepest spots of the harbor, close to the Mole of San Carlo and facing the Town Hall. Secured by four anchors, it gives an impression of such stability that it seems to stand on pillars. The upper structure rests on a raft of metal tubes (shown on the plan in dotted lines)."[68] The two swimming pools—the larger for men, the smaller for women—were of the sunken cage model, with wooden floors hanging under the raft on steel rods, internally connected with wire mesh. Springboards were fitted on the bow for those who wanted to swim in the sea. In the autumn, the Bagno Maria was towed into the Bay of Muggia where it was docked for the duration of the cold weather. What has become of this Titanic among floating pools is unknown.

The Last of the Few floating pools—the well-preserved Frauenbad (1886?) in central Zurich
Floating Pools (fig. 1.29) being an exception—have survived.[69] Having accomplished their
pioneering work, they were replaced by fixed open-air and indoor pools—*Hallenschwimmbäder* or *piscines,* as opposed to *Flussbäder* or *bains sur Seine.* The first indoor swimming *pools* (in contrast to *baths;* in the available literature there reigns persistent confusion as to the distinction between "bathing establishment" or "bathhouse" and "swimming bath" or "swimming pool") were built in Vienna. The Dianabad opened in 1842, as an addition to the already existing bathing establishment of 1804; at 36 by 12 meters, it was the largest covered swimming pool of the time.[70]

That year also saw the appearance of the first English bathing and swimming pool "for the labouring class," in Liverpool. Unlike their continental relatives, the English bathing establishments invariably included public laundries and had, in addition to the usual separation between the sexes, further division according to class.[71] But before a reasonable number of pools could be built, England had to wait for the passage of such legislation as the Promoting the Establishment of Baths and Washhouses for the Labouring Class Act or the Mansion House Act of 1844.[72] The swimming pool at the Paddington Bath House (1847) was the first of a long line of politically inspired, combined wash, bath, and swimming establishments that would soon populate London in large numbers; by 1854 the capital could count thirteen. In America the (public) swimming pool movement came on strong only in the late nineteenth century, followed swiftly by the much stronger demand for private swimming pools.[73]

The last word on the world of the floating pool belongs to Rem Koolhaas and Madelon Vriesendorp, whose revisionist–Russian constructivist dream of the Story of the Pool is a tale as simple as it is profound. On a day in Moscow shortly after the revolution, a group of architectural students decide to build a colossal floating pool (fig. 1.30).

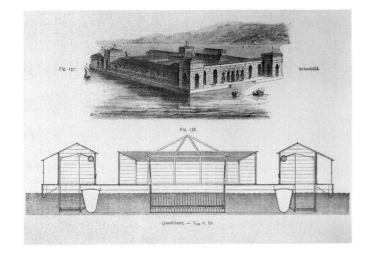

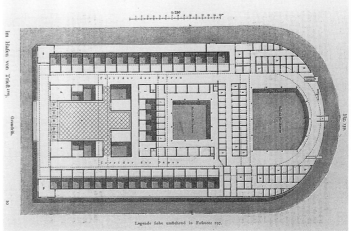

Someone *had* to invent the floating swimming pool. . . . An enclave of purity in contaminated surroundings [it] seemed a first step, modest yet radical, in a gradual program of improving the world through architecture. . . . The pool was a long rectangle of metal sheets bolted onto a steel frame. Two seemingly endless locker rooms formed its long sides—one for men, the other for women. At either end was a glass lobby with two transparent walls; one wall exposed the healthy, sometimes exciting underwater activities in the pool, and the other fish agonizing in polluted water. It was a truly *dialectical* room, used for physical exercise, artificial sunbathing and socializing between the almost naked swimmers. The prototype became the most popular structure in the history of Modern Architecture. Due to the chronic Soviet labor shortage, the architects/builders were also the lifeguards. One day they discovered that if they swam in unison—in regular synchronized laps from one end of the pool to the other—the pool would begin to move slowly in the opposite direction.

Early one morning, in an openly confessed allegiance to the Communist regime, the architects started to swim "in relentless laps in the direction of the golden onions of the Kremlin." But in fact, after four decades of incessant swimming it was Manhattan that they finally reached. Koolhaas's retroactive theory that the Manhattan block was in fact a modernist concept acquired by accident was now proven: "In a way the pool was a Manhattan block realized in Moscow, which would now reach its logical destination."[74]

"the date of the introduction of the public bath in this country" (70).
74. Rem Koolhaas, *Delirious New York: A Retroactive Manifesto for Manhattan* (New York: Oxford University Press, 1978), 253. Although of a similar nature, pools in the large passenger steamers of the first half of our century have to remain outside this essay. There are several nice pictures in Kelly Klein, *Pools,* of the swimming pools of the S.S. *Olympic* (c. 1911), the S.S. *Imperator* (c. 1912), the *Saturnia* (c. 1938), and the *Queen Mary* (1936). Recently BBC television showed interesting footage of swimming in the *Queen Mary* swimming pool. (BBC, March 24, 1992.)

1.27. *Page 45, left:* Bay of Trieste: Bagno Maria, 1858. (Genzmer, *Bade- und Schwimmanstalt,* 1899.)
1.28. *Page 45, right:* Bagno Maria, plan. (Genzmer, *Bade- und Schwimmanstalt,* 1899.)

1.29. *Opposite, top:* Zurich: Frauenbad in river Limmat. *Also plate 4.*
1.30. *Opposite, bottom:* The floating pool according to Rem Koolhaas and Madelon Vriesendorp. (Koolhaas, *Delirious New York,* 1978.)

75. Dawes, *Design and Planning of Swimming Pools,* 229–230.
76. "Paradise," *Los Angeles Times Magazine,* July 17, 1988, 19.

Floating pools had taken advantage of natural conditions, and because of their low costs of material and exploitation—using or reusing public water and often recycling used barges—they were commercially attractive. By contrast, modern-day, large-scale pools have to rely on finely filtered drinking water and to be heated to temperatures far exceeding normal room temperature. Therefore they are energy-consuming, expensive to run, and not particularly environmentally friendly.

The Ideal Is Sterile After being boxed in and separated from its original state, water loses its healthy composition, becoming stagnant. In order to restore its fitness for swimming it has to be submitted to various treatments of increasing alienation: artificial coloring, chlorination, and disinfectants. "The pool ideal is a sterile environment," expert John Dawes recommended. "Swimming pool water must be better than the water we drink, and remain so. It has to be clearer than drinking water and still contain a palatable disinfectant."[75] Dawes did not foresee that rigorous chemical purification may lead to new, often dangerous if not lethal, toxicity.

Apart from introducing less hazardous substances, the bad image of swimming pool water was fought with campaigns like that of the Ocean Park Bath House, Santa Monica, California, which in 1912 advertised the magic of modern filtering techniques with the slogan: "Some people drink filtered water. We bathe in it."[76]

Another way to counteract poisoning-through-disinfection was to reintroduce "nature" by simulating healthy precipitation in indoor swimming pools. As early as 1842 the

77. See E. Willmann, *Das Dianabad in Wien, 1842,* colored drawing in Lachmayer, Mattl-Wurm, and Gargerle, eds., *Das Bad,* 41.

78. Schleyer, *Bäder und Badeanstalten,* 332–333; Hans Krämer, ed., *Der Mensch und die Erde; die Entstehung, Gewinnung und Verwendung der Schätze der Erde als Grundlagen der Kultur* (Berlin, Leipzig, Vienna, and Stuttgart: Bong & Co., 1912), 282–283.

79. Following the American Sandwich Syndrome (piling one sensation upon the other), the Adelphi hotel in Melbourne, Florida, had its rooftop swimming pool installed in such a way that part of it "projects one meter out of the building, at which point a glass floor allows views of the street below." *House and Garden* (UK), August 1996, 49.

80. Jack Petree, "Pilings Prop Up Pool in Middle of Lake," *Pool and Spa News,* November 17, 1986, 83 and 104.

Viennese Dianabad was equipped with sprinklers to provide the swimmers with a daylong oxygenous infusion.[77] About 1910, the municipal pool of Hildesheim had showerheads fitted around the pool to shoot clouds of water from one end to the other in a conscious effort to add a strong sense of hydrotherapy to everyday use of the pool. Another way to revitalize pool water was to shake it up by means of wave-making machinery. German engineer Recknagel of Munich had his System-Höglauer patented shortly before 1910; by means of a set of hydraulically operated shovels, the contents of a swimming tank were pushed rhythmically from one side to the other, creating a cataract of white-crested waves. Recknagel's system was put into public practice in the "Undosa" Wellenbad at Dresden (fig. 1.31), before 1912.[78]

Inducing waves and simulating rainfall belonged to the Renaissance tradition of recreating nature under artificial circumstances in order to improve upon the savage state and so establish a customized *belle nature.* This tradition has come to fruition in our contemporary aquatic pleasure parks, where waterfalls, water chutes, meandering rivers, and oceanic breakers have become standard elements. In most of the aquapark attractions, the massive catering to vertiginous sensation is intended to inspire feelings of weightlessness, the sensation of floating in space being part of the dubious complex of well-being that makes up the joy of swimming.[79]

The Parasite Pool The latest word in environmentally safe swimming pools is the parasite pool, an inflatable bath that is lowered into another pool whose water quality is considered suspect. Another solution is "the pool in the lake." The town of Bellevue, Washington, has been developed for residential living around Lake Sturdevant. But the lake makes unpleasant swimming because it is surrounded by a peat bog. A local builder found the solution by building a 5-by-10.5-meter reinforced-concrete pool that was to be sunk in the middle of the lake. The pool shell had to be cast in the lake on a floating, temporary, raftlike construction, since the bog could not possibly carry its weight. After completion, the pool was launched onto its permanent, pile-supported site. How it is to be reached and whether prospective swimmers still have to wade through the bog are not explained in the report. But it is a stirring idea![80]

With increasing anxiety over global pollution and growing popular distrust of man's deleterious effects on the environment, the swimmer's next recourse will be the integral frogman suit, dramatically demonstrated by doomsday clairvoyant Dustin Hoffman in *The Graduate* (1967; see chapter 6). Together with the condom, the frogman suit must be regarded as the characteristic attribute of an increasingly autistic society that cannot communicate unreservedly or without self-protection, a society that regrettably is on the way to determining the approaching millennium.

1.31. Dresden: "Undosa" Wellenbad, before 1912.
(*Der Mensch und die Erde*, 1912.)

two

From *Maison de Plaisance* to Playhouse

Lords of the Swan I

Auch die frei, zierlich-stolz
Sanfthingleitenden Schwäne
In gesell'ger Schwimmlust
Seh'ich, ach, nicht mehr! Goethe

Ultimately, the swan is the perfect representation of lustful hypocrisy. A. P. Thomas

Epigraph: Johann Wolfgang von Goethe, *Faust* (Munich: Verlag C. H. Beck, 1977), line 9095.
1. Charles Sprawson, *Haunts of the Black Masseur: The Swimmer as Hero* (London: Jonathan Cape, 1992), 213.
2. Ibid., and Julius Desing, *Wahnsinn oder Verrat; war König Ludwig II geisteskrank?* (Lechbruck, n.d.).
3. Richard Sennett, *The Fall of Public Man* (1974; New York: Norton, 1992).

When swimming was reinvented in eighteenth-century Europe, its practice and instruction had been part of the public domain. Swimming pools were public pools, and thereby public places for instruction. Swimming was generally taught along military lines: one lap up, one down, in crisp and disciplined movements. These patterns of instruction dictated the architecture of the early public swimming pools, which were all straight lines and right angles. By contrast, it was the patterns of entertainment that determined the architecture of private pools, which initially were extremely rare. The few that were known tended to be small tanks designed for bathing and other varieties of aquatic diversion, the experimental playthings of eccentric princes.

The development and distribution of the private bath and pool house is an intricate part of the social transition from public to private and from ancien régime to capitalist society. The transition from aristocratic eccentricity to bourgeois dissipation and conspicuous waste can be best explored in that fascinating laboratory of privatization, the fin-de-siècle United States of America, where lingering memories of feudal bliss were mixed with a new sense of equality and plutocratic independence. The late nineteenth-century indoor pools of the East Coast offer interesting insights into the patterns of big-money entertainment.

From there it is just one more step to the pleasure villas of the West Coast and the hallucinations of Hollywood. After all, we are now dealing more with the entertainment value of private water than with swimming per se, and there the movie capital of the new world was the *locus logicus*. It should come as no surprise that the emperor of the entertainment industry, William Randolph Hearst, developed into the modern equivalent of the man who had more or less invented it all: Ludwig II of Bavaria. It is useful to commence the story of the private pool with the contributions of the mad monarch, who suffered from "an intense curiosity for water," as Charles Sprawson noted in his magisterial study.

"'The cold waters of the Alpsee beckon to me,' Ludwig once wrote in his diary, referring to Starnberger See," where the king drowned.[1] "One of the leading figures of late German Romanticism . . . [whose] corpse on his demise was discovered in the shallows,"[2] Ludwig II shared with Hearst an extraordinary talent for thematic eclecticism, a furious nostalgia for heroic feudalism, and this "intense curiosity for water." Naturally, there are other possible heirs to the Dream King, but what makes this specific case of artistic identification significant is that each married his veneration for water with an unquenchable lust for building. They were no mere dreamers, but frantic doers who instantly translated their whims into palpable proofs of their unique artistry. And what makes this particular line of artistry so interesting is that it established a tradition that would be indispensable to the aesthetic of the American cinema, and later of television. In homage to these two notorious figures, the following three chapters are entitled "Lords of the Swan" because, more than any other emblematic animal, the swan perfectly embodies the theatrical display of perverse hydrophobia characteristic of the domestication of water, from the Bavarian castles of Ludwig to the West Coast monuments of Hearst.

Public and Until the end of the ancien régime, bathing and swimming were performed
Private in the public domain, in pools or, in more adventurous instances, in rivers and in the sea. Gradually, however, hygienic exercises moved away from the public bathhouse and began to settle within the intimacy of the private home. The bourgeoisie withdrew to its private quarters and many formerly public services moved there too, necessarily in miniature versions, a phenomenon convincingly documented by Walter Benjamin, Philippe Ariès, and Alain Corbin.

The public realm became fragmented into segments of private authority. The bathhouse, the latrine, the wash house, and ultimately the swimming pool were sufficiently reduced in scale to be able to fit into the home. This process of civic miniaturization and privatization led to an almost complete secrecy in terms of distribution and disposition of the hygienic facilities. Communal bathing and defecation Roman style were cloaked with an ever-increasing mystery, until the Anglo-puritanical autoconfinement of the privy was reached. Intimacy, Richard Sennett tells us, has become the obsession of the post-public era,[3] and thus one could conclude that the private pool has become the obsession of public intimacy.

But civic miniaturization was not the only factor that determined the break between public and private swimming pools. After all, the private pool is much more than just a small public pool; it could be a shrine, a nymphaeum, or a monumental or practical piece of water embedded in the magical surroundings of a grotto. One recurring feature is fake naturalism. This somewhat vaguely determined tradition runs from the proto-classical shrines of nature to Renaissance grottoes, and passes through the Venusgrotte and the Villa Vizcaya to the free-form pools of the fifties.

The evolution from free or "wild" swimming, to the princely interest in the art of swimming in the period of Enlightenment, to the age of public instruction at the beginning of the nineteenth century, demonstrates an increasing interest in the art of survival as well as in the theatrical and medical aspects of life in water. This was the age of the Theatrum Mundi—society as the stage—where performers and audience contributed in equal terms to the spectacle. Public instruction, as it was known from the Roman *thermae* to the medieval marketplace,

4. See Samuel John Klingensmith, *The Utility of Splendor: Ceremony, Social Life, and Architecture at the Court of Bavaria, 1600–1800* (Chicago: University of Chicago Press, 1993), 102–103. Klingensmith did not consider the Badenburg tank as a place to swim in. W. Schleyer, on the other hand, in his *Bäder und Badeanstalten* (Leipzig, 1909), 264, did not hesitate to call the *Baderaum* a "tief in das Sockelgeschoss hinabreichendes Schwimmbassin."

"The only other roughly contemporary examples," Klingensmith added, "are French—Robert de Cotte's bathing pavilion at Severne and that at the Prince de Conti's Château d'Issy of around 1705. The latter pavilion also contained a Festsaal and limited living quarters; its bath chamber, however, was not nearly as large as that of the Badenburg. This was also true of Louis XIV's 'appartement des bains' at Versailles (1671–77), where the basin was hardly larger than a modern bathtub. The Badenburg may also have been inspired by Turkish thermae, which Max Emanuel would undoubtedly have become aquainted with during his campaign in Hungary." The bathtub in the "Badehaus" at Schwetzingen, built after the plans of Nicolas de Pigage, the plans for a bathroom for double occupancy by Jacques François Blondel, *De la décoration des édifices en général* (1737), and the Marmorbad in the Karlsaue in Kassel (1722–1728) should be added to the list. See Herbert Lachmayer, in Herbert Lachmayer, Sylvia Mattl-Wurm, and Christian Gargerle, eds., *Das Bad; eine Geschichte der Badekultur im 19. und 20. Jahrhundert* (Salzburg: Residenz Verlag, 1991), 51–52. For an update of the history of princely bathing pavilions and bathrooms see Ulrika Kiby, *Bäder und Badekultur in Orient und Okzident; Antike bis Spätbarock* (Cologne: DuMont, 1995), especially 209–227.

5. See, for example, the bathing tank commissioned in 1567 for Schloss Ambras near Innsbruck by Philippine Melser, the progressive wife of Archduke Ferdinand, cited by Kiby, *Bäder und Badekultur*, 222.

6. It is not clear what material was used originally for waterproofing. Lead and tar are possibilities.

remained even when the populist character had been left behind. Take as example the Nymphenburger Badenburg.

The Badenburg This "bathing palace" is a medium-sized pavilion of restrained frivolity, erected on a slightly elevated socle preceded by a series of steps that connect the building with what we would now call a Roman-end pool (a rectangle with one or two apsidal endings).[4] This pond was part of the extensive waterworks of the Nymphenburg park; it was inhabited by a flock of swans and enlivened by two fountains. Built in 1718 by the elector Max Emanuel and his architect, Joseph Effner the Younger, it was intended as a *maison de plaisance,* a pleasure pavilion that, like the Pagodenburg and the Magdalenenklause (Hermitage), was an architectural focal point in the ceremonial use of the park. The main—and unique—attraction of the Badenburg, from which the building derived its name, was the generously proportioned bathing room, some 9 by 6 meters, which occupied one wing of the building that it shared with a dining room, a main hall, and a "Chinese room" (fig. 2.1).

Set in the basement, the pool proper, with its tiled walls, reaches to the level of the *piano nobile.* The spectator who enters at this level immediately experiences a sinking sensation, since the expected floor has disappeared and one looks straight down into the basement. A narrow gallery, supported by elegantly carved consoles and defined by intricate railings of gilt bronze and wrought iron, frames the pool below. A spiral staircase hidden in a corner leads to the bottom, which has been waterproofed by fine concrete. There are two faucets, one for cold and one for hot water, which probably could have filled the basin within several hours.

The bathing room's actual function is difficult to ascertain. Marble benches were provided at the entrance side, inviting bathers to sit and soak, as in many Renaissance bathing tanks.[5] The zinc-plated tank, too big for a mere quick bathe but too small for making swimstrokes, resembles the typical *Bewegungsbad* of a nineteenth-century spa. Of particular interest is the stool in the middle of the bath to give bathers some hold. Since the Badenburg tank is too shallow for swimming, it may be assumed that its visitors experimented with dog-paddle-style propulsion, usually accomplished by keeping the feet in contact with the floor in a limited floating action. In the early eighteenth century, the dog paddle was the closest one could get to real swimming.

The uniqueness of the art of swimming and its spectacular possibilities of instructive entertainment are emphasized by the presence of the gallery. From there curious guests were offered a first look at something generally forbidden to commoners, something only the most privileged could witness. The bathing room (fig. 2.2) seems a cross between the operating amphitheater of an academic hospital and the lecture room of a Society of Dilettanti, except for the frivolous chandelier and the rocailles adorning the marble-encrusted gallery zone, which are in such contrast to the crisp tiled walls and cement-clad floor of the pool.[6]

2.1. *Left:* Nymphenburg, Bavaria: Badenburg, 1718, interior. Joseph Effner the Younger. (Konrad Ottenheym, Utrecht.) *Also plate 5.*

2.2. Badenburg, plan. (Schleyer, *Bäder und Badeanstalten,* 1909.)

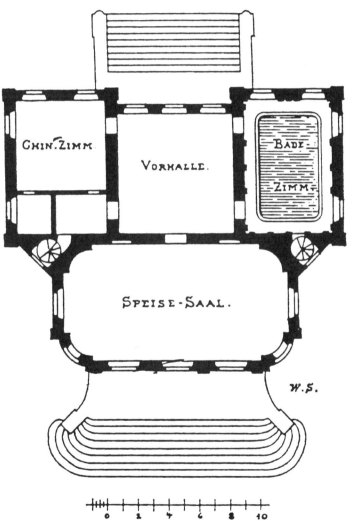

7. Herbert Lachmayer, "Inszeniertes Wohlbehagen-Funktion und Luxus des privaten Bades," in Lachmayer, Mattl-Wurm, and Gargerle, eds., *Das Bad,* 51.

8. See Ernst Hartwig Kantorowicz, *The King's Two Bodies* (1957; Princeton: Princeton University Press, 1966). On the whole, actions undertaken in a state of total or partial undressing such as bathing, swimming, urination, and defecation had, until relatively recent times, been performed in the company of others. Extra importance was given to the proximity of persons of elevated, preferably regal, authority. There are many instances of this transition from public to private; let us illustrate the point using two reasonably well known paintings. The first is the early sixteenth-century *Susanna and the Stoning of the Elders,* by Albrecht Altdorfer, a painting thoroughly analyzed to illustrate this very point. It could be stated that Altdorfer's staging of the scene is one of overwhelming public interest in a scene of minimal erotic impact.

The other picture, Degas's pastel study of a girl squatting in a shallow tub scrubbing herself is, by contrast, a hyperindividual scene, in which the bather is not bathed by others but by herself. And where the assistants are lacking, the observers are reduced to merely the artist who had witnessed the scene and made the picture. The two pictures play well into Richard Sennett's famous distinction between the private and the public, in the latter of which not only the communality of bathing is stressed but more emphatically the scene is rendered as a staged performance, with an interested audience and a willing players. See Wolfgang Pircher, "Artemis, Bathseba und Susanna im Bade. Verletzte Intimität," in Lachmayer, Mattl-Warm, and Gargerle, eds., *Das Bad,* 9–18.

9. Schleyer, *Bäder und Badeanstalten,* 268–269.

10. Lachmayer, "Inszeniertes Wohlbehagen-Funktion," 51.

Invoking an atmosphere of alchemical entertainment, the entire arrangement is reminiscent of the secretive way Faust observed the movements of the bathing nymphs in the lower Peneios.[7]

The split-level arrangement of the *sala terrena* and *piano nobile* might be explained in several ways. It may have facilitated participation in the rituals of court life, of which the bath was part of the ceremony of the *lever et coucher* of the king. Together with the *lit de parade,* the bath was the ideal place to observe the "king's other body" at close range and to display public intimacy in a ceremonial manner.[8] Another possibility is that the bathing tank was a place of scientific observation, a sort of anatomical theater in which the movements of the bathers/swimmers could be followed and studied from above. Finally, with reference to the tradition of the Renaissance garden with its multitude of hydraulic surprises, the bath might have found employment as the magical wet-theater in which daring contemporary plays of risqué character could be performed by professional artists acting the roles of shepherds or of nymphs and satyrs. After all, the many connotations of the unusual name of the estate—Nymphenburg—must have been obvious to most of the audience.

What is certain, in any case, is that even if it had been intended as a place to practice swimming, the size of the basin did not permit more than a couple of strokes, with no opportunity to lift the feet from the bottom. The degree of realism that the aspiring swimmer had to face was about the same as in the Roman *frigidaria,* in which the water generally stood at 1.1 meters, about the height of the navel. Swimming was play, a spectacle of make-believe in which survival was not at issue and the risk of drowning was vastly less than that of scraping one's knee on the mosaics of the bottom. A document that may help us interpret the activities performed in basins of such a size is the creative reconstruction of a Roman *frigidarium* that Claude Perrault made for his annotated translation of Vitruvius of 1684, wherein a balustrade separates the onlookers from the bathers and the water reaches no higher than the groin.

Smaller than the Badenburg pool, and perhaps not even intended for serious bathing, let alone swimming, was the Marmorbad in Kassel (fig. 2.3). The marble bath, incorporated into the Orangerieschloss in the Karlsaue in Kassel, was built between 1722 and 1728 by Marcus Schlichting for the Landgraf Karl.[9] It is a richly decorated, marble-faced room, 13 meters square, that accommodates an octagonal sunken bath, 6.15 meters wide, with marble benches in the four corners. Since plumbing had never been provided, it must have been either filled and emptied by hand or else never made operational.[10]

Such *maisons de plaisance* were aristocratic playthings that were part of the general layout of gardens. Because of its accessibility and its open structure, the Marmorbad, more than the Badenburg, was an architectonic but domestically scaled replacement of the nymphaeum or garden grotto. Gradually, typical garden features like fountains, ponds, and grottoes seem to follow a trend of domestication and privatization. The next step would be to dig out the nymphaeum—rocks, grotto, waterfall, and all—and reinstall it entire in the living room.

2.3. Kassel: Marmorbad, 1722–1728. Marcus
Schlichting. (Schleyer, *Bäder und
Badeanstalten*, 1909.)

11. Wilfrid Blunt, *The Dream King: Ludwig II of Bavaria* (London: Hamilton, 1970), 152.

That this was indeed the line of future development may be best demonstrated with the most exotic of Bavarian country houses, the Linderhof, favorite refuge of the most picturesque member of the Wittelsbach dynasty, Ludwig II. Although Ludwig's colorful building activities are not unheralded, they should be briefly summarized here because they so clearly illustrate that displacement of swimming exclusively from the public sphere, where theory and practice were developed in military swimming schools and in bathing establishments for the lower classes, to the more private world of the upper echelons of society. The aristocracy and the haute bourgeoisie began to indulge in a process of miniaturization and privatization that led to indoor grottoes and pools, which then gradually lost their educational, hygienic, and athletic functions in favor of mere ornamental value. This trend continued into the twentieth century.

Ludwig II and the Padre Patufet Syndrome Born at the palace of Nymphenburg in 1845, Ludwig must have been familiar with the Badenburg. It is generally taken for granted that he "was a strong swimmer," although in 1886 he managed to drown in the shallow part of the Starnberger See.[11] We may surmise, therefore, that if he had ever received instruction in swimming in the tank of the Badenburg, it could hardly have been that effective.

After all, most of the swimming done in the eighteenth and nineteenth centuries was wild swimming *à la naturelle,* in rivers, ponds, lakes, canals, whatever was available. Salt water was considered to be particularly healthful for therapeutic bathing as well as for swimming. Since the open sea was considered uncooperative, more tranquil spots like rock and tide pools and secluded bays, such as those in Naples and Capri, were preferred. Indoor pools were extremely rare, and, it is probably safe to say, only eccentric kings like Ludwig ever thought of building one. His pool was in all respects a transitional affair standing halfway between the garden grotto and the paradise pool, designed to be floated on as well as swum in.

The model was Richard Wagner's Venusgrotte, designed for his opera *Tannhäuser,* for generations an inexhaustible source of psychoanalytical enjoyment. It is significant that these two historical figures, Richard Wagner and Ludwig II, both obsessed by water and both suffering from sexual repression, not only chose the swan as their pet emblem but also displayed uncommon interest in the anthropomorphic grotto.

Grottoes and secret hiding places from the Renaissance onward were mostly schematic simulacrums of the female sex organ. Arguably the largest of its kind was the Grotto of Thétis by Hubert Robert, François Boucher, and the sculptor Thévenin, hidden in a *bosquet sauvage* in the gardens of Versailles, a place Ludwig admired and had copied at random in different instances. Usually such structures followed simple organic precepts in which easily legible forms were employed, such as oval openings, bulging masses, mossy cliffs, coral-colored stalactites, and so on. The intended meanings were reinforced by figure groups of fauns and nymphs that often depicted scenes from Ovid's *Metamorphoses*. Of all grotto designs, those drawn by Jean-Jacques Lequeu (fig. 2.4) had the naive charm of being the most literal. His sketches were unambiguous anthropomorphic remodelings of the vagina, often preceded by sketches of the real thing in order to facilitate the evolutionary sequence.[12]

When Richard Wagner described the sets for the interior of the Venusberg in scene 1, act 1, of *Tannhäuser,* he followed traditional lines. Despite his characteristic scrupulous disdain for overt sexuality, Wagner ventured further than anyone before him, including Lequeu, into what in later cinematic terms would be called a sense-surround simulation, in this case of a gigantic uterus on stage. "Die Bühne stellt das Innere des Venusberges dar. Eine weite Grotte, welche sich im Hintergrunde durch eine Biegung nach Rechts [an extraordinary gyneco-logical detail, following the characteristic bend in the uterine tube] wie unabsehbar dahin zieht."[13] The naturalism is astounding! Then, in well-chosen but thoroughly traditional anthropomorphic analogies, he prescribes streams and waterfalls that flow into a pool where naiads and sirens bathe. The physiognomic source can be recognized in the description of the walls as "unregelmässiger Form, mit wunderbaren, korallenartigen tropischen Gewächsen bewachsen" (irregular forms covered with wonderful, coral-like tropical growth).

Then the composer switches to a larger scale. First, instead of having a narrow, make-believe stream and waterfall trickle over the stage, Wagner decided to flood it with a sizable pool, probably the very first swimming pool placed on an opera stage. Next, in his irresistible urge for scenic realism, Wagner added color to the scene with the help of colored light. Venus lies on a bed in the foreground, surrounded by the closely intertwined bodies of graces and amoretti. As in the most vulgar of brothels, the group is bathed in the light of a "zarter, rosiger Dämmer." The realistic touches of soft red and pink are brought to a climax in the lighting of the foreground: "Der ganze Vordergrund is von einem zauberhaften, von unten herdringenden, röthlichen Lichte beleuchtet" (the entire foreground is bathed in a mysterious reddish light, magically rising up from below). To creative psychologists such as Salvador Dalí, the will to build grottoes of this remarkable naturalism was an indication of strongly regressive desires—were not caverns like the Venusgrotte the chosen places to relive prenatal memories?

"Playing at Making Grottoes" Dalí began his explorations of regression with a thorough analysis of Jean-Auguste-Dominique Ingres's *Le bain turc* of 1863 (fig. 2.5), the last in the artist's series of Turco-Persian hydraulic impressions. Succinctly stated, the picture appears to be a one-person keyhole observation of minimal public participation but optimal erotic effect. Dalí, who exhibited a keen interest in the picture, convincingly interpreted it not only as a model of solitary erotic enjoyment, but predominantly as a detailed image of "intra-uterine memories."[14] An enthusiastic and devoted follower of Freud,

12. See Jean-Jacques Marty-L'Herme, "Les cas de Jean-Jacques Lequeu," *Macula* 3/4 (1979), 138–149.

13. "The stage represents the interior of the Venusberg, a capacious grotto which, because of a curving to the right, disappears out of sight." Quotations are taken from Tilman Osterwold, "Die Natur auf der Bühne," in Ilse Czigens, Franziska Schmitt, and Detlev Zinke, eds., *Naturbetrachtung/ Naturverfremdung* (Stuttgart: Württembergischer Kunstverein, 1977), 61–71. It must be coincidental, but this specific configuration of the uterus is unique to the human species. See Elaine Morgan, *The Scars of Evolution: What Our Bodies Tell Us about Human Origins* (London: Souvenir Press, 1990).

14. Salvador Dalí, *The Secret Life of Salvador Dalí,* trans. H. M. Chevalier (New York: Dial Press, 1942), 27: "Intra Uterine Memories." For other interpretations of *Le bain turc,* see John L. Connolly, Jr., "Ingres and the Erotic Intellect," in Thomas B. Hess and Linda Nochlin, eds., *Woman as Sex Object: Studies in Erotic Art, 1730–1970* (London: Allen Lane, 1973), 16–32.

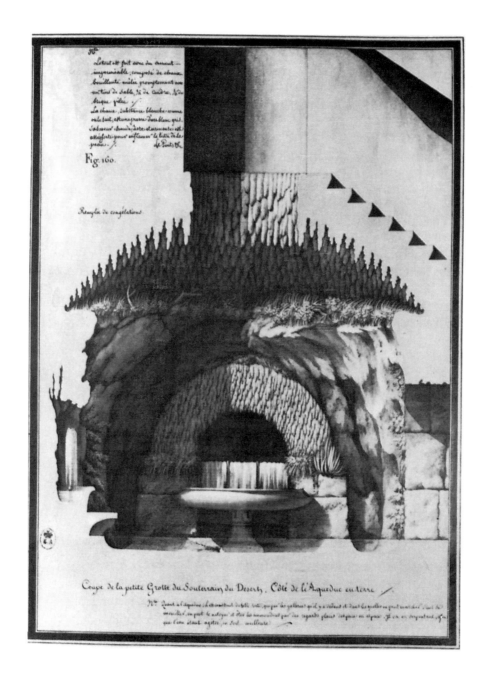

2.4. Jean-Jacques Lequeu, grotto design. (*Macula,*
      3/6 [1979].)
2.5. Jean-Auguste-Dominique Ingres, *Le bain turc,*
      1863. (Paris, Musées Nationaux.)

Dalí expounded a theory of prenatal experience based upon Freud's thesis that birth is a disruption of the motherly paradise and that a large number of human dreams and desires are to be traced back to a regressive longing for a prolonged stay in the uterus: "Indeed if you ask me how it was 'in there' I shall immediately answer, 'It was divine, it was paradise.' But what was this paradise like? Have no fear; details will not be lacking. But allow me to begin with a general description: The intra-uterine paradise was the color of hell, that is to say red, orange, yellow and bluish, the color of flames, of fire; above all it was soft, immobile, warm, symmetrical, double, gluey."[15] Ingres's *Turkish Bath* was the "preeminent unconscious expression of the intra-uterine paradise." Dalí dramatically illustrated his point by juxtaposing Ingres's tondo with a photograph (fig. 2.6) of himself posing in a supine fetal position—his favorite sleeping pose—inside a chicken's egg.[16]

> External danger has the virtue of provoking and enhancing the phantasms and representations of our intra-uterine memories. When I was small I remember that at the approach of great summer storms we children would run frantically with one accord and hide under the tables covered with cloths. . . . All curled up in there we especially liked to eat sweets, to drink warm sugar water, all the while trying to make believe our life was then transpiring into another world. I had named that stormy weather game "Playing at making grottoes," or else "Playing at Padre Patufet." Padre Patufet has been since olden times the most popular childhood hero of Catalonia; he was so small that one day he got lost in the country. An ox swallowed him to protect him. His parents looked for him . . . and heard the voice of Patufet answering: "I am in the belly of an ox where it does not snow and it does not rain."[17]

15. Dalí, *The Secret Life,* 27
16. Ibid., illustration facing page 70.
17. Ibid., 31. Dalí had observed this syndrome during the war: "The present war has furnished me several striking examples on this subject: during the air raid alarms in Paris I would draw the curled up and foetus-like attitudes that people would adopt in the shelters. There the external danger was further augmented by the intra-uterine evocations inherent in the darkness, the dimensions etc. of the cellars. People would often go to sleep with ecstasies of happiness, and a secret illusion was constantly betrayed by smiles appropriate to a satisfaction absolutely unjustified by logic." Ibid.

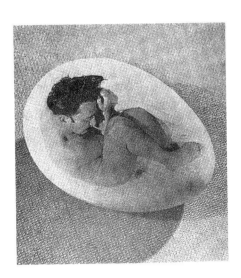

2.6. Salvador Dalí, self-portrait in egg. (*The Secret Life of Salvador Dalí*, 1942.)

18. For an interesting analysis, see Harald Szeemann and Jean Clair, *Le macchine celibi/The Bachelor Machines* (Venice: Alfieri, 1975), 79, and Michael Balint, *Thrills and Regressions* (New York: International Universities Press, 1959).
Epigraph: J.-J. Rousseau, *Emile ou de l'éducation* (Paris, 1933), I, book III, 190.
19. Michael Petzet, *König Ludwig II und die Kunst* (Munich: Münchener Residenz, 1968), 36.
20. Alain Corbin, *The Lure of the Sea: The Discovery of the Seaside in the Western World, 1750–1840* (Berkeley: University of California Press, 1994), 223, quoting from E. Richer, *Voyage pittoresque dans le département de la Loire inférieure* (Nantes, 1823). See also Ulrich Schmidt, *Inseln; Streifzüge von Geschichte und Gegenwart einer zauberhaften Welt. Von Atlantis bis Mallorca* (Lucerne and Frankfurt: E. J. Bücher, 1972).
21. The archetypal eroticized island is that of Cytherea in the *Hypnerotomachia Poliphili* of 1499. An interesting study of the geocultural aspects of the Island of Cytherea is being prepared by Dutch art historian Renée Borgonjen, Amstelveen. In modern literature, Michel Tournier, *Vendredi, ou les l'Indes du Pacific* (Paris: Gallimard, 1976), creates a gripping combination of an enlightened *Hypnerotomachia* and an uncensored *Robinson Crusoe*.
22. See Gabrielle Wittkop-Ménardeau, "Capri ist wie das Leben; Inselgefühle und Inselgedanken," *Frankfurter Allgemeine Zeitung*, August 29, 1996, R 5, and Ron Hall, "The Secret Mediterranean," *The Condé Nast Traveller*, April 1990, 118–132.
In 1876 an American colonel, John Clay

Dalí reasoned that the traumatization attendant on birth was due to the abrupt separation from the uterus, comparable to the physical and spiritual experience of the expulsion from paradise. In order to undo this unfortunate course of events, man had developed the tendency to create a new paradise, based upon his intrauterine memories, as illustrated by the Padre Patufet syndrome. In this sense the Turkish bath is a vision of the intrauterine paradise, a womblike sauna, padded with bouncy female bodies. Ingres's vision was contemporary with the exploits of Wagner and Ludwig and serves as an explanatory model of their respective grotto buildings.

After an exhaustive correspondence with Wagner, Ludwig in 1876 had an enlargement of the entire *Tannhäuser* set rebuilt in the park of Linderhof by the landscape designer August Dirigl, and commenced refining it into a comfortable but haunting "machine célibataire."[18] Electric light had been made operational a short time before, and Ludwig was the first to test its possibilities. Initially the grotto was bathed in Wagnerian boudoir-pink, but after the discovery of the erotic potentials of the Blue Grotto of Capri, the king thought it necessary to have pink and blue light both.

Intermezzo: *L'île du genre humain, c'est la terre.*   J.-J. ROUSSEAU
Isola Erotica

To get some idea of the range of influence of Capri in the nineteenth century, let us briefly study the meaning of the "Isola Erotica." Its Blue Grotto was highly fashionable; for example, in 1861, visitors to the Hofoper in Berlin could witness the protagonist riding in a gondola through the Gulf of Naples; when he finally reached Capri, the stage changed into the Blue Grotto.[19]

In a peculiar yet not illogical way, small idyllic islands have a certain affinity with swimming pools. The Greek word for island—*nasos* or *nesos*—derives from *neo*, to swim; an island is *nasos*, "he who swims" or rather "she who swims," because *nasos* is feminine. The discovery of the island as a place of pleasure cannot be attributed to one period in particular. From Homer to Hadrian and Pliny, the island could be regarded as the haunt of a faun, a nymph, or a beautiful sorceress, or equally as a place of agreeable and secure "isolation." In times when the relation between man and nature existed mainly in terms of fear and domination, the island offered a clean, manageable piece of nature that could be possessed, charted, and defended. In romantic interpretations, the island became an object of aesthetic contemplation or a secure refuge and place of social idealism, conveying a feeling of security evoked by Shelley's phrase "the oasis of the island." Rousseau, in imitation of Hadrian at his villa in Tivoli, had his tomb erected on the "isola" in the pond at Ermenonville outside Paris. Caspar David Friedrich and Heinrich Heine sought reclusive solitude on the Baltic and North Sea islands of Ruegen and Norderney, respectively.

Furthermore, small uninhabited islands were the ideal nursery of naive utopias, as the various "Robinsonades" have proven over the centuries. Social and spiritual regression, as Alain Corbin has written, were projected onto the island as a return to the motherly womb, the island thus becoming "that mythical image of woman, the virgin, the mother."[20] The eroticization of the island, later intensified by romantics like Byron and Shelley, derives from the Venus legends, which frequently assigned to the goddess the island of Cythera.[21] To emphasize the sweet surprise of the semisavage wilderness, islands could be appointed with yet more miniature secluded places, like secret springs and hidden creeks, grottoes and ponds. The island grotto thus becomes the substitute for an eroticized Mother Earth.

Corbin has described how romantic travelers journeyed to such northern islands as the Hebrides, Skye, Staffa, Rum, and the Isle of Man in order to study the grottoes and the craggy coastlines. Later tourists concentrated on warmer, more hospitable places. In the wake of Byron's erotic representations of the Mediterranean islands, Capri increasingly became the focal point of many more or less lewd excursionists. Its Blue Grotto was touristically discovered in 1826 by two Germans, August Kopisch and Ernst Fries, assisted by the local notary Giuseppe Pagano. The massive travel activity that followed was the beginning of the exploitation of the Côte d'Azur as a modern touristic paradise. In the case of the Blue Grotto, it was not solely its delightful location that made it the particular goal of amatory pilgrimages, but also its traditional anthropomorphic explicitness.[22] None of this was lost on Ludwig II when he was busily designing his Venusgrotte at the Linderhof estate.

Ludwig was highly susceptible to the politics of seclusion. His passion for grottoes was matched by his love of islands, demonstrated in the gradiose redoing of the three islands in the Herrenchiemsee in southern Bavaria. The first island is the Herreninsel, once occupied by the Augustinian canons; then there is the Fraueninsel, which accommodated an

Mackowen, settled on Capri, where he bought a house and wrote a book. He was said to have collected statuettes and pictures of the catamites and ephebi that Capri had been notorious for since the days of Tiberius, who came to the island for the cruel eroticons with male slaves and the infamous satyricons that Suetonius and Petronius commented upon. The colonel was murdered in 1901, supposedly in relation to his too enthusiastic collecting of erotic antiquities.

2.7. Frolics on Max Emden's islands in Lago
     Maggiore. (Landmann, *Ascona–Monte Verità*,
     1983.)

abbey of Benedictine nuns; finally, there is the Krautinsel, where the nuns and monks reputedly held their amorous rendezvous.[23]

Something similar was taking place in northern Italy, where in 1885 the Russian baroness Antonietta de Saint-Léger bought two little islands in the northern part of Lago Maggiore: San Pancrazio and Sant'Apollinare. The islands were named after the two convents that had found refuge there; today they are known as the Brissago or Saint-Léger islands. Baroness de Saint-Léger must have been a charming eccentric; she cherished the great ambition of transforming the islands into lush paradisical gardens. In the shortest possible time they were converted from inhospitable clumps of rock—so inhospitable that even the monks had fled—into a resplendent Eden. After erecting a villa and planting a botanical garden of considerable scientific value, Madame began to organize garden parties, concerts, ballets, and plays, to which she invited the cultural beau monde, whom she expected to be participants as well as spectators. The new civilization culminated in the establishment of an autonomous post office, which issued its own stamps.

After the death of the baroness in 1927, the islands were acquired by the German department store millionaire Dr. Max Emden. Whereas the baroness was a sort of philatelic latter-day Eve, Dr. Emden was a sensualist. For him, Die Inseln der Glückseligen— "The Islands of the Blissful Spirits"—were a place to develop a radically hedonistic strategy, to which end he converted one of the islands to a theater of soft-core pornographic euphoria (fig. 2.7). Under the guidance of the Berlin architect Breslauer, a neo-Renaissance palace was built and the garden, with its exotic foliage, extended. But the most interestingly salacious aspect of Emden's ambitions was that he determined to devote all the time that old age allotted him to the study of frisky young girls in the nude. Therefore he commissioned Breslauer to build him a swimming pool of tasteful proportions and the most beautiful materials, so that the girls would stand out well against it. Roman in inspiration, completely covered with precious marble, the pool was probably based on the paintings of Sir Lawrence Alma Tadema. Its total length was 33 meters, for Europeans an unusual dimension, but it translates into about 100 feet, which justifies the suspicion that the pool was designed by an American, rather than a continental, firm.

The exact range of the blissful pensionnaire's interests may be gauged by the commission he gave the popular Hamburg sculptor, Wrba, for the statue of an attractive female nude to be placed at the entrance of the pool. When the great businessman found time for an hour or so of study, he would ensconce himself comfortably in a custom-made rocking chair of generous proportions placed in the shelter of the loggia, to watch a specially choreographed spectacle of simple bathing pleasures. Unlike most of his contemporaries, Emden devoted his old age exclusively to the viewing of delicately tanned bathing nymphs. "Max Emden loved to surround himself with beautiful young women, the way other men loved to collect bronze statues. . . . Every day he could be seen driving his motor boat over the lake, the deck covered with tanned bodies sunning themselves."[24]

23. Blunt, The Dream King, 152–153.
24. "Wie andere männer Bronzestatuen sammeln, so liebte es Max Emden, von schönen, jungen Frauen umgeben zu sein. . . . Täglich konnte man Max Emden in seinem Motorboot, auf dessen Deck sich braungebrannte Körper sonnten, über den See fahren sehen." Robert Landmann, Ascona–Monte Verità; auf der Suche nach dem Paradies (Zurich and Cologne: Benzinger, 1973), 260–261.

Islands and swimming pools are closely related, bound together by their strong negative-positive character. Islands float on the water, like swimmers; the pool is an oasis, a fertile place. What the pool is to the earth, the island is to water. Linking them is their capacity for separation; nowhere are the elements so abruptly severed as where the beach meets the ocean, the rim of the pool the water. The abruptness of the transition inspires strong feelings of erotic intimacy.

This breakdown of the space-time continuum and its effect on our capacity for erotic excitement may be illustrated by the "boudoir frenzy." Not the smallness of the room, nor its suggestive furnishings, but the sudden transition between the formal and the informal, the public and the private, creates a moment of intense anticipation. This anticipatory tension could very well be observed in those countless ultrafamiliar desert island cartoons. The island/paradise theme invites fantasies of immediate erotic opportunism, for there is not a moment to be wasted. Time has become an extraordinary incentive. The sensation of longing, for example, is a time-directed experience. Cartoons of desert islands and oases thus make manifest intimations of desire. In this sense longing is but the result of the tension between space and time. For the unhappy desert traveler, the distance to the oasis is measured in units of the desire/time continuum.

A sudden dissolution of the desire/space-time continuum causes a release of erotic energy, easily observable, in the case of the boudoir, in a sexual frenzy that has become the object of countless erotic fantasies. Here, of course, the relative spaces are interchangeable so long as they are of extreme confinement. Thus monks' and nuns' cells, toilets, changing cabins, islands, and swimming pools represent conceptually the *hortus conclusus* of the hedonistic spirit. And so the Emden island was an overall reinforcement of the sensualist's closed garden.

Hollywood's idea of a playground for the pleasure-loving spirit was much less realistic. Here the imagery is conceived symbolically, and metaphorical circumlocution dominates. A beautiful example of thoroughly disguised hedonism is demonstrated by a photograph of English-born movie star Joan Fontaine posing with her newly acquired "island pool" in the miniature garden of her Los Angeles home (fig. 2.8). Miss Fontaine, wearing a flower-patterned dress, sits in a deck chair near the side of an irregularly shaped swimming pool with a rocky island in the middle. The scene is of an exaggerated quaintness.

But let us not be fooled. Miss Fontaine is a wolf in floral dress! Looking away from her pool, she stares into the distance, allowing her thoughts to travel back to the times when she was a mermaid. With no dress to cover her gracious limbs, garbed only in the tail of a dolphin, she imagines herself on the beach of a paradise island. Swimming pool builder Philip Ilsley, who had decades of experience with customers who desired designs that matched their dreams, remembered: "Most of the unusual patterns are dreamed up by customers who can afford to satisfy some latent longing. Actress Joan Fontaine apparently dreamed of being a

2.8.   *Below:* Joan Fontaine by her Philip Ilsley pool in
        Los Angeles. (Marc Wanamaker/Bison Archives.)
        On page 69:

2.9. *Top:* Linderhof: Grotto of Venus, 1876–1877, in Tannhäuser pink. (Jervis and Hojer, *Designs for the Dream King,* 1978.) *Also plate 6.*

2.10. *Bottom:* Grotto of Venus in Capri blue. (Jervis and Hojer, *Designs for the Dream King,* 1978.) *Also plate 7.*

25. Frank J. Taylor, "Those High Jinks in Hollywood Pools!" *Saturday Evening Post,* August 11, 1951, 34–35; 66–69.
26. *New York Times,* June 27, 1991, C1.

mermaid stranded on a rocky island, so my men sprayed, with the so-called 'gunnite' method, her pool with an island in the middle."[25] Numerous modern swimming pool designs have tuned into these paradise island fantasies. Among the newest fads is the "beach entry" pool, a quasi-natural concrete hole in the ground with a lazy ramp on one side, covered with sand, gradually leading into a free-form pool. Recently the National Spa and Pool Institute rewarded such a "Beach Entry Pool," located in Phoenix, Arizona, with an award. Where water is scarce and beaches are rare or nonexistent, such a pool is bound to deserve a prize.[26]

The Swan Has No Fun Within this context, the rosy pink and blue color schemes of the Venusgrotte make perfect sense (figs. 2.9, 2.10). In order to realize his chromatic dream, Ludwig sent forth his most aesthetically sensitive equerry, Richard Hornig, to the island of Capri to study the right kind of *Grotta Azzurra* blue. Shortly after Hornig had returned from his mission, the grotto was illuminated alternatively in Tannhäuser pink and Capri blue, so that it could be experienced in the two different moods excited by these colors.

This intensified interest in the island of Capri, its blue grotto, and the surrounding bay is significant. Capri, as far as wild swimming and bathing and of course diving were concerned, was the most advanced, the most daring place to visit. Ludwig, although unable to leave his own trusted territory, was able not merely to reconstruct the matter but to recreate the spirit of that most seductive spot on Earth.

The exact functions Ludwig assigned to his pool-grotto are not entirely known. It is certain that he kept two of his favorite swans in permanent residence, and that he was fond of riding in a boat shaped like a cockleshell. This organically shaped contraption

27. Petzet, *König Ludwig II und die Kunst,* 36.
28. Shot on location, the film shows many interesting scenes, including the ride of the cockle boat. See also Mattias Theodor Vogt, "Taking the Waters at Bayreuth," in Barry Millington and Stewart Spencer, eds., *Wagner in Performance* (New Haven: Yale University Press, 1992), 130–153.
29. Petzet, *König Ludwig II und die Kunst,* 36.
30. Ibid.
31. Sprawson, *Haunts of the Black Masseur,* 213–214.
32. See also Jeannot Simmen and Uwe Drepper, *Der Fahrstuhl; die Geschichte der vertikalen Eroberung* (Munich: Prestel, 1983), 189ff.

was manned by a servant who, in full view of his monarch, who well knew that in reality it was on rails and was propelled electrically, manipulated a pair of oars in pantomime fashion (see fig. 6.3), not dissimilar to the phantom engineer on a totally computer-controlled Japanese bullet train.

It is less certain whether Ludwig used the pool as a swimming bath; he was known to perform most of his physical exercises, among which bathing/swimming was included, at night. It might be deduced that he intended the Venusgrotte to be employed as a swimming pool on the basis of directions he issued in 1876 concerning its coloring. The king wrote that the bottom of the pool should be painted blue so as to intensify the azure lighting, "but," he added, fearing some kind of chemical pollution, "the paint should not be harmful, since the lake [i.e., the pool] must at the same time be able to serve as a bathing pool [*zugleich als Bad benützt werden muss können*]."[27] That the basic concept of the Venusgrotte was "a grotto accommodating a bath," rather than "a nonswimmable pool in a grotto," appears from a letter that Hornig sent to court secretary Düfflipp. Referring to His Majesty's earlier idea to build "a bath thought of as a grotto" in his castle of Neuschwanstein, Hornig orders Düfflipp to do likewise at Linderhof.

In view of the king's theatrical ambitions, it seems equally likely that the water of the grotto was also used for performances, or water ballets, of scenes taken from Wagner's operas, or perhaps even something that might have satisfied Dr. Max Emden's interests, a point that Luchino Visconti suggested in his film *Ludwig*.[28]

The king was fascinated by all kinds of advanced machinery, welcoming anything that could help him to realize his meta-world, so long as he did not have to understand its operations. "I don't want to know how it works. I just want to see that it works," the great man was reported to have said.[29] The whole grotto was a completely integrated system of electrically operated simulation devices. Michael Petzet, the specialist on Ludwig, has explained: "Behind the illusion of the cast-iron-framed artificial rocks stood the most modern technical apparatus. There was a hot-air heating system that was designed to keep the temperature at a constant level of 16 degrees Réaumur (20 degrees centigrade). Then there were 25 electric generators, installed by their inventor Werner von Siemens, making it the first electric power station in the kingdom."[30] Another hydrotechnical invention Ludwig seems to have furthered was the artificial wave-making machine credited to Wilhelm Bauer, the inventor of the submarine.[31]

Relying totally on his wealth and on the supremacy of his technicians, Ludwig always asked for the impossible. His ambition to have a flying machine built in the shape of a peacock—Ludwig's other favorite bird and one of the few that have no flying ability to speak of—which was to carry him over to the far side of the alpine lake, is illustrative of his disregard for technicalities.

If Ludwig indeed used Linderhof's Venusgrotte as a place to swim, it would probably count as the first free-form swimming extravaganza of the modern world, easily outdoing most present-day tropical aqua-amusement parks. And although "modern" sounds oddly out of place when used in relation to the Bavarian "fairy king," it should be recognized that reclusive dreamers such as Ludwig were among the first to call in the help of the most sophisticated modern contraptions.[32]

In addition to Ludwig's obsessions with Wagner, the womb, and other regressional tendencies, he also entertained an intimate relationship with swans. Traditionally swans have belonged to the emblematic household of the aristocracy, and in that sense Ludwig had inherited the connection from his father. But seen in the dim light of the Wagnerian resuscitation of the bird as a symbol of metamorphosis and eroticism, it is worth analyzing the meaning of the swan, not least as a metaphor for restrained hydro-enjoyment.

Unlike our other symbolic beasts, the swan has absolutely no intention of enjoying itself. Completely devoid of a sense of humor, without social abilities of any kind, it principally functions as the emblem of refined loneliness. The swan's melancholic sense of displacement makes it ideally suited to the theatrical representation of tragic abandonment and to the grave enjoyment for which Ludwig employed his pool.

Pool on the Another swan pond that the king frequented was constructed on top of his
Roof palace in Munich. If the Linderhof grotto was an erotic underground playground inspired by the uterine myth of the island of love, the Munich Wintergarten was a water fantasy based on the Turco-Moorish tastes of the period. In 1867, over the old banquet hall on the roof of the Residenz, a greenhouse was erected which, technically speaking, was very much in line with the most refined iron and glass conservatories of the time. It sheltered a free-form pool, surrounded by tropical foliage and inhabited by two swans, a peacock, and an authentic "Lohengrinjum" (fig. 2.11). Hidden behind ferns and palms were an "Indian" cabin and a "Moorish" kiosk.

One evening Ludwig invited the Spanish Infantin Maria de la Paz to his roof garden, and she ecstatically remembered this scene:

> Crossing by a primitive wooden bridge over an illuminated lake we saw behind us, between two chestnut trees, an Indian town. . . . We came to a tent made of blue silk covered with roses, within which was a stool supported by two carved elephants and in front of it a lion's skin. The king conducted us further along a narrow path to the lake, in which was reflected an artificial moon that magically illuminated the flowers and water plants. . . . Next we came to an Indian hut, from whose roof native fans and weapons were hang-

2.11. Munich: Residenz with Wintergarten, 1867.
(Petzet, *Ludwig II und seine Schlösser,* 1995.)

ing. Automatically I stopped, but the King urged me forward. Suddenly I felt as if I had been transported by magic to the Alhambra: a little Moorish room, in the centre of which was a fountain surrounded by flowers, carried me to my homeland. Against the walls were two splendid divans, and in an adjoining circular pavilion behind a Moorish arch supper had been laid. The King invited me to take the center seat at the table and gently rang a little handbell. . . . Suddenly a rainbow appeared. "Heavens!" I involuntary cried. "This must be a dream!" "You must also see my [Herren]chiemsee castle" said the King. [Was he hinting at the palace's generously dimensioned bath?] "So I was not dreaming after all. . . ."[33]

In bell-ringing also the king had developed a certain adroitness: witness the charming story of the "Singer in the Pool," retold by Wilfrid Blunt with alluring compactness. "Either Josephine Scheffsky or some other singer is said to have fallen 'accidentally' into the shallow artificial lake in the Winter Garden in the confident hope that the King would himself come to her rescue. But she misjudged her man; Ludwig merely rang the bell for a servant for her to be fished out, dried and removed permanently from the royal presence." As if that were not enough for the long-suffering roof of the old Residenz, Ludwig ordered more exotic livestock for his penthouse paradise: "Get me at once a pair of gazelles and make inquiries about a young elephant."[34]

"It Is Unreal but True" His capriciousness, his wild eclecticism, and his aesthetic volatility make Ludwig a worthy forerunner of the various hypersensitive virtuosi who made popular fashion, the movie industry, and the amusement park into what they are today. Disneyland and its parthenogenetic offspring are chiefly dependent on Ludwig's example. To him, architecture was ephemeral in the sense that it had to be instantly realized according to his whims. It had no other status than as a medium of entertainment. The king's submission to the great magician of thematic composition, Wagner, was of course in complete harmony with his own ideas of using architecture to express moods and fancies. The lewd moods of bathing and swimming, and the seductive presence of water, were supported by sets of oriental derivation. The Persian paradise was represented by the peacock throne and a host of peacock effigies throughout the Linderhof. Then there were the Moorish kiosk and the Moroccan house, both aquired at the Paris universal exposition of 1867 and erected in the same park as the Venusgrotte. Ludwig succumbed instantly to his fantasies, most of them truly brilliant. What is more, he had those fantasies realized, virtually the next day. He shared with the American robber barons, the movie industry, and the nervously tuned designers of today a compellingly perverse relation to reality. In the words of Orson Welles: "It is unreal, but true."[35]

33. The translation is taken from Blunt, *The Dream King*, 92. The Wintergarten was demolished in 1897.
34. Ibid.
35. Interview with Orson Welles on TNT television, February 6, 1993.

2.12. Paris: apartment house pool, 1891. F. Gaillard.
(*La Construction Moderne*, 1891.)

Had it not been America that subsequently pushed the private pool to such monumental heights, it might have been Paris. During the *belle époque* several initiatives were taken to make the modern apartment buildings in the super-rich areas near the Bois de Boulogne into the most luxurious dwellings ever seen. The *Construction Moderne* of 1891 proudly presented an apartment building of "great luxury," designed by the architect F. Gaillard, that was embellished with "une belle piscine" (fig. 2.12). The design of the pool is typically transitional, in the sense that it combines the hygienic starkness of the basin with the grottesque decoration of the nymphaeum. This somewhat Badenburgian pool, located on the ground floor next to the courtyard, was republished by Paul Planat in his widely read *Encyclopédie de l'architecture*.[36]

The last of the great European privately owned indoor pools was that installed by gun manufacturer Alfred Krupp in his Villa Hügel in Essen, Germany, just before the outbreak of World War I.[37] It is located in the basement, receives no daylight, and is much less ornate than its predecessors. The Krupp pool features underwater handrails, large circular wall filters, and waterspouts. Roughly contemporary, and similar in its generous distribution of grips and railings but differing considerably in its architectural attire, is the Gothic swimming pool of the Marquis of Bute in his house, Mount Stuart, on the Island of Bute. The use of Gothic-style vaults is an improvement over the flat ceiling of the Krupp pool, since vaults and domes are superior in dealing with condensation.[38]

When in the 1990s suburbia—and with it the garden swimming pool—experienced a decline, the indoor pool underwent an unexpected revival. The wealthy and famous began to install luxurious swimming pools in their Manhattan apartments. Recently the BBC's Terry Wogan, visiting the fashionable scene of New York for his famous talk show, proclaimed that on Fifth Avenue people now had pools in their homes and that some "master of the universe" had fitted a swimming pool in his top-floor apartment.

Of course this development had been foreseen in the 1920s, as Ford Madox Ford had noted in his *New York Is Not America*: "Later one began to hear of millionaire owners of vast edifices who had bungalows on their roofs, poplar groves, garages, I daresay golf courses . . . who knows what? That sort of imagination is very easy to have and to cap. There is no reason why you should not have a lake with sailing boats. Indeed, the swimming pool of the Illinois Women's Athletic Club is on the roof of a Chicago Skyscraper."[39] Well, half a century earlier, Ludwig had had all that, and more, condensed into a single roof garden on top of his own palace. America was not Bavaria. Not yet.

36. Monique Eleb-Vidal, *Architectures de la vie privée; maisons et mentalités XVIIe et XIXe siècles* (Brussels: Archives d'architecture moderne, 1989), 276–277.
37. See Tilmann Buddensieg, *Das Wohnhaus Krupp in Essen* (Bonn, 1984). Thanks to Dr. Manfred Bock, Amsterdam.
38. Early British developments in private pool building include a marble pool built for Andrew Carnegie in Skibo Castle, Scotland, around 1900, and the outdoor pool for Sir Philip Sassoon at Port Lympne, Kent, about 1920.
39. Ford Madox Ford, *New York Is Not America* (New York, 1927), 68.

three

The Playhouse, the Pool House, and the Pool

Lords of the Swan II

Epigraph: Thorstein Veblen, *The Theory of the Leisure Class* (1899; Harmondsworth: Pelican Books, 1979), 259.
1. Susan M. Ward, ed., *Biltmore Estate: A National Historic Landmark* (Asheville, N.C.: Biltmore Estate, 1989), 92.

The leisure-class canon demands strict and comprehensive futility. . . . Sports satisfy these requirements together with a colourable make-believe of purpose.   THORSTEIN VEBLEN

The earliest American private pools were indoors, and the earliest of the indoor pools were built at the end of the nineteenth century on the East Coast, on the estates of the extremely rich. Indoor pools were, for a relatively short period, the status-bearing playthings of the Vanderbilts, the Astors, the Whitneys, and other Veblenian collectors of money and property.

Technically the difference between public and private pools is minimal. Only size and social function distinguish them. Public pools were first used for instruction and later for pleasure; private pools from the very beginning were intended for pleasure, and little instruction. The private pool was a bauble, a thing to play with and in, yet what exactly was played is hard to say. It is fair to assume that some pools were expressly designed to accommodate the master's ambition to become an all-round, English-style gentleman-athlete. They were also intended to impress guests, the guinea pigs of the moneyed aristocrats, who served as touchstones for the hospitality that was lavished on them. Guests came in flocks to admire the newest fads and gadgets, and they were inevitably invited to play as many games as they could stand. Naturally this could be extremely demanding physically, and thus large houses such as Biltmore were equipped with Swedish-style fitness and recovery rooms to keep the guests from collapsing. Part of that recovery circuit was often the indoor swimming pool.

The indoor pool of George Vanderbilt's Loire Valley château, Biltmore (1890–1895), near Asheville, North Carolina, was most probably the earliest of its kind and the model for them all (fig. 3.1). It was designed by, or under the auspices of, Vanderbilt court architect Richard Morris Hunt. Dug deep into the core of the mansion, the room is shaped like a crypt, covered by a groined vault, and closed by an apsidal ending. Vault and walls are faced with glazed tiles and brick. The basin, with its steep walls and a deep trough that allows the use of a diving board, is relatively small, roughly the dimensions of a soaking pool in a Turkish bath, but is distinguished by its depth. In size and spatial concept it follows the model set by the Badenburg at Nymphenburg. In contrast to the rest of the house, which loudly indulges in rich ornamentation, the pool is a rather stark affair. Accessible only via a series of confusing passageways, it lives in the darkest part of the house with no daylight entering. Every available square foot is covered with white tiles, giving the pool a clinical, anxiously hygienic character. Like most of its successors, it looks more like the delousing facilities at Ellis Island than a swimming pool for athletic entertainment.

Pools like the one at Biltmore were part of a subterranean fitness and physical entertainment system that included bowling alleys, dressing rooms, bathing facilities, gymnasiums, smoking rooms, and billiard rooms. The Biltmore facilities featured Spaulding exercise machines and parallel bars, a rowing machine, dumbbells, and a spa-type shower.[1] The entertainment discipline at such millionaires' estates was very demanding, the pursuit of mainly

3.1. Asheville, North Carolina: Biltmore, 1890–1895,
indoor pool. Richard Morris Hunt.

2. See John Armitage, *Man at Play: Nine Centuries of Pleasure Making* (London and New York: F. Warner, 1977), 101–102.
3. Veblen, *Theory of the Leisure Class,* 249, 259.
4. Jules Huret, *L'Amérique moderne,* 2 vols. (Paris: Pierre Lafitte, 1910), 1:37: "Mais ces énergiques émigrants apportent dans la nature, au lieu de notre flânerie tranquille et reposante, la même fièvre du mouvement et de bataille qui les énerve dans la ville...."
5. Ibid., 39. "Tout est arrangé pour pouvoir chaque instant remuer, agir, faire quelque chose, pour n'être pas obliger de parler...."
6. David Chase, "Superb Privacies: The Later Domestic Commissions of Richard Morris Hunt, 1878–1895," in Susan R. Stein, ed., *The Architecture of Richard Morris Hunt* (Chicago: University of Chicago Press, 1986), 153.

physical happiness occupying almost the entire twenty-four hours of the day. Such money aristocrats as the Vanderbilts took it as their duty to develop new court-style ceremonies of such overwhelming generosity that they might be suspected of trying to compensate for the loss of absolutist court life after the French revolution. It was not so much continental court life that was taken as a model, however, but its British counterpart, in which sports and games had long since uprooted all forms of cultural refinement.[2]

This entailed diverse sorts of physical activities like hunting, horse racing, boating, and a variety of ball-related games such as tennis and golf. The "emulative ferocity"— to speak in Veblenian terms—of the sportsman found its application in ball games and athletics as replacement for the duel as a socially acceptable "survival of bellicose chivalry." In Veblen's America, the leisure scene instantly reverted to sports and the outdoor life in order to procure the desired conjunction of substantial futility and "make-believe of purpose."[3]

Battle of This overdose of physical amusement was considered by Europeans like *Leisure* French travel writer Jules Huret to be typical of the energetic behavior of the American. After visiting some of the great châteaux of Long Island during the first decade of this century, Huret wrote: "Unlike the quiet strolls that we take when enjoying the outdoors, the energetic Americans take along the turmoil and the frenetic activities of their daily business in the city.... As work stops on Saturdays at about one o'clock, the cities pump their workers out into the suburbs, and there everyone starts to participate in a variety of sports: hockey, football, baseball, riding, running, bicycling, or—and this is particularly characteristic of young women—one goes out to watch a game. From the frozen plains of the North to the sunny Eldorados of Louisiana and California you find a veritable explosion of New World muscles."[4]

The situation scarcely differed in the highest echelons of society, in the circles of the Hydes, the Goulds, and the Mackays of Long Island. "Everything," Huret goes on, "is so arranged that at any chosen moment one can get moving and do something, without having to talk at all." "Do something" is the key phrase. Americans seem best to express their spiritual energy by moving their bodies, by running, walking fast, and competing in sports.

Take for example this seventeen-year-old debutante heiress to one of the largest railroad fortunes of the nation.... She leaves the house after breakfast for a ride in the fields, returns for lunch ... then sets out again for a tour in an automobile, in a buggy, or taking out the bicycle or a tandem. An hour and a half later she is back again, only to appear in the salon where I observe her challenging one of the young men to a run. But she is back in no time, maybe thirty minutes, to start a game of ping pong. However, the day is not yet over!

3.2. Biltmore, outdoor pool, c. 1914.

[The mere recollection of all this pushes poor Huret to the edge of exhaustion.] She still has not played her game of indoor tennis! And then, in a screened-off hall adjoining the gallery, there she is, for about an hour, busily indulging in that exhausting game of indoor tennis they call "squash."

But there is more torture to come. "One would suppose that after such an excruciating program, the poor girl would like to take some rest. But no. After dinner there is another game of ping pong and one evening I have observed her trying to play the hunting horn." For reading and conversation, Huret concluded, there was certainly no time available. Or was there? "Yes, the charming mademoiselle was quite positive in her reaction. Reading and conversation she did indeed. But when? 'Oh, when I ride, drive, or eat.' 'Which is when you're busy doing something else?' 'Indeed yes!'"[5]

Although these strenuous programs were designed primarily for the benefit of the lord of the manor and his guests, they were directed to a broader audience. A contemporary newspaper (1890) observed that "the millionaire is the Paladin of our day. . . . The habits of millionaires today excite as much interest and curiosity as those of European royalty." David Chase, in an essay on Richard Morris Hunt's later palaces, concluded rightly that "in an era before sports heroes, Hollywood and television, celebrity was largely the province of the rich and none of the accoutrements of the American millionaire's way of life excited more interest than his habitation."[6]

All that knightly, dapper, athletic behavior was as much a spectator sport as a private exercise. In that respect it had much in common with the hygienic exercises and the *lever et coucher* of the absolutist monarch, which belonged to the public domain in much the

7. See Ernst Hartwig Kantorowicz, *The King's Two Bodies* (1959; Princeton: Princeton University Press, 1966). This study defined the rituals of intimate corporeal proximity in the royal circles of fifteenth- and sixteenth-century France. The "two bodies" of the king represented the abstract body of authority as well as the concrete body of physical prowess and military might: the king as a man. Physical presence was necessary to establish his power. Conflating the two bodies resulted in the proximity frenzy of the courtiers, for whom the most intimate visual or palpable contact with the body of the king was proof of high rank.

8. Ishbel Ross, *Taste in America* (New York, 1967), 126; Sigfried Giedion, *Mechanization Takes Command* (New York: Oxford University Press, 1948), 686.

9. Nancy Weinberg, "The Gold Coast: The Battlements of Wealth and Privilege That Gatsby Tried to Conquer," *On the Sound* 4, no. 3 (April 1974), 30.

10. Monica Randall, *The Mansions of Long Island's Gold Coast* (1979; New York: Rizzoli, 1987), 20.

11. *Avenue* (New York) 14, no. 6 (January 1990), 90.

12. Randall, *Mansions,* 15. Similarly August Belmont is said to have had "a stuffed deer and moose on a steel framed motorized rails-mounted sled to practice shooting." Ibid.

13. According to Giedion (*Mechanization Takes Command,* 670), the promotional campaign of David Urquhart and the establishment of the first public Turkish bath in England, the "Hammam," in Jermyn Street, London, 1862, were instrumental in the popularization of the Turkish bath in America.

same way as the American president of today is expected to invite a TV crew to record his morning excursions in jogging dress. The "fitness" of the president—Theodore Roosevelt was the original example—reassured the public about the well-being of the nation.[7]

Similarly, Americans immersed themselves in contemplation of the hygienic facilities of their own very wealthy citizens. In her study of taste in America, Ishbel Ross noted that "the bathrooms of famous men became matters of public interest in the 1890s." Descriptions of J. P. Morgan's twelve-foot bathtub and the luxurious bathroom in George Vanderbilt's Fifth Avenue mansion were enough to fill entire newspaper columns.[8] If the location of George K. Vanderbilt's North Carolina swimming pool in the darkest depths of the château was the wrong response to this American trend, it was not out of line with the traditional character of continental private pools of the nineteenth century. The rigging of the Biltmore pool, shown in its present-day reconstruction, with gallows-like lifelines and expandable ladder, and without a diving board, is more suggestive of anxious instruction than of insouciant enjoyment.

The outdoor pool at Biltmore (fig. 3.2) is of a later date. Nevertheless, with its uneven surfaces, its hand-shaped scum gutters, its railings made of gas pipe, and the large wrought-iron rings that hold the lifelines, it is a surviving, and therefore interesting, example of the crude application of concrete during the first decades of our century, c. 1914. The steps in those days were made of stone slabs, arranged like garden steps, that reached in long lazy flights to the bottom of the pool.

New York's Plutocracy Traditionally Long Island had been the country life outlet of New York's plutocracy. In the 1870s, yachting in Long Island Sound, and some occasional fox hunting, represented the beginnings of a more organized club life modeled after British examples. "Members of the two clubs," Nancy Weinberg wrote in 1974, "were quite separate: those who enjoyed one sport generally had little interest in the other. While yachting always began in the same place, fox hunters would gather at various locations, including the Garden City Hotel and William C. Whitney's estate in Old Westbury."[9] "The horse became the root of North Shore life," Monica Randall observed in 1979, and it was around their daily occupation, British-style fox hunting, that August Belmont and his circle of friends established the first country club, the Meadowbrook Hunt Club, in 1881.[10]

After the clubs came the private lodges, to be followed by the oversized weekend and summer houses and finally the colossal mansions. The increasing variety of sports available and the growing numbers of sportsmen resulted in more clubs, more houses, and larger mansions. Horse-related sports, like hunting, riding, and polo, enjoyed the highest status, but ball-related sports like tennis and golf were in close competition. As more and more individuals began to participate in the leisure frenzy, public space grew smaller and smaller. The wild hunting parties gave way to polo and riding, sports less prodigal of space. Although

3.3. Oakdale, New York: Indian Neck Hall, 1900, exterior. Ernest Flagg.

the number of clubs kept pace with the expanding diversity of sports, many gamesmen began to concentrate a number of sports facilities on their own estates. Tennis courts, shooting ranges, and small private golf courses appeared, complemented by swimming pools, Turkish baths, bowling alleys, billiard rooms, and so forth. "Far more American aristocrats maintained private golf courses in the first half of this century than they do today," *Avenue* magazine recently revealed. "In the early 1900's John Jacob Astor, A. G. Spalding and Theodore Havemeyer all trod their own golf lay-outs. In the late 1920s, the Du Pont clan built a course for themselves near Wilmington, Delaware, and the great film comedian Harold Lloyd owned a private spread near Los Angeles."[11] A fine example of the small-scale domestication of outdoor sport was the shooting lodge of Clarence Mackay, heir to a fortune based on gold and telegraph and cable. Mackay and his friends used to practice their marksmanship on "an electrically operated stuffed moose, complete with antlers, that ran outside a secluded log cabin."[12]

Although the love for outdoor recreation may be traced directly to English country life, the introduction of hydraulic entertainment must have had another source. Until late in the nineteenth century, the English landed gentry was reputedly hydrophobic. If swimming was practiced at all, it was done in rivers, lakes, and the sea. It is remarkable that the Anglo-Dutch scions of the established "backbone of American society"—Vanderbilt, Whitney, Astor, etc.—were quick to adopt strict physical cleanliness at a time when their European counterparts considered bathing of no immediate concern. Turkish-style bathing and modern swimming quickly became incorporated into the lifestyle of the American squirearchy.[13]

14. Stylistically, the house triggered some interesting ambiguities: "Although the original concept was italianate, the exterior declares Georgian while the inside does whisper the Italian villa influence." (James Fordyce, "Frederick Bourne and Indian Neck Hall," *Long Island Forum*, March 1987, 54.) "Thus the style of the Bourne House was a hybrid: neo-Georgian and Federal Revival forms the exterior, 'modern French Renaissance' the interiors." (Mardges Bacon, *Ernest Flagg: Beaux-Arts Architect and Urban Reformer* [Cambridge: MIT Press, 1986], 160). Whatever stirs one's imagination!

15. Bacon, *Ernest Flagg*, 158.

16. Fordyce, "Frederick Bourne," 54, and newspaper clipping, *Suffolk County News,* February 5, 1987. It is interesting to note that apart from these toys, Bourne, like some other kindred spirits of his time, also developed a predilection for gigantic pipe organs. In the music room he had installed a $20,000 organ, which was replaced several years later, in 1908, by a much larger one: "The music room built to accommodate this massive new organ measured approximately 40 feet by 100 feet, and the organ was described by its manufacturer as 'the largest and most complete house organ in the world.' Constructed by the Aeolian Company, it contained over 7,000 pipes and cost well over $100,000." (Fordyce, "Frederick Bourne," 54.) Domestic organs of the period ranged between something like an eighteenth-century private orchestra of the Haydn/Esterhazy kind and something like a modern home entertainment stereo set, and were extremely popular among the very wealthy. F. W. Woolworth, Captain DeLamar (see below), and Henry Frick enjoyed them (Frick's is still in situ in his Fifth Avenue mansion, now the Frick Museum), and in Europe entrepreneur and maecenas H. C. van der Leeuw had one in his modernist villa at the Kralingse Plas, Rotterdam. An article is under way exploring this interesting phenomenon.

17. The lower part of the house, especially where the baths and pool are situated, was by 1990 in a state of severe abandonment. One hopes the present owners might find the funds to restore this monument of American hydrophilia to its original splendor.

18. Apparently taken by its charm, Flagg translated the private family pool into the terms of communal housing when he and his firm ventured to build an apartment block on 7200 Ridge Boulevard, Brooklyn, 1932–1937. Flagg Court, as it was modestly called, was built around an elongated court in which both a tennis court and a sizable swimming pool were accommodated. The pool is installed below grade

Bourne's Baths Frederick Bourne belonged neither to the backbone nor to the outer fringe.

He came from a modest New England family and ascended through the ranks of the Singer Sewing Machine company until, in 1890, he became its president. In 1897, Bourne commissioned Ernest Flagg, the company's official architect (who between 1896 and 1908 designed no fewer than seven buildings for it, including the famous Singer skyscraper of 1908), to build him an estate near Oakdale on Long Island. At the time of its completion in 1900, Indian Neck Hall was the largest mansion on the island (fig. 3.3). With uncompromising lack of fantasy, Flagg had set the house on a large plot of land facing Great South Bay. Indian Neck Hall is a colossal palace of hybrid origins, with a central body situated on the vast south lawn and two short wings, placed at angles facing north, sheltering the entrance.[14]

It was said of Bourne that he was quite "a sportsman." He had started his upwardly mobile outdoor career in the company of those hydrophilic plutocrats, W. K. Vanderbilt, W. Bayard Cutting, and Captain Nicholas Ludlow, at the Southside Sports Club, which was the "wet" counterpart of the landlocked Meadowbrook (fox hunting) Country Club. On the south shore of Long Island, sports were commonly understood as water sports; Bourne, after he had climbed to power, frantically started to practice all water-related activities simultaneously. Flagg was asked to create on the Indian Neck estate a boathouse, an artificial lake, and "a three mile canal system originally filled with 1,200 trout."[15]

Bourne reached the pinnacle of his social aspirations when he became president of the New York Yacht Club in 1903, entitling him to add to his name the imposing title of Commodore, just as his successor and defender of the America's Cup, Harold Vanderbilt, was to do. Having been taken up by the Long Island sports set at a relatively late stage in his life, Bourne made it a point to have all imaginable hydraulic pleasures installed on his premises at one and the same time. Besides the lake, the canal, and the boathouse, Bourne had the basement reserved for an impressive array of exercise facilities. "A skating rink, bowling alley, Turkish bath, and swimming pool with underwater lighting could be found there, along with the electric power plant and boilers."[16] The indoor pool belongs to the same order of austerity as the one at Biltmore, and since it was planned and executed within the context of the house it can be dated between 1897 and 1900.[17] It is smaller than the pool at Biltmore, but its dimensions of 32.3 by 6.9 feet (9.8 by 2.1 meters) made it possible to swim at least a few strokes. The bottom shows no diving trough, so a springboard must not have been included. Currently the Bourne estate is home to the La Salle Military Academy.

Pools in Ernest Flagg, with whom Bourne had become friendly, although financially
Houses not able to keep pace with people like Bourne, was socially his superior.

From an old and respectable New England family, he was related to the Vanderbilts, of whom his family did not think very highly but whom they enthusiastically accepted

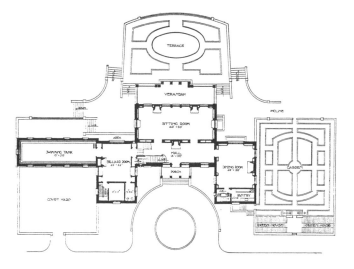

3.4. Staten Island, New York: Stone Court, 1898–1899, plan. Ernest Flagg. (Bacon, *Ernest Flagg*, 1986.)

because of their enormous wealth. It is therefore not surprising that the architect not only could maintain friendly relationships with his clients, but also could compete openly with them in terms of such highly valued status symbols as home sports facilities. In the late 1890s, Flagg had accumulated enough money to build himself a country house on Staten Island. Stone Court, erected between 1898 and 1899, included all the niceties of the Gold Coast mansions.

From the outside it looked rather quaint, with its gambrel roof and large double chimneys and its friendly verandah and porch. But the plan (fig. 3.4) gives away Stone Court's secret: it is an unadulterated playhouse. The central part of the ground floor is taken up by the sitting room and a hall of elongated dimensions, flanked by the dining room and the billiard room. Adjoining the billiard room and mirroring the dimensions of the hall is an indoor swimming pool measuring 50 by 15 feet (15.2 by 4.6 meters). Billiard room and swimming pool account for half the living space on the ground floor. With this pool, at the time the second-largest private indoor swimming pool in the United States, the architect easily surpassed his client, Bourne. Later Flagg installed an outside swimming pool in the garden of his expanding real estate development; it was of such titanic dimensions that it equaled the total surface of the main house![18]

Between 1900 and the outbreak of the First World War several indoor pools worthy of study appeared on Long Island's Gold Coast. Of special architectural interest was the pool of Coindre Hall, built in 1906 by George McKesson Brown, owner of a large pharmaceutical firm. Coindre Hall is well known for its tall water tower which, as in most large properties, had to supply the estate's own water. Like Indian Neck Hall, Coindre Hall was conceived as a water sportsman's paradise. Situated near the North Shore, it had an extensive boathouse and in the main house, on the first-floor level, a sauna and a 15-foot bathing/swimming pool.[19]

and fills all of the available space. Wide shallow gutters surround it, and as a romantic touch two Indian pergolas, or *chattris*, were put at the short ends. See Bacon, *Ernest Flagg*, 264, fig. 134.
19. Randall, *Mansions*, 33. In 1990 the house still stood but was threatened by demolition.

20. See Kelly Klein, *Pools* (New York: Knopf, 1992), 62. The photo is unidentified, but the elaborate roof trusses link the structure to pictures of Idle Hour's playhouse.

21. Leland Roth, *McKim, Mead & White, Architects* (New York: Harper and Row, 1983), 265; see also *A Monograph of the Works of McKim, Mead & White* (New York: Architectural Book Publishing Co., 1915), 113–114. The main house at Ferncliff is now owned by Mr. James McGuire. Following the layout of Ferncliff was another McKim, Mead & White extravaganza, Florham (standing for "Florence" and "Hamilton" as so often happens when houses are more quickly built than names are found), for Florence Vanderbilt Twombly, at Convent Station, New Jersey. In the main house an indoor pool of great sophistication was accommodated. See Robert King, *The Vanderbilt Homes* (New York: Rizzoli, 1989), 122ff. See also Paul Baker, *Stanny: The Gilded Life of Stanford White* (New York: Macmillan, 1989), 299; "For some reason, the Ferncliff commission led to a dispute with the owners, and White admitted afterward that he was 'not on architectural speaking terms' with the Astors, owing to the rumpus over their athletic courts at Rhinebeck."

22. Arthur Schlesinger, Jr., and John Dominis, "Profiles: Brooke Astor," *Architectural Digest*, May 1986, 167.

23. Randall, *Mansions*, 143.

One of the largest swimming pools of the first decade could be found in the playhouse on William Kissam Vanderbilt, Sr.'s estate, Idle Hour, at Oakdale, Long Island (1906).[20] It was built by Hunt & Hunt, the successor firm to Richard Morris Hunt; the two sons more or less inherited their father's elite clientele and successfully continued the family expertise in civilized opulence. The major competitor in their field, of course, was the firm of McKim, Mead & White, among whose partners it was Stanford White who had adjusted most naturally to plutocratic demands. Contemporary with Idle Hour was the casino on the Ferncliff estate at Rhinebeck, New York, that White had created for John Jacob Astor in the years between 1902 and 1905 (figs. 3.5, 3.6).

According to the firm's biographer, Leland Roth, at Ferncliff "Jack [Astor] and his spirited wife, Ava, had White build a guest home and recreational pavilion incorporating squash courts, swimming pool, and enclosed tennis court."[21] The casino was conceived as a freestanding garden pavilion on the model of the Grand Trianon; its architecture of arched walls with pilasters and freestanding Corinthian columns bearing the stuccoed groin vault recalled the hallway of a Renaissance palazzo. Light came in from the front as well as from above, where light drums were let in through the vaults. The tennis court was protected by Guastavino tiles and suffered, as the architect admitted, from acoustical problems. The swimming pool was situated in a loggia that could be screened off by windows.

The Ferncliff casino's priority as one of the earliest private swimming pools in the country was recently confirmed by Mrs. Brooke Astor.[22] Its classical elegance set it apart from the bathroom starkness of the Biltmore pool. The architectural detailing, too refined for a garden shed and too pompous for simple hydroentertainment, was nevertheless aimed at a more-casual-than-the-main-house degree of sociability. It seems that the pool, open on one side, was not fit for year-round use. The harsh winter conditions of upstate New York would have made it impossible to heat.

On Long Island, large pool-and-tennis houses now appeared in rapid succession. In the beginning, the plans and distribution, and the degree of hydraulic sophistication, differed greatly. What they had in common was the glaring incongruity in space and volume between the sports facilities and the living quarters. The playhouse Greentree, on the John Hay Whitney estate at Manhasset, was much larger than the main house, whereas the greenhouse-nymphaeum-pool annex of Pembroke, the estate of Captain DeLamar at Glen Cove, existed merely in spatial parity with the house.

Greentree, built between 1910 and 1927, is a colossal emporium of sport facilities (fig. 3.7). The playhouse consists of two stories, allowing an over-under position of tennis court and swimming pool. "The size of the place is overpowering," Monica Randall observed; "the tallest man would be dwarfed by its proportions. Inside the all-glass roofed court, heads of deer, boar and other wildlife reflect the big game hunting days of the owner. There is a balcony lounge with dressing rooms for guests at the other end, overlooking a perfectly maintained clay tennis court. Below, on another level, is the Olympic-size indoor swimming-pool."[23]

3.5. *Top:* Rhinebeck, New York: Ferncliff, 1902–1905, casino. Stanford White. (*Architectural Record,* July 1905.)

3.6. Ferncliff, swimming pool in casino. (*A Monograph of the Work of McKim, Mead & White,* 1915.)

3.7. *Top:* Manhasset, New York: Greentree,
      1910–1927, aerial view. (Randall, *Mansions of
      Long Island's Gold Coast,* 1979.)
3.8. Glen Cove, New York: Pembroke, 1916, plan.
      Cass Gilbert. (*The American Architect,*
      September 17, 1919.)

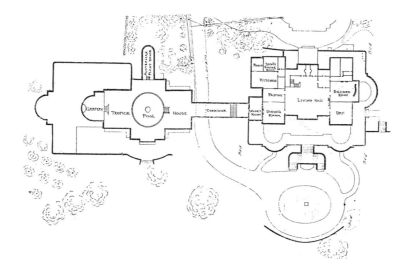

Pembroke was built in 1914 by renowned society architect and skyscraper builder Cass Gilbert, for the eccentric billionaire who had made his fortune in ship salvaging and gold claims and later became a state senator and large-scale industrialist. The most interesting part of DeLamar's fifty-room house, apart from its size, is the greenhouse extension (fig. 3.8), measuring almost an acre.

> Designed as a horticultural museum, its palm trees towered some thirty-five feet amid the luxuriant flowering foliage. At the far end of the room was a curious, almost sinister looking cave, or grotto, encrusted with stalactites. . . . A statue of a nude woman stood in the shallow water [of a pool] and was reflected by a mirror set deep in the cave. At one time water cascaded down its rocky surface and flowed into a stream that wound its way through all parts of the room. . . . There were two ornate metal bridges so one could cross from one wing to the other. In the center of the main section, where the room towered up some sixty feet at its highest point, there was a large round tiled swimming pool. A gazebo or pavilion made of ornamental metal work and Tiffany-style glass stood on a rise in the center of the pool. Directly over it was a circular gallery with a metal railing from where guests could dive into the pool below.[24]

Needless to say, at Pembroke all the necessary accompaniments, like indoor tennis court, pipe organ, and billiard room, were incorporated. There was also a boathouse and a Parisian-style stone bridge extending into Long Island Sound. There was a movie theater as well, in which the captain could show anything, it seems, that celluloid could stand.

Hydraulic Entertainment The DeLamar pool serves as a good example of the theatrical *maison de plaisance* way of using domestic water. The captain does not strike one as being a swimmer for swimming's sake; as a sailor it is highly likely that he would have been a nonswimmer. Furthermore, he had not started building the property until the age of seventy-one, his active life mostly behind him. And when he finally took possession of the house he did not live long enough to see it completed, dying in 1918. What the captain rather liked was to watch—to peer at the nymphs and fauns emerging from the grotto landscape at the far end of the conservatory (fig. 3.9) and then, as naturally as could be arranged, venturing into the pool where some spectacular frolicking found a beginning and no end (fig. 3.10). Having others perform was normal practice in this period. Plutocrats like DeLamar hired professionals to do the frolicking, the diving, and the swimming in their place.[25]

24. Ibid., 41. Oddly enough, Randall does not mention Gilbert as the architect.
25. Captain DeLamar spent most of the brief social life that remained to him throwing one glittering poolside party after another. At his death, the movie theater mogul Arthur Loew bought the estate and continued the tradition in style. Unfortunately, the house was destroyed in 1968.

3.9. *Left:* Pembroke, pool house, interior with
nymphaeum. (Randall, *Mansions of Long
Island's Gold Coast,* 1979.)

3.10. Pembroke, poolhouse, interior with pool.
(Randall, *Mansions of Long Island's Gold Coast,*
1979.)

It should be remembered that few people, even in the highest circles of society, were able to swim. Around 1900 swimming instruction was still in its infancy. And if any serious effort was made it was probably still in the same cranky manner as Lord Gimcrack, who practiced swimming "most exquisitely on land."[26] This situation had hardly changed in 1914, when Commodore Wilbert E. Longfellow launched a "Red Cross Water Safety Program," proudly introducing the apparently new technique of teaching swimming in the wet because he believed that people "learned to swim more quickly in the water."[27]

It is not surprising, therefore, that parties thrown by the wealthy were adorned with performers, professional wet bodies who were able to dive and swim artfully and to amuse the guests with all sorts of aquatic antics. Often celebrities from the world of sport were invited to display their art and to partake in the festivities. Johnny Weissmuller and Esther Williams were frequently invited to give exhibitions. Sprawson relates the account that champion swimmer Doris O'Mara gave of her exhibition at Biltmore. "When we entered the pool, there were lackeys standing in a line with their hands out. We had on our bathing suits and caps and a towel wrapped around us, and as each one of us came by we just dropped our towels."[28]

Monica Randall, in her gossipy but valuable chronicle of the architecture of the Long Island Gold Coast, was just in time (1979) to be able to note down the juiciest stories from the most reliable sources. Some of these stories throw an interesting light on our delicate problem. The activities in the swimming pool of Josephine Hartford Douglas's playhouse at Lattingtown, Long Island, could serve as an illustration of the ubiquitous use of playhouse and pool. Like the decorations of a bordello (after all, in Victorian times the term "play-house" was used to indicate "brothel"), the paintings on the pool walls were intended to reflect and to inspire its colorful use. "The walls of the swimming pool were gaily painted by a famous Russian artist—with polar bears, moose, buffalo and flamingoes all engaged in erotic activities." Unfortunately the text does not go into details about who did what with whom, whether and how the polar bears did it with the flamingoes, and so on. But it informs us about its visitors: "Tennis greats Bill Tilden and Billie Jean King came here to play the game and attend the fabulous parties that took place here."[29] The paintings have not survived, but the decorations of the playhouse of the Dodge Sloane estate near Lattingtown might give an indication of their appearance and effect.

The Playhouse Leisure and play were the main obligations of the landed plutocracy. Until the turn of the century, most of the playing was still done within the seigneurial mansion, but already in the 1910s, a shifting of activities out of the house and into an annex becomes noticeable. From then on playing was done in the "Play-House," a weatherproof, indoors sportsground. As a building type, the playhouse is specific to the affluent regions

26. Charles Sprawson, *Haunts of the Black Masseur: The Swimmer as Hero* (London: Jonathan Cape, 1992), 24.
27. *National Geographic* 159, no. 6 (June 1981).
28. Sprawson, *Haunts of the Black Masseur*, 263. The pool in question must have been the outdoor pool, constructed in or about 1914.
29. Randall, *Mansions*, 239; and see Emmet Murphy, *The Great Bordellos of the World* (London: Quartet Books, 1983). Tilden and King were, in their respective times, quite notoriously homosexual. Lattingtown is now the Lattingtown Tennis Club.

30. From a brochure in the M. E. Hewitt Collection, Nassau County Museum: "Kiluna Farm," Manhasset, Long Island. The pool and tennis building were designed by James W. O'Connor, c. 1910.

31. See Norbert Elias, *Die höfische Gesellschaft* (1969; Frankfurt, 1992), 337.

32. Christina Geis, *Georgian Court: An Estate of the Gilded Age* (1982; Cranbury, N.J.: Alliance Press, 1991), 58.

of New England and the middle Atlantic coast. A large rectangular shed, its dimensions were customarily based on those of a tennis court; this produced a large unobstructed area in the middle (50 by 25 meters, with the roof beam reaching upward about 20 meters), which was often surrounded by spaces of smaller volume. The central area was lit from above through vast panes of glass supported by steel trusses of the railroad-shed type (fig. 3.11).

Depending on its size, the central area could be used as a riding ring, a ballroom, or a tennis court. The other rooms could contain a Turkish bath, a pool, a billiard room, a bowling alley, a gymnasium, a movie theater, squash courts, a shooting range, and anything from boudoirs and dressing rooms to bars and pantries. Most playhouses also accommodated the estate's guest quarters. Later, as hydrotechnology became more advanced, swimming pools began to take up the central space (see, for example, the Helen Miller Gould pool building, below).

Although the main houses of the great estates adopted shapes that challenge civilized description, the playhouses remained simple and unadorned, differing only in size and equipment. The interior decor was invariably the same. The main hall was left relatively barren, since it had to be occasionally decorated for balls and tournaments. On the long sides were balconies for the spectators, inevitably embellished with deer and moose heads. Fishnets, trellis work, and ivy were standard items, ivy in particular becoming the trademark of the sporting society of New England. A standard example is the interior of the George Fahys playhouse called Cheerywood, in Locust Valley, Long Island.[30]

The development of the playhouse proper covers some fifty years, beginning in the last decade of the nineteenth century and ending by World War II. Architecturally, environmentally, and socially, however, the playhouse is a monument of transition. In the eighteenth century the garden grotto was drawn into the *maison de plaisance* (Badenburg); then, at the turn of the next century, the pool was accommodated within the belly of the mansion (Biltmore; Indian Neck). As physical entertainments grew beyond the confines of the house, separate playhouses were erected. Finally, as the swimming pool in turn outgrew the playhouse, pool houses were built. In the inhospitable northeastern climate, the pools remained indoors until the introduction of sophisticated heating systems that allowed outdoor pools to become, in theory, at least, operative throughout the year.

Socially, playhouses served as theatrical marketplaces, *teatra mundi,* neutral territories where neo-aristocratic hosts could perform feudal rituals without exposing their private household to excessive publicity. In this sense playhouses acted as places of transition between the private and public spheres. It was the playhouse to which the lord of the manor invited his guests in order to have them witness his monarchic impersonations and participate in nostalgic large-scale dress balls. For the everyday life of the hyperwealthy was driven by a neurotic need for entertainment. Trainloads of guests were supplied to fill up the *horror vacui* that was so urgently felt, especially by those who had taken up the lifestyle of the landed

3.11. Oyster Bay, New York: William Coe estate, roof of pool.

gentry. In the social season, eligible people were invited for long weekends of dancing, eating, and playing. Particularly popular were masquerade balls and banquets.

Georgian Court At the grand opening ceremonies of the playhouse of Georgian Court, Lakewood, New Jersey (a new resort discovered in the 1890s by the Rockefellers, the Pulitzers, the Scribners, the Goulds, and Elihu Root), George Gould, with a perfect sense of social irony, received his guests in the disguise of a doorman.[31] Gould and his first wife, Edith, proved extremely cunning in their battle for attention. The main problem of people like the Goulds, apart from accommodating several hundred guests, was to keep them from getting bored. At Lakewood, the technology of the playhouse was aimed exclusively at the radical suppression of ennui: "Above the riding area are archways and balconies from which spectators could watch the ponies or whatever else George's ingenuity could devise. On one occasion indeed he was to bring a circus to the court for the amusement of his friends. At another time he arranged for a chess game with live chessmen. . . . Edith Gould would bring a motor-driven moving picture machine to the casino, where the latest and best picture plays were shown for Sunday evening entertainment."[32]

Georgian Court's "Casino," as the playhouse was dubbed, was three times as big as the main house (figs. 3.12, 3.13). It was inaugurated in 1899, on the 12th of December, with a splendiferous feast; Edith Gould led the ceremonies in an astronomically expensive costume of purple velvet, trimmed with semiprecious stones and a ten-foot train of pure ermine. Later in the evening Santa Claus emerged, "pushing before him a huge snow ball out of

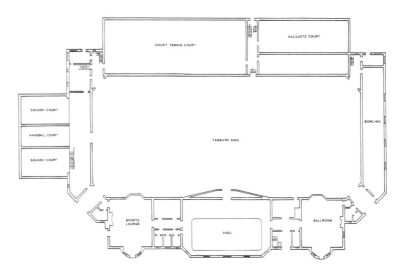

33. Ibid., 61. Thanks to Dr. Robert Twombly, West Nyack, N.Y.

34. Ibid., 17ff.

35. Huret, *L'Amérique moderne*, 43, "Même sur un socle, j'ai vu *l'Enlévement de Proserpine par Pluton*, de François Girardon, qui vient, dit une pancarte, de Versailles, pavillon Montesquiou."

which a beautiful tinsel-and-spangle clad fairy emerged, bearing gifts of gold for all the guests: bonbon dishes for the ladies and pins for the men fashioned in the shape of golf sticks or horseshoes."[33]

The first European to report on the American playhouse was Jules Huret, who experienced one of his introductions to the good life of the East Coast during a Saturday afternoon visit to Mr. and Mrs. Gould at their "Château de Lakewood," sometime between 1900 and 1910. The term "château" applied best to the vast Versailles-inspired gardens and much less to the main house, which was but a gargantuan version of a quaint colonial mansion. This dull regeneration of an old style, combined with sophisticated new technology, was typical for the period. Georgian Court (1897–1899), as it was modestly called, had been designed by Bruce Price, gentleman-architect to the wealthy (and father of Emily Post), to the exorbitant requirements of George Gould, who enjoyed an immense family fortune based on speculation and the railroads.[34]

Huret was having a wonderful time with his well-mannered hosts and was genuinely impressed by the beauty of this North American Versailles. The Goulds were proverbially Veblenian in the incessant evidence of their "pecuniary standard of taste." To display their enormous wealth was the main task, and the luxury and regal dimensions of gardens was a certain, yet civilized, way to impress.

Before dinner Huret was led around these gardens, strolling through the Goulds' private forest, promenading over the parterres, and pausing at impressive sculptural groups such as the "*Abduction of Persephone by Pluto,* by François Girardin, which comes from Versailles, a sign proclaims, from the pavillon Montesquiou," as he slyly noted.[35] But Huret is a

3.12. *Opposite:* Lakewood, New Jersey: Georgian
Court, 1897–1899, plan. Bruce Price. (Geis,
Georgian Court, 1991.)
3.13. Georgian Court, casino, interior. (Geis, *Georgian
Court*, 1991.)

36. Ibid.
37. Geis, *Georgian Court,* 54.
38. Huret, *L'Amérique moderne,* 43.
39. Ibid., 43–44.
40. Geis, *Georgian Court,* 58.

sympathetic observer; there is no snobbishess or prejudice in his comments. Unlike most of his fellow Europeans, who typically condemned American taste as vulgar and shamelessly derivative, Huret enjoys the wealth of his hosts and the generosity of the space, and he experiences an unexpected, but wonderful, sense of well-being. He is not what one could call a critical observer, and allows himself to be enthusiastically bribed by his all too charming hostess, "well-nurtured in the lap of luxury," to use another of Veblen's descriptions, but neither is he without irony, and he retains his very acute sense of proportion, seeing primarily the fun of it all.

After his tour of the house and the garden, he generously admits that this was the second time he felt that "sensation de beauté que j'ai éprouvée en Amérique." Yet there is another sensation waiting for him, sublime this time, a vast building sitting on an elevated site of the property, "le court"—the playhouse. To the eyes of Huret it appeared as a "large and spacious building made of stone and covered by a glass roof, in which all imaginable sorts of sports are accommodated."[36] Georgian Court historian M. Christina Geis explains: "The allocation of the interior space offered a unique solution to the problem of boredom among weekend guests. Dominating the entire center of the structure, a tanbark ring the size of the old Madison Square Garden in New York provided an exercise run for horses and polo ponies. . . . The large central area, 175 feet × 86 feet [53 by 26 meters], was covered by glass."[37]

Huret continued: "To begin with, there is a manège as big as a circus piste, which easily allows the running and turning of two or three horse-drawn carriages. Next there is a gymnasium in which all the equipment and gadgets invented by the maniacal ingenuity of the Americans are to be found; further on there is a squash court [*tennis de chambre*] for two players: then comes a court for tennis [*tennis pour quatre joueurs.*]" After viewing two additional large halls used for other ball games, the walls of which are fitted out with awnings or canopies ("une salle immense pour le jeu de paume, avec ses murs garnis d'auvents en pente"), Huret enters a garage where five cars are parked, including a small one for children; finally he comes to the billiard room, "furnished with comfortable chairs and settees, the walls covered with fine, antique English colorprints."[38]

But the best part is still to come: "Mais la merveille du lieu est la piscine" (fig. 3.14). The swimming pool was the most splendid of its kind, or at least the most splendid Huret had ever laid eyes on.

It is a large and deep tank of marble, measuring 15 or 20 meters long and 10 meters wide, in which clear and heated water runs. Balloons float on the surface to give swimmers some fun. For diving a platform of eight marble steps is provided. On the marble quais, benches, also made of marble, are placed against the wall, and there are vases and flower pots with azaleas and camelias, orange and palm trees. A rubber mat has been laid around the pool

3.14. Georgian Court, pool. (Geis, *Georgian Court*, 1991.)

to prevent people from slipping. On one side there are wet and dry Turkish sweat-baths, which are always in service. Everything is so arranged that with a simple pull on a cord the whole thing starts working! Having all those splendid works of art within reach, out in the open, and experiencing this sense of athleticism and physical fitness, together with the sheer luxury of all those bathing facilities amidst subtropical plants and flowers, one is overwhelmed and, for a brief moment, has the sensation of classical Rome revisited.[39]

According to Geis, this was

a swimming pool constructed of brick faced with porcelain and holding 100,000 gallons of water [about 380 cubic meters]. An artesian well sunk that year near the Casino supplied water in abundance. An elaborate pump and piping system in the basement allowed for drainage toward the lake a quarter of a mile away. Adjacent to the pool, a dressing room area with showers and a Turkish Bath led to a commodious trophy room and lounge dominated by a fireplace of medieval capacity. . . . A few steps away, on the west side of the structure, were squash courts, shooting galleries, and a billiard room. Occupying most of the north side were a huge glassroofed racquets court and a 'court tennis' court, one of six in the country at the time.[40]

Huret was utterly flabbergasted. And very justifiedly so: he was one of the first European travelers to see, and rightly appreciate, an American billionaire's playhouse. Immense

41. The photo reproduced here as fig. 3.17 was published by Kelly Klein in her giant picture book, *Pools*. The caption reads: "Lyndhurst, Tarrytown, the estate of Jay Gould. Photo c. 1880." It took a while to unravel the mystery, but thanks to Dr. Robert Twombly of West Nyack, N.Y., the right provenance could be established. The drawings were published in *The Architectural Record*, August 30, 1910.

42. I am grateful to Barbara Lister-Sink, who fixed my attention on the historic pools in that area. Another early pool is the one in Graylin House, Winston-Salem, former home of Bowman Gray, president of the Reynolds Tobacco Company. The pool was installed between 1924 and 1935. The Reynolds family must have been an enthusiastic pioneer of swimming pools. It is known that East Coast pool builder Ed L. Wagner was employed by some of the family's members. See Fay Coupe, "Pool History: A History of the Pool and Spa Industry," part 2, *Pool and Spa News*, January 12, 1987, 42.

43. *Avenue* (New York) 14, no. 6 (January 1990), 89–90.

44. Oral communication by family member.

estates, colossal city palaces, outsized skyscrapers were all well known in Europe, and the visitor was prepared for their impact. But the titanic playhouse was a definite first, and its swimming pool was the marvel of the place.

The Pool House   Another member of that family who acted as proprietor of an impressive entertainment shed was Miss Helen Miller Gould of Irvington, on New York's Hudson River. The architectural firm of Crow, Lewis and Wickenhofer of New York embellished her estate in 1910 with a pseudo Greek-Roman bathhouse and swimming pool of glorious dimensions.[41] The Irvington pool house clearly demonstrates the usurpation of the playhouse by the swimming pool (fig. 3.15). Whereas the playhouse originally harbored a peaceful symbiosis of games and pastimes, in this case the pool has pushed the others from under the roof (fig. 3.16).

The visual effects of a glass-covered swimming pool are unusually impressive. Light streams through the large expanse of glass and breaks into festive fireworks in the clear, sparkling water. An unidentified picture in Kelly Klein's picturebook shows the same pool under different circumstances. Apart from the swimmers and the potted plants, there is a rowboat in the water, which adds some mystery (fig. 3.17; cf. chapter 6 below). Since the photo must have been taken in or shortly after 1910, it must be one of the earliest American records of hydrophobic devices in swimming pools. Note that the lady in the boat is fully dressed.

The definitive separation of the swimming pool from the playhouse is magnificently illustrated by the superbly crafted pool house that tobacco magnate J. Reynolds built in the 1920s on his Reynolda estate, near Winston-Salem, North Carolina (fig. 3.18). It measures 7 by 15 meters, slopes from 1.2 to 2 meters in depth, and is covered by an elegant prewar metal and glass roof.[42]

Some Outdoor   Outdoor pools were not terribly practical in the hostile New England climate.
Pools   As water heating systems became more and more sophisticated, the outdoor pool gained favor, but it never achieved the same popularity as in California or Florida. There are, however, several important roofless pools in the Northeast that deserve attention. A particularly early one was the pool on the Rockefeller estate at Pocantico, near Tarrytown, New York. "John D. Rockefeller, following the idiosyncracies of his class, had started to build a nine hole golf course in 1899, which in the 1930s was expanded to eighteen holes."[43] Between 1910 and 1915 a swimming pool was installed near the main house. It was said that the Rockefeller boys used to dive into the pool from the second-floor windows, barely missing the canopies of the lower floors.[44] The golf course–swimming pool combination was also adopted for the estate of William Kissam Vanderbilt, Jr., Eagle's Nest, near Center Point, Long

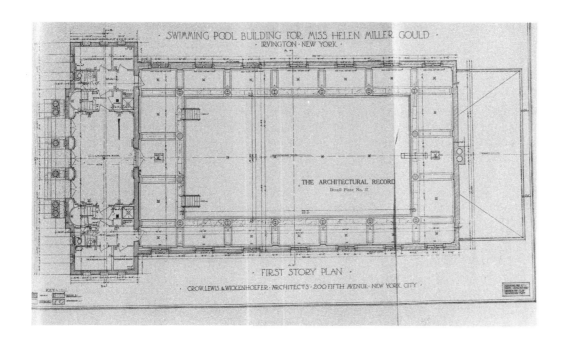

3.15. *Top:* Irvington, New York: Gould pool house, 1910, plan. Crow, Lewis and Wickenhofer. (*Architectural Record,* July 1915.)

3.16. Gould pool house, interior. (*Architectural Record,* July 1915.)

3.17. Gould pool house, c. 1910. (Klein, *Pools,* 1992.)
3.18. *Opposite:* Winston-Salem, North Carolina: Reynolda, c. 1920s, pool house.

45. See King, *Vanderbilt Homes,* 148–160, and Jerry F. Patterson, *The Vanderbilts* (New York: Abrams, 1989), 161–166.
46. See Augusta O. Patterson, *American Homes of To-day: Their Architectural Style—Their Environment—Their Characteristics* (New York: Macmillan, 1924): pool of "Mr. Samuel Untermeyer's Estate at Yonkers, N.Y."; "Swimming pool on the estate of Mr. and Mrs. Robert S. Brewster, by Delano & Aldrich, architects"; "Home of Mr. & Mrs. Joseph Clark Baldwin at Mt. Kisco, N.Y."

Island, built between 1912 and 1936, a jewel of its kind.[45] Its diminutive yet discreetly monumental garden pool is particularly interesting. At the far end of an undulating lawn, covered by the foliage of the coastal slopes, is hidden a circular swimming pool (fig. 3.19). In the summer of 1990, this delightful Hadrianic bathing theater was in a state of romantic neglect. Two semicircular flights of steps, separated by a niche that originally contained a fountain, lead down to a concrete tank about 12 meters in diameter, with a capacity of 70,000 gallons (265 cubic meters) of (salt?) water. In its present state it acts as a flower pot for an abundance of ivy, shrubs, and trees, but at strategic places pool ladders peek through the thick green (fig. 3.20). At the far side facing the entrance stands the lower half of a dismembered classical deity, flanked to either side by a small block of changing cabins.

The pool was probably part of a more extensive system of sportive entertainment, including the private nine-hole golf course, each hole of which was named after one of the nine yachts that "Willie"—William K. Vanderbilt, Jr.—possessed. A charming detail was that Willie had the first tee of his course installed on the roof of his so-called "Maritime-Museum." Willie was very proud of his collection of marine curiosities and, in order to have his low-brow sporting guests share his pride, with subtle force he manipulated the infrastructure so that teeing off was possible only after an intricate tour through his museum. The firm of Warren and Wetmore, architects for the Vanderbilt family's railroad empire, was largely responsible for the house and its grounds and perhaps also for the pool.

Pools of this type apparently were designed to play a theatrical and monumental role more than to provide mere athletic facilities. Their principal purpose was to embellish the garden and to enliven parties. The object of several other New York pools was a similarly monumental ostentation, such as those of Robert S. Brewster, c. 1924, by Delano & Aldrich (fig. 3.21), and of Joseph Clark Baldwin, both at Mt. Kisco, New York.[46]

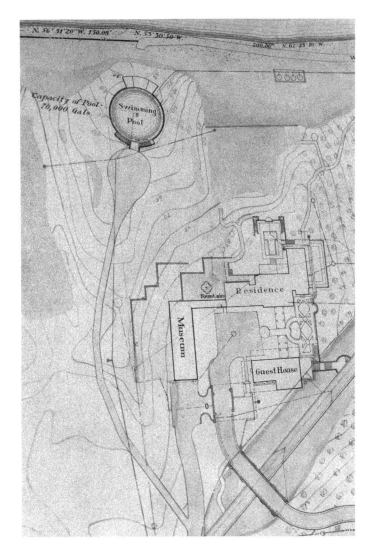

3.19. *Opposite, left:* Center Point, New York: Eagle's Nest, 1912–1936, plan.

3.20. *Opposite, right:* Eagle's Nest, pool; view in 1990.

3.21. *Above:* Mt. Kisco, New York: Brewster pool, c. 1924, with Mrs. Brewster and her children. Delano & Aldrich. (Patterson, *American Homes of To-day,* 1924.)

47. The Ralph Pulitzer pool featured in Patterson, *American Homes of To-day*, plate section, and *The Studio* (U.K.), 1917, 145.
48. See *Landscape Architecture* 49, no. 4 (Winter 1958–1959), 222–224.

Charles A. Platt, architect and author of the influential book *Italian Gardens* (1894), designed several elegant estates on Long Island, often with ponds that were later transformed into swimming pools. The authentic-looking "Roman-end" (apsidal) swimming pool at the Pratt estate called Harrison House at Glen Cove, built by Platt in 1912, is actually an enlargement, dating from 1934, of the original circular lily pond. In contrast, the pool Platt built on the estate of Ralph Pulitzer at Manhasset, Long Island (fig. 3.22), was originally designed for swimming. Widely publicized and praised for its classical grandeur, it nevertheless seems gloomy and forbidding; the contemporary photograph, taken at close range, reveals that the pool has already been taken over by dead leaves and a number of playful carp.[47]

It is true that most of these "old East Coast pools looked so forbidding," as one elderly resident remarked to the author. Especially uninviting was the pool at the Samuel Untermeyer estate Greystone, at Yonkers, New York, designed by Welles Bosworth, architect, and Charles Wellford Leavitt, landscape designer (fig. 3.23). The garden layout, with its ornamental water, Corinthian rotunda, and matching swimming pool, resembles in its ponderous monumentality a posh cemetery more than a restrained playground. Nevertheless, the complex must have left quite an impression: its marble pavilion, with marble lion's heads by sculptor Frederick J. Roth spouting water into the pool, the floor of which was decorated with sea animals in brilliant mosaic, was in its cool restraint and plutocratic grandeur the modest forerunner of W. R. Hearst's marble showcase at San Simeon, California.

Halfway between the sheer ostentation of suburbia and the simplicity of the country lies the swimming pool in the botanic gardens of Dumbarton Oaks, Washington, D.C. (fig. 3.24). Swimming pool and tennis court were designed in the mid-1920s by noted landscape architect Beatrix Farrand for the owners, Mr. and Mrs. Robert Woods Bliss.[48] The pool measures c. 20 by 8 meters and goes from a depth of 1.2 to 2.4 meters. The tennis court has been replaced by a pebble garden and fountains, but the charming pool with its dressing rooms—now public facilities—is still there. It holds 88,000 gallons (about 330 cubic meters), with the diving dip near the middle and a lazy three-step stone entry on the shallow side. The mosaic decorations of the dressing rooms by artist Allyn Cox are particularly noteworthy.

Rural Pools   From the mid-twenties onward, pools gradually became the domain of professional builders. The early mansion and playhouse pools were usually part of the overall architectural design of the house and were drawn by the architect and his team. But for the more moderate-sized open-air pools, a pool builder was contracted. One of the first self-proclaimed pool builders on the East Coast was Ed L. Wagner of Darien, Connecticut. In 1919 Wagner had started a company to build sewage and water systems, including reservoirs. Almost automatically he applied his reservoir-building experience to swimming pools. These pools were of the "fill-and-draw" type: concrete was poured into a hole in the ground and water let into it. Since the water could not circulate and since chemical treatment was grossly

3.22. Manhasset, New York: Pulitzer estate, pool.
Charles Platt. (*The Studio*, 1917.)

3.23. *Left:* Yonkers, New York: Greystone, pool. Welles
Bosworth and C. W. Leavitt. (Patterson,
American Homes of To-day, 1924.)

3.24. Washington, D.C.: Dumbarton Oaks, 1920s,
pool. Beatrix Farrand, architect. *Also plate 8.*

insufficient, the pool became unsanitary and unsafe for swimming so that after a couple of weeks, sometimes after only a few days, the water had to be drawn off. Wagner's masterpiece was the uncommonly large pool for movie producer Adolph Zukor, built in 1927 on Zukor's Hudson River estate in New York as a simple concrete box measuring 40 by 110 feet (12 by 33 meters).[49] But it is only after World War II that pool building became an industry and the various firms began to "sign" their work with their trademarks on pieces of equipment such as ladders and filters (fig. 3.25). For pools built before that time, determination of the authorship depends on guesswork and hearsay.

How simple and how primitive those early open-air swimming pools for non-millionaires actually were is revealed in the following report on the construction of a 1913 rectangular poured concrete swimming tank (fig. 3.26), published in *American House and Gardens,* September 1913. The pool in question was installed by J. P. Putnam, architect of Boston, in the gardens of Old Farm House, Medfield, Norfolk County, Massachusetts. Pools of this type often had to rely on the availability of natural water. "If the country house should be as fortunate as to have a small stream flowing through its grounds," it was pointed out in the magazine, "the problem may be greatly simplified. . . . A very successful swimming pool was once constructed by merely broadening out one spot in its course."[50]

If water had to be mechanically pumped into the tank, it generally sat there until it became stagnant and unhealthful. When that occurred, the tank had to be drained through an outlet at the bottom. For that reason pools were best built on a slope, so that the fresh water could come in from the top end and the draining be accomplished at the lower. For building materials, *American House and Gardens* suggested bricks for the sides and for the bottom: "Concrete is frequently used and in other instances walls are merely bricked up, the floors being also made of brick with the surface covered with cement. Tile in various forms may be used and in fact any material which represents a surface easily kept clean would be suitable." Amid all this frugality, would a springboard not be something of a frivolity? Perhaps, but here, too, local material could be successfully employed: "A spring board, which may be easily arranged by using a plank of oak or pine, would, of course, add greatly to the enjoyment of the bathers either large or small."[51]

Phoebe Westcott Humphreys, in *The Practical Book of Garden Architecture* (1914), provided her readers with practical information for the do-it-yourself installation of garden swimming pools. Most of the information came from a William Walter Smith, "who," she said, "has become famous throughout the country as 'the concrete man.' 'For a rectangular-shaped pool fifteen by fifty feet in the clear,' the concrete man advised, 'the bottom is made sloping in order to provide a shallow end for the children and a greater depth at the spring-board end for those who care to dive.'" The rest of the instructions read like a recipe: "The best method for constructing a pool of this size is to lay out the excavation seventeen by fifty-two feet. With a plow, scraper, and team remove the dirt. . . . Drag the dirt out at the shallow end.[!] Trim the ends and sides vertical with a spade." And so on. The result is shown in a photograph (see fig.

49. Coupe, "Pool History," part 1, *Pool and Spa News,* November 17, 1986, 68. Wagner's son remembered: "The pool was completely tiled and used ultraviolet rays for purification. It is still in use today as part of a country club complex." Which one is not disclosed.
50. *American House and Gardens,* September 1913, 304.
51. Joseph B. Pearman, "A Swimming Pool at Home," *American House and Gardens,* May 1913, vi–viii.

3.25. *Right:* Glen Cove, New York: Pratt pool with Pascal Paddock's trademark.

3.26. Medfield, Massachusetts: Old Farm House, poured concrete swimming tank, c. 1913. (*American House and Gardens,* September 1913.)

3.27. Near Ashokan Reservoir, New York: Breuchaud pool, 1909–1910.

I.3), accompanied by the unrelated caption "A pool screened by a tall privet hedge," shrouding the ongoing drama in more mystery than should have been necessary.[52]

In this period of experimentation, many different kinds of building materials might find their way to the pool side, depending on the craftsmanship available. An eloquent example is provided by the majestic swimming pool (fig. 3.27) that Ashokan Reservoir engineer Breuchaud built for himself and his family between 1909 and 1910 in upstate New York.[53] This sublimely situated pool, measuring 75 by 25 feet (23 by 7.6 meters) and sloping from 3½ feet to 10 feet (1.1 to 3 meters), is built with the local bluestone. The tank is dug into an elevated site overlooking the reservoir and is naturally fed by a nearby artesian well. As was customary in this period, it would be drained only several times a year. The unique feature of the pool is its construction and the use of local materials. Breuchaud started building the pool at the time of the construction of the reservoir, even before he had broken ground for the foundation of his own house. After the tank was excavated, the sides were packed with concrete. Tall logs were chained together to keep the box in shape. Finally the concrete sides were faced with the local bluestone, which was cut so finely that the slabs could be fitted with no danger of seepage (compare the Dumbarton Oaks pool, fig. 3.24).

For the job Breuchaud had recruited the very best immigrant stone cutters and fitters, Italians who were widely admired for their art.[54] This simple yet noble pool is a miniature reflection of the gigantic collector of drinking water it so magnificently overlooks. Of somewhat later date is the adjacent oval swimming pool which, smaller and shallower, was conceived as a play pool for children. The entire system of pools, overflow systems, pumps, and canals has the atmosphere of a private laboratory of hydrotechnology, scaled down to observe the flow of water and to test its taste and feeling within the confinement of the home.

52. Phoebe Westcott Humphreys, *The Practical Book of Garden Architecture* (Philadelphia: J. B. Lippincott, 1914), 76–83.
53. Information has been kindly provided by Mr. David Chrispell of High Point Springs Farm, Olive Bridge, N.Y.
54. Bob Steuding, *The Last of the Hand-made Dams: The Story of the Ashokan Reservoir* (New York, 1989), 50–51.

four

W. R. Hearst, a West Coast Lohengrin

Lords of the Swan III

I didn't know anything about swans; I didn't even know what the swans know. I only knew Gloria Swanson.   MARION DAVIES

The woods decay, the woods decay and fall,
The vapours weep their burthen to the ground,
Man comes and tills the field and lies beneath,
And after many a summer dies the swan.   TENNYSON, QUOTED BY ALDOUS HUXLEY

Epigraphs: Marion Davies, *The Times We Had* (New York: Ballantine, 1975), 202; Aldous Huxley, *After Many a Summer Dies the Swan* (London: Tauschnitz, 1939).
1. Gaston Bachelard, *L'eau et les rêves* (1942; Paris: José Corti, 1989), 50.
2. Johann Wolfgang von Goethe, *Faust* (Munich: Verlag C. H. Beck, 1977), part 2, act II.

Among the obsessions that bedeviled William Randolph Hearst was one that may endear him to us: he was enthralled by swimming pools. Whereas his fellow plutocrats built towers in the air, Hearst dug holes in the ground. From beginning to end, his activities in the field of real estate were dictated by his urge to buy or build pools, and his were the fairest in the land. For every student of private pools, the Hearst contribution is of prime importance.

Seen in the light of the period, Hearst's building mania was not unusual, but the scale and originality of his works made him outshine all his competitors. The only one who might have been in his class was the Swan King of Bavaria. Ludwig (1845–1889) and Hearst (1863–1951) would have been congenial spirits, captivated as they both were by the discreet figure of the swan.

Swans have no fun (fig. 4.1). The swan's relationship with water is one of restraint, detachment. Of all amphibians, the swan seems to like water least, its standoffishness suggesting hydrophobia. The swan sits on the water in resignation, the way Jesus sat on the cold stone. It has frequently struck the contemplative observer that the swan strongly suggests displacement, alienation—the wrong spirit in the wrong body in the wrong place. However elegant and majestic it may appear, seldom is it credited with a genuine individuality but more frequently is regarded as the phenomenal guise of a forensic spirit. Its doubtful authenticity has inspired poets, thinkers, and artists to conceive of the swan as a majestic body inhabited by some other being.

Gaston Bachelard has seen the swan as a metaphor for nostalgic eroticism. Whereas the frog could be viewed in terms of bawdy physical merrymaking, the swan suggests tragic love in a terminal phase, its haughty whiteness a nude (not naked), distant (not reachable) woman (not girl): "un ersatz de la femme nue. C'est la nudité permise, c'est la blancheur immaculée et cependant ostensible. . . . Qui adore le cygne désire la baigneuse."[1] To which should be added that by "la baigneuse" is meant not "la nageuse" but the land-bound variety of swimmer who is permitted to reach into the water no deeper than ankle height. Bachelard's "baigneuse" should be imagined as a Victorian Susannah, a Biedermeier Bathsheba.

But this tableau is not merely nudity with restraint, it is Eros with second thoughts. For his interesting thesis, Bachelard turned to Goethe's *Faust*, in which the landscape evokes the desire and the voyeur imagines himself in the place of an approaching swan.[2] The

4.1. Disneyland, California.
Photo by Diane Arbus. (Postcard.)

3. The swan was highly valued for its sexual prowess. Midas Dekkers recently pointed out, in his entertaining study on bestiality, that the whiteness of its feathers merely acts as an effective cover for its dark and indefatigable sexuality, the reason Jupiter chose the swan as the medium to surprise Leda. No one, especially an innocent nymph of Leda's standing, would suspect that under such immaculate plumage would hide a veritable sex machine. Few are aware of the biological oddity that the swan possesses an uncommonly large penis. It is this paradoxical ambiguity—overlooked by Bachelard, incidentally—that makes the swan the ideal vehicle to secretly transmit feelings of lust and longing and at the same time be able to fulfill them. See Midas Dekkers, *Lief Dier: Over Bestialiteit* (Amsterdam, 1992), 13–14.

4. See also David King Dunaway, *Huxley in Hollywood* (New York: Doubleday, 1989), 85ff.

5. Huxley, *After Many a Summer*, 39

6. See Sara Holmes Boutelle's monumental monograph, *Julia Morgan Architect* (New York: Abbeville Press, 1988). For the Berkeley pools, see 53–56.

scene is set in the second act, during Walpurgisnacht when, at the Lower Peneios, nymphs are playing "at the water's edge," splashing, wading, performing a beguiling water battle, a classic spectacle for the voyeur. The hidden observer, passionately torn between guilt, fear, and his mother on the one hand and the outright enjoyment of watching scenes of secret delight on the other, has no intention of partaking in the frolic but, for a closer look, must be represented by an alter ego, in this case the swan, which is going to stir up a ballet of the "healthy limbs of young girls."

A group of swans approaches round the bend, showing no interest in what is going on except for one. By its action, Bachelard recognizes the otherwise neutral and androgynous bird as a male. Detached from the group, his chest inflated like a macho Adonis from muscle beach, this male swan chases the girls, "glistening, doubled by the water mirror," in a confusion of lust and bashfulness, finally "penetrating into the sacred spot," an obvious metaphor. To the imagination of the romantic, the apparently genderless bird is a distant, controlled representative of the Faustian voyeur: white, chivalrous, and proud he may look, but at the same time he is a merciless and potent fornicator (fig. 4.2), and ultimately the perfect symbol of lustful hypocrisy.[3]

Yet the greatest strength of the swan lies in its weakness, its loneliness, and its melancolia. Bachelard formulated this brilliantly when he recognized the swan as a metaphor for a lost melancholy. The swan suggests frustrated sexuality, dissatisfaction, and obsessive loneliness; combined with the more obvious characteristics of adoration, sacrifice, and intense jealousy, these were the traits Aldous Huxley had selected for the swan as key to the persona of W. R. Hearst in his roman à clef, *After Many a Summer Dies the Swan* (1939).[4]

Huxley portrays Hearst as a despotic billionaire, the pathetically jealous lover of former Ziegfeld Follies girl Marion Davies. "Through his dark glasses Mr. Stoyte [Hearst] looked up at her with an expression of possessiveness at once gluttonous and paternal. Virginia [Davies] was his baby, not only figuratively and colloquially, but also in the literal sense of the word. His sentiments were simultaneously those of the purest father love and the most violent eroticism."[5] Stoyte/Hearst was "on the verge of breaking up completely. Forty pounds overweight and having had a stroke," he was a man at the end of his physical possibilities, longing for something which would probably never happen. At San Simeon, Hearst lived the life of a quasi-bachelor, obsessed by the concept of longevity, convinced that the protracted construction on La Cuesta Encantada kept him alive. (It was never finished, and the moment that Hearst, for reasons of health and money, was separated from it, he died.) He drew his strength from the very process of building; La Cuesta Encantada at San Simeon was his *machine célibataire*.

While maintaining his splendid isolation, Hearst invited countless weekend guests and watched parties develop in and around the swimming pool without taking part. His pleasure consisted in observing the golden adolescents of the movies, brought in by the train-

4.2. A. H. Branchot, *Leda,* Salon of 1888. (Salon catalogue, 137.)

load from Los Angeles, perform their rites of passage, trying to erase the memories of his own lonely years of growing up as the only son of the formidable and domineering widow, Phoebe Apperson Hearst.

Early in her career as promoter of women's position in American life, especially academic life, Mrs. Hearst had compiled an enviable record as a patron of architecture, particularly with regard to gymnasia and swimming pools for the Young Women's Christian Association. The quality of these buildings was outstanding, thanks to her choice of architects, first Bernard Maybeck, later Julia Morgan, the nation's (if not the world's) first major woman architect.

Together with a gigantic fortune, William Randolph Hearst inherited his mother's architects, whom he employed to erect, after her death in 1919, the Phoebe Apperson Hearst Memorial Gymnasium for Women at the University of California at Berkeley (fig. 4.3), completed in 1925–1926.[6] The original idea was the harmonious combination of physical exercise and cultural enlightenment within a single establishment. Not unlike San Francisco's Sutro Baths on the Pacific coast (see below), the Hearst Gymnasium was conceived as a place to bring together a theater, a music hall, a museum, and athletic facilities, but ultimately the grandiose scheme had to be reduced in scope.

What remains is an elegant ensemble of hydrophilic architecture, a classically decorated complex of indoor exercise rooms and outdoor pools. The layout offers a large forecourt into which is sunk an outside swimming pool measuring 80 by 40 feet (some 24 by 12 meters), guarded by two corner pavilions and visible from the street on one side and, on the other, screened off from the main building by a blank wall enlivened by balustrades and two

4.3.   Berkeley, California: Phoebe Apperson Hearst
Memorial Gymnasium, 1925–1926, pool. Julia
Morgan and Bernard Maybeck.

replicas of Roman sarcophagi in reinforced concrete. On the cross axis of the pool, a monumental portal opens to the main building and leads to the gymnasia downstairs. Two ornamental basins are situated at the short sides of the main pool, and a second swimming pool, about half the size of the main one, is tucked in between two projecting blocks at the southern side of the complex.

The Hearst Memorial Gymnasium is a good example of the immensely ingratiating, if somewhat conservative, style of Julia Morgan, who, after a brief moment of indecision, became W. R.'s loyal in-house designer, serving him for more than twenty-five years. Two skills in particular recommended her to Hearst. First, Morgan was an early aficionado of the architectural use of reinforced concrete, at the time more typically a European enthusiasm. During her study at the Ecole des Beaux-Arts in Paris, she had enrolled in the school's course on the use of ferroconcrete, a wise decision considering that she would return to an area where earthquakes posed a serious threat to the stability of a building, along with the dreaded menace of fire. Morgan's employment of ferroconcrete was as effective as it was original, many of her most important commissions on or near the San Andreas Fault, including Hearst Castle at San Simeon, the Examiner Building in Los Angeles, and the Berkeley Women's City Club, being constructed in this earthquake-resistant, fireproof material. The other qualification that suited Hearst perfectly was her expertise as a builder of swimming pools. Through her contacts with Phoebe Hearst and the YWCA, Morgan had become the foremost swimming pool architect of the West Coast.[7]

The Bower Bird *When the "bower" or ball-room is completed, the reader may well ask the use to* **(Ptilonorynchus** *which it can be put. It is not a nest, [but] serves as an assembly room, in which a* **holocericeus)** *number of birds take their amusement. Not only do the architects use it, but many of the other birds of both sexes resort to it, and continually run through and round it, chasing one another in a very sportive fashion.* REV. J. G. WOOD

The precise moment when W. R. Hearst became aware of the part of his subconscious that urged him to amass a collection of swimming pools is difficult to determine, but from 1919, the year that Memorial Pool was begun, until 1930–1931, when the unbuilt Mausoleum Pool at Wyntoon was designed, he manifested the compulsion to create the largest and most conspicuous pools of the modern age. During this time he had secured the devoted assistance of the frail, unathletic, and sexually uncertain Morgan, who would design all of the "bowers" for Hearst's Faustian strategies to win the favors of Marion Davies.

The drama of the newspaper magnate's efforts to conquer the ex-Ziegfeld Follies actress runs parallel to the history of his architectural exploits. In fact, all of the residential buildings he built or converted in the period between 1919 and his death in 1951 were

7. See Boutelle, *Julia Morgan,* for the following: Honolulu YWCA courtyard swimming pool, 1926; Berkeley YWCA, indoor plunge, 1929–1930; Long Beach YWCA and indoor pool, 1923; pools at the Hacienda del Pozo, Pleasanton, 1910; as well as the many houses, pools, and remodelings for members of the Hearst family.

Epigraph: Rev. J. G. Wood, *Homes without Hands: Being a Description of the Habitations of Animals, Classed According to Their Principle of Construction* (London: Longmans, Green and Company, 1866), 340.

4.4. The bower bird. (Wood, *Homes without Hands*, 1866.)

8. G. H. Edgell, *The American Architecture of To-day* (New York: Charles Scribner's Sons, 1928), 135–141; Kathryn Chapman Harwood, *The Lives of Vizcaya: Annals of a Great House* (Miami, 1985); Augusta Owen Patterson, *American Homes of To-day: Their Architectural Style—Their Environment—Their Characteristics* (New York: Macmillan, 1924), 263–271.

9. Hap Hatton, *Tropical Splendor: An Architectural History of Florida* (New York: Knopf, 1987), 35.

10. Ibid., 34–36. The painful suppression of Deering's feelings toward Chalfin is made manifest in a handwritten letter of 1916 to Chalfin, which Vizcaya's biographer, Kathryn C. Harwood, printed in full to illustrate that Chalfin's "association with Deering from early 1911 had something rather mystical about it, almost as though he manipulated Deering, who seemed only too willing." The letter started and ended with the following sentences: "Do you realize that it will soon be five years since you and I hitched our horses together? In all that time except for intervals of food, water and flirtation you have given your time, labor and thought to me.... In my mind there is much sympathy between us. We ought to have even more." (Harwood, *Lives of Vizcaya*, 9.)

11. Harwood, *Lives of Vizcaya*, 28.

12. Ibid., 130.

13. Davies, *The Times We Had*, 14.

designed for the same purpose as the bower bird's dance pavilions: to bring the chosen female under his spell by means of seductive architecture (fig. 4.4). It is probably safe to assume that the constructional frenzy that kept him obsessed until his death struck him the instant he met Davies at Vizcaya, near Miami, the exotic palace of James Deering, another character who could have come directly from literature, for in all respects Christoph Aschenbach, of Thomas Mann's *Death in Venice*, could have been based on Deering.

Death in Vizcaya The Villa Vizcaya (c. 1914–1916), which would exercise a powerful influence on projects like Hearst's La Cuesta Encantada, may be seen as an important synthesis of the gestalt associated with Florida and Deering's historical models. In its capricious frailty and its anachronistic mid-nineteenth-century nostalgia, Vizcaya seems to connect with the palaces of Ludwig II of Bavaria. James Deering, bachelor-heir to the International Harvester Corporation of Chicago, was a man of the most delicate sensibilities. His emotional life, complex and unstable like his decaying physical constitution, had led him to invest all his efforts in one aesthetic action: the recreation of a palace that would incorporate the past beauties of Mediterranean Europe with the promises of colonial Florida.[8] Houses like Vizcaya seem to have been built with the tenacious fantasy of offering to Christopher Columbus—the demigod who had made all this possible—a proper place to spend his well-deserved old age.

Deering, aesthetically obsessed but architecturally indecisive, was bound to sell his soul to the powerfully imaginative interior designer Paul Chalfin. The history of Vizcaya, from the first plans to the last detail, is the history of Deering's morbid love-hate relationship with his designer and sensitive alter ego. Deering and Chalfin went on several scavenging trips to Europe, especially France and Italy, where they would buy and then ship home "everything from entire rooms and their furnishings to medieval altars, Roman sarcophagi, even part of a fireplace from one of Marie de Medici's chateaux. All furnishings and accoutrements were purchased for specific locations in the Deering home, which was modeled after the Villa Rezzonico on the Brenta near Venice."[9]

It was Chalfin who devised and implemented the program following Deering's hints and suggestions. It was also Chalfin who brought his patron to the brink of ruin by constantly overextending the budget. Characteristic of the situation was Deering's helpless abandonment to the irresistible Chalfin: "When I started to build a house here, I did not expect to have anything so large and important and costly as it has turned out to be. . . . Must we be so grand?"[10] People with too much money, wavering characters with vague but persistent ideas of what they want but not how they want it done, readily become engulfed by armies of aesthetic opportunists, not unlike the entourage around Ludwig of Bavaria a half-century earlier. The syndrome is all too familiar: enormous sums spent on trifling details, endless discussions and ensuing lamentations on silly topics like doorknobs and birdcages delayed completion until 1922, just four years before the owner's premature death.

The Ludwig syndrome is clearly discernible in most of Deering's dealings at Vizcaya. His frail, sickly constitution had sent him around the spas of Europe and now held him prisoner to the Florida climate. The inviting character and the ostentatious luxury of the estate coexisted in sharp contrast with the reclusive misanthropy of its owner. To the intense displeasure of his neighbors, Deering, in the interests of his own privacy, adamantly insisted that the existing tropical forest remain untouched and that an impenetrable wall, eventually reinforced with a moat, be erected around the property.[11]

As far as hydraulic gadgets were concerned, the Deering-Chalfin tandem emulated the spirit of the Lords of the Swan. The bathtub in the master bathroom was fitted with four gold faucets shaped like swans, their long necks pouring forth fresh and salt water, hot and cold.[12] When it came to the pool, Deering, not much a swimmer, aimed more for a grotto that ended up resembling the Venusgrotte at Linderhof crossed with the Palazzo del Te in Mantua (figs. 4.5, 4.6).

The Deering folly was again the setting when Hearst met Marion Davies a second time, somewhere between 1916 and 1919; Miss Davies remembered: "The next time I met Mr. Hearst [whom she thought 'a very lonesome man'] was down in Florida at Jim Deering's house, after the show [Ziegfeld's Follies] had closed. His place was called Vizcaya Villa . . . an enormous white marble house that looked like a Venetian palace. Outside, there was a sort of canal with Venetian poles and a big marble ship. There was a huge garden on one side, and the swimming pool was half indoors and half outside. On the other side was a sand beach— just an imitation beach, not a real one."[13]

4.5. Near Miami, Florida: Vizcaya, 1914–1922,
indoor part of pool. James Deering and Paul
Chalfin. (Hatton, *Tropical Splendor*, 1987.)

4.6. *Opposite:* Vizcaya, pool. (Patterson, *American
Homes of To-day*, 1924.)

14. Patterson, *American Homes of To-day*, 266–267.

The idea of an interior-exterior pool must have been quite a novelty and a clear sign of luxury. Such a pool would be pictured in the movie *Dancing Lady* (1933), where Joan Crawford and Franchot Tone are vigorously executing an athletic synchronized crawl in the outdoor pool of a large Long Island mansion. Through an opening in the wall, articulated by French doors, they smoothly enter the indoor pool, round in dramatic contrast to the rectangular form of the one outside. Encased in glass, this pool is of the most outrageous luxury, appointed with all sorts of gadgets including a hydraulically operated telescopic wet bar (see fig. 5.20), and when the characters arrive here, their originally sportive and sexually indifferent attitude changes into one of elegant eroticism. Whereas they first traveled in a fast crawl, following the rigid lines of the outdoor pool, they now twirl in an aquatic ballet, encircling each other in upward and downward spirals, tracing the cylindrical shape of the indoor pool. The provocative architectural choreography of the film is a retrospective illustration of the tragic relationship Deering entertained with the outside world. In 1931, when Hearst would plan his last great pool sanctuary, the same relationship materialized in the outside sand beach and the inside swimming pool.

The Vizcaya pool was merely a small-scale illustration of the total program of integrating water—particularly its music—and site. Augusta Owen Patterson, society matron and art editor of *Town and Country*, wrote in the early 1920s, when she experienced the house still in its original splendor: "So skillfully has the estate been planned that the progress along the allée, with its low-voiced waterways hidden under ilex-trees, is full of pleasant surprises. . . . The climax of the unexpected is the house itself. . . . Here the sounds of water, remote and near, dropping, falling, rushing water, water in fountains, are heard." The swimming pool, with bas-reliefs of fish and a border of shells, marked the threshold where the water quasi-naturally entered the house. Patterson had perspicaciously observed that it was not an ostentatious piece of gleaming tile, marble, and steel, but a mysterious place of transition. Therefore it was hidden in the *sous-sol* and decorated more like a garden grotto than a Roman bath. In conclusion she wrote: "The descriptions have the color and romantic inflection of an Arabian Night's adventure. . . . Certainly there has been no more magnificently exotic building in this country, nothing more consistently lavish, more extravagantly complete than Mr. Deering's romantic plaything in Florida."[14]

Deering and Vizcaya were often visited by Davies and Hearst, who must have been impressed by the estate's elegance and luxury. Even if he might not have expressed himself in the manicured words of Mrs. Patterson, Hearst must have shared her feelings for Vizcaya's mystique. In that same period in the early twenties, he began to play with the idea of spanning the American continent with a chain of swimming pools. If one traces the trajectory of Hearst's acquisitions, one finds that he was thinking in similar terms to those European kings who plotted their castles each a day's journey apart. However, it was not just castles that he wanted, but pools. Pools and castles, in that order.

There were four strategic points in this Maginot Line of leisure: Long Island, California, Europe, and Florida. To continue his Floridian happiness Hearst sought to do business with the wonder boy of Florida's real estate, the Californian developer, businessman, and self-proclaimed architect Addison Mizner, the man credited with one of the most popular formal syntheses of the period, the "bastard-spanish-moorish-romanesque-gothic-renaissance-bull-market-damn-the-expense style."[15]

Like his predecessors in the recreation of the myth of the continuing Spanish colonial expansion, Mizner fashioned an Iberian presence in the southern United States with even more conviction than had the Spanish Mission cult in southern California. The villas of Palm Beach, Coral Gables, and Cocoanut (sic) Grove looked as charming as could be; witness Casa Bendita, the "palatial"—as they all were, by the way—vacation home (now demolished) of John S. Phipps, at North County Road, Palm Beach, built in 1921.[16] Meant, like all these winter residences, to offer hospitality to a never-ending stream of guests that had to be entertained for the season, with the time divided between daytime divertissements on the tennis court, golf course, and bridle path, and dining, the Phipps house possessed a particularly interesting covered swimming pool in one of the loggias. Although Florida had no swimming pool culture that could match that of California, there were some outstanding examples.

15. Donald W. Curl, *Mizner's Florida* (Cambridge: MIT Press, 1984), 130.
16. See *The Architectural Forum*, May 1923, plates 49–52, and Curl, *Mizner's Florida*, 121.
Epigraphs: Wood, *Homes without Hands;* Phoebe Humphreys, *The Practical Book of Garden Architecture* (Philadelphia: Lippincott, 1914), 76. On Martyn, see the first note of my Introduction.

Spanish Schwangau   Ornament is also employed by the bower bird, both entrances of the bower being decorated with bright and shining objects. The bird is not in the least fastidious about the articles with which it decorates its bower, provided only that they shine and are conspicuous.   REVEREND J. G. WOOD

Just as the gothic vault was an indoor imitation of the forest aisles, so the marble pool is just a high-born adaptation of the old "swimming hole."   PAYNE MARTYN

Hearst's greatest work was the castle on La Cuesta Encantada (Enchanted Hill) near San Simeon, midway between San Francisco and Los Angeles. The property had been purchased by his father, Senator George Hearst, in 1865 and had remained in the possession of the family. In or around the year of his mother's death, William Randolph started to make plans to reinforce the location with a castle, somewhat in line with Ludwig's reconstruction of the old ruin Hohenschwangau on a high crag in the Bavarian Alps. Hearst selected the dominant hilltop overlooking the fishing village of San Simeon as the ideal site. Just as Ludwig had wished to recreate the aura of ancestral Bavarian knights, it was only logical that the new castle should follow the spirit of the early Spanish settlers. But at the same time Hearst blended his serious intentions with darker, more complex ambitions.

17. Umberto Eco, *Travels in Hyperreality* (London: Picador, 1986), 23–24.

18. Boutelle, *Julia Morgan*, 176.

19. Thematic clustering is a technique of mixing themes and moods rather than styles, more or less in the manner employed by Ludwig II. It should come as no surprise that the Dream King's work was quickly integrated in America, at that time the only place able to recognize and truly appreciate his creative imagination. Ludwig was definitively original in two respects: one, his enthusiastic promotion of the technique of illusion, of *son et lumière*, as a means to shape architecture; two, his creation, with the help of illusory techniques, of a great variety of "moods." The techniques for creating these moods were already well tested in the world of the opera and the theater, just as later they would be tested in the world of the cinema. Architecture was mostly employed as ephemeral or as a mnemonic device, serving not as stylistic reconstruction but as thematic evocation. Master of the unconventional, Ludwig had developed the strategy of thematic clustering, subordinating everything to a general leitmotif in which diverse motives could be incorporated, anachronistically, without requirements of stylistic coherence or historical unity. The great American theme parks, from the Coney Island Luna Park to the most recent Disneylands, are inconceivable without Ludwig's preparatory work. Other examples of illusory techniques and thematic clustering are the Las Vegas establishments, which challenged the novelties of the 1970s Caesar's Palace with new delirious fantasies; these include the MGM Grand, the Luxor Pyramid, and the Excalibur Ritterburg.

Many of America's architectural exploits, especially those on the West Coast, are thematically conceived: Bertram Goodhue's El Fureidis, in the Persian Style, at Santa Barbara; the Theosophical Temple and Homestead at Point Loma; and the townships of Naples and Venice in greater Los Angeles, as well as the thousand others that are rightful heirs to Ludwig's magic kingdom.

20. W. A. Swanberg, *Citizen Hearst: A Biography of William Randolph Hearst* (New York: Charles Scribner's Sons, 1961), 14.

Umberto Eco has sensed quite rightly that although the place unquestionably had its own wild flavor, it also had "its own pathetic sadness, barbarian grandeur and sensual perversity, redolent of contamination, blasphemy, the Black Mass. It is like making love in a confessional with a prostitute dressed in a prelate's liturgical robes reciting Baudelaire while ten electronic organs reproduce the Well Tempered Clavier played by Scriabin."[17] Not surprisingly, then, the first source for the Cuesta Encantada was not a castle but a church.

The model that Julia Morgan had made as a means of visualizing "the mass and volume" of the project was in fact based on the church and tower of Ronda in southern Spain.[18] Moreover, the final result shows clearly an ecclesiastical, double cruciform plan with Ottonian west work and eastern transept. The perversity lies in the radical mixing of functions and moods, of the profane and the sacred, the chaste and the erotic. The castle is not a castle but an abbey church, yet its function is utterly secular. The colossal dining hall is called the "refectory," yet it was to accommodate guests for hasty meals on paper plates, since they were generally on the way to the billiard room or the movie theater. The most excruciating clash of moods, however, is achieved by the opposition of the pious church facade of the main building and the overwhelming ostentation of the classical marble swimming pool. The technique of blending a variety of unrelated, often contrasting moods, which might be best characterized as "thematic clustering,"[19] dominated all of the Hearst/Morgan environmental undertakings. At the end, as we will see, the long-awaited superclash would be realized in Wyntoon, where an abbey church was to be reerected—this time with an indoor swimming pool that was not, as at San Simeon, in a separate building but consumed the entire nave of the "church," a predictable yet audacious move indeed.

From his formative years, Hearst had been nourished by massive doses of European, especially Germanic, culture. His southern Germanic side was developed early in his life. As a youth of seventeen, when most boys chase girls or sublimate their impulses in athletic exhaustion, Hearst "read German legends as he sailed up the Rhine with his mother and Tutor Barry." As one of his biographers, the aptly named William Swanberg, reported: "They stayed for a time in Dresden, where he was given daily German lessons and was required to speak the language at meals."[20]

Hearst loved to dress up in Bavarian *Tracht* (folkloric costume), complete with felt hat and *Lederhosen* (fig. 4.7). At the same time he collected predominantly medieval art, sculpture, and architectural fragments, taken from deserted monasteries in southern Europe or purchased at auctions. For the task of welding all this into a more or less coherent whole, Hearst had secured the assistance of Morgan, a most devoted "thematic assembler" and the epitome of the West Coast architectural chameleon, who adapted naturally to the most diverse conditions while retaining her highly original sense of structural methods and materials.

When Hearst invited Morgan to design his fairy castle, he could not have asked a more accomplished practitioner. To erect a castle almost astride the San Andreas Fault

4.7. William Randolph Hearst in Bavarian costume.
(Swanberg, *Citizen Hearst,* 1961.)

4.8. *Right:* San Simeon, California, plot plan. Julia Morgan. (Boutelle, *Julia Morgan,* 1988.)

4.9. San Simeon, first outdoor pool, 1924. Julia Morgan. (Boutelle, *Julia Morgan,* 1988.)

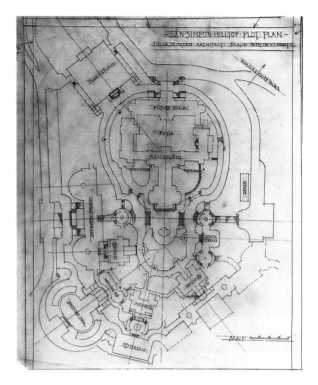

required not only courage and unlimited funds but a keen sense of engineering. Yet there was more to it. In addition to challenging the dangerous sublimity of the spot, Hearst's demand for at least two swimming pools required building large tanks of water on the shaky terrain. Even here Morgan did not falter but, on the contrary, probably did better than anyone else in the profession could have. The plan she drew for the San Simeon hilltop may be appreciated chiefly as an Haussmannian dictate that she imposed without hesitation on the hugely problematic site (fig. 4.8).

The first outdoor pool at San Simeon, completed in 1924, was T-shaped in plan, with semicircular apses on the east-west axis. A simple diving board was fitted at the far end (fig. 4.9). Although its location was unparalleled, its size was far from impressive and certainly smaller than the 55 by 100 feet (17 by 30 meters) of the Pickfair pool of 1920 (see fig. 5.27). Hearst and Morgan wasted little time in correcting the implied imbalance and, just before the official housewarming party in 1925, made ready a second, larger version. But the pool that would become the extraordinary urbanistic marvel that made San Simeon famous only came into existence during the 1930s.

Meanwhile, in 1922, on one of his European buying sprees, Hearst had acquired a temple front of unattributed origin, which he thought to use as a backdrop for a reflecting pond, never built.[21] Yet the image persisted, in further enlargements and in the sculptural groups that were ordered to emphasize the monumental character of the temple front. During the Depression, French sculptor Charles Cassou was commissioned to make three groups: a colossal Neptune, like the Neptune of the Trevi Fountain and the Apollo of Versailles surrounded by Nereids, naiads, and four hippogriffs; a Diana fountain; and a more restrained and quite successful composition of the birth of Venus. It was the Venus group that finally made it to San Simeon, after being exhibited at the Paris Salon of 1930. The Diana fountain never passed beyond the design stage and Neptune remained, unpaid for, in Hearst's New York warehouse.

Nevertheless the ensemble was called Neptune Pool, although in fact it was dedicated to Venus and, to an unexpectedly large degree, to the Swan (fig. 4.10). Surrounding the poolside are groups of amoretti and swans in various postures. To disguise the electric lighting, four marble candelabra were designed in the Piranesian manner by Morgan's associate Thaddeus Joy; carried by a quadriga of swans on tiptoes, these are placed at various strategic spots around the pool (figs. 4.11, 4.12). For the rest, Venus in all her artful manifestations holds sway: there are Cassou's *Birth of Venus,* copies of the *Crouching Venus* and the *Venus* by Canova, and other representations of her heady power, such as Galatea, and of course Leda and the Swan.

Although the academic urbanism and the intricate bouquets of sculpture suggest late nineteenth-century Parisian models (the plan might be read as a simplified adaptation of Paul Abadie's Sacré-Coeur), the overall character was intended to suggest a Roman bath, a

21. Taylor Coffmann, *Hearst Castle: The Story of William Randolph Hearst and San Simeon* (Santa Barbara: Sequoia Books, 1989), 59.

4.10. San Simeon, Neptune Pool, 1930s. Julia
Morgan, architect. *Also plate 9.*

4.11. *Left:* Neptune Pool, detail of swan candelabra by Thaddeus Joy.

4.12. G. B. Piranesi, view of an antique candelabra in marble, from *Vasi, candelabra, cippi, sarcofagi* (1778).

22. Patterson, *American Homes of To-day,* picture section of Garden Design. No page numbers given.
23. Boutelle, *Julia Morgan,* 206.
24. Ibid.
25. Ibid.

logical choice at the time. The previously cited arbiter of the appropriate style for country homes for the very rich, Mrs. Patterson, had decreed that architecturally, swimming pools should "recall the memory of Roman antecedents."[22] She illustrated her dictum with the swimming pool of Samuel Untermeyer at Greystone (see fig. 3.23), similar in *romanitas* to the Neptune pool and possibly a formal source.

Nevertheless, the Neptune Pool defies comparison in all respects. Morgan's mastery shows especially in the detailing; she had developed an unparalleled sense for finding the right solution for the right problem, as is demonstrated in the shaping of the pool ladders, which are composed of two oversized reversed consoles that resemble the side fenders of a Roman racing chariot (fig. 4.13). The pool itself is a colossal but disproportionately shallow basin, surrounded by marble colonnades and the old temple front, which found its final destination as a screen facing the Pacific Ocean. Two balustraded stairways encompassing the Venus group lead to a terrace overlooking the pool where seventeen dressing rooms, with baths and full-length mirrors, are situated.

Extended in 1930 beyond 100 feet in length, the pool is an outstanding example of ferroconcrete engineering. Julia Morgan's biographer, Sara Holmes Boutelle, has summarized it as follows: "On a site excavated from the steep hillside, the pool is hung by reinforced-concrete beams from the concrete retaining wall in such a way that a seismic movement would let it sway but not break. Water flows in from natural springs above, piped into two reserve tanks of tremendous capacity, one of 345,000 gallons, the other 1,200,000 gallons [about 1,300 and 4,500 cubic meters, respectively]. Below the pool is a large room housing a complex filter system based on the purifying power of sand [i.e., the traditional pre–World War II technique] and an electrical heating unit used to keep the water at a brisk 70 degrees Fahrenheit."[23]

The indoor pool (fig. 4.14), inexplicably dubbed the Roman Pool, was originally intended to be filled with salt water.[24] Hearst, extremely health-conscious and suffering from kidney ailments, had taken the cure in Bad Nauheim for years and was convinced of the healing qualities of salt water. He and his architect quickly realized that bringing the ocean to the hilltop (1,600 feet above sea level) was heretical as well as impractical and decided instead upon a "combination orchid-greenhouse and indoor pool—with plate glass partition for sharks!"[25] Work started in 1927, and by 1932 the most splendid indoor pool ever constructed, measuring 81 by 31 feet (24.7 by 9.5 meters) with a uniform depth of 10 feet (3.0 meters), was ready for its inauguration. A wading pool was projected on the entrance side. Light came from above, through glass bricks in the roof, which doubled as the base for a pair of tennis courts. As far as reinforced concrete construction is concerned, this inside-outside athletic palace is probably the most accomplished of Morgan's career.

Of course, judged solely as large tanks to swim in, the two pools are colossal architectural overstatements. But as bathing palaces, as theaters of physical entertainment,

4.13. Neptune Pool with "racing chariot" consoles.

4.14. San Simeon, Roman Pool, 1927–1932. Julia
Morgan. (Boutelle, *Julia Morgan*, 1988.) *Also
plate 10.*

they are in the same league with Charles Garnier's Opéra in Paris, Gottfried Semper's Opera House in Dresden, indeed with almost any other great architectural feat of the immediate past.

Although it is undeniably true that Hearst was obsessed by water, he was hardly an avid swimmer. More of a quiet floater, he left most of the swimming to others, including Marion Davies. The original concept of the Neptune/Venus pool as a reflecting pond continued to determine not only the spirit of the place but its use. Not surprisingly, considering the private pool's history—Badenburg, the Venusgrotte, the fin-de-siècle playhouse—Hearst's pond was first of all intended for theatrical use by professional performers. "Stars of the day," Charles Sprawson wrote, "Weissmuller, Crabbe, Gertrude Ederle, Esther Williams—would be invited up to submerge in 345,000 gallons of spring water, that sparkled in the California sun above the marble slabs patterned with antique green mosaics. Hearst would emerge to answer phones hidden in plant boxes, behind trees and beneath rocks."[26]

Floating, rather than swimming, was also the theme Huxley had chosen as the specific impetus behind the Neptune Pool: "From that swimming-pool at the top of the donjon, the view was prodigious. Floating on the translucent water, one had only to turn one's head to see, between the battlement, successive vistas of plain and mountain of green and tawny and violet and faint blue. One floated, one looked, and one thought."[27] Nothing could better illustrate this technique of surface swimming than the emblematic bird itself, "gliding silently on its mirror, without desire."[28]

Asked to swim-test it, Miss Williams reportedly judged the pool too small, claiming that she "couldn't do her thing." Thus it was decided to enlarge it, which indeed was accordingly done.[29] The anecdote emphasizes yet again that swimming was not the main purpose. Not that the Neptune Pool was not big or deep enough; it was simply no more a swimming pool than Wagner's *Lohengrin* was dance music.

A Theater of Metaphors The Enchanted Hill is too complex a structure to reduce to its designated function. The more we know about Hearst and his often delirious ambitions and desires, the more primary levels of observation lose their meaning in favor of secondary levels of interpretation. La Cuesta Encantada, prophetically named, was a project that intentionally ran out of control, starting as an encampment, then becoming successively a ranch, a church, an abbey, and a castle. The meaning of one, let alone two, swimming pools, is open to speculation. During the extended period, between 1919 and 1951, of changing, enlarging, reviewing, and redrawing, the initial concept was long overtaken, and the final result (although the place would never actually be completed) became a colossal scenography of complex and arcane desires: a theater of metaphors, metaphors in intention, thematic clustering in practice.

26. Charles Sprawson, *Haunts of the Black Masseur: The Swimmer as Hero* (London: Jonathan Cape, 1992), 277.
27. Ibid., and Huxley, *After Many a Summer*, 37.
28. "Le cygne glisse silencieux sur son miroir sans désir." Jacques Mercanton, *Les châteaux magiques de Louis II de Bavière* (Lausanne, 1963), 91.
29. Source: Sara Holmes Boutelle, Santa Cruz, California.

4.15. Las Vegas: pool at Caesar's Palace. *Also plate 11.*

30. Sprawson, *Haunts of the Black Masseur*, 280.

"In conception," Sprawson noted, the outdoor pool of Caesar's Palace in Las Vegas (fig. 4.15) "owes much to San Simeon's Neptune Pool . . . but the diving-boards and ladders are plated with gold, and the surrounding rotundas made of concrete rather than the ancient fragments assembled by Hearst."[30] Here Sprawson has hinted at the obsessive will to find allegorical ties with one's favorite fantasy. Be it the Roman Empire, Ludwig, or the Swan, everything, down to the smallest detail, must submit to the dominant motif. Thematic clustering, the strategy by which the personal theme is forced on the environment in the most meticulous, most tenacious way, represents the all-encompassing creative power of America. It was once the driving force of Europe too, of England's Victorian and Edwardian eras, of France's Belle Epoque. But such dreams and childish utopias left the aged continent long ago.

In their building of fantasy empires, Hearst, Ludwig, and the entrepreneur of Caesar's Palace developed an "eclectic eccentricity" apparently insulting to "good taste," but finally they created, almost as a by-product, an unforgettable, unworldly beauty surpassing those works that originated in the painful agony of reality. It could hardly have been more appropriate. When Aldous Huxley came to Los Angeles in 1938, he quickly adapted himself to what he believed was "the city of dreadful joy." How dreadful depended very much on one's access to the dollar, but a joy it certainly was.

An Empire of Pools Ludwig's junior by eighteen years, Hearst outlived him by more than six decades. In personality as well as in their building frenzy, the two *rois manqués* were remarkably similar, and showed the same patterns of chaste eroticism and reconstructive nostalgia. The major force that motivated both men seems to have been solitude and loneliness. Unable to sustain relationships on a normal social level, they practiced a solitary creativity aimed at the construction of a protective yet extremely realistic dream world (manifesting a *Weltfluchtideologie*), into which they could withdraw, paradoxically without sacrificing their contacts with the outer world.

In his restless search for *Einsamkeit* (solitude plus loneliness), Hearst owned several "castles": Saint Joan at Sands Point, Long Island, St. Donats in Wales, San Simeon, and Wyntoon, of which the latter two especially were decorative reconstructions of mysterious nonexistent pasts. Hearst's "castles" were comparable, perhaps, to Ludwig's own line of defense: Linderhof, Neuschwanstein, and Herrenchiemsee, as well as the Residenz in Munich. Driven by the same hyperaesthetic sensibility as Wagner and Ludwig, equally unhindered by restrictions of traditional good taste, Hearst was thoroughly satisfied with the way he could, through his intuitive powers, acquire a unique if improbable array of artworks, from all over the world and of many different periods.

Meanwhile it becomes apparent that the same characteristic could be identified among most American hyperplutocrats of the period. The wild array of French, Italian, and

31. Maurice Culot, "Portrait de François Spoerry," *Archives d'Architecture Moderne* 12 (November 1977), 7.

32. Davies, *The Times We Had,* 173–176.

33. Ibid., 173. See also John Tebbel, *The Life and Good Times of William Randolph Hearst* (New York: Dutton, 1952), 39: "But the final touch was one only Hearst would have thought of. He laid a velvety sward in the moat and played croquet on it."

34. Davies, *The Times We Had,* 175.

35. Monica Randall, *The Mansions of Long Island's Gold Coast* (New York: Rizzoli, 1979), 10, 20, and 26–27: "Beekman [*sic*] Towers, built by August Belmont, is the house I believe Fitzgerald described in his *The Great Gatsby.* The feudal Castle 'was a colossal affair by any standard—it was a factual imitation of some Hotel de Ville in Normandy, with a tower on one side.'" My fig. 4.17 was taken from Patterson, *American Homes of To-day,* 15, where it is captioned: "No architect given."

36. In 1896 Alva had divorced William K. Vanderbilt, Sr., in order to marry, one year later, Oliver Hazard Perry Belmont, son of the notorious fiscal manipulator and founder of the Meadowbrook Fox Hunting Club, August O. Belmont. Both Belmont and Vanderbilt had been clients of Richard Morris Hunt. Robert B. King, *The Vanderbilt Homes* (New York: Rizzoli, 1989), 165–166.

37. Architectural League of New York, *Yearbook,* 1914, advertisement section.

British castles and palaces resurrected on the East Coast is a token of the same selective search for a fitting set of secondhand roots. Spurious coats of arms, manufactured genealogies, and fake castles, gardens, and antique furnishings were produced with lightning speed. The solitude of these newly self-appointed aristocrats was not so much the effect of a traumatized mind as of a complete lack of a circle of old friends and relatives belonging to the same echelons of society; whoever appoints himself king overnight cannot expect his friends and acquaintances to be royal as well. Instead, to fill the vacuum, they encircled themselves with guests, never-ending streams of social zombies, often total strangers knowing neither their hosts nor each other, moving through the ostentatious surroundings, exhaustively entertained in a ceaseless parade of attractions that, besides eating and drinking, were generally of a sporting, often outdoors character.

In the frenzy to make up the time lost in generations of dark ignominy, the pursuit of class-conscious happiness was practiced with round-the-clock tenacity. Riding, hunting, swimming, sailing, buying, collecting, and erecting houses were the preferred activities. To the Vanderbilt family, the F. W. Woolworth circle, and of course to W. R. Hearst and his mother, acquiring palatial real estate and building on it was just another way of manifesting neofeudal power. Among these, the Hearsts' architectural taste was the most Ludwigian. Thus Wyntoon, for example, was an almost literal transplant from the Bavarian Alps. Commenced by his mother with the help of architect and second-generation German wood sculptor Bernard Maybeck, it would be transformed by Hearst and Morgan into a fairy-tale south German village, with "Hansel und Gretel" half-timbered houses and a stone fountain on the village square.

Wales Why Hearst, after strengthening his ties with Germany, should wish to occupy a small part of Celtic culture remains unfathomed, but it may be due to the fact that at the very moment he was in the market for a new castle, there came up for sale St. Donats, in South Glamorgan on the southwestern tip of Wales. Other incentives may have played a role; Wales had long been a favorite spot for Hearst's pursuit of antiques, and its harbors were extremely romantic. One of these, a hundred kilometers to the north of St. Donats, was Portmeirion, a dream village on the Glasdyl that was the life's work of the eccentric Sir Clough Williams-Ellis, a thematic assembleur on an almost American scale. His pastel-colored fantasy with no particular function was built between 1919 and 1926 as a free interpretation of something between Portofino and, perhaps, Vizcaya.[31]

The comparison of Portmeirion with Vizcaya is thrust upon the observer by the presence, on the narrow beach of the hotel, of an antique, 70-ton, two-masted vessel, neither wholly ship nor building, intended to serve as an instrument of nostalgic education. It acts as a metaphoric model which, with the help of naive images, represents the process of "mnemonic debarcation." The "ship" carries its cargo of memories to the selected coast and unloads it for ever and ever. Deering's marble Columbian barge in the bay of Vizcaya, Flagler's Spanish caravel in the harbor of Florida's Saint Augustine, and Gabriele d'Annunzio's cruiser *Puglia,* safely anchored in the hills of Gardone, are all demonstrably doing their mnemonic work.

Hearst and Davies encountered Portmeirion during their exhaustive sightseeing trips through the Welsh countryside, trips that were, according to Davies, exhausting as well: "That constant routine of getting up early, motoring all day long, resting at night and seeing the town the next day was really hard on the system."[32] Hearst began to remodel St. Donats from the very moment he bought it in 1925, the same period when Williams-Ellis was building his magic village not far away. Not surprisingly, the first thing Hearst wanted to install was his totem, a large swimming pool (fig. 4.16).

Since he was convinced that England counted no pool specialists worth mentioning, he had asked Julia Morgan to act as consultant to the architect in designing and constructing the pool. Davies, who was remarkably observant about the uncommonly large property, recalled: "WR added two tennis courts and a new, modern swimming pool about two hundred feet long and a hundred wide," necessary for the amusement of the guests who thronged there, all the way from London, for the weekends. "WR kept St. Donats open all year round. There were numerous guest apartments and there was a staff of about thirty or forty. The entertainment, as far as mealtimes were concerned, was predominantly English. But for the rest of the day it was Californian. Cards and charades in the evening. Tennis, swimming and riding in the afternoon."[33] Hearst put St. Donats up for sale in 1938, but before it could be sold it was requisitioned by the army in 1940. In 1960 it was converted into the United World College of the Atlantic.[34]

Saint Joan of Sands Points, Long Island   Of the many quirkly architectural creations of the Long Island Gold Coast, Beacon Towers (fig. 4.17), on the beach of Sands Point, was probably the most idiotic.[35] It was designed in 1915 by the firm of Hunt & Hunt for Alva Vanderbilt Belmont, as a seaside castle for leisurely use in spring and autumn.[36] The eighteen-acre property was adjacent to the Sands Point Lighthouse, perhaps the inspiration for the client's command that the brothers Hunt devise something tall and defiant (Alva was, after all, a leading suffragette) in the same radically eclectic style that their father had practiced. She urged them to incorporate elements from Viollet-le-Duc's Pierrefonds, from Neuschwanstein, and from the town halls of Normandy, insisting that the building taper upward into a single block of towers. This was no difficult task for the Hunts, specialists in Gothic nostalgia as they had shown in other work for the Belmonts, such as the family "mortuary chapel" at Woodlawn Cemetery, New York, 1913, a neomedieval curiosity replete with references to August O.'s passion for hunting, such as the four sets of deer antlers fitted into the steeple.[37]

4.16. *Top:* St. Donats, Wales, pool. (Swanberg, *Citizen Hearst,* 1961.)

4.17. Sands Point, New York: Beacon Towers, 1915. Hunt & Hunt. (Patterson, *American Homes of To-day,* 1924.)

38. King, *Vanderbilt Homes,* 166.

What makes Beacon Towers so endearing is its undisguised amateurism, its candor unspoiled by borrowed connoisseurship. The exterior bristled with five stories of battlements, turrets, and balconies; the interior was dominated by a vast hall and stairwell. This was decorated, like several of the rooms, with paintings "depicting scenes from the life of Saint Joan of Arc, painted on canvas by Italian artist Vincent Aderente. . . . A two-storey-high trinal arched Gothic window," Vanderbilt scholar Robert King wrote, "illuminated the stairwell, creating almost a cathedral effect. . . . In the master bedroom Alva incorporated a private elevator hidden among the panelled walls, which ran directly down to the beach, permitting the owner access undisturbed and unnoticed."[38]

Alva apparently was a swimming enthusiast with a craving for seclusion. To afford her a high degree of privacy, while maintaining the thrill of a dip in the sea, an outdoor swimming pool had been installed on an elevated platform at the south side of the castle. An arcaded loggia containing the dressing rooms screened off the view from the land side. The advantage of this layout was that the swimmer could look out over the parapet and imagine herself swimming in Long Island Sound, while retaining the privacy and hygienic quality of her own pool. Often such pools were filled with salt water from the nearby sea. This preference for salt-water pools was most immediately due to the vaunted therapeutic value of sea water, but it may also have enhanced the illusion of ocean bathing.

In 1924 Mrs. Belmont, in her endless quest for still more privacy, extended her property by five and a half acres, including the lighthouse, at a cost of one hundred thousand dollars, a futile expenditure since three years later she put Beacon Towers on the market and left for France. It seemed unlikely that anyone of sane mind would be interested in this unhappy folly, which featured an anguished Joan of Arc in the stairwell, a perpetual light-tower in the garden, a secret elevator behind the paneling, and an outdoor swimming pool located almost directly on the beach. But there was someone—Hearst, well acquainted with the Belmonts, who at one time had supported Alva's husband in his political ambitions. Although neither the rambling shingle-style mansions of Newport and Long Island nor the impressive neoclassical palaces of Rhode Island and Connecticut could seduce him, Hearst eventually succumbed to this insane Mont-Saint-Michel on the Long Island Sound, purchasing Beacon Towers in 1929.

Its exciting vulgarity and quasi-aristocratic opulence charmed Hearst instantly. Although he may have been aware of its dark side, he was unable to resist. "The castle at Sands Point, Long Island is where he lived least," wrote Hearst biographer Tebbell. "It was bought in 1929, presumably as part of a settlement with Mrs. Hearst, who by that time was his wife, as the saying goes, in name only . . . and he was not a stranger to St. Joan, as they named it, either at the formal occasion of its opening in 1930, or in the months preceding. . . . It quickly took on the familiar characteristics of a Hearst home: the great hall with an enormous fireplace

39. Tebbel, *Life of Hearst*, 35.
40. Cornelius Vanderbilt, Jr., *Farewell to Fifth Avenue* (New York: Simon and Schuster, 1935), 58.
41. F. Scott Fitzgerald, *The Great Gatsby* (1925; New York: Scribners, 1953), 5. For Randall's observation, see note 35 above.
42. Tebbel, *Life of Hearst*, 70–71.
43. Swanberg, *Citizen Hearst*, 367.
44. Perhaps Orson Welles was alluding to this connection between Ludwig and Hearst when, in *Citizen Kane*, he fashioned the Marion role as that of an unfortunate opera singer.
45. Bachelard, *L'eau et les rêves*, 62.
46. Ibid., 52.

would be crammed with carloads of objects . . . and furniture of every period from the early Louis to Early American."[39]

We have seen that Hearst was very fond of everything old, particularly things medieval and church-related. He collected religious paraphernalia on a large scale and bought entire interiors of churches and monasteries. Invariably he transformed profane real estate into castles of a sacred nature: St. Donats, San Simeon, Saint Joan. With Saint Joan it was the more significant because the original name had been Beacon Towers and "Saint Joan" was his own invention, though based of course on the scenes that were painted there from the life of the saint with whom Alva, the suffragette, had conveniently identified herself.

Alva's cousin Cornelius Vanderbilt, Jr., a newspaperman himself, recollecting his meeting with Hearst, characterized him as "a walking anachronism" and was fascinated by

> his medieval personality. I say medieval because except for his conventional twentieth-century clothes nothing about him suggested his connection with the world of today. If there is such a thing as reincarnation, he must have been, centuries ago, a Duke of Burgundy engaged in merciless combat with a King of France. . . . A walking anachronism in New York, he should be observed on his immense ranch at San Simeon where he is Lord and Master of everything he surveys, where his numerous vassals would not so much as raise their eyebrows were he to declare his Secession from the United States. His quarrels with Wilson, Hoover, Theodore and Franklin D. Roosevelt, could have been easily avoided had the inhabitants of the White House disclosed a better knowledge of the Middle Ages. . . . It never dawned on them that he was (and is) a Sovereign Power, not unlike Burgundy under King Louis XI.[40]

Vanderbilt's identification of Hearst with Charles the Bold—"Charles le Téméraire"—of Burgundy (1433–1477), whose heraldic device, incidentally, was the swan, and who defeated Louis XI in 1465, besides being flattering to the powerful publisher, associates him with the times of Joan of Arc (1412–1431), and may help to explain his fascination with places like St. Donats, San Simeon, and Beacon Towers.

It was Monica Randall who recognized Beacon Towers as the house Fitzgerald described in *The Great Gatsby*. Fitzgerald's own text discloses an indispensable detail: this "factual imitation of some Hôtel de Ville . . . spanking new under a thin beard of raw ivy, [had] a marble swimming pool, and more than forty acres of lawn and garden. It was Gatsby's mansion."[41] The swimming pool, of course, was that other essential element, apart from castles and saints, that had attracted Hearst's attention to Beacon Towers.

After he had bought the place, Hearst thought it only proper to present his acquisition to New York society: "As late as October 8, 1930, *The New York Times* reported that the Hearsts had entertained a formal dinner marking the opening of the Sands Point house. The formidable guest list, headed by [former] President and Mrs. Coolidge, included such New York society names as Young, Swope, Astor and Stewart."[42] Saint Joan of Sands Point was demolished in 1945.

Hearst's East Coast real estate campaign never seemed to have the same conviction as his architectural activities on the West Coast. Whether his heart was not in it, or whether prestigious property was not available, the fact is that even in Florida he was not able to get a decent foothold. Yet the old money estates there never failed to excite him. One of the "absolute musts" was the Phipps mansion, built by Addison Mizner in 1924, "a stylish hispanic house with a monumental semi-outside swimming pool. Naturally Hearst had to meet Mizner.... Early in 1924 he was in Palm Beach ... [and] encountered ... the huge, eccentric San Franciscan who had taken up architecture without benefit of formal education. It was reported that Hearst set Mizner to planning the most elaborate residence in Palm Beach for him, one that would surpass Edward Stotesbury's El Mirasol, which even had a reception room for guests' chauffeurs."[43] But evidently this was just talk, for Hearst turned again to Morgan to make plans for the largest single bathing complex to be devoted to his water baby Davies. In 1926, house and pool would arise on the beach of Santa Monica.

Santa Monica Beach House Whereas Ludwig's unrelenting love for the arts was compressed into an adoration of Richard Wagner, Hearst's admittedly less developed artistic ambitions were directed toward the ex-Ziegfeld girl and movie star Marion Davies.[44] But in comparison to Linderhof or Neuschwanstein, La Cuesta Encantada is a mausoleum. A marble monument to "a lost love," it has the color and the aspirations of the moon: "La lune, ce beau cygne du ciel, promenait son blanc plumage du Vésuve au sommet du firmament" (Jean-Paul, quoted by Bachelard).[45]

The beauty of the enchanted hill is uncontested. It is the best work Morgan or Hearst ever did. It is also their final real work. I do not wish to crush the reader under the banality of the idea of the swan song, but there is a relevant truth in it. The Swan Song, following Bachelard's interpretation, is the most beautiful, the most eloquent anthem of the lover, "la voix chaude du séducteur avant l'instant suprême, avant ce terme si fatal à l'exaltation qu'il est vraiment 'une mort amoureuse.' "[46] After the monument to Venus at San Simeon, Hearst's architectural inspiration could only go downward until the Santa Monica beach house was reached. Where the former was consecrated to the serene beauty of the moon, this became a center for worshiping the sun. Intended as a love nest of unheard-of proportions for the aquatic Pavilion Bird, it looked to everyone just like a big hotel. His adoration for Marion Davies in San Simeon was distant, tragic, romantic. In Santa Monica it turns into vulgarity. Even Julia Morgan seems to have lost control, her thoughts elsewhere.

4.18. Santa Monica, California: Marion Davies beach
house. Julia Morgan. (Postcard.)

As Hearst wanted to accommodate Davies in the Los Angeles area, he had Morgan draw up plans for a seaside fun palace on the Santa Monica beach (fig. 4.18), with a rectangular, far less ceremonial swimming pool. Located in front of the "hotel," the swimming pool looks like a fire break dug between the Coastal Highway and the ocean. Originally the pool could be crossed by a bridge, endowing a Venetian flavor to a composition that more and more resembled a colonnaded Villa Malcontenta on the Brenta joined by the Rialto Bridge. After all, Venice, California, was only a mile or so away (see fig. 5.35). A few years later the bridge was removed, and the pool acquired a semblance of serenity.

The materials used in San Simeon and Santa Monica were identical. Tiles and chariot-type pool ladders came straight from the San Simeon workshop (fig. 4.19). Whatever the faults of the main building, the pool still has the Amazonian freshness of all Morgan's pools, a freshness especially apparent when they are set against the murky grottoes and nymphaea of dirty old men like Captain DeLamar. In Santa Monica, Morgan has recycled San Simeon materials for an apparent reinstatement of the Phoebe Hearst Memorial pool at Berkeley (see fig. 4.3).

The mainly wooden beach house was

> a white-pillared manse, huge as a railway terminal. . . . Like its companion piece to the north [San Simeon], it was constantly saturated with guests, probably more so because it was handier to Hollywood and the gregarious Marion urged her innumerable friends to come see her anytime. Life at the beach house was endless fun. There was swimming, of course, not in the ocean but in the inevitable swimming pool laid out beside it. . . . Her bedroom was enormous, facing the ocean, and it boasted two baths, one at each end. As Ilka Chase remarked, this was "the kind of thing which haunts one when waking up in the middle of the night, and brings hazily to mind the story of the donkey who starved to death between two bales of hay."[47]

Partially demolished, the beach house on its extreme western flank survives as part of a beach club (fig. 4.20). So does the pool, curtailed by about a third, but under the protective mats the original tiles are still visible. Holes in the tiles mark the position of one of the three, now removed, springboards.

After the war, just a few years before his death, Hearst bought the Milton E. Getz residence (see also chapter 6), exactly the sort of property that would suit Hearst as a surrogate San Simeon. Situated just north of the Beverly Hills Hotel, on fashionable Beverly Drive, it offered the very best in luxurious living.[48] A banker, Getz had bought the land in 1925 and commissioned the English-born "man of style" Gordon Kaufmann to build him an estate in the Mediterranean mood for which Kaufmann was justly famed. Paul Thiene was given the task of making from the barren grounds a lush, water-rich garden that included an orchard, a

47. Tebbel, *Life of Hearst,* 40–41.
48. For the Getz house see Charles Lockwood and Jeff Hyland, *The Estates of Beverly Hills* (Los Angeles: Lockwood and Hyland, 1989), 18–25. Subdivided in 1966, the estate's mansion and waterworks nevertheless have been kept in such good repair that they were used in several major films, such as *The Godfather;* most recently, in *Bodyguard,* pop star Whitney Houston poses near and in the Hearst pool.

4.19. Davies beach house, pool. (San Marino, Huntington Library.)
4.20. *Opposite:* Remains of Davies beach house as Sand & Sea beach club, 1990.

utility garden, and a "swimming lake" (fig. 4.21).[49] A characteristic and very photogenic feature of the garden was the threefold, cascading reflecting pool, which ran down from the terrace to an octagonal fountain. To accentuate the narrowness of this path of water, Thiene had planted lines of tall palms. When Hearst bought the property in 1947, he immediately started to replace the lower decorative fountain with a sizable swimming pool (fig. 4.22). The avenue of palms was left untouched; the only liberty Hearst permitted himself was to have several carloads of his smaller San Simeon garden statuary brought down to mingle with the natural decor.

Hearst died in the former Getz house on August 14, 1951. On October 31, Marion Davies married a captain of the merchant marine, Horace Brown. To demonstrate her new position, she sadly posed in the upper cascade of the water path, in a rowboat (see fig. 6.15). It is a puzzlingly provocative photograph. The once gloriously hydrophilic siren now poses fully dressed in conservatively tailored tweeds, holding the oars, keeping the unwieldy boat from tumbling down the cascade. In another, almost identical picture of that scene, the captain has disappeared, leaving his wife alone with the elements. A miserable ending.

Nostalgia for a *Mr. Stoyte nodded, and explained that his Spanish agents had brought some sculp-*
Lost *ture and iron work from the chapel of a convent that had been wrecked by the anar-*
Melancholy *chists at the beginning of the civil war. "They sent some nuns along too," he added.*
"Embalmed, I guess. Or maybe sun-dried: I don't know." ALDOUS HUXLEY

49. Much interesting material was generously provided by Charles Lockwood. The Getz house and grounds were justly famous. See, for example, Winifred Starr Dobyns, *California Gardens* (New York: Macmillan, 1931), plate 19; *The Architectural Digest* 7, no. 2 (1929), 50, 103–111. Epigraph: Huxley, *After Many a Summer*, 33.

4.21. Getz estate: landscaping by Paul Thiene.
(*Landscape Architecture*, 1926.)

4.22. *Below:* Beverly Hills, California: Milton E. Getz
estate, 1925. Gordon Kauffman and Paul
Thiene. Aerial view in 1980s. (Lockwood and
Hyland, *The Estates of Beverly Hills*, 1989.)

50. Davies, *The Times We Had*, 181.
51. Bachelard, *L'eau et les rêves*, 59.

It was during the late twenties that Hearst was most active as a buyer of old buildings and works of art. During his days in Wales he acquired the abbey of St. Bradenstoke, in Wiltshire, and moved it to St. Donats because he needed it as a dining room. "WR was very clever at doing that," Marion Davies remembered understandingly, "if he had his heart at something he'd get it.... It didn't matter how much it cost. He bought a cloister in France and it ended up in San Simeon in the warehouse [this, by the way, was reconstructed in Orson Welles's *Citizen Kane*]; it was never unpacked. He wanted to give it to San Francisco, but I don't think they took it; they were afraid it would cost too much to put up."[50]

This is a fascinating yet flawed account. The cloister came not from France but from Spain, and it was intended not for San Simeon but for Wyntoon. Yet it ended up in San Francisco, indeed, and there it still is, in Golden Gate Park, overgrown with decades of neglect. The story of the transplant of the monastery of Santa Maria de Oliva began with its rediscovery during a trip Hearst and hispanicist Arthur Byne made c. 1928 to the hills near Burgos.

It was to be expected that the last building Hearst should want to construct would be devoted exclusively to his *amour épuisé*. In this light San Simeon was to be merely a mighty monument on the way to a still mightier one. San Simeon's complex of swimming pools, its Roman starkness, excess of marble, dramatic location on the crest of a promontory, all looked very much—apart from being a terrific "ol' swimming hole"—like a *Heldendenkmal,* an American Valhalla, a Vittoriale, the sort of thing Gabriele D'Annunzio was building between 1923 and 1930 in the hills overlooking the Lago di Garda. The heroic scale of San Simeon's Venus pool—and precisely because of its uninviting masculinity intuitively, if incorrectly, iden-tified with Neptune—was not the thing Hearst felt should represent his never-ending passion for the woman he could not possess. But the *mort amoureuse* or *amour épuisé* was merely the symptom of a much larger ensemble of a more profound darkness. The lost love was only a small detail in a total clustering of things lost. The complex of the swan illustrates not so much lost love, or erotic penitence, or the melancholy of love, as it alludes to the grief over the loss of that melancholy. The complex of the swan is exactly that: "la nostalgie d'une mélancholie perdue" (Bachelard). It is this all-encompassing dark nostalgia that unites Ludwig, Deering, Hearst, and D'Annunzio. All their bile, their feelings of displacement, their longing for a lost age were compacted in that one metaphor, the swan.

D'Annunzio, for example, lived by the power of the metaphor and the meta-morphosis. To him the swan—witness his poem "Leda"—was the image that could explain everything. The body of the swan, sculpted by the power of the waves, could explain the shape of the skiff's hull; its wings could give meaning to sails billowing in the wind.[51] When D'Annun-zio, nostalgic soldier and gifted theme park designer, had the cruiser *Puglia* hauled up to the hills of his estate at unimaginable cost and effort, he had in fact erected a monument to a melancholic swan: a perverse swimming pool resting forever between two rows of cypresses (see fig. 6.18). A little higher up the hill D'Annunzio built the actual Valhalla, a circular marble

52. D'Annunzio must have known of Hearst's ambition to run for president and of his efforts in 1898 to draw America into a merry old-fashioned war with Spain. And he must have loved the feudal sound of that ridiculous telegram sent by the publisher to Western heroics specialist Frederick Remington: "Please remain in Cuba. You furnish the pictures and I'll furnish the war."

53. Boutelle, *Julia Morgan*, 218.

54. Robert Clements, in Alison Sky and Michelle Stone, *Unbuilt America* (New York: McGraw-Hill, 1976), 182–184. Clements at the time was also preparing an article for *American Heritage*, but I have not been able to trace this.

55. For William Beckford, "England's richest son" (Byron), see John Wilton-Ely, "The Genesis and Evolution of Fonthill Abbey," *Architectural History* 23 (1980), 40–51.

56. Clements, in Sky and Stone, *Unbuilt America*, 184.

mausoleum crowned with the stele of his fallen comrades in arms. Looking down toward the lake, one finds the *Puglia* waiting, halfway, ready to sail out to the lost battlefields. The "Vittoriale degli Italiani" is a study in the "complexe du Cygne"; as a monument, it educates in metaphorical terms about nostalgic love, nostalgic heroism, lost beauty, and, of course, surviving political rancor.[52] They were very much of a kind, those Knights of the Swan, united by their common distrust of reality. By a rigorous twist in their perceptional mechanism, they enabled themselves to live their lives metaphorically.

Thus the compelling force that drove Hearst to build one aquatic monument after another was part of a larger complex of living his life metaphorically. The castles he built were thematic assemblages intended to provoke specific moods and attitudes. Some were intended as bowers for his bride, others were temples for the Grail, and others again were Bavarian cottages where he could entertain the villagers in folkloristic dress. But none of these places was able to please Miss Davies in such a way that she would make it a home. As Ludwig had built his chain of castles as a series of emotional mousetraps, so Hearst encircled Davies with a string of water castles and, not being able to catch her ever-receding love, decided to build her a thing he would never play a role in: the beach house. The beach house was a heartless thing, only substance and no passion, where Marion could play and be on her own, without the oppressive presence of her master. At the Santa Monica house she could do freely what she in her role as amphibious bird was instructed to do: sleep, sun herself, and swim.

But that operation had merely been a diversionary tactic while Hearst was plotting his largest and last great battle. In retrospect it all seems so self-evident, but it took time before the final piece would fit well into the predetermined slot. The last of the chain of pavilions had to be a mausoleum, a building of heroic yet tragic proportions, commemorating his obsessional triad: water, unattainable love, and nostalgia. It must be a quest of Wagnerian proportions and tone—"blood, lust and death." For an age, Hearst had been seeking the ideal form to fit his concept, and then, in 1930, he found it, in Spain: the Cistercian monastery of Santa Maria de Oliva, near Burgos, discovered in a state of extreme decay by Byne, one of Hearst's professional scavengers, who felt instantly that Hearst would not to be able to resist it. And indeed he could not. Or better, he should not—it was as if his mother had risen from her grave and ordered him to buy the convent, have it shipped to San Francisco, and use it as building material to reconstruct her castle of Wyntoon, destroyed by fire during the winter of 1929–1930.[53] Having become an instrument of fate, he called upon Julia Morgan, already busy designing a Bavarian village at Wyntoon with a belt of half-timber houses of the "Hansel und Gretel" variety surrounding the castle, to make plans for the grandest of all his undertakings.

The brief was of an amazing unworldliness, for Hearst required a medieval castle situated on the bend of the river which would "rise in commanding towers and bastions to eight storeys of pure fairy tale splendour. It would have sixty-one bedrooms divided over six floors, and the eighth floor, at the top of the tallest tower, would contain only a solitary round study for 'the Chief.' "[54] The sublime madness that had struck William Beckford,[55] Ludwig II, and to a lesser degree Napoleon III (when he commissioned Viollet-le-Duc to rebuild the colossal castle of Pierrefonds as his imperial residence) had now manifested itself in Hearst. But the real beauty of this brilliant plan was yet to come.

Robert Clements, who unearthed the drawings in 1976, described the progress of the redesign of the monastery's "chapel" in terms of a purely logical answer to an architectural problem of a too-long nave and a too-short transept: "The final solution was breathtaking—the chapel was to become an enormous swimming pool. It was to be 150 feet long [46 meters; an Olympic-size pool is 50 meters] with the diving board where the altar had been" (fig. 4.23). This seems to be a misreading. The plan shows a springboard at the "west end" or vestibule (actually to be placed to the north). Clements continues: "And the two side chapels converted into a lounge and a women's toilet. Around the apse there was to be a very wide deck with a southern exposure, filled to a depth of two or three feet with sand, so that one could sunbathe on the beach and proceed into the chapel for a swim."[56]

The depth of "the plunge" would run from three feet near the steps in the presbyterium to eleven feet in the nave and even more in the vicinity of the diving board. The transept arms accommodated two semioctagons of decreasing depth (three feet). Along the eastern flank were situated the dressing rooms for women and men, totaling a staggering fifteen rooms for each sex. To separate the dressing rooms a gymnasium was wedged between the transept and the west block, five bays long and three wide. Adjoining the women's dressing rooms was to be a squash court, while at the opposite side, on the axis of the western transept, was situated a bowling alley.

Clearly, the functional organization is based on the New England playhouse, whereas the architectural layout refers to the monastery. If this ensemble had been realized, the effects would have been shattering. Imagine a Cistercian monastery constructed in thirteenth-century Spain, transplanted onto the banks of the McCloud River, partly hidden by the dense forest of Wyntoon. Picture the traveler who, attracted by lights playing through the fir trees, approaches its massive silhouette, throws open the archway, and finds himself blinded by pool lights, deafened by the echoing cries of seminude men and women, and utterly amazed by this northern Californian Walpurgisnacht.

The project may remind us of some of the fantastic architectural recycling projects dreamed up during the French Revolution, especially those for the suddenly redundant religious structures. One example is especially appropriate: the cathedral of Saint-André at Bordeaux, which in 1793 was imagined transformed into a winter garden (fig. 4.24). The charm of the plan by Alexandre-Théodore Brongniart is the inversion of the processional direction of the building. Through a triumphal arch one enters the apse, which is covered with the mixture of pebbles and sand characteristic of the parks of the day. At the transept the park narrows into a serpentine path leading into the nave, where a picturesque, quasi-oriental garden is

4.23. Wyntoon, California, plan. Julia Morgan. (Sky and Stone, *Unbuilt America*, 1976.)

4.24. *Opposite:* Alexandre-Théodore Brongniart, project for a mountain in the cathedral church of Saint-André, Bordeaux, for the Festival of Liberty and Reason, 1793. (*Les architectes de la liberté*, 1990.)

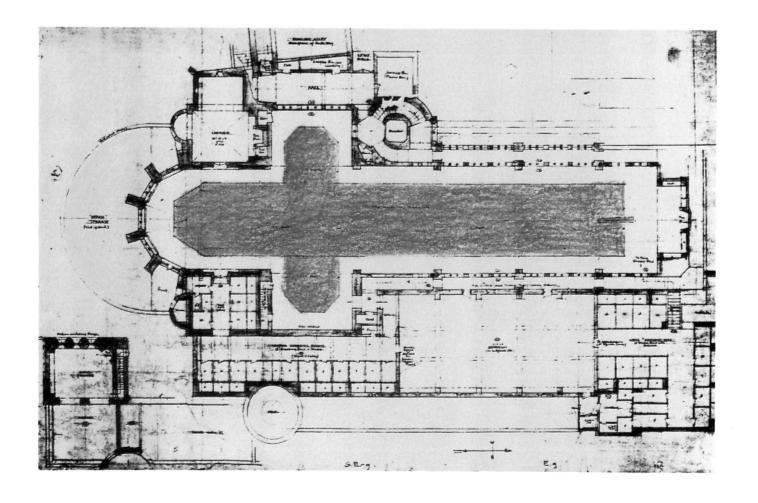

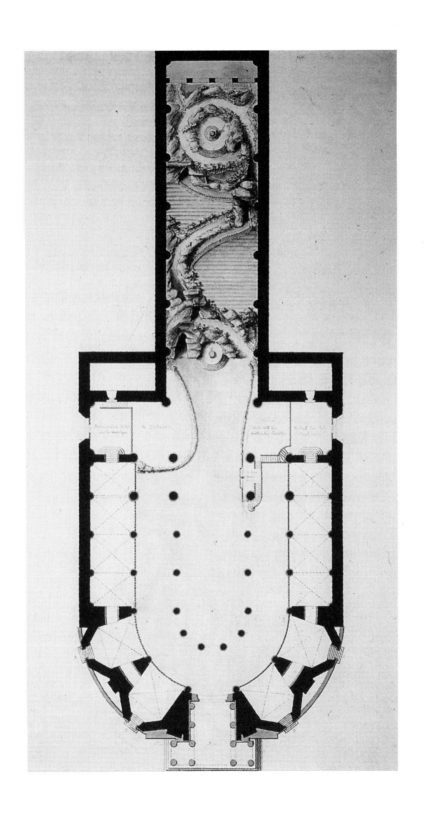

57. *Les architectes de la liberté, 1789–1799* (Paris: Ecole nationale supérieure des Beaux-Arts, 1989–1990), 224, plate 164.

58. The artifically heated pool—not open in July because that is when the city annually repairs its hot-water system—graced many a front page with its steaming surface and its lifeguards stomping about the icy banks in fur coats and hats.

59. "Nowadays the interior looks clean... The swimming pool has been built in the nave, the aisles adapted to accommodate dressing rooms. Showers have been installed in the ambulatory.... The springboard has replaced the altar, but for environmental reasons is little used." "Erst Gemüselager und dann Badeanstalt," *Frankfurter Allgemeine Zeitung,* March 30, 1992. I am grateful to Konrad Ottenheym for sending me this invaluable information. The church, built 1832–1838, was by the local architect Alexander Brjullow.

accommodated. The culminating point is the mountain of reason, a circular platform in the form of a ziggurat.[57]

Under Communist rule, a number of Russian churches also lost their religious purposes, if not their very fabric. In 1931, the nineteenth-century cathedral of Christ Saviour in Moscow was blown up to make way for the winning design by Boris Iofan in the competition (to which Le Corbusier had contributed a significant entry) for the Palace of Soviets. Intended as the Soviet answer to the Statue of Liberty, with an unsteadily orating Lenin atop a gargantuan pedestal, the Palace rose no further than the perpetually flooded foundations. Thereupon the site was reused for the open-air Moskva Pool, a popular institution that accommodated 10,000 visitors daily in its 90-meter-diameter basin. With the fall of the Soviet regime, however, the cathedral is being reconstructed on its original site, usurping the Moskva Pool.[58] In St. Petersburg, on the other hand, the neo-Romanesque German Protestant Church, into which a swimming pool was installed in 1959–1963 (fig. 4.25), in 1992 had that facility nicely refurbished.[59]

What Hearst's objectives could have been in his own remarkable travesty of form and function may only be surmised. A pious Christian might have imagined that, like Don Juan, Hearst would be burning in hell. A cultured man of musical upbringing might have responded as if he were watching Auber's *Fra Diavolo* or Rossini's *Comte Ory.* Hearst himself, being an aesthetic eclectic, would have conceived this sacrilegious pool as a thematic cluster gathered from *Tannhäuser*'s Venus Grotto, *Lohengrin*'s Swan Lake, and *Parsifal*'s Temple of the Holy Grail.

Unlike Ludwig who, being a literary eclectic, had surrounded himself with literal reconstructions of favorite scenes from Wagner's operas, Hearst followed a purely visual eclecticism, a tactic that allowed him to incorporate all sorts of elements with no literal attachment to their sources into one single piece of art. All of Hearst's grand creations were therefore of a radically random origin, so utterly inconsistent with historical logic that the presence of a swimming pool never seemed out of place. Every one of his projects had a swimming pool as the center of concentration. Hearst's aesthetic precursors, William Beckford and King Ludwig, reserved their centers of concentration to stage their favorite pieces of literature or music. But for "America's wealthiest son," literary indulgence was replaced by athletic indulgence. Therefore, the swimming pool in the Temple of the Holy Grail is no less inadmissible than the Venusgrotte in the Linderhof garden. They are merely different interpretations of the same Wagnerian dilemma: how far and when should man give priority to the spiritual or to the corporeal part of his being? Instead of choosing between the two, Hearst opted to accept the whole dilemma as leading principle, in the process becoming the slightly comic combination of a knight of somewhat distant sexuality and a champion of carnal awareness. Thus the theatrical stages he built were the amphitheaters of the human substance. And Marion Davies, to speak in Heideggerian terms, was simply the substance in which the collective being was incorporated.

4.25. St. Petersburg: German Protestant Church of 1832–1838 as a swimming pool. (*Frankfurter Allgemeine Zeitung*, March 30, 1992.)

five

Love, Death, and the Swimming Pool

The Aquatic Ape and Hollywood

Epigraphs: Dick Powell in *Hollywood Hotel*, dir. Busby Berkeley (1937); Gaston Bachelard, *L'eau et les rêves; essai sur l'imagination de la matière* (1942; Paris: José Corti, 1989), 100. Bachelard is quoting Jung here, but it was impossible to trace the exact locus.

1. Bachelard, *L'eau et les rêves*, 17: "L'eau en groupant les images, en dissolvant les substances, aide l'imagination dans sa tâche de désobjectivation, dans sa tâche d'assimilation."

2. European water films from the period included Jean Vigo's *Taris roi de l'eau* (1932) and J. H. Lartigue's *Le roi Pausole* (1932).

3. The number of movies in which swimming and swimming pools play a prominent part is impressive: *Daughter of the Gods* (1914), *The Old Swimming Hole* (1921), *Figures Don't Lie* (1927), *Les mystères du Château du Dé* (1927), *The Floating College* (1928), *Her Summer Hero* (1928), *Kid Boots* (1926), *Swim Girl Swim* (1927), *The Kid from Spain* (1932), *Le sang d'un poète* (1932), *Gold Diggers of 1933* (1933), *Dancing Lady* (1933), *Hollywood Hotel* (1937), *A Star Is Born* (1937), *Sullivan's Travels* (1941), *Arabian Nights* (1942), *Bathing Beauty* (1944), *Leave Her to Heaven* (1945), *Mr. Blandings Builds His Dream House* (1947), *Neptune's Daughter* (1949), *Sunset Boulevard* (1950), *Million Dollar Mermaid* (1952), and *Blind Date* (1987), to name just a few. An interesting selection of swim films and pool movies was presented as *Film op Waterbasis* in the Amsterdam Zuiderbad, October 1990.

4. Bachelard, *L'eau et les rêves* 9: "L'être voué à l'eau est un être en vertige. Il meurt à chaque minute, sans cesse quelque chose de sa substance s'écroule."

Hollywood? Oh, what a life! Falling in and out swimming pools.   Hollywood Hotel, 1937

Le désir de l'homme, c'est que les sombres eaux de la mort deviennent les eaux de la vie.   Bachelard

If each element has its corollary in human states, water is the element of dreams, the element that in helping us dematerialize the objective world inspires us to dream. In Bachelard's words, "By gathering images and dissolving substances, water assists the imagination with its task of dematerialization, its task of assimilation."[1] And so it is logical to assume that in a world where dreams are manufactured, water is of paramount importance. Thus in Hollywood, a place as dry as the nearby desert, the element appears as a dream living in concrete or plastic containers called private swimming pools. Hollywood, mass producer of popular lifestyles, doused its merchandise with generous quantities of water. The movies of the 1930s that coincided with the Depression are difficult to imagine without scenes of water-rich estates and luxurious swimming pools.

Among the classics are *Palmy Days* (1931; fig. 5.1), *The Kid From Spain* (1932), and Busby Berkeley water shows like *Footlight Parade* (1929–1933) and *Gold Diggers of 1933* (1933/1935).[3] The pool scene in *Dancing Lady* (1933) makes it a historical document, and the pool entertainment with lots of nymphs, ball playing, and diving in slapstick movies of the 1940s, like Abbott and Costello's *In Society* (1944), lifts these to unexpected heights. Russell Sturges, himself a pool enthusiast, made swimming pools a leitmotif of his Depression drama *Sullivan's Travels* (1941). As a springboard spectacular, especially in the superb musical number "Watch the Birdie" (fig. 5.2), the fast-moving *Hellzapoppin'* (1941) is still unparalleled.[3]

The theme of Eros and Thanatos, of love—particularly carnal love—and death, is as old as the world. Its double-sidedness, effectively coupled to the similar ambiguity of water, has been thoroughly exploited by the moviemakers. On the one hand there is the erotic, life-giving element, on the other the equally erotic but life-taking element. Bachelard observed that when man feels himself attracted to water, he will soon find himself in a state of vertigo. Every minute he will die and every time he will lose some of his substance.[4] In the movies, at least, there is hardly a pool to be found that is not intrinsically connected to death and love. In the two versions of *Cat People* (1942 and 1982), death is menacingly present in a modernistic indoor pool enveloped in meaningful darkness. The locus classicus for death in the pool is, of course, *Sunset Boulevard* (1950), in which the dead body of a scriptwriter (played by William Holden) is found by the police, floating on the surface like a water spider. "Poor dope," the detective says, "he always wanted a pool. Well, in the end he got himself a pool. Only the price turned out to be a little high." The film opens and closes with the view of that same pool. At the conclusion it is drained, dark, and teeming with rats.

The pool as a death trap is a popular trope, as in the film where the very location has become the title, *La piscine* (1969). Here a criminal, amphibious pair, played by

5.1. *Below:* Penthouse swimming pool, *Palmy Days*, 1931. (Ramirez, *La arquitectura en el cine,* 1986.)

5.2. *Right:* "Watch the Birdie," *Hellzapoppin'*, 1941. (Publicity still.)

5. The pool acquired a certain popularity through Michael Curtiz's film *Female* (1933). See Donald Albrecht, *Designing Dreams: Modern Architecture in the Movies* (London: Thames and Hudson, 1986), 127.

6. Mieke Bernink, "Een brekingsindex van 1.3.; De filmische aantrekkingskracht van zwembaden," *Film op Waterbasis* (Amsterdam, 1990), 10.

7. Ibid., 11.

8. Ibid., 7.

9. On the erotic potentialities of surreptitious observation, especially of undressed people in paintings, photos, and other public image carriers, see the excellent contribution of Silvia Eibelmayr, "Das Primat der Materie über den Gedanken; Transformationen des Weiblichen in Bad der Moderne," in Herbert Lachmayer, Sylvia Mattl-Wurm, and Christian Gargerle, eds., *Das Bad; eine Geschichte der Badekultur im 19. und 20. Jahrhundert* (Salzburg: Residenz Verlag, 1991), 86–94.

10. To some scientists the East African Rift could be equated with our idea of the Garden of Eden, which is represented by so many amazingly similar images in most civilizations. To scientists like Gordon Orians, this similarity could easily point to a theory of a genetically transferred memory of Paradise. Orians's concept of Eden and Edward Wilson's Biophilia seem to agree that our idea of Paradise found its origin in our original midevolutional habitat, where the great jump was made from animal to man and where our senses were so profoundly stimulated that the picture of that *locus amoenissimus* never left our genetic memory, acting as the touchstone of natural beauty. See chapter 1 above, and Dieter E. Zimmer, "Der Garten Eden," *Zeitmagazin* 45 (October 8, 1991), 56–66.

11. References to the frog as a representative of radical hedonism are countless. "The frog in the folktale," Beryl Rowland wrote in *Animals with Human Faces: A Guide to Animal Symbolism* (Knoxville: University of Tennessee Press, 1973), viii, "is symbol of sexual initiation: as everyone knows, the princess, after much persuasion, kisses it: it turns into a prince." Bruno Bettelheim, in *The Uses of Enchantment: The Meaning and Importance of Fairy Tales* (New York: Alfred A. Knopf, 1976), argued that stories like this one acted as metaphoric preparations for the actual sexual initiation. Essential in the story of the frog and the princess is that subconsciously the princess recognizes the erotic potential of the frog and that, although aesthetically the slimy creature initially disgusts her, emotionally it is able to inspire feelings of erotic desire. Having overcome her abhorrence and given in to

Romi Schneider and Alain Delon, use the pool as a murder weapon. *The Dead Pool,* a Dirty Harry movie with Clint Eastwood, Peter Greenaway's *Drowning by Numbers* (1988), plus *The Drowning Pool* (1976) and *Deep End* (1971), employ the mechanics of death by drowning as their thrilling attraction. In *Deep End* the pool is left empty, leading to an uneasy anticipation on the part of the viewer. When the two lovers have taken their places in the deep end, the pool is quickly filled up, engulfing the occupants. The execution of the bathers is guaranteed to cause shivers. The plot of Georges Clouzot's *Les diaboliques* (1954) elaborates on a suggestion that a corpse lies on the bottom of the château's classical swimming pool. When the pool is eventually drained, the long-awaited corpse does materialize and a negative suspense sets in. Dead bodies and pools form an almost inseparable cinematographic entity. *The Christine Keeler Affair* (1964), *The Alphabet Murders* (1966), and *The Day of the Locust* (1975) produced floating corpses, soaked cadavers, and animal carcasses like the horse, apparently of rubber, that was adrift in the narrow pool of Frank Lloyd Wright's Ennis House.[5]

The erotic appeal of the swimming pool in the movies has proven immense. As long as love, sex, and desire were popular themes, the pool would remain a favorite location.[6] Following the lead of archetypally hydroerotic films like *Bird of Paradise* (1932), even an intrinsically innocent film such as *The Last Picture Show* (1971) would select an indoor swimming pool as an excuse for an adolescent group striptease. In contrast, *A Bigger Splash* (1974) stages a naumachia of homoerotic fantasies. It seems self-evident that swimming pools and "sexuality, love, and desire" find each other in a natural symbiosis. For filmmakers such as Eric de Kuyper, it means an opportunity "to present the viewer with human bodies, preferably naked bodies."[7]

De Kuyper exploited this opportunity in *Casta Diva* (1983), where he shows the voyeur, his back to the camera, lounging on the edge of a swimming pool, nervously plucking at his swimming trunks while observing an attractive body at the opposite edge. "For a moviemaker," De Kuyper explained, "a swimming pool presents two highly important principles: Basically, a pool is a beautiful composition of clear, straight lines. . . . And to swim in a pool allows the [semi-]nude body to be shown either in a restful pose or in action."[8]

Nudity, swimming pool, and voyeurism combine to produce the ingredients of the puritanical-creative experience of lust. The nude body is not lascivious in itself, especially during the act of swimming. It is the observer, aware of his spying, who creates his own guilt and therewith the puritanical conditions of his lust, lust through guilt, the golden formula. The geometric *encadrement* of the bath provides a frame around the naked body and transforms the commonplace into a special occasion. Substituting for the neutral act of observation, the specific act of spying elevates a banal procedure to the state of a unique aesthetics. It could be the old story of Susannah or Bathsheba, who became objects of lust simply because they unwittingly created the conditions for lascivious observation.[9]

The pictorial arts, which since the late nineteenth century have included photography and cinema, are the ideal media for the voyeuristic experience. Since voyeuristic lust is universal and since America, including Hollywood, is emphatically puritanical and therefore hypocritical, the introduction of the swimming pool as a pretext to show nude or seminude bodies was a spectacular opportunity. Eros could be shown in an athletic and hygienic context, providing legal as well as tasteful entertainment for the voyeur as a family man. The best-known products of this development were pinups (see chapter 6) and the innocent/not-so-innocent family swimming spectaculars featuring Esther Williams, like *Neptune's Daughter* (1949) and *Dangerous When Wet* (1953), the title of the latter conveying the lascivious undercurrent.

The Aquatic Ape The water's edge is the domain of the insouciant, pleasure-seeking amphibian. The water's edge is also the wet counterpart of the forest edge, the transition to the African savannah, thought before the aquatic ape theory to be the testing grounds of *Homo sapiens*. Now the wetlands of the East African Rift are believed to have acted as the perfect habitat where primates were stimulated to evolve into the intelligent, furless, bipedal, ventro-ventral copulating, and water-loving *Homo sapiens*.[10] So the water's edge could well serve as the archetypal model of modern recreation/re-creation in the sense of a return to a happy, precivilized existence.

Modern man has displayed a miraculous desire to dwell in an area that could be best characterized as the marginal territory between the wet and the dry, the converging ecosphere of land and water, banks, shores, and beaches. It is a no-man's land where the security of the uneventful dry metamorphoses into the adventurous insecurity of the wet.

It is the perfect place to get acquainted with the Goethian *Feuchtgefühl* and to relive the frivolity of the metaphoric frog.[11] The power of Hollywood has always been to create something out of nothing. In California the natural conditions for a lush frog pond are nonexistent, but, at the same time, its attraction is irresistible. With the precision and pictorial rhetoric of the set designer, the biotopos of the cultivated amphibian was therefore forced upon the bone-dry environment of Los Angeles. Henceforth the movie industry exploited the appeal of the water's edge to the limit.[12]

The first amphibious film, in which not only swimming but also a scantily clad female body were shown, was *A Daughter of the Gods* (1916), in which the Swedish child of nature and champion swimmer Annette Kellerman showed her one-piece swimsuit to the world. Kellerman's attire turned the overdressed affair of "bathing" into the physically conscious, athletic act of "swimming." But it was not just her suit that stirred the imagination. "Her chief attractions," explains Charles Sprawson, "were her novel one-piece bathing costume and an athletic body later described by a Harvard professor as physically the most perfect out

her desire, she is rewarded for her choice as the frog turns into a socially most acceptable nobleman. She now lives happily ever after, *knowing* that deep inside her socially correct husband lives a savage of unlimited sexual prowess. And he knows that she knows; it is here that ultimate marital happiness is to be found.

12. The term "the water's edge" has been selected as being analogous as to what Robert Geddes had called "The Forest Edge," in his homonymous article in *Architectural Design* 52, nos. 11/12 (1982), 2ff. Illustrative of this specific environment are the photographs of J. H. Lartigue, who in the 1930s recorded scenes of people who haunted the water's edge in a variety of activities and postures, photographs republished in the volume *Watersides* (Paris: Bookking International, 1990). Lartigue's water movie *Le roi Pausole* (1932) is the kinetic elaboration of this genre.

5.3.   Esther Williams as Annette Kellerman in the
"one-piece swimming suit," *Million Dollar
Mermaid*, 1952. (Publicity still.)

of 'ten thousand women scientifically tested.'"[13] "The symmetry and grace of her figure so simply clad was indisputable," wrote Ishbel Ross, "and by 1913 Jantzen was manufacturing one-piece suits for daring swimmers." The suit that changed "Bathing into Swimming" became a well-known slogan,[14] and from that moment swimming became a fashionable activity throughout Europe and America.

It was the manifest destiny of another national champion, hundred-meter Olympic finalist Esther Williams, to become the postwar Hollywood incarnation of the great Swedish revolutionary. In *Million Dollar Mermaid* (1952), the romanticized remake of *Daughter of the Gods*, Williams used the extraordinary configuration of the one-piece suit to transform herself into a futuristic mermaid (fig. 5.3). With her natural technique and hydrodynamically streamlined swimmer's body, she became the ideal model of the latter-day amphibian. The healthily limbed Williams was a delight to the eye and had no trouble explaining the theory of the water's edge in readily comprehensible, strictly physical, terms. Meanwhile, Eros was kept wet and alive in the atavistic fertility rituals performed in such Busby Berkeley spectaculars as *Footlight Parade* and the various *Gold Diggers* films.

Metamorphosis The cycle of life is but an extended metamorphosis. The fluids of the uterus and the waters of Tartarus are at the beginning and the end. Crossing the waters is necessarily a rite of passage, preparing one for another, perhaps higher, phase of existence. Anyone who has successfully crossed a particularly dangerous stretch of water has seen death with his own eyes. He is akin to the Orpheus/Christ figure who returned from the underworld and thus achieved eternal life. The beginning and the end, love and death, Eros and Thanatos, entertain a connection of extreme opposites. This relationship is often articulated in the depictions of water as both a male and a female element. In most cultures the male element is represented as the wildly moving sea or the torrential river, whereas the female element is the calm, subterranean water of the source. On the one hand there are the tempestuous river gods and on the other hand the nymphs of the spring.[15] Hartmuth Boehme has convincingly analyzed Goethe's erotic water fantasies from the 1770s, in which the so-called temptation of drowning is treated as the erotic fusion of the killer pool and the irresistible attraction of *das feuchte Weib*: the perfect, and therefore fatal, metamorphosis of the totally eroticized woman into the neutral, senseless, but lethal element H_2O.[16] Mythology and popular imagination are lavishly furnished with those hydraulic femmes fatales: Lorelei, sirens, mermaids, nymphs, naiads, Neriads, ondines, and all the other wet creatures of the tempting depths.[17]

In literature the woman-water identification is a recurring theme. A fine example is the beautifully stylized story by John Cheever, "Metamorphosis III," in which Nerissa, the amiable but unattractive daughter of the imperious, aristocratic widow Mrs. Peranger, after

13. Charles Sprawson, *Haunts of the Black Masseur: The Swimmer as Hero* (London: Jonathan Cape, 1992), 34–35.

14. Ishbel Ross, *Taste in America: An Illustrated History of the Evolution of Architecture, Furnishings, Fashions, and Customs of the American People* (New York: Crowell, 1967), 188–189.

15. For the cultural history of water, see Hartmuth Böhme, ed., *Kulturgeschichte des Wassers* (Frankfurt: Suhrkamp, 1988). Several contributions, such as the ones by Böhme, Heimo Reinitzer, and Inge Stephan, deal directly with the theme of Eros, Thanatos, and Water.

16. Hartmuth Böhme, "Eros und Tod im Wasser–'Bändigen und Entlassen der Elemente.' Das Wasser bei Goethe," in Böhme, ed., *Kulturgeschichte des Wassers*, 212ff.

17. It is well known that among mariners there is a manifest resistance to learning to swim. But what is amazing is that there is also a distinct longing for a death by water. Somewhere the sirens of the deep call on them to become engulfed by the waters of the sea. The mariner does not swim lest he not be prepared to become one with his mistress, the lethal wave.

18. John Cheever, *The Stories of John Cheever* (New York: Knopf, 1978), 648–649. The name Nerissa derives from Shakespeare's *Merchant of Venice*.
19. Böhme, ed., *Kulturgeschichte des Wassers*, 105.
20. Bachelard, *L'eau et les rêves*, 113: "L'eau est l'élément de la mort jeune et belle." Examples of "la mort jeune et belle" are countless. Gottfried Keller's romantic drama *Romeo und Julia auf dem Dorfe* (1856), in which the youthful lovers find their ultimate union by drowning themselves in the river, remains especially impressive. Frederick Delius used the story as the basis for his musical poem of 1900–1901, *A Village Romeo and Juliet.*

years of unsuccessful "nuptiosis" suddenly befriends a very nice young man of no particular social ranking. One fine summer evening the two take "an innocent swim" in the family swimming pool and just as innocently kiss. But when Nerissa tells her mother she has found the man she wishes to marry, Mrs. Peranger is of a totally different opinion. The nice young man is expelled from town; Nerissa pines away and dies. Mrs. Peranger goes through a brief period of atypical grief, but at the end is her unyielding, imperious self. One afternoon something strange occurs. Seated in her study, she becomes aware of the sound of water coming from the swimming pool. "Mrs. Peranger very clearly hears the water murmuring 'Mother, Mother, I've found the man I want to marry.' Crossing the lawn and standing on the curb of the pool Mrs. Peranger calls: 'Nerissa! Nerissa!' but all the water says was 'Mother, Mother, I've found the man I want to marry.' Her only daughter had been turned into a swimming pool."[18]

It is a moving story with an interesting twist. The metamorphosis is tragic but not heroic. Instead of changing the unhappy "nymphlike" Nerissa into a being of corresponding character—traditionally a tree, a deer, a waterfall—Cheever turns her into a monument of bourgeois banality.

More generally, a metamorphosis takes place whereby water becomes steam, mist, a cloud, a wave. From Ovid to the Japanese, water is the element through which a change of form is effected.[19] Yet the water-shrouded metamorphosis is almost always the final one. Death in water is the ultimate change, occurring in the same element in which life begins. Ophelia entrusted her unhappy life to the river from which she would eventually arise. Bachelard has beautifully demonstrated the cycle of existence represented by this element, concentrating on death by water as an intrinsically female form of mortality. According to him, death by water is in particular the death of youth and beauty.[20]

That the heroine's metamorphosis takes the shape of a swimming pool is a twist Cheever kept to the last moments of his story. The provocation lies in the friction between the phenomenal power of water and the leaden materiality of the pool. The swimming pool's capacity to represent bourgeois materialism is used by Cheever to great avail in another brilliant story, "The Swimmer," made into an equally brilliant film by Frank Perry in 1968 (fig. 5.4), with Burt Lancaster in the starring role. In this story the pool functions in part, but only in part, as a status symbol. Since the last quarter of the nineteenth century, the mastery of several branches of sport was considered a sign of social refinement because it indicated that the sportsman had nearly unlimited time at his disposal and a comparable fortune. After the Second World War, swimming pools still retained their reference to higher social achievement. The pool into which Nerissa was transformed was not just an arbitrary garden prop, but a fetish of conservative, aristocratic power. Mrs. Peranger's object of devotion was her own conservatism, of which the pool was the sublimation.

Another quality of the pool, especially as it appears in Perry's filmed masterpiece, is the double-sided representation of water as a metaphor of both memory and forgetful-

5.4. Burt Lancaster in *The Swimmer,* 1968. (Publicity
still.)

5.5. Peter Steiner, "Orpheus and Eurydice in Connecticut." (*The New Yorker,* 1991.)

ness.[21] In *The Swimmer,* the protagonist takes a tour back through his own life, swimming through one long "river of pools"; traversing an upper middle-class part of suburban Connecticut, the swimmer reconstitutes his former social existence. But when he returns home, the water becomes a river of forgetfulness, the river Lethe in Hades, making the swimmer into a modern Orpheus. Peter Steiner's cartoon "Orpheus and Eurydice in Connecticut" (1991) offers an apt commentary on this classical theme (fig. 5.5).

What makes the filmed version of *The Swimmer* so extraordinary is the obvious intention of the filmmaker to weave the variety of pool shapes into the fabric of the narrative. There are eleven pools, as typologically different as possible: rectangular, circular, kidney-shaped, and so forth, each with its own social, psychological, and aesthetic dimension. Pools and their shapes entertain a meaningful relationship with their owners, expressing their ambitions in a way comparable to their houses, gardens, cars, pets, and lovers.

Early Mules and Fresno Yet the pool itself, straight and rectangular, didn't really fit the idea of the wet Paradise. Its shape was like that of the contemporary automobile, angular; the material was concrete or, more rarely, finely cut natural stone. Apart from those of a few plutocrats, pools were designed and built by the owner in collaboration with a contractor who, at best, had only limited experience. If the owner knew what he wanted and the contractor could execute it, the pool materialized, but with difficulty and at great cost.

The first private outdoor swimming pools appear after World War I, golden years for pool builders, the most renowned of whom were Edward P. Wagner of New York,

H. H. Enbody of Illinois, and Richard Valenzuela of southern California. Not surprisingly, Valenzuela had the fastest-growing market; time and place conspired in this. It was a period in which sports became increasingly integrated into the lives not only of the superrich but also of the very rich and of a new group that aspired to wealth and leisure, the movie class. Swimming joined British-inspired upper-class sports such as hunting, riding, and tennis in respectability. Bathing had changed into swimming, and women started to join the men in swimming instruction. Although southern California has one of the most benign climates in the world and magnificent beaches, the water of the Pacific Ocean is not particularly suited for swimming. Fresh water had always been a rarity until November 1914, when Fred Eaton and the legendary William Mulholland (see Roman Polanski's *Chinatown* of 1974) brought the Owens River to the San Fernando Valley by means of the longest—375 miles—aqueduct in existence.[22] From then on Los Angeles started to grow in swift jolts; new water shortages arose, new springs were tapped until subsequent growth waves caused new shortages, and so on until the last drop of water was consumed.

But the construction of swimming pools never suffered from the recurrent droughts. In the 1950s, Los Angeles counted one million swimming pools, more than the rest of the United States put together. People like Lawrence Cline, Pascal Paddock, Philip Ilsley, and Phil Anthony exploited the pool-building frenzy as much as they could. Excavating was done the primitive way by digging a hole in the ground, making a formwork, and pouring the concrete into it. This process was called "with mules and fresno," referring to the unsophisticated machinery and the old-fashioned material (the wood of the "fresno," the local ash tree).[23]

The method of construction was by trial and error. "All these pools," explains Rudy Thompson, "except for very large public pools, were of the fill and draw type, with no filtration. The pools were dosed with chlorine for a sanitizer and with soda-ash to counteract the acidic effects of the chlorine, to keep the water as swimmable as long as possible. Then they were drained and refilled."[24] Water was kept in a reservoir located above the pool, usually near a spring or a stream. When the water became too dirty to swim in, it would be drawn off and replenished by the water from the reservoir, by gravity, without the use of a pump. Pumps and valves were not endemic to the pioneering pool industry but were bought from marine suppliers and were thus of a cruder breed. Filters had to be provided by the petroleum and dry-cleaning industries and modified for pool service. This changed in 1925 when a pool supply business was set up by former chemical engineer John Mudge. From then on water recirculation systems were developed and installed, alleviating the immense waste and allowing for sites that were not necessarily dependent on a nearby source. This in a land without abundant natural sources of water meant a great breakthrough. Less obvious but equally essential were water-heating systems and pool-cleaning machinery. Cleaning, heretofore done manually by the gardener and his staff, was taken over by professional pool cleaners who appeared on the job with menacing vacuum cleaner machines.

21. See Ivan Illich, *H₂O and the Waters of Forgetfulness* (London: Boyars, 1986).
22. See Kevin Starr, *Material Dreams: Southern California through the 1920s* (New York: Oxford University Press, 1990), 60.
23. Rudy Thompson, *A History of the Southern California Swimming Pool and Spa Industry* (Los Angeles: National Spa and Pool Institute, 1988), 2. Thanks to Michael Lerner for the etymology.
24. Thompson, *History,* 2.

25. Ibid.
26. An early example of the Roman end pool could be found in the estate of an early movie mogul in the Topanga Canyon, near Glenview, Los Angeles. Sid Beller, experienced swimming pool cleaner, remembered the location but not the name of the owner. Since the pool had been filled in, it had to be dug out again to be restored to its original state (1990).

The first swimming pool cleaning firm, Chemtech, was founded in 1929 by that same Mudge and headed by Dave Cavanah, a most imaginative equipment inventor. His first job, supposedly, was to clean the pool of world champion heavyweight pugilist Jack Dempsey: "When Cavanah arrived on his service call, he and Dempsey would get into their swimming trunks and dive for leaves at the bottom of the pool."[25] Other hydro-entrepreneurs followed: Barton Bainbridge, Lawrence Cline, Jim Carney, Pascal Paddock, Philip Ilsley, and a gentleman called Nightingale, who was reputedly the inventor of an underwater lighting system that did not collect dirt and was claimed to be safe under all circumstances. A notable innovator, Lew Weirich, started his career selling heaters for baptismal fonts but soon discovered that there was considerably more money to be made in the secular sector, a beautiful illustration of the transition from sacred to profane in the matter of the *piscine.*

In the 1930s pool construction became more streamlined, physically as well as organizationally. The straight-sided tank lost its dominance to more varied shapes like ovals, circles, and combinations such as the "Roman end," based upon the *caldarium* of the Baths of Caracalla: a rectangle terminated by two apses at the short ends.[26] This presents a major difficulty in pool history: old pools, with their original equipment, are almost impossible to locate; normally owners updated their pools as frequently as they had their bathrooms modernized.

The most frequent problem was leakage. The walls were thick enough—from 8 inches on the West Coast to 12 inches in New England where freezing could cause damage—but since they were poured in sections to allow for expansion, leaks were bound to occur. Water-resistant ceramic tiles solved the problem only partially. Philip Ilsley, a Canadian who had come to Los Angeles in 1925 to set up a landscaping firm, began to include swimming pools as part of the garden layout. He dug his pools in curvilinear patterns to suggest mountain streams, constructing them with hand-packed concrete over wire mesh, called "dry pack." He was the inventor of the serpentine jungle pool and as such could be held responsible for the free-form movement that first took off in the thirties and became a great rage in the fifties. Meanwhile Pascal Paddock had gone into the concrete business; his contribution to leak-free pool construction was the "monolithic pool," consisting simply of continuous pouring in one single operation. His tour de force was the Santa Barbara Biltmore hotel pool, built into the unstable ground of the nearby beach and having to withstand the resulting hydrostatic forces. The concrete was poured nonstop in seventy-two hours. The gorgeous, only slightly modified, Olympic-size Biltmore pool is still in operation. But such a labor-intensive operation couldn't be profitable, and when Ilsley came up with the technique of the "inverted dome" it meant a revolution.

Changing Under the influence of such movies as Busby Berkeley's *The Kid from Spain*
Shapes (1932; fig. 5.6), *Footlight Parade,* and *Gold Diggers of 1933,* which developed more
adventurous, exotic settings, the pools of the late twenties exhibited a
greater variety of form. It is not entirely clear why Berkeley suddenly introduced water into his
films; where before the musical was filled with dancing and parading, now diving, swimming,
and treading water were de rigueur. The stage turned into a swimming pool.

Three reasons for this change suggest themselves. The first two are fairly
obvious: the novelty of the medium and the anticipated sex appeal of wet female bodies in
swimsuits. In *Footlight Parade,* Berkeley gave a hint, through the mouth of the leading man,
James Cagney, of what drove him to include water in his shows. While in a taxi, driving around
desperately trying to find a prologue for a new musical, Cagney ends up in Harlem. It is a
sizzling hot day and a group of black kids are playing in the spray of a fire hydrant. Cagney:
"That is what the prologue needs: A mountain waterfall splashing on those beautiful wet bodies." "It can't be done!" shouts the partner in despair. But Cagney replies, still shouting: "It can
be done." And so it was. The purely erotic-aesthetic motive remains: the naked black youths
are filtered out and replaced by swimsuit-clad white nymphs who stage a wet T-shirt contest
that moves from one intricate swimming pool to another, to come to rest in a peculiar landscape of transition between culture and nature, dry and wet. The strictly geometrical stage
pools give way to those of organic shape. A waterfall comes into view, and from under the
individual jets amphibious beings emerge (fig. 5.7), sirens dressed only in their own long
strands of hair, which gradually changes into swimsuits of seaweed. They are personifications
of "the wet woman," *das feuchte Weib,* the feminine metamorphosis of water. The accompanying
song, "By a Waterfall," is orchestrated to create the illusion that it is the water that is singing,
with the seductive voice of Nature herself:

There is a magic melody,
Mother Nature sings to me.

It is remarkable how the heretofore militaristically mechanized Berkeley now
becomes meditative—this is the third rationale—and introduces atavistic rituals. This Jungian
twist is fascinating. Berkeley appropriates an interpretation of Paradise as a midpoint in which
man and his environment are fixed during the transition from primate to man, from nature to
culture. In the Renaissance this transitional state was visualized by the grotto, hidden in a
remote corner of the garden, artificially humidified and overgrown by mossy substances, where
the denizens of the civilized world assembled to honor, in their own hypercultivated way,
quasi-uncultivated nature. This state of transition, commonly represented by a variety of erotically inclined hybrids such as satyrs, centaurs, mermaids, the wild man, the werewolf, or the
ape man, is gratefully exploited in the movie world. Famed were Esther Williams as the mer-

5.6. Scene from Busby Berkeley's *The Kid from Spain*, 1932. (Ramirez, *La arquitectura en el cine*, 1986.)

5.7.   A waterfall of "wet women" in *Footlight Parade*,
       1929–1933. (Publicity still.)

maid, Johnny Weissmuller as ape man, and King Kong, who was so tragically afflicted with human emotions. The moral superiority of these beings confirms the traditional reputation of the "noble savage," the unspoiled original denizen of Paradise not yet suffocated by society.

"Paradise— Now that the original inhabitant of Paradise had been discovered, his habitat **The Secluded** had to be designed, a task confided to the great filmmakers of the period. In **Island of Lani"** the early thirties David O. Selznick, with the cooperation of his director King Vidor (and with Busby Berkeley supervising the choreography of the girls from the South Pacific), made two major films that would forever define the tropical Eden: *Bird of Paradise* (1932; fig. 5.8) and its sequel *Green Mansions* (1933), which unfortunately never made it to the screen. To represent primordial physical lust in acceptable terms, an ethically correct environment had to be selected. In popular belief this could only be the unspoiled islands of the South Pacific, with their lush vegetation, brilliant beaches, and blue lagoons, inhabited by innocent, pure-minded children. The two Selznick films were the most sensual Hollywood had thus far produced.

An important element, also present in the contemporary Tarzan movies, was that sexual exploration, foreplay (the act itself was never shown), took place *in,* or on the edge of, the water. *Bird of Paradise* excels in that respect, situating the mating ritual entirely *under* water, which entailed sophisticated pre–Jacques Cousteau subaquatic cinematography. The marine paradise is intelligently and tastefully depicted in relation to the archetypal ambiguity of water: Eros and Thanatos. Sensual love sizzles through the length of the film, but at the end death is the price to pay. Joel McCrea (Johnny) is the proverbial unwary American and Dolores Del Rio personifies the irresistible, wildly erotic Pacific priestess. Her mission is of Rousseauesque sincerity—to establish an imaginative connection between the degenerate West and the pure, unspoiled world of the savage. Essentially it is intended as a search for the essence of human existence and a campaign against bourgeois hypocrisy. Teacher Del Rio and pupil McCrea spend their lustful days undisturbed on a fairy island, in the company of a goat, a banana tree, and a coconut palm. While reconnoitering "the secluded island of Lani," they find the perfect place: a pond fed by a small waterfall. "This will be home," they cry in bilingual unison. A house is easily built of bamboo and palm leaves to create the ideal home: bedroom, porch, and swimming pool. Then the island's holy volcano becomes restless. To pacify its fire a sacrifice must be made—inevitably, the beautiful Dolores.

Bird of Paradise is the ultimate hydrophilic narrative. From the very beginning the two lovers splash about the screen, and when they are not in the water, fluids are produced to keep their bodies constantly wet. Two such scenes are unsurpassed in their eroticism. First, after landing on their paradise island and searching for food, Miss Del Rio cuts open a coconut and trickles the milky liquid over her lover and then over herself—a most eloquent expression.

5.8. Advertisement for *Bird of Paradise*, 1932.
(Haver, *David O. Selznick's Hollywood*, 1980.)

27. Ronald Haver, *David O. Selznick's Hollywood* (London: Secker and Warburg, 1980), 80–81.
28. Mircea Eliade, *Mythes, rêves et mystères* (Paris: Gallimard, 1957), 89–90. See also "le mythe du bon sauvage," 40ff.

At the end of the movie, when Johnny lies wounded and near death in his bunk on board the yacht, the priestess comes to his rescue for the last time. Ronald Haver has movingly described the final scene: "She knows she will never see him again, that indeed she goes to her death when she leaves him. The two are alone. He moans for water; she finds an orange and, sucking the juice out of it, lets it trickle from her mouth to his in a series of nibbling kisses shot in extreme close ups."[27] Then the priestess, forced to die by ceremonial suicide, walks up the side of the volcano and throws herself into the fiery pit, returning metaphorically to the source of her passion.

Bird of Paradise, despite a million-dollar budget, was never successful enough to return the investment. Perhaps its imagery was too explicit, its ending too sad, or maybe the rest of America was just not interested in Hollywood's specific idea of paradise. *Tarzan the Ape Man,* far less daring, did much better.

Tarzan Strongly related, and not as guileless as one might think, were the countless Tarzan movies. Tarzan was the ideal interpreter of the role Californians have assumed as the latter-day inhabitants of paradise. Few places on earth have inspired such feelings of natural and religious nostalgia as California. Mircea Eliade has identified the activities of those who want to restore *illud tempus* (the good old times before civilization); besides a convincing dialogue with the Creator, they indulge in strong leanings toward friendship and love with animals.[28] Being himself a transitional creature, at least socially, Tarzan is able to communicate with the animals of the forest as well as with the folks back home. His whole existence is a demonstration of a liaison between the ideal and the real. The ideal was translated and explained in terms of the common; thus Tarzan's habitat is not a real jungle but a customized forest, quite savage yet having convenient little spots with which the viewer could comfortably identify. Tarzan lives in a sophisticated part of the jungle, with a pleasant swimming hole in the front yard of his tree house.

The first of the long series was *Tarzan the Ape Man,* of 1932. The choice of swimming champion Johnny Weissmuller as Tarzan suggests a secret knowledge of the aquatic ape theory: how else could it be explained that a baby raised by the apes of the jungle could have learned to swim? The ape man's amphibious traits are instantly revealed in his first encounter with Jane (Maureen O'Sullivan), who, in a paraphrase of the princess-frog fable, is irresistibly attracted to the mysterious potency of Tarzan. How this potency is to be conveyed to the audience is demonstrated in one of the film's most bewildering publicity stills (fig. 5.9).

Why swimmers with their smooth, seallike bodies, rather than the hard-muscled weightlifters of today, were chosen to represent the noble ape-man is a question worthy of study. It might have to do with public acceptance of the seminude male body in what looks like swimming trunks. It might also be associated with the swimmer's athletic omnipo-

5.9. Johnny Weissmuller as the erotic *Tarzan the Ape Man*, 1932. (Publicity still.)

5.10. *Below:* Buster Crabbe as the erotically charged Tarzan. (Publicity still.)

29. Mary Astor, *A Life on Film* (New York: Delacorte Press, 1971), 64.

30. Ibid., 158–159. The pool can be dated with the help of some events mentioned in the book that seem to coincide in time (see p. 151, for example). I am grateful to Mark Pentz, architect, who, while working in the area, discovered this unusual piece of historic architecture for me. The present owner was very helpful in allowing me to document it.

tence: swift, lithe, supple, strong, and who knows what more. In any case, Weissmuller was not the only one. Buster Crabbe, another famous champion swimmer, followed Weissmuller in the Tarzan role, even inheriting his erotic attraction to an almost frightening degree (fig. 5.10).

Just as in *Bird of Paradise,* it is the noble savage, driven by his insouciant temperament, who takes the initiative in the mating ceremonies. The spot Tarzan has selected is his favorite "plunge" or "swimming hole." He cunningly maneuvers Jane into a state of imbalance so he can draw her elegantly under water where the love act may be performed (fig. 5.11). *Tarzan the Ape Man* draws on a number of enlightened bourgeois utopias. It was inevitable that once demonstrated on screen, these utopias would find their way back to the same society that had created them. Thus Tarzan's "swimming hole," just like the one in *Bird of Paradise,* is a reflection of the swimming pool, just as his tree house is a reflection of the California bungalow. But in its turn that same "swimming hole" becomes the model for an entirely new trend in pool design, the serpentine jungle pool. The two environments, the South Pacific and Tarzan's swimming hole, could easily be combined, as for example in the charming shallow studio pool in *Aloma of the South Seas* (1941), with Dorothy Lamour and "Not the Real Tarzan" Jon Hall (fig. 5.12).

Jungle Pool The serpentine jungle pool is an extraordinary example of swimming pool ingenuity. It is so designed that it imitates a natural stream, following the meandering lines the virgin water cuts into the tough soil of the Hollywood Hills. An early example could be found in the garden of the former estate of Mary Astor, on Temple Hill Drive, originally built by her father, who had been toying with this idea since the autumn of 1927 (fig. 5.13).

As Miss Astor later recalled, "he made plans to put in an enormous swimming pool with a sandy beach and a waterfall."[29] Probably he wanted to emulate the great stars in whose company his daughter found herself professionally, such as Douglas Fairbanks, whose banana-shaped pool was in 1927 the largest in existence. However, this ambitious enterprise quickly impoverished the elder Astor and caused financial problems for the two other legal owners of the property, his wife and daughter. In her autobiography Miss Astor reported with cool restraint: "Daddy finally put a mortgage of $22,500 on the house and went ahead with his swimming pool. It was typically elaborate, built into the side of the hill and shaped like a lagoon, about a hundred feet and of varying widths and depths, with a little sandy beach at one end and overhanging foliage, and even a small bridge over it." To indicate the vast discrepancy between the value of the house and the cost of the pool, she added with dismay: "It cost eighteen thousand dollars. Daddy was offered eight thousand dollars for the house."[30]

The pool is still there, although, after decades of neglect, it has lost its former glamour. Neither water nor swimmers has it known for a long time, and the original bridge

5.11. Johnny Weissmuller as Tarzan, drawing Jane
into the "plunge." (Publicity still.)

5.12. *Below:* Dorothy Lamour and Jon Hall in *Aloma
of the South Seas,* 1941. (Publicity still.)

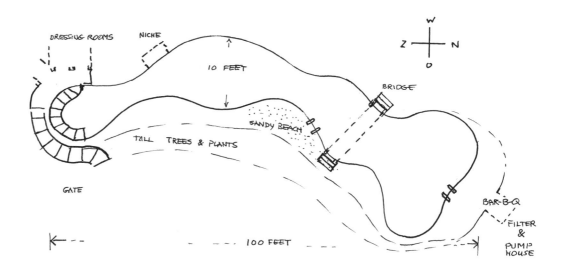

31. Data on the Zublin estate have been generously provided by the Los Angeles Conservancy, Los Angeles. Recently a monograph on Williams appeared by his granddaughter Karen Grigsby Bates: *Paul R. Williams, Architect: A Legend of Style* (New York: Rizzoli, 1993).

and the springboard have been removed. The sides are smudged with graffiti, the *mene tekel* of our anti-civilization. Yet the effect that was originally intended is still noticeable; the riverbed has been cut deep and narrow, the steep banks covered with concrete packed onto a mesh of steel wire. The imitation rocky slope dives steeply into the narrow canyon (fig. 5.14). At irregular intervals steel eyes are drilled into the concrete, perhaps to hold lifelines or fine nets to keep out leaves and debris. Or was it to add to the jungle atmosphere and have artificial lianas dangle to offer the swimmer escape routes when the river became too wild for comfort? He would begin his adventurous trip at the southern end where a series of steps curved down from the changing cabins. After a hundred yards of curves and a frantic struggle with the elements, the brave swimmer would find an oval pool, a dark lagoon full of romantic thrills. A sandy beach nearby can be reached by a ladder. It is an inviting spot warmed by the southwestern sun and screened by lush vegetation. Since outdoor adventure and cookouts are closely teamed in the West, a cavern fitted out with a barbecue stand and a drinking fountain was provided. Today ferns, prickly pear, and melancholically drooping branches dominate the scene. The trained eye of a horticulturist could estimate the period of nonuse by the height of the eucalyptus tree that has shot up in front of the pool house toilet, blocking the entrance.

      An almost identical Tarzan-like pool came to light in the garden of the deserted estate of businessman John Zublin, at St. Pierre Road in Bel-Air, a community inspired by the Côte d'Azur (fig. 5.15). The Zublin palazzo was designed by society architect Paul Williams in 1931.[31] The waterworks in the garden were constructed exactly like those on Temple Hill Drive. The color and the uneven texture of the pool's lining are similar, as well as the system of scum gutters. Like the Astor pool's, the bottom is flat and the sides straight; here

5.13. *Opposite:* Los Angeles: Mary Astor estate, Temple Hill Drive, sketch plan of swimming pool in 1990.

5.14. A graffiti-smudged portion of the former Astor pool. *Also plate 12.*

5.15. *Left:* Bel-Air, California: John Zublin estate,
1931. "The veritable swimming river."
5.16. Advertisement for Paddock Pools, c. 1950.

too is a bridge, which appears to be in its original state. The arrangement of plants is almost identical. However, the scale is much larger—this is not a swimming stream but a veritable swimming river, its length of 300 feet exceeding by three times that of the Astor pool. Moreover, there are several plateaus of varying height over which the water is led, following the design pioneered by the great landscaper of the mid-twenties, Paul Thiene.

Zublin was one of the odd but not unheard-of swimming pool owners who could not swim themselves. His pool was the work of Philip Ilsley, Brentwood real estate developer and self-appointed garden architect, who was commissioned to build a pool big enough for Zublin to row his boat in, but also "long and narrow, so that he could touch both sides with the oars of his boat." It resembled a moat crossed by several small bridges. "His urge satisfied," Ilsley concluded with the quiet wisdom of the successful businessman, "Zublin sold the property, and Miss Davies, one of the film colony's large real-estate owners, picked it up." It was said that Johnny Weissmuller visited the Zublin pool for a dip now and then. Since it might fairly be assumed that both pools were done by the same builder, very likely the Astor pool was also Ilsley's work. The Zublin estate and its serpentine pool are still there and in good condition.

Ilsley "In California the pool became a necessity, not a luxury," explained Philip Ilsley.

From 1939 on, Ilsley started to experiment with rounded surfaces, in what became known as the "inverted dome" method of construction. The fluid curves of the shell offered much better resistance to the shifting earth, and leaking was considerably minimized. Just before World War II, Ilsley became the owner of Paddock Pools and began to operate on a much larger scale. Construction became more and more industrialized: with the availability of cheaper as well as more advanced materials, mass production replaced the manual craft that had served pool makers for over thirty years. The privilege once reserved for the millionaire and the movie star was to become the right of the middle class: the private pool became the family pool.[32]

In 1950–1951, Paddock Pools launched a campaign to promote adventurous free-form pools of the *Tarzan/Bird of Paradise* type. Thanks to new methods of fabrication, the serpentine pool was placed within the financial range of the not-so-wealthy.[33] A Paddock advertisement (fig. 5.16) illustrates the dramatic technical possibilities of the postwar period. The free plan has been maintained, and now the flat bottom is replaced by one that is curved: the serpentine shape of the thirties is incorporated within the organic free form of the fifties.

The photo repays close study. The rather contrived posture of the swimmer is reminiscent of Dolores Del Rio in *Bird of Paradise,* but the atmosphere has changed. Her lover has disappeared and so has her purity. Instead of nudity and free-flowing tresses, we see a bathing costume and—fascinating detail—a bathing cap. Although not precisely a novelty, as a suggestion of paradise it fails completely, for the bathing cap is the condom of aquatic free-

Epigraph: *Saturday Evening Post,* August 11, 1951, 69.

32. Between 1986 and 1990, a detailed history of the pool and spa industry in southern California was compiled by Fay Coupe, former editor of the magazine: Fay Coupe, "Pool History: A History of the Pool and Spa Industry," *Pool and Spa News,* fifteen installments numbered I–XV ranging from November 17, 1986, to October 23, 1989. I am grateful to Mrs. Coupe for having provided me with otherwise inaccessible material.

33. From *California Arts and Architecture,* March 1951, 41.

34. See Robert Sklar, *Movie-Made America: A Cultural History of American Movies* (New York: Vintage Books, 1975), 173.
35. *Landscape Architecture* 47, no. 4 (July 1957), 502.

dom. By restraining its free flow, the cap has robbed the hair of its mythical expression of sexuality. Was this merely a hygienic measure, or was it a consequence of Hollywood's Production Code of 1930, enhanced by the Legion of Decency, which prohibited innocence and promoted hypocrisy?[34] The sequel to *Bird of Paradise, Green Mansions,* with the same cast and an even steamier scenario, was never distributed.

If *Bird of Paradise* was not a financial success, it nevertheless caused a considerable impact on West Coast mores and fashions. Dresses, beach wear, and bathing costumes, sporting flower and leaf patterns reminiscent of the sarongs Miss Del Rio was wearing in the film, were styled "Bird of Paradise" in the department stores. But let us be candid: the posture of the swimming figure in the Paddock Pools advertisement is not at all like that of Miss Del Rio, but is the bent-back, drawn-up-knee pose of the synchronized swimmers of the Billy Rose Aquacades, a sort of water vaudeville from the same decade, the 1930s. It might well have been modeled after the plastic-caped figure of Esther Williams doing her Aquacade-inspired underwater frolics in films like *Dangerous When Wet* and *Neptune's Daughter,* or, still better, the underwater scene in the *Ziegfeld Follies* from 1946 (fig. 5.17). How remarkable is this change in posture. The wholesome naturalness that Johnny Weissmuller and Dolores Del Rio displayed is now translated into the corporeal commercialism of the striptease, a choreographed sensuality that echoes the sexual dissoluteness of a golden age. The free-form swimming pool became the suburban version of the jungle serpentine pool. After the war, however, swimming pools lost their erotic double entendre and turned into family pools, absorbed, together with the station wagon and the barbecue, into the family-values complex of the virtuous bourgeois. But wealth, or at least its status symbols, remained high on the priority list. In 1957 *Landscape Architecture* intoned: "Of all the symbols of wealth you can imagine, having a private swimming pool for your own family probably would rank among the highest."[35]

Gunite and Free-Form Pools   As we have seen, comprehension of the swimming pool requires studying the evolution of swimming, for the pool obediently follows the lines of the swimmer's progress. The first pools had been rectangular, in sympathy with the military drill of lap swimming. In the 1930s, the rectangle gave way to the serpentine plan, because swimming, rather than an exercise, had become a fantasy. Fantasies of various merit had entered the world of swimming: the savoring of weightlessness, the adventurous call of the jungle, the carnal joy of the erotic.

In the original edition of *Experiencing Architecture* (1959), Steen Eiler Rasmussen called attention to this change in human kinetics. The shaping of the pool's basic form, he argued, ran parallel with the systematics of military training, but in the thirties, when "the new freedom" was introduced (from the perspective of architectural historians of the period, this was identical with modernism), it entailed a new architectural shape. Rasmussen wrote:

5.17. Esther Williams in "goldfish position," *Ziegfeld Follies*, 1946. (Publicity still.)

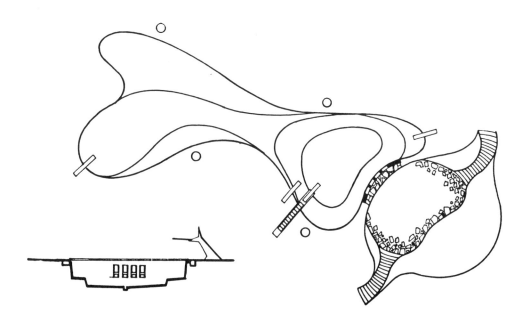

36. Steen Eiler Rasmussen, *Experiencing Architecture* (1959; Cambridge: MIT Press, 1962), 148.

37. See further Rudolf Ortner, *Sportbauten; Anlage, Bau, Gestaltung* (Munich: Callwey, 1953), 207: "Schwimmbad in Monza, Italien, architekt Giulio Minoletti, Mailand ... Bewusst wurde eine von der ueblichen Rechteckform abweichende Anlage gewaehlt, um eine moeglichst organische Einfuegung in der Parklandschft zu erreichen. Durch Fenster in der Beckenwand sieht man die Unterwasserschwimmer."

38. Rasmussen, *Experiencing Architecture*, 148.

39. D. A. Armbruster et al., *Swimming and Diving* (St. Louis: Mosby, 1968); Daniel Pautrat, *Zwemmen* (Antwerp: Standard, 1977), 19.

40. Fay Coupe, "Pool History," *Pool and Spa News*, June 15, 1987, 66; Francis S. Onderdonk, *The Ferro-Concrete Style* (New York: Architectural Book Publishing Co., 1928), 44–45.

"But it is probably in swimming that the new rhythm most clearly manifests itself. For centuries swimming, too, bore the stamp of military drill; the breast stroke was taught to a count of four. In contrast to walking, it was a completely symmetrical form of motion, well suited to soldiers who had to force a river with full marching equipment on their shoulders."[36]

To illustrate his idea Rasmussen selected not an American but a European example: a pool at Monza, Italy (fig. 5.18), by Giulio Minoletti, which has an unusual plan midway between a dog's favorite knucklebone and an amoeboid blob.[37] No previous design had ever come so close to such formal anarchy. The shape suggests no moment of repose, but changes incessantly. This was the new kinetic free form for freestyle swimming. At the bottom other strange forms appear, serving as playthings for the swimmers, who move about in a happy state of weightlessness, like goldfish in a bowl (fig. 5.19). Rasmussen compellingly compares the floating swimmers with the figures in a painting by Tintoretto: "This change in the field of sports recalls the change that came in the visual arts with Rafael, Michelangelo, and Tintoretto, a change from a rigid, frontal style to a more plastic one with movement and rhythm. Tintoretto's figures seem to float through space in a weird, gliding manner. In 1951, four hundred years after Tintoretto's painting, the Italian architect Giulio Minoletti designed a swimming pool with a very similar rhythm."[38]

The comparison could easily be extended to the subaquatic cavorting of Hollywood's contemporary aquatic apes, such as Esther Williams and her companions, Tom and Jerry and the lovesick Octopus (possibly a parody of Hokusai's print *Wife of the Fisherman*), in *Dangerous When Wet* (1953) and *Neptune's Daughter* (1949).

5.18. *Opposite:* Monza, Italy: free-form pool, 1951, plan. Giulio Minoletti. (Rasmussen, *Experiencing Architecture,* 1962.)

5.19. Monza pool. (Rasmussen, *Experiencing Architecture,* 1962.)

But this was not unique to the postwar period. On the contrary, the free style of swimming had been introduced much earlier, in 1873, when Arthur Trudgen demonstrated his version of front crawl, which became known the world over as "Trudgeon" or the "Trudgeon stroke." In 1888, his fellow Englishman, J. Nutall, established a 100-yard record of 1 minute 6 ⅘ seconds by employing the new "Trudgeon" or "crawling" style.[39] In the 1930s, freestyle swimming had been shown on the screen in movies such as *Bird of Paradise* and, in an architecturally and cinematographically more sophisticated version, *Dancing Lady* (1933; fig. 5.20). This is a fast-moving chorus-line movie, directed by Frank Leonard, starring Joan Crawford, Franchot Tone, and a young Fred Astaire in his first film role, which features a flamboyant Long Island swimming pool consisting of two separate basins, one outside, the other indoors. The indoor pool was designed as a glass-encased aquarium, with plants and rocks and tunnels. Crawford and playboy Tone are filmed from below, moving about in the slow, smooth curvature of a couple of amorous sea lions. It should be noted that scenes like this one were repeated in the forties and fifties films discussed above.

Although some unorthodox pools had been constructed in the prewar period, the largest number appeared after the war when a new, almost total freedom in construction was permitted by the application of a technique of concrete spraying called the gunite method (fig. 5.21), whereby dry sand, cement, and water are pneumatically blown over steel mesh by the force of compressed air. Gunite was invented and patented by Dr. Carl Akeley, a curator of the Chicago Museum of Natural History, who had constructed a "concrete gun to apply a concrete skin to life-size models of prehistoric animals."[40] A few guns according to Akeley's specifi-

5.20. Joan Crawford and Franchot Tone in the pool, *Dancing Lady*, 1933. (Haver, *David O. Selznick's Hollywood*, 1980.)

5.21. Hollywood Hills, California: Philip Ilsley pool being "shot" with gunite. (*Saturday Evening Post*, 1951.)

41. Thomas S. Hines, *Richard Neutra and the Search for Modern Architecture* (Oxford: Oxford University Press, 1982), 84.
42. Coupe, "Pool History," June 15, 1987, 66.

cations were manufactured, and in 1910 the Cement Gun Factory was founded in Allentown, Pennsylvania.

It is characteristic of the playful nature of the West Coast that gun-shot concrete was almost exclusively used for swimming pools. When in 1927 Richard Neutra constructed the Los Angeles residence of physical fitness enthusiast Dr. Philip Lovell, he had a rectangular swimming pool created where other people would have built a terrace. The pool inhabited the concrete foundation slab that, balanced on a dangerously steep slope, carried the steel frame of the house as a waiter carries a tray on his outstretched fingers. The pool, half outside, half inside, sharing the lower main floor with the "Belvedere," was constructed of wire mesh and gunite. Neutra's biographer, Thomas Hines, explained that "the concrete 'gunite' was 'shot' onto the wire lath by long hoses extending from the mixers on the street."[41] The first free-form pool constructed in this manner, according to the historian of the American swimming pool industry Fay Coupe, was built in 1940 "on the corner of Sunset Boulevard and Layton Drive in West Los Angeles, by a local gunite firm, Johnson and Western Gunite."[42]

Also improved at this time were water filter systems. In the prewar period, the majority of pools were equipped with a shallow channel on all sides of the inner wall to catch surface scum: the so-called scum gutters, with which all the pools discussed thus far were equipped (fig. 5.22). But with irregular pool shapes, this technology had to change. During World War II the Paddock firm had invented the floating plastic "skimmer." "Connected to a vacuum fitting, the skimmer had the terrific advantage that it could be adjusted to any possible shape. Around 1952, fixed 'in-wall skimmers' came into use, the first being operated by the

5.22. Scum gutter made by Malibu Potteries, 1930.
(Malibu, Adamson House Museum Collection.)

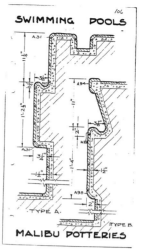
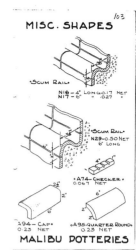

43. Coupe, "Pool History," November 16, 1987, 53.
44. Thomas Hine, *Populuxe* (New York: Knopf, 1986), 108, 109.
45. Thomas D. Church, *Gardens Are for People: How to Plan for Outdoor Living* (New York: Reinhold, 1955), 142.

The variety in free-form pool shapes is seemingly unlimited. There are the kidney, cookie cutter, plain vanilla, heart, hepatica leaf, lazy-L, double-radii oval, and many others; to which must be added the endless stream of pools in the shapes of pianos, guitars, Coca-Cola bottles, airplanes, boxing gloves, and so on. And see, for example, Ed Rusha, *Nine Swimming Pools and a Broken Glass,* 1968; Claes Oldenburg's sculptures based on swimming pool shapes; and Mike Sheridan, "Dive In!," *Sky,* September 1989.

46. *Architectural Record's Treasury of Contemporary Houses,* 1953, v.
47. David de Long et al., *Design in America: The Cranbrook Vision* (New York: Abrams, 1983), fig. 58: "Inexpensive injection molded dispenser eliminates nuisance of individual wrapping and strongly appeals to men." The people at Gillette certainly knew their customers.
48. Coupe, "Pool History," June 15, 1987, 68.
49. Ibid., 66.

workings of a simple toilet-tank valve as a control."[43] Both of these dirt-collecting systems allowed the pool architect to draw any form he liked, without having to worry about technical problems.

The free-form pool craze was but part of a much larger context: "The entire environment had an image of open-endedness," wrote Thomas Hine in *Populuxe.* "Things were shaped in loosely defined forms and their relationships were often vague or dispersed," a sensibility that was most positively and successfully expressed in Alexander Calder's mobiles.[44] The individual pieces of Calder's mobiles were shaped in the same "amoeboid" forms as Joan Miró's "blobs," Matisse's cutouts, Picasso's earthenware pots, and, as Bevis Hillier has claimed, World War II camouflage patterns. Designed to merge with the natural environment, these patterns followed the organic shapes of things natural. In the man-made world, these shapes fitted into the repertoire of the architects of the organicist movement, such as the Finns Alvar Aalto and Eero Saarinen and, in his late phase, Le Corbusier. To Hine the family of amoeboid shapes was best represented by the boomerang, with its air of organic aerodynamism that appealed to the lay public and professional designers alike. Furniture by Ray and Charles Eames and the young firm of Knoll—chairs like the Hardoy and butterfly chairs, plus coffee tables—and lamps, office equipment, household appliances, and, naturally, the swimming pool, followed the lines of the boomerang, the shape of freedom, informality, and above all mobility. "There is no fixed rule about what shape a pool should be. The shape may be influenced by your own convictions and prejudices. . . . Rectangles, circles, ovals, classic shapes and a free form may all be possibilities," explained Thomas Church, authoritative free-form pool designer of the period.[45]

What had been predominantly rectangular became curvilinear, including the house. *Architectural Record's Treasury of Contemporary Houses* of 1953 shows a delirious array of

Pl 1   Paris: Bains Deligny after reconstruction of 1953.

Pl 2   Jacob Alt, watercolor of the Kaiserliche und
        Königliche Militärschwimmschule in Vienna, 1815.
        (Vienna: Historisches Museum der Stadt Wien.)

3

4

5

6

7

8

9

Pl 8 Washington, D.C.: Dumbarton Oaks, 1920s, pool.
Beatrix Ferrand, architect.

Pl 9 San Simeon, California: Neptune Pool, 1930s. Julia
Morgan, architect.

Pl 10 San Simeon, Roman Pool, 1927–1932. Julia Morgan.
       (Boutelle, *Julia Morgan,* 1988.)

Pl 11 Las Vegas: pool at Caesar's Palace.

10

11

13

12

14

16

15

17

Pl 17 Carpinteria, California: Isham estate, 1927. George
       Washington Smith.

Pl 18 San Simeon, California: Casa del Sol. Tile tableau.

Pl 19 Southern California subdivision, aerial view.

Pl 20 Naples, California, canals.

18

19

20

21

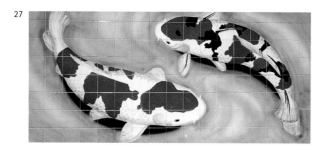

27

Pl 21 Beverly Hills: Pendleton estate, photo of pool by Slim
       Aarons. (Aarons, *A Wonderful Time*, 1974.)

Pl 27 Santa Barbara, California: Nishiki-Koi nursery,
       Montecito Street, mural.

Pl 22 Jack Benny's pool with its octopus guardian.
       (*Saturday Evening Post,* 1951.)

Pl 23 Brentwood, California: Troy Pool, 1987. James
       Pulliam.

Pl 24 Pacific Palisades, California: Whitney Pool, 1981.
       Frank Gehry and Mark Mack.

24

22

23

25

26

free-form houses, gardens, and pools. Emerson Goble, managing editor of the magazine, wrote in the introduction: "Why shouldn't it [a house] have anything its owners really want, including a curve or two, even a Victorian curve?"[46]

The War After the war, the transport industry was given a lift by a defunct war industry that was flogging its surplus airplanes and ground vehicles. Civil air transport was reshaped by the smooth, muscular forms of fighter planes and bombers; reminiscences of warplanes and other lethal machinery merged with streamlining experiments of the thirties to caress into shape automobiles, trains, refrigerators, and TV sets. The most famous example was the 1948 Cadillac which, with tail fins borrowed from the Lockheed P38 fighter plane, became the first of a generation of wingmobiles.

The war spirit also infected the design of more modest objects. Such household tools as electric drills were shaped like hand guns, the butt lying comfortably in the home soldier's hand, the barrel pointing at the job. Razor blades, in packs of five, got dispensed in belligerent-looking cartridges from which a manly thumb could push a blade as if it were a bullet in an ammo clip.[47] After the war, high-tech, lightweight war materials such as aluminum suddenly became available for civilian industry. Although still relatively expensive, aluminum was introduced for kitchen appliances, in the leisure industry, and in low-cost housing. Its unique pliability contributed to the rounded shapes of camping cars—most notably the Airstream trailer—and toasters.

The swimming pool industry, too, became part of the great aluminum fire sale. Diving boards, traditionally made of wood, were now manufactured of aluminum, which, probably unintentionally, began to revolutionize the art of diving. The material's greater flexibility and resilience propelled the divers higher into the air. Consequently, because the braking distance had to be longer, pools had to be deeper.

During the war, pools were generally not a priority. Pools were built for the military, to increase the physical fitness and swimming skills of the soldier. In an emergency, swimming pools could also be used for fire-fighting and as a potable water supply.[48] Finally, since the movie industry was encouraged to produce morale-boosting films featuring the newly invented pinup girl, pools, however modest, were considered a wartime necessity in that arena. Those films made during the war that featured swimming adopted the prescribed materials for the pools, which consequently changed in appearance. *Leave Her to Heaven* (1942) features a large, concrete shell-pool of undetermined outline. To boost the army's morale, most of the swimming is done by a dazzling Gene Tierney. Another task for the movie world was to blur the differences between the military and the glamour class. Movie stars were urgently invited to open up their pools to service men![49]

50. Coupe, "Pool History," November 16, 1987, 54.
51. *Saturday Evening Post,* August 11, 1951, 66. I am very grateful to Mrs. Fay Coupe for her generous provision of this material.
52. Edla Muir, in the prewar period, was associated with John Byers. They built over twenty-five houses in the region, in several "moods," although they seemed to have favored the ranch or craftsman bungalow moods.
53. *Los Angeles Times,* Home Section, August 7, 1949, 3–4.

Other factors that determined the future of the pool were restrictions on the use of chlorine and the promotion of the use of concrete. The fighting forces required large quantities of chlorine and it was inevitable that many private as well as public pools would have to close. Although chlorine is still the disinfectant of choice in almost every public pool, this prepared the search for less hazardous disinfectants. Furthermore there was the forced acceleration of the use of concrete as a building material. Since steel and other ferrous metals were needed for the war effort, concrete, previously not as popular in the United States as in Europe, where labor costs were lower and steel very expensive, finally got its chance. The promotion of concrete, combined with the ready availability of gunite spraying, drastically speeded the development of the free-form pool.

Builder, Dieter, Watcher A key monument in the history of the postwar free-form swimming pool is the one built for himself by Philip Ilsley in 1949, in the Hollywood Hills overlooking the San Fernando Valley. "Probably the most famous private pool in the world," wrote Fay Coupe, "it had many innovative features—as befitted a pool belonging to the head of the largest pool building company in the world—and was featured in many national and local magazines."[50] In fact the *Los Angeles Times,* as well as the *Saturday Evening Post,* fully illustrated it with luxurious color and black-and-white photographs (figs. 5.23, 5.24, 5.25). The *Post's* description is vivid: "It nestles between his modernistic house and a steep slope, and was dug and sprayed in the shape of a hepatica leaf, which, in turn, resembles an elongated three-leaf clover. Ilsley insists he chose the hepatica leaf, not to outdo his whimsical customers, but because it is beautiful and functional as well." This point required a lot of explaining, which Ilsley did with convincing rhetoric: "To begin with, the hepatica shape provides the most swimming and diving space for the least water. Its three lobes separate the sun-tanners, who like to loll on the warm brink without getting wet, from the divers, who splash and splash around the springboard on the opposite side, while the athletic types who like to swim can tee off at the far end of the leaf and paddle right up the stem, winding up—in the Ilsley pool—in an alcove of the living room of his house" (fig. 5.24).[51]

The idea of the "threshold" pool had been first introduced c. 1916 in James Deering's Vizcaya, and repeated in the streamlined perfection of *Dancing Lady* (see fig. 5.20). Also taken from the movies was Ilsley's "view room" beneath the deck, with windows looking out into the pool at both underwater and water level (fig. 5.25). It is revealing that the house—designed by architect Edla Muir—was conceived more or less as an accessory to the pool.[52] But as the critic of the *Los Angeles Times* observed, "there is nothing of the beach house or bath house about it."[53] On the contrary, the Ilsley residence was appointed in such a way that every association with the swimming pool was rigorously banned. As might be expected, Ilsley was not very fond of swimming but "would rather build pools than swim in them, and would rather

5.23. Hollywood, California: Philip Ilsley estate,
hepatica-leaf pool. (*Saturday Evening Post,*
August 1951.) *Also plate 13.*

5.24. Ilsley pool and living room. (*Saturday Evening Post*, August 1951.) *Also plate 14.*

54. *Saturday Evening Post,* August 11, 1951, 68.

55. It is probably no coincidence that devotees of the open air such as Rudolf Schindler and Richard Neutra came from Austria to California to implement their ideas in a region where the climate was considerably more reliable for this kind of experiment, the model being Schindler's own house at North Kings Road in West Hollywood with its sleeping porches (already a familiar device in Greene & Greene's Pasadena bungalows) and outdoor living room. See August Sarnitz, *R. M. Schindler, Architekt* (Vienna and Munich: Brandstätter, 1986), 21, 44ff.

keep his waistline slim by dieting than by swimming."[54] May we surmise that Mr. Ilsley was not only a builder and a dieter but also a watcher? The glass wall in the cellar of his house explains a lot. And if the photo used for his 1951 advertising campaign (fig. 5.16) was taken in his own pool, there were a sufficient number of bathing beauties in the area that could have posed for him. A photograph used for the *Post* article is eloquent proof of how much a camera-wielding landlubber Ilsley really was (fig. 5.23). None of the nine people in the picture is in the water. The three bathing beauties, in various positions, distributed over strategic points on the poolside, are posing for three men holding cameras! The man with his back to the fourth camera (that of the *Post*'s photographer's) seems to be Ilsley himself. It is an amazingly revealing picture.

Thematic Clustering To other Americans, California was what America had been to the Europeans, the generous fulfillment of a dream-wish of more than biblical proportions, a combination of the Garden of Allah, Promised Land, Garden of Eden, and Shangri-La. All elements that could possibly contribute to the *Lustbild* were frantically collected and meticulously staged. Inevitably the character of this *Lustbild* changed over the years, but one aspect was securely fixed: the predominance of physical well-being. More than any other American aspirant to paradise, the southern Californian sought a beautifully proportioned body, tenderly bronzed by the California sun, a goal that many contemporary Europeans shared wholeheartedly, as witness the Scandinavian and Austro-German naturalist and health movements.[55] Moreover, Californians knew quite well how to deal with their privileged exis-

5.25. Ilsley pool through basement windows. (*Los Angeles Times*, August 1949.)

56. *California Arts and Architecture,* July 1933.

57. Although not in California, closely related in its paradisiac mood was the leisure suburb of Coral Gables near Miami, Florida. The architect George E. Merrick conceived the architecture and landscaping as being expressive of "Beauty, romance, inspiration and home" (Alan Gowans, *Images of American Living: Four Centuries of Architecture and Furniture as Cultural Expression* [New York: Harper and Row, 1976], 380). The late Reyner Banham, as always, sensed long ago the total inaptitude of art historical classificatory method in relation to the Californian built environment (*Los Angeles: The Architecture of Four Ecologies* [New York: Harper and Row, 1971], 21–25).

58. Compilers of architectural guides seem to be quite addicted to this method of classification. To give an impression of just how senseless such a system is, I quote the individual stylistic denominations that were used to bring some order to the relatively modest architectural heritage of Santa Barbara, as it appeared in Herb Andree and Noel Young, *Santa Barbara Architecture: From Spanish Colonial to Modern* (Santa Barbara: Capra Press, 1980): Spanish Colonial, Mexican, Victorian, Gothic Revival, Italianate, Second Empire, Queen Anne, Cottages, Post Victorian, Revivalism, American Colonial, Mission Revival, Medieval, Mediterranean, Classical, Craftsmen [*sic*] Movement, Bay Region Tradition, Bungalows, Prairie Style, Secessionist, Spanish Colonial Revival, Medieval French, Medieval English, Hänsel and Gretel, Fairytale, Monterey, Colonial Revival, French, Italian, Capetown, Southwest Indian, Second Bay Tradition, Modern, International Style, Postwar Modern, Brutalist, Third Bay Region Tradition, Woodsy, Second Spanish Period, Traditional, not to mention the innumerable mutants, crossings, and modifications also appearing in the text.

tence. *California Arts and Architecture,* tasteful propagator of the good life, often illustrated its points with pictures of bronzed locals sipping drinks on the sun-drenched beaches, for "Californians know the art of living" (fig. 5.26).[56]

To properly communicate these values in architectural terms, a large repertoire of signs had to be developed. In California signs had to be less academic, less Vitruvian, and more directly appealing to the sensations than elsewhere. So in the shortest possible time, radical associationism ran rampant. Just as, in the ice cream business, existing flavors were quickly exhausted and new, composite ones had to be invented, similarly every owner, through his residence, pool, or garden, could send off his own message of poetic licence.[57] Although historians are accustomed to classify houses by their stylistic appearance, such a system loses its clarifying purpose when it comes to contain—as with varieties of ice cream—as many denominations as there are items.[58]

People don't live "Queen Anne" or "colonial" but follow the fashion of the day, the moods of the time. They dress themselves, their cars, and their houses in a self-evident, noncritical acceptance of whatever seems to be in harmony with the general temper. A desire to follow the "wilderness mood" might entail residing in a "craftsman" bungalow, which comes as a complete lifestyle package: interiors equipped with bucolic fireplaces, handcrafted rugs and pottery, a corduroy suit, and an easily maintained garden—no pools, just ponds—in harmony with the good rustic life. The suggestive package of the wilderness atmosphere was part of a whole set of related humors, most of which were directed to the rediscovered landscape, which was believed capable of regeneration so long as the proper mood-matching art and architecture could be found.

This important process of suggesting and selecting took place, among other sites, in the newspapers and magazines. *California Arts and Architecture,* founded originally as two separate magazines in 1911 and 1918, took as its mission the propagation of an architecture that would match, or better still incorporate, the regional lifestyle. Much effort was spent on determining the relation of the house to the outdoors—the particular climate, the spirit of the place. A significant role for the magazine consisted of inventing gardens and houses that would fit the idiosyncrasies, the particular expectations, of their owners. It ran various series on Mediterranean gardens, Hispanic architecture, Indian culture, Near Eastern travel impressions. In 1936 the regional emphasis was dropped and the world "California," printed in still smaller type, was tucked away into the farthest corners of the magazine's cover, until, from 1944 onward, it disappeared entirely. From 1938, under John Entenza's inspired proprietorship, the magazine went through its international modern—and most famous—phase as *Arts and Architecture.* After 1960 the direction again was altered, and it was overwhelmed by a stream of more glossy, less tasteful magazines. Some of its original objectives, however, have been carried on by *Sunset,* based in Menlo Park near Palo Alto.

5.26. "Californians know the art of living." (*California Arts and Architecture*, July 1933.)

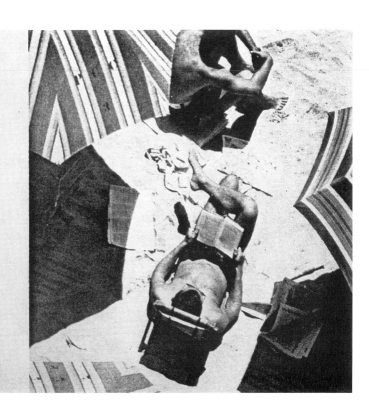

CALIFORNIANS KNOW THE ART OF LIVING

In this photograph as with the one reproduced on the front cover, Will Connell, distinguished California artist-photographer interprets his subject with skill and a modern touch. The Pacific Coast Club of Long Beach is crowded on Sundays with those seeking the soothing effects of sun and ocean.

Below is a colorful and comfortable patio setting arranged by J. W. Robinson Company of Los Angeles. Out-of-door furniture is selected as the ideal complement to the beach home. Rope webbing lends distinction as well as comfort. Solid wooden wheels are not only a decorative addition but make the furniture easily movable about the patio or garden. Rush rugs, plaid linens and pottery fruit service complete the picture now so common in southern California homes.

59. Paul C. Johnson, ed., *The Early Sunset Magazine, 1898–1928* (San Francisco: California Historical Society, 1973), 11. I thank Daniel Gregory for his friendly assistance.

60. *California Arts and Architecture*, October 1931, 17.

61. See, for the architectural implementation of those ambitions, Timothy Anderson, Eudorah Moore, and Robert Winter, *California Design 1910* (Salt Lake City: Gibbs and Smith, 1980). And for local utopianism, Robert V. Hine, *California's Utopian Colonies* (1953; Berkeley: University of California Press, 1966).

62. *Saturday Evening Post*, August 11, 1951, 66.

63. Ronald L. Rindge and Thomas W. Doyle, *Ceramic Art of the Malibu Potteries, 1926–1932* (Malibu: Malibu Lagoon Museum, 1988), 12–13.

64. Charles Lockwood, *Dream Palaces: Hollywood at Home* (New York: Viking Press, 1981), 94. The quotation is from Mary Pickford, *Sunshine and Shadow* (Garden City, N.Y.: Doubleday, 1955).

65. "Thomas Ince's death was just as confused and improvized as his architecture," wrote Charles Lockwood. "On the day of Tom's death, an early edition of the Los Angeles *Times* ran the headline 'Movie Producer Shot on Hearst Yacht.' ... But what really happened in this much repeated Hollywood tale? Charlie Chaplin had been on board *The Oneida* [Hearst's yacht].... He wasn't saying anything, but his Japanese chauffeur, Kono, told friends that he'd seen Ince carried off the yacht with a bullet wound in his head. That lent some credibility to the rumor that Hearst had caught Tom playing around with Marion Davies, his movie-star mistress, on a lower deck and shot him in a fit of rage." And so on. There was no autopsy and Ince's death remained unsolved. (Lockwood, *Dream Palaces*, 165.)

Sunset was founded in 1898 as a romantic introduction to life on the Pacific Coast. Its mission was to publicize for easterners the "resources of this great western empire for the husbandman, stockman and miner, and for the tourist and healthseeker."[59] As a promotor of what it called "western living," it amalgamated the genius of the place and the dreams of the owner into an attractive package of fantasy architecture and design. Compared to *California Arts and Architecture, Sunset* emerges as the more practical, quaint, simple, and distinctly less artistic of the two.

Considering that these magazines all claimed to provide the prospective owner with "The Typical Home Life of California—Choose Your Own Architect and Then Develop a Neighborhood,"[60] they must have generated a wide variety of architectural phenomena. Wasn't it just as reasonable to champion the revitalization of the local Spanish mission architecture as of the indigenous Indian monuments that still could be found in California itself and in the neighboring state of Arizona? During the mid-nineteenth century, the unfaltering efforts of Arthur J. Lummis to restore the traces of the original Spanish mission settlement were popularly appreciated. Yet although extremely fitting and easy to understand, the mission style was insufficient to satisfy the need for stronger, more associative and picturesque eclectic impulses on the part of those who wanted to escape it all for the fantastic world of yet unfulfilled religious, idealistic, and utopian ambitions.[61]

Those ambitions and dreams often resulted in playful waterworks that repay close scrutiny. As we have seen above, the private swimming pool in California's Southland achieved its early form by following the example of Long Island's Gold Coast and the aristocratic estates further south, from New Jersey to Florida. There were several possible routes of influence. One was through the monumental gardens of old-money San Francisco and its wealthy suburbs, followed by William R. Hearst, who was able to dominate the Los Angeles swimming pool scene from 1931 until his death in 1951. Marion Davies herself owned seven houses in Los Angeles alone equipped with pools,[62] quite a remarkable record.

A second line of inspiration originated not in the demonstration of the power of one man, but less grandiosely by the authority of pictorial persuasion, most notably through the magazines and books on garden architecture and design. These promoted the Mediterranean landscape as the proper surroundings for the cultivated denizen of Paradise.

An American Riviera With an unerring if casual sense for the right architecture for the right place, Frederick H. Rindge, founder of Malibu Potteries and author of *Happy Days in Southern California* (1898), proclaimed southern California "The American Riviera." In his vision, this part of the state could pose as a picturesque resuscitation of the cities of Venice, Naples, and Seville, combined with landscape touches from the Côte d'Azur, Tuscany, and the Campagna.[63]

As is so often the case, clients and architects found each other as a matter of course and cooperated in such a way as to achieve an original and most harmonious result. The swimming pool had represented from its earliest beginnings a sign of paradisiac, almost unreal luxury. Movie stars also belonged to another world. Stage actors may have belonged to the theater, to the city, to civilization, but movie "stars" inhabited an extraterrestrial, heavenly space. Stars were paid enormous—"astronomical"!—salaries; in return they were obliged to maintain the lifestyle that was thought to befit their rank. Very expensive and relatively useless, swimming pools were indispensable to that lifestyle, as well as being useful instruments to enhance the brilliance of the star. The pool was a mechanistic looking glass, a shining hall of mirrors, excavated from the soft turf of the traditional garden, surrounded by trees and flowers. Whereas the garden breathed the greens and browns of the earth, the pool radiated the pale azure hues of the daytime sky, and the deeper blue of the sky at night.

One of the earliest and certainly most famous star-enhancing hydrophilic ensembles was Pickfair in Beverly Hills, the Hollywood counterpart of the Villa d'Este and Versailles combined. The property of Douglas Fairbanks and Mary Pickford, darlings of the movie public of the 1920s, the house was a quaint thing of vaguely Cape Cod ancestry and totally uninteresting. The hydraulic equipment, on the other hand, was breathtaking. After purchase in 1919, the grounds were augmented by several highly unusual pools. Pickford told the press, "Doug liked to swim, but usually didn't have time to drive to the Pacific Ocean, in the middle of the week when he was shooting a picture. That was no problem. He brought the Pacific Ocean to the estate, or at least a scaled-down version: a 55 × 100-foot [18-by-33-meter] swimming-pool, with a sandy beach along one side." Because Fairbanks also enjoyed canoeing, he had dug a series of small ponds where he and his friends could paddle canoes amid the arid Santa Monica Mountains.[64] The big Pickfair pool was not only one of the largest private pools of its time, it was also one of the least conventional. Its plan was that of a flattened-out banana, dangerously balanced on the brow of the hill. Safety ladders were positioned at strategic places and a springboard and chute placed at the short end (fig. 5.27).

A similar treatment transformed the grounds belonging to former Broadway actor and independent film producer Thomas Ince, notorious for his death in 1924 on the yacht, and supposedly at the hands, of the jealous W. R. Hearst.[65] Four years earlier, in the same year as the happy Fairbanks-Pickford couple, Ince commissioned the Paddock firm to construct a large squarish pool, embedded in all sorts of natural foliage and reminiscent of the lily ponds his neighbors used to have in their gardens. Partially rectangular, its irregular shape also anticipated the jungle pool (fig. 5.28). This interesting milestone of pool design was destroyed in 1950.

Not far away, also in Benedict Canyon, Beverly Hills, the celebrated comedian Harold Lloyd had acquired a vast property of slightly over twenty-two acres which—in a grotesque challenge to the arid natural condition of the place—he called Greenacres. Here he commissioned the largest, and thus far the costliest—over three million dollars—estate to be

5.27. Beverly Hills, California: Pickfair pool, 1920.
     (Marc Wanamaker/Bison Archives.)
5.28. *Below:* Beverly Hills, California: Thomas Ince
     pool, 1920. (Marc Wanamaker/Bison Archives.)

built in the entire area, and the first movie-star residence that aimed at eclipsing the aristo-cratic homes of the East Coast millionaires. In fact it showed all the stigmata of the Long Island mansion-plus-playhouse. From the air the estate looked very much like one of the Medici villas in the Tuscan hills, but instead of the usual agricultural buildings, one encountered a sports complex of the most outrageous dimensions (figs. 5.29, 5.30), which encompassed courts for handball, squash, and tennis, a miniature nine-hole golf course, several ponds and streams, a gigantic swimming pool, a smaller swimming pool, and an 800-foot "canoe stream" (see also chapter 6).[66]

The eastern side of Lloyd's palazzo was extended into a "cascade," not unlike the one in the Villa Aldobrandini, Frascati, lined with specially imported cypresses. The gardens were designed by A. E. Hansen, an artist who apparently had a number of traditional examples at the ready. Lloyd had insisted that the gardens not only look, but sound, "green." The quanti-ties of water that daily had to course through the grounds is mind-boggling. Apart from the irrigation of the gardens and the golf course, a miniature swamp had to be kept at the right humidity and a plethora of fountains activated. In 1962 Lloyd told the press: "We loved the effect of the fountains. There isn't a corner anywhere on this property where you can't hear the sound of water."[67]

Southern California architects like Paul Williams, Gordon Kaufmann, Stiles Clements, George Washington Smith, and Wallace Neff were wonderfully able to execute the fantasies of their clients, and what they created was more to please than to glorify. There is a certain sweetness, if not quaintness, to the architecture of the very rich of that period, con-ceived as it is with great charm and a tremendous sensitivity to place and climate. It is for the latter quality, it seems, that the architecture of the *garden* so often surpassed that of the house in originality and taste. Garden designers like Paul Thiene and A. E. Hansen provided the es-tates of Bel-Air and Beverly Hills with the gorgeous landscaping that is still one of the ultimate delights of our time.

The largest property that Kaufmann designed and Thiene landscaped was the gigantic park and Norman Gothic castle in gray stone of oil trillionaire, and legendary founder of Beverly Hills, E. L. Doheny, between 1925 and 1927. The waterworks of Greystone, as it was called, included pools, ponds, and wild cascades that were among the largest ever built (fig. 5.31). When the estate was subdivided and the house acquired by the City of Beverly Hills in 1964, an enormous reservoir was discovered.

It requires little visual memory to recognize the sources of those great houses in popular architectural books of the early twentieth century, the best known and perhaps most infuential of which were Charles A. Platt, *Italian Gardens* (1894), and Edith Wharton, *Italian Villas and Their Gardens* (1904), with exciting plates by Maxfield Parrish.[68] Other information could have been found in general magazines like *Scribner's* and *Harper's,* or the more specialized *Gar-den Design, American Homes and Gardens,* and, from the 1920s on, *Garden Architecture, California*

66. *Life,* August 1, 1938, 28. "Except for the estate of the late Edward Doheny, Jr., it is the greatest in Southern California. From the big Spanish house with its 27 telephones, to the 800 ft canoe stream and the waterfall which can be lighted up at night, Green Acres is a rich man's dream. Six gardeners care for the lavish grounds. Mr. Lloyd can play golf on a pri-vate nine-hole course, swim in spacious pools or play handball in the best court on the West Coast. The Lloyd children have their own four room play house." The Lloyd estate was a perfect illustration of the urge to privatize public services (e.g., the golf course), just as the East Coast robber barons had compacted ancien régime amenities within their own estates. Mr. Charles Lockwood, great connoisseur of the movie kingdom, provided me most generously with information.
After Lloyd's death in 1971 the estate was subdivided and the gardens and pools disappeared.
67. "The House That Harold Built," *Show Business Illustrated,* April 1962. For the requirement that the sound of a splashing fountain always be within reach, the locus classicus is Pliny on his villa in Tuscany: "By every chair (marble bench) is a tiny fountain, and throughout the riding grounds can be heard the sound of the streams directed into it." (*The Letters of Pliny the Younger,* trans. Betty Radice [Harmondsworth: Penguin, 1969].) The "cascade" of the Villa Aldobrandini was frequently imitated in American garden design of the early twentieth century. On the East Coast the Charles M. Schwab es-tate, Loreto, Pennsylvania, by Charles W. Leavitt (c. 1920) and on the West Coast, apart from the Lloyd gardens, the former Milton Getz, later Hearst-Davies, estate in Bel-Air, were the best known.
68. See Charles A. Platt, *Italian Gardens,* republished, with an overview by Keith N. Morgan (London: Thames and Hudson, 1993).

5.29. Beverly Hills, California: Greenacres, the estate of Harold Lloyd. (Charles Lockwood, Los Angeles.)

5.30. Harold Lloyd by his Olympic pool at Greenacres.
(Marc Wanamaker/Bison Archives.)

5.31. Beverly Hills, California: Greystone, the estate
of E. L. Doheny, 1925–1927, cascade. Gordon
Kaufmann and Paul Thiene. (*Landscape
Architecture*, 1927.)

Arts and Architecture, and *Sunset*. To find the most celebrated designs of early Southland gardens with more or less elaborate waterworks, it suffices to leaf through books like *California Gardens* by Winifred Starr Dobyns (1931), with a foreword by star-society architect Myron Hunt, or through magazines like *Garden Architecture* and *American Homes and Gardens*. The communities most frequently represented were Pasadena, Beverly Hills, and Montecito, near Santa Barbara. The largest swimming and ornamental pools, and the greenest gardens, are encountered where water is rarest. This golden rule has been successfully applied to the environs of Santa Barbara where, in the community of Montecito, the lushest estates were built in the years before and, even more, after the great stock market crash of 1929. Two large water gardens deserve special mention. The gardens of the Las Tejas estate of the Oakleigh Thornes featured a series of cascades ending in a pool, which, following the example of the Villa d'Este at Tivoli, was screened off by a system of box hedges. The gardens, very appropriately, were designed by Mrs. Thorne herself. The nearby Charles Boldt house, with an impressively monumental swimming pool, was landscaped by Ralph Stevens,[69] responsible also for the gardens and oversized swimming pool of Las Terrasas, the estate of Harold Stuart Chase at Hope Ranch, outside Santa Barbara.

Two other colossal monuments that both appeared in Beverly Hills in 1928, the homes of Buster Keaton and of real estate entrepreneur Edwin Janss, were frequently represented in various periodicals, including the *Architectural Digest*. The Keaton mansion, a pompous variation of the Tuscan villa model designed by Gene Verge, featured an oval swimming pool at the foot of some very solemn steps. Janss obviously invested more in his garden and waterworks than Keaton, resulting in two splendid pools, one for show and one for swimming. Both have become famous since their appearance in David O. Selznick's *A Star Is Born* (1937), and are also featured in the Abbott and Costello slapstick comedy *In Society* (1944).

The work of architects Wallace Neff and Roland E. Coate, and of landscape designer Florence Yoch, was also featured in *Architectural Digest*. The collaborations of the English-born (but archetypally California-style) architect Kaufmann and the landscape designer Thiene were particularly esteemed. Frequently published, in addition to Greystone, are their enchanting water gardens for John L. Severance in Pasadena and the estate of Isidore Eisner in the Hancock Park neighborhood of Los Angeles, in which an ornamental pool was placed at right angles to the main house, creating a pattern that had a widespread following.[70] Another work that was published with recurring prominence was the estate of financier Ben R. Meyer, in the eastern part of Beverly Hills.

Electric Hair Dryers The Ben Meyer pool, pool house, and garden form a most interesting example of Thiene's craft (figs. 5.32, 5.33). The north-south-oriented rectangular plot is five and one-half times longer than wide and is situated on the

69. *California Arts and Architecture*, May 1931, 44–45. The gardens of the Villa d'Este provided a popular model in California, which gives some indication of their colossal scale. See Thomas D. Church, "The Villa d'Este at Tivoli: An Outstanding Example of the Principles of Garden Design in the Renaissance," *California Arts and Architecture*, October 1933, 14–15.
70. The popularity of the Eisner house is easily explained: it appeared often in the magazines sponsored by producers of clay products. Mr. Eisner was president of the Gladding, McBean & Co. ceramic tile factory.

5.32. *Left:* Beverly Hills, California: Ben Meyer estate,
1920–1927, site plan. Gordon Kaufmann and
Paul Thiene.
5.33. Ben Meyer pool. (*Landscape Architecture,*
1927.)

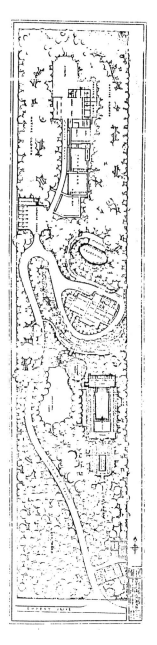

higher slopes of Beverly Hills. In order to create a picturesque illusion of Renaissance Italy on this rectangular strip of land, Thiene had to rely on the irregular slope and meandering paths. Alternating plantings of orchards, flower and water gardens ("plans d'eau") were to distract attention from the straight-cut boundaries. The house was situated high on a cliff, overlooking the pool and orchard, while a steep walkway was cut out in the rock and meandered down to the pool. Filters and pumping systems were housed under the pool. Landscape and architectural design went on concurrently from 1920 and, judging from their comments, both Thiene and Kaufmann considered the collaboration most successful.[71]

Thiene was decidedly pleased with the result and subsequently discussed the garden, but more especially the swimming pool, in the Boston-based magazine *Landscape Architecture*. The Ben Meyer pool, Thiene argued, could well be considered a model for an open-air pool in the typical Mediterranean conditions of southern California. As a friendly concession to the current Beverly Hills desiderata, pool and pool house were outfitted with the newest gadgetry. Thiene wrote:

> In the back of the pavilion are six dressing rooms for ladies and six for men, each section provided with shower, lavatory, etc. Electric hair dryers and other modern conveniences in the ladies' section were not overlooked. The top of the pavilion is provided with beach chairs so as to give the bathers in their wet bathing suits an opportunity for a sun bath. A kitchenette completely equipped is very helpful in entertaining. The pool itself contains approximately 160,000 gallons of water filtered by two eighty-four inch Roberts Vertical Pressure water filters capable of a total filtration of 15,000 gallons per hour. A ten horsepower Westinghouse electric motor is directly connected to a single stage centrifugal Byron Jackson pump which forces the water from the swimming pool through the filters and in turn through the Ultra Violet Ray for sterilization. In order to eliminate algae, a daily application of one pound of copper sulphate is used for each million gallons of water. . . . A vacuum cleaner is used for cleaning the floor and a suction system is provided to take care of any leaves that may fall on the surface of the water.[72]

Water for the pool was stored in a large oval reservoir in the higher reaches of the garden that doubled as an ornamental pool in front of the main house. The swimming pool, of the modest size of 18 by 10.5 meters, was, and still is, beautifully tucked into shrubs, bushes, and creeping evergreens in the lower part of the estate. Thanks to the drop in the terrain, the machinery under the swimming pool is easily accessible from the lower platform. The disposition into the three different levels of pool house, pool, and filter/pump shed has proven very popular and may be seen at many places throughout the country.

71. Alson Clark, "The 'Californian' Architecture of Gordon B. Kaufmann," *Journal of the Society of Architectural Historians, Southern California Chapter* 1, no. 3 (Summer 1982), 3.
72. Paul G. Thiene, "Water Features: Notes on Experience in California Gardens," *Landscape Architecture* 18 (October 1927–July 1928), 43–44.

5.34. Ben Meyer pool in 1990. *Also plate 15.*

The Meyer estate has been split into a lower and a higher unit; the lower, where originally the orchard and the pool were situated, has been modified over the years, but the pool and pool house are carefully preserved (fig. 5.34)—fortunately, since they came to stand as a model for later architects. Florence Yoch, working as a landscape designer for producers and directors like David O. Selznick and George Cukor, followed the solution devised by Kaufmann and Thiene in her garden, pool, and pool house of 1936 for Cukor.[73]

Winifred Dobyns alluringly described the "outdoor living rooms" of Mediterranean-inspired Californian houses and gardens. They may take the form of "cloistered patios" or "a flagged sitting area beneath the spreading branches of a majestic live oak. They may be small sun-bathed walled gardens with a lawn panel and bright flower borders where chairs and benches are arranged in a friendly fashion under the orange trees."[74] And if that is so, then in California the swimming pool must be the open-air bed- or bathroom.

Oriental Water In the radical associationism that governed southern California in the age of its becoming, the Mediterranean impulse accounted for only half the field. The other half—the interest in bodily hygiene, the daily bath, and the therapeutic qualities of water—was associated with the Islamic Orient.

As Pierre Goubert noted in *The Conquest of Water*, "Dr Delabarre's Toothpastes were touting their 'Oriental Water,' their 'Oriental Powder,' and their 'Oriental Paste.'"[75] Historically, the reintroduction of institutional hydro-enthusiasm for therapeutic as well as recreational purposes often occurred in the context of Roman or Turkish baths (the so-called hammams). But the real aura of the exotic, as Giedion noted, came only after the publications of the noted British hydrophile and traveler David Urquhart, around the mid-nineteenth century. Urquhart's "Hammam" in Jermyn Street of 1863 became "the prototype of hot-air baths both in Europe and America." Something like an "Islamic Bath Movement," as Giedion called it, was very much in the air.[76]

It was in America that the Moghul/Moorish mood was tackled with the greatest vigor. Perhaps because the signs were stronger and more alluring, and because they were not in thrall to the already existing, often classically outfitted *Kurorte* and *villes d'eaux*, the American bathing establishments could more directly follow the Moghul mood that had been set by the sixteenth-century works of Shah Jehan, particularly the Taj Mahal, and the water temple of Hyderabad. The Salt Air Bathing Pavilion on the Great Salt Lake, the Great Bath House of Hot Springs, Montana, the Santa Cruz Beach Casino of 1904, and the Bath House of Venice beach of 1912 (fig. 5.35), were among the most eloquent examples.[77]

Among the earliest West Coast Islamic fantasies were the estate of James Waldron Gillespie in Montecito (1902) and the house of the developer Leslie C. Brand who, together with his architect Nathaniel Dryden, founded the borough of Glendale in 1904. Al-

73. James J. Yoch, *Landscaping the American Dream: The Gardens and Film Sets of Florence Yoch, 1890–1972* (New York: Abrams/Sagapress, 1989), 85–91. "View of pool" on 87.
74. Winifred Starr Dobyns, *California Gardens*, with a foreword by Myron Hunt (New York: Macmillan, 1931), 20.
75. Jean-Pierre Goubert, *The Conquest of Water: The Advent of Health in the Industrial Age* (Oxford: Polity Press, 1989), 123.
76. Sigfried Giedion, *Mechanization Takes Command: A Contribution to Anonymous History* (1948; New York: Oxford University Press, 1969), 670, 668. Seaside resorts and their demonstrative piers often followed the Oriental mode. The Brighton (1866) and Blackpool piers were distinctly "Indian." The first Blackpool Pier of 1874 was called the "Indian Pavilion." See Simon Adamson, *Seaside Piers* (London: Batsford, 1977), 30, 79–80.
77. Gary Kyriazi, *The Great American Amusement Parks* (Secaucus, N.J.: Castle Books, 1978), 136ff.

5.35. Venice, California: bathhouse and beach. (Postcard.)

78. Richard Oliver, *Bertram Grosvenor Goodhue* (Cambridge: MIT Press, 1983), 40–41.

79. Horatio Stoll, "A Persian Garden in California," *American Homes and Gardens* 10, no. 12 (1913), 426–427. See also Dobyns, *California Gardens*.

80. Charles Moore, *The City Observed: Los Angeles, a Guide to Its Architecture and Landscapes* (New York: Vintage, 1984), 302, and Richard Alleman, *The Movie Lover's Guide to Hollywood* (New York: Harper and Row, 1985), 296.

81. For the thematic clustering in West Coast architecture, see Louis Marin, *Utopics: Spatial Play* (1982; Atlantic Highlands, N.J.: Humanities Press, 1984), chapter 12, and Umberto Eco, *Travels in Hyperreality* (London: Picador, 1986), 3–58; Banham, *Los Angeles: The Architecture of Four Ecologies;* Thomas Hines, "Los Angeles Architecture: The Issue of Tradition in a Twentieth Century City," in David G. De Long, Helen Searing, and Robert A. M. Stern, eds., *American Architecture: Innovation and Tradition* (New York: Rizzoli, 1985), 112–129; and Anderson, Moore, and Winter, *California Design 1910*.

The Arabesque mood, the Mediterranean cluster, the Classical Graeco-Roman mode, and the Californian Spanish Mission Renaissance are probably the most illustrative. Rindge and Doyle, *Ceramic Art of the Malibu Potteries*, 93. The Malibu Potteries produced architectural ceramic tiles and catered to the current tastes in lifestyle. Tiles were designed, among others, for the newly constructed Los Angeles

though the Gillespie house was modeled after a Roman villa, the complex was expressly intended to be a Persian water garden called El Fureidis, Arabic for "pleasant place." The owner had developed a special interest in the Persian garden and had commissioned his architect, Bertram G. Goodhue (a gifted eclectic who later would foster the Spanish style in California through his work for the San Diego Exposition of 1911–1915 and his buildings at the California Institute of Technology in Pasadena), to design him a house in the Persian style. To facilitate this, Gillespie invited Goodhue on a research trip to trace architectural trails from the Caspian Sea to the Persian Gulf.[78]

Of the result, *American Homes and Gardens* opined, "In treatment it is suggestive of the hillside gardens of the Kasr Kajar, near Teheran, or of the Naib-i-Sultan in the Shimran, and its splashing fountains, its lotus covered pools, its brick paved walls, shadow flecked by great trees, and its suburban outlook are the wonder of everyone who has the privilege of viewing them. Unlike most Persian gardens, where every drop of water is treasured owing to its scarcity"—the reviewer remarked with slight critical wonder—"the Gillespie estate has a plentiful and constant supply."[79] Most of the garden is taken up by several sequences of decorative pools, each finally trickling down in narrow and shallow water steps and cascades.

The Brand estate is of a less serious but equally surprising character. By building this resplendent minareted house at the foot of Mount Verdugo, the owner could overlook from there his newly created borough (he named his place El Miradero, meaning "the lookout"). The Islamic quality of the house was, like so many American stylistic derivatives, based upon a visit to one of the great exhibitions, this time the World's Columbian Exposition at Chicago, 1893, with its East Indian Pavilion.[80] As in El Fureidis, the intention was not to construct an actual replica but to reinvent the desired image stripped of its unwelcome memories, as something that existed only in fantasy—or more precisely, in utopian fantasy, since it is the exotic mood as it ought to be or should have been, not as it is. No European would be able to recognize the "European" styles of architecture as they appear in California, any more than a Frenchman could understand the French waiter in a Los Angeles restaurant or an Arab feel kinship with Douglas Fairbanks in *The Thief of Baghdad*. But that is because none of these—the European, the Frenchman, or the Arab—were the ideal representatives of their own utopian image.

Huitzilipochtli Usually memories and fantasies like these are communicated in thematic clusters. Sometimes haphazardly chosen on the basis of a popular movie, or inspired by the accidental reading of a book, sometimes simply there because they belong to the actual past or the "wish history" of the place, always these thematic clusters are presented in meticulous, "almost real" detail.[81] An advertisement (*Architectural Digest,* 1928) for the stone manufacturer who supplied ornament for the Los Angeles Theater read: "Huitzilipochtli, The God of War, has been reborn to a new environment. His image, high on the facade of the Mayan Theater, was not tediously carved by hand as was done in the Ancient Temple of the Mayans; but was cast in versatile and economical art stone by the Mission Staff and Stone Co., Inc."

There are some superb examples of Huitzilipochtli's building activities to be found in Los Angeles. If one can't visit the archaeological sites in Mexico, a trip to Los Angeles will provide some outstanding if ersatz representatives of Mayan and Aztec architecture.[82] Frank Lloyd Wright's Hollyhock House for oil heiress and artistic eccentric Aline Barnsdall (1918–1921) and his Ennis House (1924) are the best known. Both are equipped with pools, that of the Ennis House being an especially photogenic one. Wright's son, naturalized Californian Lloyd, also created some superb pools, although they are not easy to locate because pools, even by renowned architects, do not feature in architectural guides. A particularly attractive Lloyd Wright pool, with the customary terraces and decorations, can be found at 1825 Curzon Street in the Hollywood Hills (fig. 5.36).

In the house that Lloyd Wright built between 1926 and 1928 for the legendary star Ramon Novarro, he created a breathtaking balancing act on the most awkward site one could imagine. The foundations are placed the way a rock climber positions himself, one foot high above the other. The top floor of the house clings to a steep cliff, whereas the ground floor tiptoes on a narrow strip off the road. The late and celebrated architect Charles Moore described the situation with characteristic bravura: "This four story slab of white stucco thrusts from a bend in the road like a shear plane of the San Andreas Fault [reminding us of the ever-present menace of the local geology]. This single-family house, which is even wider than it is tall, has the bulk of an apartment building as it dams up the end of a sizable ravine."[83]

City Hall, 1927. Among the firm's clients, the architects Austin, Parkinson & Martin were determined *not* "to confine themselves to any particular style, which ruled out the Moorish-Spanish type architecture so prevalent in Southern California at the time" (ibid., 84). The firm designed tiles in product lines entitled "Saracen," "Persian," "Mayan," "Moroccan," and "Espanol."

82. See Marjorie Ingle, *The Mayan Revival Style* (Albuquerque: University of New Mexico Press, 1984).

83. Moore, *City Observed,* 250.

5.36. Lloyd Wright, drawing for pool and terrace
decorations at 1825 Curzon Street, Hollywood
Hills. (Courtesy the owners.)

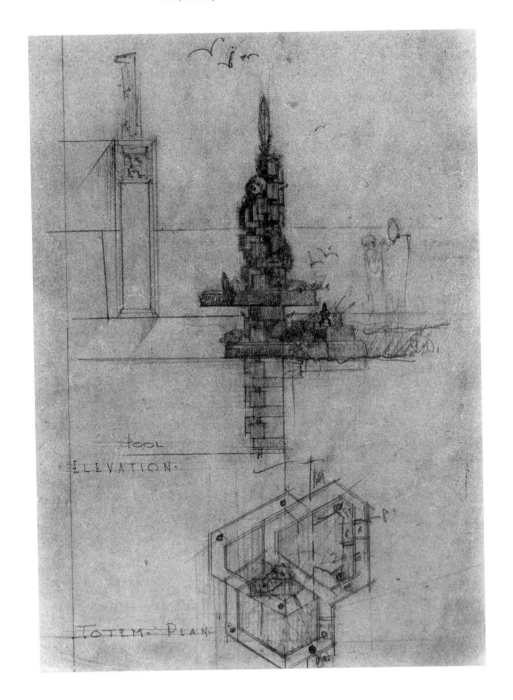

"Single-family house" was already a banal appellation for a dwelling designed for a single man who had the daring to express his sexual preference overtly in the accoutrements of his quarters.[84] *California Arts and Architecture* published a vivid description: "The dining room is a symphony in black and silver, the aluminum legged table having an onyx glass top, the chairs black satin seats and the black walls being covered with strands of dull silver chain hung from the ceiling to floor. The result constitutes the most unusual decor in the whole residence." The writer added daintily, "It is said that MGM set designer Cedric Gibbons, husband of Dolores Del Rio and cousin of Novarro, had decorated the place." But what makes the house as exciting as its location is the swimming pool. "On an axis with the living room and dining room entrances," the magazine continued, "which tie the two 'al fresco' features of the plan together, French doors open upon the chief delight of Mr. Wright's design, an outdoor swimming-pool surrounded by walls and conveniently situated for one to tumble from bed directly into the morning plunge [fig. 5.37]. At night the water is blessed with a convincingly realistic electric moonlight, of which aquatically minded guests are not slow to take advantage."[85]

Several owners since have tried to accommodate to the house's restricted configuration. When architectural critic Brendan Gill visited the house to make pictures for his book *The Dream Come True* the pool was roofed over and he could only wonder about the unusual arrangement: "Was this pool originally in the open air and enclosed by Wright at the behest of some later owner of the property?"[86] The answer is that although it was originally designed to be solidly "protected from intruders," it was probably one of the few pools of which it was possible to have a good view from the road above (fig. 5.38). The house is now owned by actress Diane Keaton, who has diligently restored it to its original state.[87]

Garden of Allah   *There will always be a poet to extol the streams of Arcadia and the cool springs of the Garden of Allah.*   PIERRE RESTANY

Of the many other moods and thematic clusters of the Southland, only a few can figure here as the eloquent representatives of the various hydraulic fantasies. Speaking directly to the heart were the semimystical, quasi-biblical hallucinations of the original paradise. *Paradeisos* is a Greco-Persian word that means "garden," but in an arid environment "garden" means more than just a piece of greenery; it connotes cultivation, water, civilization, and religion. The Persian garden was created in the desert with the help of God and water, the exclusive privilege of princes and of the blessed deceased; consequently the term became synonymous with the hereafter. The traditional representation of *paradeisos* is a walled-in square through which one or two small streams flow, crossing in the middle, in a decorative small basin. Paradise is earth and water, and the final habitat of the faithful.[88]

84. Alleman, *The Movie Lover's Guide to Hollywood*, 60.
85. *California Arts and Architecture*, July 1933, 13–31.
86. Brendan Gill, *The Dream Come True: Great Houses of Los Angeles* (New York: Lippincott, 1980), 96–97.
87. *Maison et Jardin*, no. 390 (February 1993), 124–130. The quotation is from *California Arts and Architecture*, July 1933, 13–31.
Epigraph: From *Domus*, "Aqua/Water," no. 611 (1988), 2–7.
88. Annemarie Schimmel et al., *Water and Architecture*, special issue of *A.A.R.P. Environmental Design Journal of the Islamic Environmental Design Research Centre* 2 (1985), 6–9. Islamic-Egyptian architecture was thought fitting to shape the Temple and Homestead of the Theosophical Society at Point Loma, San Diego, which was begun in 1897 and which took up other moods—Indian, Florentine—during the process of construction. Most of it is demolished now, but in its heyday it was certainly famous. See Hine, *California's Utopian Colonies*, 33ff.

5.37. Los Angeles: Ramon Novarro (later Taggart) house, 1926–1928. Lloyd Wright. Mr. Novarro at his pool. (*California Arts and Architecture,* Summer 1933.)

5.38. *Below:* Former Novarro house in 1990. *Also plate 16.*

The parallel with California is unmistakable: those whose faith was strongest traveled the long and arduous road over the Rocky Mountains and at the end were rewarded with paradise. In that sense the swimming pool could hardly be other than a replica of *paradeisos*. The idea of southern California as the desert made to bloom with water by the beneficence of God was also the first myth of the early settlers. The biblical Garden of Eden and noble Moorish Spain offered fabled reminiscences that were highly respected; but it should not be forgotten that their exact opposite, the decadent luxury of the harem, of the palace of the houris, was a very lively sign as well. There is a long semantic tradition that identifies the Moorish style with a lush bordello. According to Emmet Murphy, "For some reason or other, the Moorish Castle idea captured the fancy of many of the leading madams in the United States. From New York to Miami, Chicago and Los Angeles, captains of American industry would be able to take their sexual pleasures in surroundings in which only a Moor should have found himself comfortable. The madams of America somehow managed to confuse the architecture of northwest Africa with the harem-settings of fabled Baghdad, Damascus and Istanbul."[89]

The Arabic mood was further set by films such as *The Sheik* (1921) and its sequel, *Son of the Sheik* (1926), in which Rudolf Valentino played an elegant desert vagabond who had developed a knack for seducing European ladies. Other films that contributed to the fashion were the numerous adaptations of *Arabian Nights*. The most influential Arabesque movie was *The Thief of Baghdad* (1924) with Douglas Fairbanks, whose marriage to Mary Pickford put him and his film in the pages of the women's magazines of the period, including *Ladies' Home Journal*.[90] The lavish sets for the *Thief* were designed by William Cameron Menzies, whose glorious career as an art director got its start with this film.[91] Another cinematic hit was *Arabian Nights,* among the many remakes that of 1947 being the most memorable from a hydrotechnological point of view. A bank of bathtubs is filled with exotic princesses who, like geese, have drifted to the shallow side and, unable to swim, hold on firmly to a lifeline bolted to the inside of the tubs (fig. 5.39).

As early as 1904, Robert Hichen's novel *The Garden of Allah* began a successful ascent to the movie screen. It was also a success as a play in 1911 and was filmed again in 1927. In 1936, David O. Selznick launched his version of the story, but, despite the use of Technicolor and the participation of Marlene Dietrich and Charles Boyer, his *Garden of Allah* was unsuccessful.[92] (Dietrich had already appeared in 1930, amid similar scenery, with Gary Cooper in *Morocco.*) While filmmakers could make ample use of the natural Californian landscape, in the studio they had to rely on set designers. For the landscaping of *The Garden of Allah* Selznick called upon the popular garden architect Florence Yoch, who had worked for other movie moguls like Jack Warner and George Cukor.[93]

In January 1927, the picturesque condominium named the Garden of Allah was built as an extension to the home of the popular silent film actress, Russian-born Alla

89. Emmet Murphy, *The Great Bordellos of the World* (London: Quartet Books, 1983), 171.
90. Lockwood, *Dream Palaces,* 102.
91. Michael Webb, *Hollywood: Legend and Reality* (New York: Little, Brown, 1986), 86.
92. Ronald Haver, *David O. Selznick's Hollywood* (London: Secker and Warburg, 1980), 182–190.
93. Yoch, *Landscaping the American Dream,* 93–107.

5.39. Bathing beauties in *Arabian Nights*, 1947.
(Ramirez, *La arquitectura en el cine*, 1986.)

Nazimova. Its designation may have owed something to the Hichen novel, or to the famed San Francisco bordello of the same name, run by the legendary Sally Stanford during the interbellum years, but is primarily a play on Nazimova's forename. *Photoplay* gave a brisk description: "Alla Nazimova's beautiful estate, the one far out on Sunset Boulevard, has been converted into a residential hotel of twenty-five separate villas. . . . Rooms over the great garage of the 'Garden of Allah,' as it is now called, have been transformed into a studio where Nazimova lives. At the moment, however, Madame is making vaudeville appearances."[94]

Sheilah Graham recollected that "when Alla's garden and home were transformed into a bungalow hotel, the 'h' was added to her name, to give an aura of the Arabian Nights."[95] The architecture was nondescript—traditional Hispano-Californian—but the gigantic swimming pool was a great attraction (fig. 5.40). Situated in the middle of the compound, its shape purportedly was inspired by that of the Black Sea, a tribute to Nazimova's native locale. In an epoch when private pools were the privilege of the very wealthy, even in Los Angeles, the Garden's pool acted as a social magnet.

Gossip columnists had a great time, for ambitious young film stars came to live there and, with the permissive atmosphere and presence of the big pool, many scandalous scenes could be recorded. Starlets arrived to undress, show themselves, and take part in the general carnal fun. "In the thirty-two year span of its life, the *Garden* would witness robbery, murder, drunkenness, despair, divorce, marriage, orgies, pranks, fights, suicides, frustration and hope."[96] Among the memorable swimming pool scenes, the one with Johnny Weissmuller and Tallulah Bankhead deserves special mention. Graham writes:

> Bill O'Brian, a top agent and manager . . . living at the Garden, was awakened . . . one morning at about five by an unearthly din. He got out of bed and hastened to the window. The scene was straight from a Hollywood movie. A group of people in full evening dress had obviously had one hell of a party, and two of them, Tallulah Bankhead and Johnny Weissmuller, proceeded to dive off the top board, fully clad, into the pool. Tallulah, weighed down with a heavy beaded dress and diamonds, sunk to the bottom like a stone. Having an instinct for survival, she shed her clothes and jewels while weaving at the bottom of the Black Sea, emerging completely naked. "Everybody's been dying to see my body," she croaked. "Now they can see it." Weissmuller took to the hills after dragging his intoxicated companion—who could not swim—out of the pool, where she lay panting. A Filipino gardener, coming on early duty, tried to snatch a hose from her neck—she was wearing it like a snake—whereupon she chased him around the garden, intending, no doubt, to murder him if she caught him. Dredging operations to recover Miss Bankhead's jewelry took some time, while Tallulah removed the "Gar" from the big sign on the outside wall leaving it "The den of Allah."[97]

94. Quoted in Sheilah Graham, *The Garden of Allah* (New York: Crown, 1970), 18. For a description of the San Francisco brothel, see Murphy, *Great Bordellos of the World*, 225–226.
95. Graham, *Garden of Allah*, 18.
96. Ibid., 27.
97. Ibid., 45–47.

98. Dick Adler, "The Garden of Allah," *Angeles*, July 1990, 56.
99. Alleman, *The Movie Lover's Guide to Hollywood*, 168–169.

Of all the remarkable things that went on that morning, what stands out in the light of our investigation is that Bankhead, celebrated star of the twenties, could not swim, yet she dove off the highest board! Reminiscent of suicidal Etonian swimming of the mid-nineteenth century and the nonswimming poet Shelley's abandonment to the Mediterranean waves, it shows once more how rarely practiced the art of swimming actually was. In more general terms the story also shows the ascent of the swimming pool as the arena of sex and suicidal entertainment. Wild pool stories were the gist of Hollywood gossip in the pre–World War II years; the most popular ones involved high schoolers, who would round off the evening by jumping fully clothed into a pool.

"The jaded insouciance of the time was cultivated by guests such as Louis Calhern . . . [who] liked to finish off an evening of partying with a dip, fully dressed, in the Garden pool. And he wasn't the only one: everyone from [Robert] Benchley to the Barrymore brothers and Tallulah Bankhead tried the same stunt."[98] Nazimova died in 1945; the Garden was demolished in 1959 to make place for a parking lot and a bank, which keeps a model of the compound in a glass bubble at the back.[99]

Casa Blanca It is hardly surprising that people who came to Hollywood to enjoy its particular atmosphere of exotic eroticism were easily intoxicated. Take Albert Keep Isham, son of the Chicago manufacturer and multimillionaire Ralph Isham, who arrived in Los Angeles in the early twenties for no other reason than to have a great time. After inspecting the in places, he set out to build a pleasure palace for himself on a sandy beach—

5.40. *Opposite:* Los Angeles: "Garden of Allah"
      condominium, with swimming pool. (Graham,
      The Garden of Allah, 1970.)
5.41. Carpinteria, California: Isham estate, 1927,
      entrance, with convertible. George Washington
      Smith.

5.42. Isham pool, convertible roof down. *Also plate 17.*
5.43. *Opposite, left:* Isham pool, convertible roof up.
5.44. *Opposite, right:* Isham pool machinery.

100. The older pumps were obtained from Isham's home town; the inscription reads: "Yeomans Bros., Pumping Machinery, Chicago."

Sandyland—south of Santa Barbara near the community of Carpinteria (fig. 5.41). Isham wanted to incorporate into his own secluded erotic paradise everything from the Garden of Allah and *The Thief of Baghdad* to Moorish-style bawdy houses. In 1927, he commissioned Santa Barbara society architect George Washington Smith to design a complex in the Arabesque mood, called Casa Blanca, which was to contain in its very center a hammam-inspired swimming pool. Together with those at San Simeon, this is probably the most handsome pool in the United States. Its design is simple: a rectangular basin of 16 by 6.5 meters, trimmed with colorful tiles of superb quality and surrounded by the characteristic scum gutters of the period, the walls following the lines of the pool. There is a clerestory of tiled niches admitting light from above. An extraordinary feature of the pool is that when weather allows—not always the case on the foggy Pacific Coast—the roof opens electrically, rather like those on the boat-sized American convertible automobiles. The roof consists of a glass canopy, set in a finely decorated wooden frame and split in the middle so that each half can slide soundlessly out of sight (figs. 5.42, 5.43). Several dozen meters from the sea, Isham's pool was filled alternatively with salt or fresh water, which required sophisticated machinery (fig. 5.44).[100] Because of tidal fluctuations of several inches, the concrete tank had to be protected by deeply sunk walls heavily reinforced with cables. As was customary in the period, the lighting fixtures were sunken in the pool sides; if this provided sensual effects it also was responsible for electrical problems, because that same shifting sea water table penetrated the porous sandy soil.

To give the pool its allure of an Islamic (Islam = Isham?) hammam, Isham incorporated a great number of tiles that looked authentically Oriental—in fact they were said to come from Tunisia, but were almost certainly made by local tile manufacturers. Some of the

5.45. *Top:* Isham pool, tile by Malibu Potteries.
5.46. San Simeon, California: Casa del Sol, tile
tableau. *Also plate 18.*

ceramic work comes straight from the catalogues of the nearby Malibu Potteries (see fig. 5.22). At the shallow end, a large tile tableau crowned by a Moorish window and preceded by a small, delicately shaped fountain depicts underwater scenes with fishes and plants. At the opposite end, under a series of arches near the entrance, a mural of exquisite beauty is discreetly incorporated in the wall (fig. 5.45). It depicts a courtly scene of a prince and a princess in a garden done in the Moghul fashion and, although neither signed nor dated, may conceivably be by the same artist, perhaps manufactured by the same firm, as the tableau (fig. 5.46) in the outer wall of the guest cottage "C," later named Casa del Sol, at San Simeon.[101]

The Isham house was originally conceived as a beach house and comprised an entrance porch, a courtyard with an octagonal tiled fountain, and several smaller courtyards and pavilions (fig. 5.47). The main building was in fact no more than the shell that accommodated its main attraction, the swimming pool with a squash court and bowling alley alongside, in the tradition of keeping guests constantly amused.[102] Every year, in the fashion of the time, Isham "would go abroad and travel. And when he got back he would go to George Washington Smith and commission him to build a new house on the land in the style of wherever he had been," recalled Smith's former collaborator Lutah Maria Riggs in an interview.[103] Most of the additions were washed away by storms in the thirties and forties and, although heavy breakwaters and reinforced concrete walls were built, only half of the suicidally dangerous site remains undamaged.

A house built around such an extravagantly decorated and generously dimensioned "convertible" pool is, even for California, an oddity. But it is less so if one thinks of it not so much as a house as the modish hideaway of a hyperhedonistic voluptuary. It seems obvious that Isham, although the scarce literature on him does not dare to mention it, intended the house as his very private erotic amusement center, not unlike a Victorian "sporting-house," for the exclusive use of one man. Shy, and homely to the point of being repulsive, with too much money and nothing serious to do, Isham became an alcoholic and, by energetically pursuing all that was hazardous to his health, managed to die before he had reached forty. During the few years he spent among the Hollywood demimonde, he quickly became the fastest playboy in what was already the fastest set one could find. He spent lavishly and bought all the pleasures he wanted. Of the many stories that surrounded him, one will suffice here to illustrate the point: "The pool warming party was in full swing, with bathtub gin flowing freely, but no Isham. Then the big wooden doors opened and he came roaring into the building in a convertible Duesenberg. . . . Each fender was adorned by a champagne drinking starlet. . . . He drove it right into the pool, where of course it sank, and his white yachting cap came floating up to the surface. A few seconds later so did he."[104]

After Isham's death in 1931, the house was selectively vandalized. A decade or so later, the estate was bought and consecutively enlarged by a series of starkly unpleasant reflecting pools and some residential buildings whose designers desperately but unsuccessfully

101. P. Failing, "William Randolph Hearst's Enchanted Hill," *Art News* 78, no. 1 (January 1979), 53–59.
102. For a filmed revitalization of the fitness facilities, see one particular sequence of the Inspector Columbo sleuth series, "Lovely but Lethal," from 1971(?).
103. Georgia Sargeant, "Casa Blanca by the Sea," *Santa Barbara Magazine* 8, no. 3 (June/July 1982), 47. Thanks to Michael Redmon, Santa Barbara Historical Society.
104. Ibid., 49.

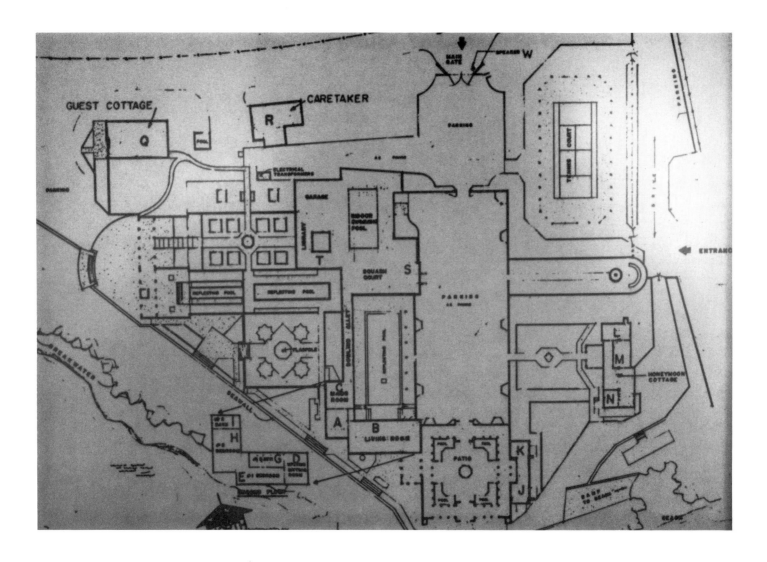

5.47. Isham estate, plan.

tried to recapture the original tone of the place. After a well-meaning but unfinished restoration in the early eighties, the property has been, not entirely unlovingly, developed into a luxury condominium of single-family dwellings, in which the original elements are being restored and kept as the main attractions of the compound.

Tiles for Pools Tile manufacturers such as the local Malibu Potteries, and the larger nationwide firm of Gladding, McBean & Co., based in San Francisco, are important links in the chain of swimming pool history.[105] Malibu Potteries was founded in 1926 "as a response to the strong demand for decorative ceramic tile used in the then prevalent Mediterranean and Spanish Revival architecture."[106] The most popular motifs were multicolored geometric and floral patterns, the product lines being listed in the Standard and Salesman's Pocket Catalogues as "Saracen" and "Moorish." Commonly used for floors, murals, architectural ornament, door trimmings, and stair treads and risers, the tiles also appeared in ornamental fountains, bathrooms, and swimming pools.

Although polychrome glazed tiles had been employed in bathrooms and pools for some time, their use was still regarded as something of a novelty during the teens. In 1911, for example, the predominantly Midwest and East Coast-oriented magazine *The Brickbuilder*, keen to promote clay products, noted that "another development in architectural terra cotta directly due to the polychrome possibilities is its use for interior decoration. . . . The practical sanitary qualities of the bright glaze were partly responsible for the inception of this development. . . . For the same reason polychrome [i.e., bright glazed] water resistant terra cotta has been used in several instances for the decoration of swimming pools and natatoriums. It will be readily seen that the bright glaze is admirably suited for this purpose."[107] These extraordinary tiles—unique in the world—created a totally new pattern of artistic coherence among hydroenthusiastic Pacific Coast hideouts, from San Simeon south to the gardens of Montecito, Isham's Casa Blanca, and the home of the Adamson family, the owners of Malibu Potteries, at Malibu.[108]

For those who could not afford a private pool, the next best thing to have was a fountain. Anderson McCully observed in 1931, "What the open fireplace is to the homes of the North, the tinkle of water in pool and wall fountain is to those beneath a warmer sun. The Moors revered their water with almost the fervor they displayed toward their Koran. Their lasting influence came down to us today through the Spanish heritage of our Southwest to such an extent that our walls seem incomplete without somewhere the splash and shimmer of water breaking."[109] (To create the same auditory effect, Hollywood set designer Cedric Gibbons outfitted his modernist house in the Santa Monica Canyon with "water sprinklers on the copper roof above to create the sound of rain.")[110] California tile manufacturers provided a great number of these wet "fireplaces." Many a splendid fountain still can be found in and around Los Angeles. One of the most splendid waterscapes was created for Bertram Goodhue's Los Angeles

105. *Shapes of Clay* was first issued in 1925 as a quarterly magazine for Gladding, McBean & Co., 660 Market Street, San Francisco. The idea was to publish articles and photos of the many applications of terra-cotta facings and trims for buildings, roofing tiles, faience tiles, fire clay, fire bricks and tiles, garden pottery, and furniture. Swimming pool tiles were not explicitly mentioned then. After gobbling up the Los Angeles Pressed Brick Co. and the Glendale-based Tropico Potteries, Gladding, McBean & Co became in 1927 the largest tile manufacturer on the West Coast. (*Shapes of Clay,* April–May 1927, 23.)
106. Rindge and Doyle, *Ceramic Art of the Malibu Potteries.*
107. *Brickbuilder* 20, no. 12, 65.
108. The tiles for the main house of La Cuesta Encantada, for example, were designed and produced by California Faience, a company that together with Gladding, McBean & Co. and the Malibu Potteries factory supplied most of California's architectural demands. The firm was cofounded and run by William Bragdon who, after its demise, went to work for Gladding, McBean & Co. See Hans van Lemmen, *Tiles in Architecture* (London: Laurence King, 1993), 189.
109. Anderson McCully, [Wall Fountains and Various Materials: The Link between the Garden and the House,] *California Arts and Architecture,* October 1931, 22.
110. Albrecht, *Designing Dreams,* 91.

111. *California Arts and Architecture*, October 1931, 51.
112. Suggested by Charlotte Laubach, Malibu Beach State Museum.
113. [The Beach Home of Mr. and Mrs. M. H. Adamson, Santa Monica,] *California Arts and Architecture*, March 1930, 40–41.

Public Library, with tiles furnished by the Malibu firm. Both the Adamson and Isham houses had octagonal fountains, which became familiar features in houses of comparable scope. George Washington Smith included wall fountains in his work for clients as well as for himself, while the Paul Fagan House at Pebble Beach, which he designed in 1931, featured an Oriental-inspired bathroom. The Hilgartner Marble Company of Los Angeles, responsible for its execution in marble and mosaic, proudly represented it in an ad in *California Arts and Architecture*, explaining that "the lavatory is cut from a solid block of marble; an inspired combination of Byzantine art and modern convenience and luxury."[111]

Swimming pools of the pre–World War II period were usually made of concrete hand-packed onto mesh, finished with either a painted or a tiled surface. The trimmings were executed in decorative tiles, often hand-painted. Scum gutters, characteristic in shape and typical for early swimming pool construction, appeared in the tile firms' catalogues as prefabricated arrangements. The famed pool in Frank Lloyd Wright's Arizona Biltmore Hotel in Phoenix apparently had tiles from the Malibu factory.[112]

One avid client of the tile manufacturers was Merritt H. Adamson, son-in-law of Frederick Rindge, the founder of Malibu Potteries. In an effort to help the ailing firm through the Depression years, Adamson had his weekend house on the Malibu beach (fig. 5.48) almost entirely covered with tiles.[113] The house, pool house, and pool were designed by Stiles O. Clements, of the commercial architectural firm of Morgan, Wall & Clements, who were responsible for several of the more impressive midrise skyscrapers in nearby Los Angeles—among them the former Pellissier Building and the resplendent, tile-covered Richfield Building. In the Adamson house, not only are kitchens and bathrooms but also bedrooms, corridors, halls, and living rooms ceramicized from bottom to top; even rugs have been replaced by imitation tile patterns. Adamson's mania made his dwelling into a showcase/laboratory testing the limits of the product's application. As an extension of the experimental character of the house, the swimming pool, charmingly situated on the Pacific's floodline and therefore subject to the same damaging fluctuations as the Isham pool, served a similar goal, this time for (salt)water-resistant tiles. It also served the staff of the Potteries who, in the interests of empirical knowledge, needed to run a check here and there. It was the rule that at lunchtime everybody took to the wet, either in the nearby Pacific Ocean or the nearby pool (fig. 5.49). It is fitting that the well-preserved Adamson house is the museum for Malibu Potteries, which ceased production after a devastating fire in 1932.

The Price of Los Angeles has two opposing passions: an obsessive fear of earthquakes
Paradise and an equally obsessive desire for swimming pools. Yet this is neither contradictory nor unique, for apocalyptic ruin has often been the price for miraculous healing. In California, the natural forces of destruction are held in high esteem, and

5.48. *Top:* Malibu, California: Adamson house, 1929–1930. Stiles O. Clements. (*California Arts and Architecture,* March 1930.)

5.49. Adamson house, pool house. (*California Arts and Architecture,* March 1930.)

114. Most revealing in this respect is Gladys Hansen and Emmet Condon, *Denial of Disaster: The Untold Story and Photographs of the San Francisco Earthquake and Fire of 1906* (1989; San Francisco: Cameron, 1990). For fear of damaging the image of paradise, the real extent of this greatest of urban devastations was never revealed.

115. Robert H. Boyle, *Sport: Mirror of American Life* (Boston: Little Brown, 1963), 50–51.

even inspire local pride—fire and quake, quake and fire. They belong to the same family of paradoxes that nurtures the belief in paradise; just as America knows total freedom for the elements as well as the inhabitants, at the same time the destructive forces are categorically denied.

Every fall when the tropical storms hit Florida, flimsy wooden structures fly through the air in a willful repetition of last year's disaster. In California, where earthquakes and fires rage annually, people continue to challenge fate by putting up wooden houses, in the belief that wood is cheaper and safer than reinforced concrete. Even after the gruesome devastation of San Francisco in 1906, its inhabitants clung to their tradition of denying the actual dangers of their environment.[114]

Earth and water entertain an uneven relationship there: lots of earth and no water. The little water there is manifestly to be spilled. Amid the fourth consecutive year of drought in 1990, the *Los Angeles Times* of May 6 reported that people—apparently caught in an obsessional neurosis—were, despite the dire circumstances, continuing to water *the sidewalk*. Promotional photographs of real estate agents provide overwhelming illustrative proof of this self-destructive folklore: a 7.25-million-dollar "romantic hideaway" in Bel-Air was promoted for sale in a brochure featuring irresistible color pictures of the house's two sundrenched, yet thoroughly wetted, courtyards.

Wetting the street is a remarkable yet not altogether inexplicable habit. In arid environments the presence of water is a source of life and wealth. In some cultures, such as that of imperial Rome, the spilling of water was considered a sign of great prosperity and power. Roman emperors, in their desire to show their godlike *magnificentia,* almost flooded the capital with the costliest drinking water. Water was brought to the city over hundreds of kilometers of aqueducts at the greatest expense. When it finally arrived, often depleted due to theft and evaporation, it was literally dumped into fountains with no holding capacity, so that it simply rushed away, through the Tiber, ending its brief glittering appearance in the sea. It is scarcely different in southern California, where evaporation of swimming pool water alone accounts for an annual loss of at least 15 percent of the valuable drinking water. During one of the annual droughts it was announced on local television that car washing must be no more frequent than *once a week,* a frequency that would seem prodigal to even the most hyperhydrated and car-loving areas of western Europe. Californians sprinkle their lawn twice a day to make it look like a lush English country garden, rather than adjusting the vegetation to the natural desert conditions.

Sprinkling lawns, wetting sidewalks, washing cars, or filling up swimming pools are all part of the same ideology of making the desert bloom. Southern California is the epitomal perversion of the elements. The dry should be made wet, the hot should be made cold. The ultimate luxury is to turn the world into what it is not.

5.50. Southern California subdivision, aerial view.
Postcard. *Also plate 19.*

All in all, the insatiable appetite for swimming pools and swampy gardens fits logically within this frame. Environmentally speaking, there is one positive side to the swimming pool: a well-filled pool acts as an excellent fire extinguisher. Pool owners are advised to keep a powerful water pump at hand, however, because otherwise it will not work. Often it does not work in any case, because when there is an earthquake-related fire, there usually is no electricity.

The greater Los Angeles area has the largest density of private swimming pools in the world. Flying over the city gives a true indication of the sheer mass of blue patches of pool spread over the landscape. "In 1962, the Outdoor Recreation Commission, established by Congress to evaluate the needs of the Americans by the year 2000, made the first of its reports. . . . The commission found swimming to be the most popular activity. The postwar increase in swimming pools alone had been fantastic. In 1947, there were 11,000 pools in the United States. Now [1962–1963] there are more than 310,000, of which 113,500 are in California. A passenger flying over the Mexican desert can tell when he has crossed the United States border by the swimming pools that suddenly appear below" (fig. 5.50).[115]

six

The Medusa Complex, or the Dark Side of the Pool

Perverse Hydrophobia

. . . Un cygne qui s'était évadé de sa cage,
Et, de ses pieds palmés frottant le pavé sec,
Sur le sol raboteux traînait son blanc plumage.
Près d'un ruisseau sans eau la bête ouvrant le bec

Baignait nerveusement ses ailes dans la poudre,
Et disait, le cœur plein de son beau lac natal:
"Eau, quand donc pleuvras-tu? Quand tonneras-tu, foudre?"
Je vois ce malheureux, mythe étrange et fatal . . .   BAUDELAIRE

In the world of the swimming pool hydrophobia is an ever-present guest.   DARK DICTUM

Epigraph: Charles Baudelaire, "Le cygne," from *Les fleurs du mal* (*Oeuvres complètes,* vol. 1 [Paris: Gallimard, 1975], 86).
1. Sigfried Giedion, *Mechanization Takes Command: A Contribution to Anonymous History* (1948; New York: Oxford University Press, 1969), 35.

Perverse Aquatic restraint is best demonstrated by the swan. The swan is not *in* but **Hydrophobia** on the water; it does not swim but, as Goethe had observed, "glides softly away from us." The swan's performance illustrates one of the basic attitudes toward swimming. Where the summer frog is joyful, irresponsible, and vulgar, the movements of the swan are solemn, disdainful, and respectable. Aristocrats and others naturally appropriate the beast as a heraldic device, seeking to capitalize for social advantage on those very characteristics. Swans really don't seem to enjoy being in the water; they merely stay afloat (fig. 6.2).

The swan's restrained mechanicality has inspired several techniques of perverse hydrophobia. Aquatic anxiety has been successfully counteracted with the help of life preservers, small boats, inflatable mattresses, and rubber beasts. Especially in the period of the Enlightenment, this combination of curiosity and anxiety led to a variety of contraptions, machine- and pedal-driven waterfowl being recurrent themes. In 1738, for example, the legendary mechanical duck of inventor Jacques de Vaucasson made a lasting impression on encyclopedist and leading technophile Denis Diderot, because it could "waddle and swim. It would wag its head, quack and pick up grain, the passage of which could be observed in swallowing movements. A mechanism inside ground up the grain and caused its exit from the body much as in natural circumstances."[1]

Despite his bravura and the general atmosphere of blood, death, and romance surrounding him, the swan king Ludwig II was the least adventurous of all naval explorers. In his exotic indoor swan-pond-cum-swimming-pool in the Linderhof he used to enjoy himself in an incongruous quasi-swan-drawn cockle boat that ran on underwater rails and was driven by an electric motor (fig. 6.3). Little imagination is required to recognize in Ludwig's subterranean Luna Park an experimental Tunnel of Love. Ludwig is here at his radically theatrical best, for his tunnel of love is a derivative of Wagner's biomorphic Venusgrotte. The boat is the tradi-

6.1. *Below: De Stem van het Water* (The Voice of the Water) by Bert Haanstra shown during the cinemaquatic event Film op Waterbasis, at the Amsterdam Zuiderbad, 1990.

6.2. *Right:* Hamburg's swans being taken by boat to their winter quarters. (*NRC Handelsblad,* November 16, 1995; AP photo.)

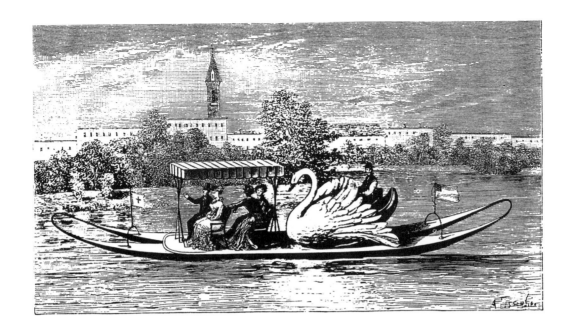

6.3. *Opposite:* Ludwig II and his boatman in his electrically driven cockleshell skiff at Linderhof. (Blunt, *The Dream King*, 1973.)

6.4. Swan boats in Boston Public Garden. (Tissandier, *Six mois aux Etats-Unis*, 1886?)

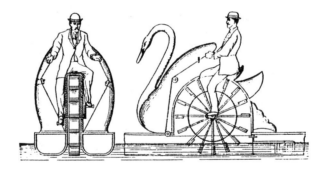

6.5. Olivia de Havilland in a poor man's version of the swan boat. (Lencek and Bosker, *Making Waves*, 1989.)

2. Louise von Kobell, as quoted by Tilman Osterwold, *Ludwig II von Bayern und die Kunst* (1898), cited by Michael Petzet, ed., *König Ludwig II und die Kunst* (Munich: Prestel, 1968), 67.

3. Albert Tissandier, *Six mois aux Etats-Unis; voyage d'un touriste dans l'Amérique du Nord suivi d'une excursion à Panama* (Paris: G. Masson, 1886 [?]), 219–221.

4. Lena Lencek and Gideon Bosker, *Making Waves: Swimsuits and the Undressing of America* (San Francisco: Chronicle Books, 1989), 75.

tional Lohengrinjum, while its scallop shell shape is a clear reference to the birth of Venus. In a brutal travesty of mythology, Venus has metamorphosed into a washed-out Ludwig burdened with the task of dispensing love to himself or his oarsman. The fixed trajectory of the vessel makes the whole thing into the perfect *machine célibataire*. These excursions were submitted to strict programming: "The royal visit took place mostly during the night," reported a contemporary. "First the monarch started to feed the two resident swans . . . then, assisted by a valet, he boarded a gold and silver plated canoe in the shape of a cockle. He then let himself row about the pool, although it was at the same time moved by an underwater electric device."[2]

Lohengrin's swan boats and Ludwig's scallop shell canoe, compacted into the Lohengrinjum, were the forerunners of the pool dinghies, floating mattresses, and inflatable dinosaurs of our time. Among the many punts and park skiffs of early twentieth-century America, the swan boats of the Boston Public Garden were world-famous. In William Cullen Bryant's *Picturesque America* (1872 and later editors), they were extensively illustrated, paddling proudly on the lake. But the most detailed and highly technophilic description is by a Frenchman, Albert Tissandier, in *Six mois aux Etats-Unis* (1886?; fig. 6.4). Tissandier described the swan boats as *vélocipèdes aquatiques,* or *bateaux vélocipèdes.* Such a "water bike," he wrote, "consists of a double hull, connected by a wooden deck, which makes the boat rigid. In front there are fixed seats for four passengers; a light tent protects them from the sun. At the rear is the driver who, with the help of a set of bicycle pedals and a chain, operates a large paddle wheel. This paddle wheel is shrouded by a cover molded in the shape of the raised wings of a gigantic swan." If the voyage was not swift, it nevertheless was elegant: "but in the artificial lakes and rivers of a park, its appearance is graceful and quite original."[3]

Swan-shaped vessels, the gracious Lohengrinjums, continued to do their work in exactly the same environment as Ludwig's tunnel of love. A fine example could be found in the 1937 Gershwin musical *A Damsel in Distress,* directed by George Stevens, with Fred Astaire, Joan Fontaine, George Burns, and Gracie Allen. At one point in the film the dancers are shown at work in and around a tunnel of love through which they travel in pure white Lohengrinjums, ending their journey on water chutes that dump them into an artificial lake. This sophisticated moving stage was used by choreographer Hermes Pan in the rather puzzling dance act for which, amazingly enough, he received an Oscar. Hollywood was equally responsible for the revival of Jacques de Vaucasson's invention, in the form of the monstrously inflated bathtub duck with paddle propulsion that carried Olivia de Havilland as she posed in the "typically tubular suit of the day" (fig. 6.5).[4]

People are drawn to water for a variety of reasons, some frivolous, others philosophical, religious, practical, or macabre. In general the attitude toward water is two-sided—out or in, alive or dead; indeed, one might regard swimming and drowning as the obverse and reverse of the same coin. Still there is, and always has been, a middle way: neither alive nor dead, neither out nor in, but *on* the water. This position is highly ambiguous. The water attracts and rejects at the same time. Somebody who takes to the pool on a rubber mattress is distributing his fears and joys over his vehicle of choice; it is uncertain which of the two has the upper hand, but in boating the scale has tipped in favor of fear as the major mover.

Boating is a latent form of hydrophobia, an impossible love for the element most feared, the dominant complex of the mariner. There is a profound truth in the old saying, "Mariners don't swim." Lord Nelson, to mention just one famous nonswimming mariner, was so intensely hydrophobic that he asked to be buried in St. Paul's and not in Westminster, where he had been consigned to rest in accordance with his status. A swamp originally, the soil of Westminster was still too humid for his eternal peace of mind.

The Medusa Complex Canoeing, punting, boating—all belong to the same category of perverse hydrophobia. Recreative boating has always been a romantic balancing act on the tightrope between danger and safety. The melancholy of the gondolier's song, the fragility of the English punt, and the majesty of the Adirondacks explored in an Indian canoe all represent man's tender submission to the elements. Nothing could better illustrate the subtleties of confrontation than a comparison between two pictures. One is Géricault's painting *The Raft of La Méduse,* 1819 (fig. 6.6), the other a photograph taken by Jacques-Henri Lartigue in 1932 (fig. 6.7) during the filming of *Le roi Pausole* at Eden Roc, Cap d'Antibes. Both display an abundance of seminude bodies scattered over a sailing vessel, and they are quite similar in a compositional sense. The spatial play of legs and arms, pointing in various

6.6. *Above:* Samuel W. Reynolds after Théodore
Géricault, *The Raft of La Méduse*, 1819. (Bazin,
Théodore Géricault, 1987.)
6.7. Jacques-Henri Lartigue, photograph on the set
of *Le roi Pausole*, 1932.

directions, slung over the sides, trailing in the sea, reaching out toward the water, are deceptively similar. In Lartigue's picture, the charming movie extras are suffering from heavy, lazy, summer afternoon languor. Every movement is directed toward the comfort of the cooling water. Limbs are lead-heavy, dangling over the side, skimming the surface of the Mediterranean. Sensuality is also present in the Géricault picture, but it is more exhibitionistic, more provocative. Géricault's bodies are of the muscle beach variety, whereas Lartigue's extras are caught in the nonact of heavy lounging.

What the two pictures have in common is total abandon. All the coquetrie of delightful death is represented: languorous limbs, legs spread wide, a hip upturned provocatively, socks coquettishly slipping off some lazy feet trailing in the wake. Where the two scenes seem similar in a formal sense, the difference is between life and death, between floating and drowning, between Eros and Thanatos. In fact, the shift is deceptive: there is no difference at all. Form and content, although differently intended, converge perfectly. Hydrophobia is what the top half of the raft expresses; the lower half whispers hydrophilia. This is the Medusa complex, the tragic side of hydrophilia: abandon at all costs.

In America, where the relationship between civilization and nature has been more drastically exploited than anywhere in the world, boating and canoeing enlivened family recreation with allusions to the history of adventurous exploration. The sheer number of canoes, rowboats, and gondolas that plied the waters of the American park systems around the beginning of our century must have been overwhelming.[5] Scarcely a postcard sent home by happy vacationers did not show armadas of canoes in the hotel waters, forest ponds, or amusement parks. Rowboats and canoes were pictured parading in sunshine as well as by moonlight. Quite amazing is the colossal number of gondolas, the omnipresent staffage of artificial lakes, canals, and swimming pools from Florida to southern California during the 1920s. The gondola—like the punt, the canoe, and the rowboat—has two functions, one simply to travel on water and the other to add a specific effect, a particular local color, to the environment. The punt refers to the river Thames and the gondola to Venice. But why was Venice such an obligatory point of reference for all sorts of pleasure colonies from St. Augustine and Miami Beach to Los Angeles and Newport Beach? Why Venice in Florida? Why Venice in California?

Although the actual work of Abbot Kinney, cigarette manufacturer ("Sweet Caporal") and founder of Venice, California, is reasonably well documented, the motives of this delirious soul are as yet unknown. Morrow Mayo, chronicler of Los Angeles in the 1930s, recounts: "Chance took Mr. Kinney to an uninhabited stretch of the beach, twenty-five miles from Los Angeles, and there, standing upon barren sand-dunes, gazing out over the blue Pacific, he thought—for some unknown reason—of Italy, and especially of the ancient and lovely city of Venice. . . . With intense emotion he remembered the Grand Canal with its marble palaces, the gondolas slipping silently through the water past the churches, those museums of the fine arts, with their majestic façades. A great inspiration descended upon Abbot Kinney . . . he determined to create there a replica of Venice!"[6]

5. Foster Rhea Dulles, *A History of Recreation: America Learns to Play* (New York: Appleton-Century, 1965), 357.
6. On Kinney's Venice see Morrow Mayo, *Los Angeles* (New York: Knopf, 1933), 203–210.

6.8.   *Top:* Venice, California. (Mayo, *Los Angeles,*
        1933.)
6.9.   Naples, California, canals. *Also plate 20.*

6.10. Coral Gables, Florida: Venetian pool. (Postcard.)

7. Ibid., 207.

Kinney acted instantly and started to dig a maze of canals in the coastal marshes, then had the gondolas made (fig. 6.8). "Boats could be made in Southern California," Mayo innocently suggested, "but that did not appeal to Mr. Kinney. He imported from old Venice a fleet of graceful gondolas, and to man the water-taxis he brought over from the same place twenty-four real, live gondoliers." Venice in America was opened in 1905. But "the Italian gondoliers were not happy. . . . Their songs died out. Gradually they disappeared. One of them became so desolate and so desperate that he got into his gondola and propelled himself through the main canal out into the Pacific Ocean, determined to scull his way back to Italy. He was blown ashore at Ocean Park, a few miles down the beach."[7]

This nostalgic success story of urbanistic courage and childish imagination inevitably ended in bankruptcy, in 1925. The Venice adventure was matched somewhat by the foundation in 1903 of Naples, a little to the south below the city of Long Beach. The layout of this other paradise consisted of more or less concentric canals, faintly reminiscent of Amsterdam and having absolutely nothing to do with Naples. That this vision of the Old World, awarded to a certain Arthur Persons, was mistaken in its origin is irrelevant. What counted was to build an attractive system of waterways on which prospective homeowners could parade their canoes, gondolas, and a variety of other modest vessels. Even swimming through the canals was—and still is—a serious possibility (fig. 6.9).

Another quasi-urban development combining navigation and natation within the same architectural environment was George Merrick's picturesque-continental illusion at Coral Gables, near Miami, Florida. Merrick was a thematic bricoleur who, with the help of decorator Phineas Paist (who had worked for James Deering on Vizcaya) and landscape designer

8. Hap Hatton, *Tropical Splendor* (New York: Knopf, 1987), 60–62.
9. Marc Wanamaker of Los Angeles, collector of Hollywood paraphernalia and movie-related pictures, provided me with these rarities. Judging by the shape of Skelton's pool, the picture should date from the mid-forties.
10. The Benny estate was located on 1002 Roxbury, according to a photo in the Huntington Library: Paddock Engineering, 1940. 07-26-1940.
11. *Architectural Digest,* April 1992, 158. Sturges was said to have had one wish when he purchased his residence, which was to put in a kidney-shaped pool.
12. The Getz estate and pool ostensibly figured in the 1966 sleuth film *Harper,* starring Paul Newman, Janet Leigh, Robert Wagner, and Lauren Bacall. It is significant that not one single stroke is swum in this glorious pool. However, at one point Robert Wagner can be observed floating on an inflatable mattress at about the same spot as where Miss Davies performed her rowing act. In a 1973 installment of *Columbo,* the Getz pools are given extensive yet purely decorative attention.

Frank Button (who had gained pond-building experience designing Lincoln Park in Chicago), created a suburb that alluded to various European stylistic associations, one of which happened to be Venetian. The plans were drawn in 1920 and the last buildings, including the splendiferous Miami Biltmore Hotel, were finished in 1926. It was for one of the dominantly aquatic neighborhoods that Merrick employed the "Venetian" style.[8] The largest single surface was occupied by the "Venetian Pool," a construction that suggests navigable water while at the same time conforming to the hygienic and constructional restrictions of a swimming pool. To indicate its dual character, swimmers maneuver Indian canoes around picturesque obstacles (fig. 6.10). It is also the first of all those aquatic theme parks that later, in the 1980s, would become so fashionable.

Venice and Naples are inhabited water parks, not unlike the present-day golf course communities, where living and playing have been strictly interlocked and where no escape is possible, unless one chooses to follow the path of the homesick gondolier through the big waves of the Pacific. The historical theming of water, no less than its rigorous technological management, indicates a latent hydrophobia at work.

Like the mariners in the *Raft of La Méduse,* movie stars often show a passionate desire to keep dry even when wearing bathing costumes of increasing provocation. It is fascinating indeed to study promotional photographs of stars from the 1920–1950 period. They were usually shown surrounded by the attributes of their status, very often their swimming pools. The puzzling thing about these photographs is that they show the stars not in but on their pools, steering a wide variety of vessels. However modest the size of the pool, if a canoe could be wedged in, it is there. Comedian Red Skelton, for example, illustrates the hydrophobic mariner by paddling a canoe through his ill-fitting free-form pool in nautical dress (fig. 6.11).[9]

The preferred outfit for movie stars of both sexes who posed dry in their pools was heavy tweeds. On several occasions in the 1930s, Douglas Fairbanks and Mary Pickford were pictured in their canoe on the lake-sized pool of Pickfair, in an attire intended for a grouse-hunting party in the Scottish Highlands rather than a canoe ride on a Hollywood swimming pool (fig. 6.12). A portrait of Jack Benny poses him on his recently finished elegant double-apsidal pool, constructed by the firm of Paddock in 1938 (fig. 6.13); Benny is paddling through the pool dressed in tweeds, shoehorned into the tiniest of dinghies.[10] Allan Jones, Raquel Torres, and Bing Crosby had dinghies in their pools identical in size and model to the one Benny owned. Particularly telling is a photograph of writer Preston Sturges in his free-form swimming pool, paddling away in a minute dinghy (fig. 6.14).[11]

A most daring and at the same time painfully restricted boat ride was performed by Marion Davies in the waterworks of her newly aquired estate in Beverly Hills, the former Milton Getz estate, in 1952 (fig. 6.15).[12] Miss Davies is photographed from a high point, about the second floor of the house, sitting in a rowboat placed in a cascaded pool. The cascade is part of a dramatic layout, designed by the famed landscape architect Paul G. Thiene in 1927

6.11. Red Skelton on his California pool. (Marc Wanamaker/Bison Archives.)

6.12. Douglas Fairbanks and Mary Pickford on the Pickfair pool. (Marc Wanamaker/Bison Archives.)

6.13. *Opposite:* Jack Benny on his Paddock pool, 1938. (Marc Wanamaker/Bison Archives.)

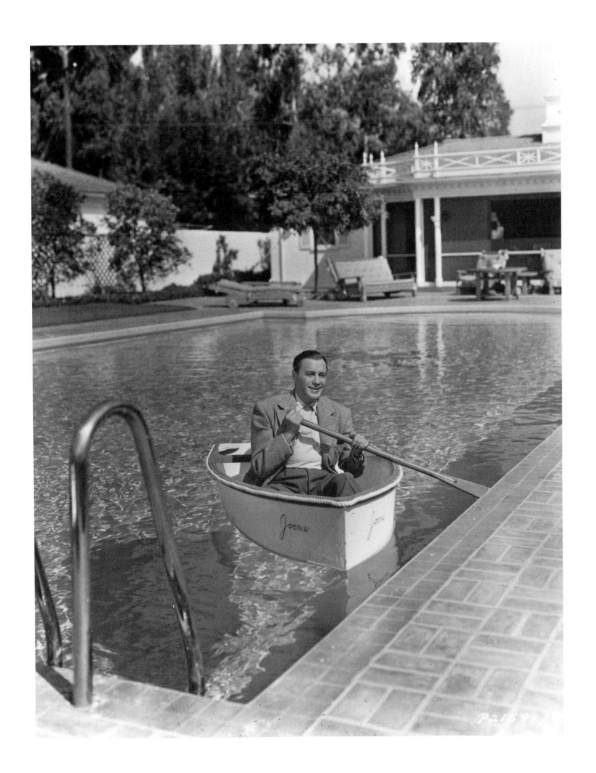

6.14. *Left:* Preston Sturges on his kidney-shaped pool. (*Architectural Digest,* April 1992.)

6.15. Marion Davies with new husband Horace Brown, on the pool of the former Getz estate; see fig. 4.22. (Charles Lockwood, Los Angeles.)

(see fig. 4.21), originally intended to include three identical ponds leading to a circular basin in which a fountain was placed. The ponds were filled with lilies and the water lazily trickled downward over generously curved thresholds.

What was the meaning of all this? In the Pickford-Fairbanks case, it might be argued that the canoe was there to measure the immense size of the pool (55 by 100 feet, about 17 by 30 meters). And in such a veritable river, the canoe and its passengers suggested necessity rather than luxury. In the case of Marion Davies, however, the presence of the boat is inexplicable. Technically, the boat had to be brought in from the (invisible) terrace, which, apart from being aesthetically jarring, was hardly an action to be performed every day. Moreover, there was no way out except being dumped twice over the concrete thresholds of the cascade that eventually led to the swimming pool at the far end. And finally, owing to the narrowness of the cascade, rowing was impossible and dangerous. It was not intended that Marion Davies would pull at the oars or cover any distance. Rather, she was meant to perform a ritual the meaning of which has since escaped us. Bragging and related vanities, common to those who like to communicate their good fortune to others, were obviously part of these astonishing stagings.[13]

But perhaps we should try to accommodate this remarkable conflict of attraction and repulsion within a number of older traditions that are reasonably well documented in the history of architecture and garden design. Take the so-called *ephemeralia,* or festive architecture, in which ships, boats, and rafts were produced to enliven garden parties and on which the partygoers—nonswimmers naturally—could be found fully dressed navigating ornamental pools and baths. It is a tradition going back as far as the *naumachiae* or naval battles of the Romans and their cultural heirs, the princes of the Renaissance (fig. 6.16), all performing mock sea battles in scaled-down warships in inundated parts of the palace grounds. Most imaginative were the ones staged in the Palazzo Pitti under Ferdinando de' Medici, Grand Duke of Tuscany, in 1589.[14] The courtyard of the palace was sealed off and quickly flooded by five feet of water. Eighteen miniature galleys manned by extravagantly dressed Christian warriors were lowered into the newly constructed pool and a marine attack against a Turkish fortress ensued.

Of a lesser magnitude were the various boating parties held in Istanbul in the seclusion of the Topkapi palace. For a long time students of Ottoman culture thought that the odalisques took an occasional bath in the pools of the harem, but recent archaeological evidence suggests that these ladies took to the pool in "small rowboats."[15]

Movie stars, like their predecessors in the public entertainment business—absolutist kings ("Sun King" and "movie star" both refer to heavenly bodies) and neo-aristocrats of the East Coast—aspired to possess in private what the common man could only enjoy as part of public provisions. Thus Douglas Fairbanks, as a manifestation of his sublime status, had brought the ocean to his home. On certain occasions he took to his miniature ocean in a canoe, demonstrating his status to the public. Like Versailles, Pickfair was a reflection of the

13. For the American culture of bragging, see Thomas A. P. van Leeuwen, *The Skyward Trend of Thought* (Cambridge: MIT Press, 1987), 137. The original owner indeed claimed that by building this pool he "brought the Pacific Ocean to Beverly Hills."

14. Roy Strong, *Art and Power: Renaissance Spectacles, 1450–1650* (Berkeley: University of California Press, 1984), 55, 80, 144. Not entirely in the same vein and certainly less bellicose were the so-called "magnificences" of Fontainebleau, staged by Catherine de Médicis in 1564, and the festival at Bayonne of 1565. A number of them were depicted in the Valois tapestries. The Bayonne festival was concluded by a water feast in which Catherine and her party sailed through a series of canals—although, alas, not specially dug for the occasion—and as they journeyed they passed a series of scenes depicting all sorts of marine marvels: an attack on a whale, Tritons riding a tortoise, etc. The whole thing must have looked like the Cave of the Pirates in Disneyland, California.

15. Leslie Pierce, "Topkapi: The Sultanate of Women," *FMR* 15 (October 1985), 71, 100. "In the large pond outside the building [the Kiosk of Osman III], discovered during recent excavations, the women of the harem amused themselves in small rowboats."

16. Charles Lockwood, *Dream Palaces: Hollywood at Home* (New York: Viking Press, 1981), 183.

17. Angelo Cantoni et al., *La Villa Lante di Bagnaia* (Milan: Electa, 1961), 40, 42, 48, and fig. 34, showing the *quadrato* in a remarkable drawing by Robert Adam of 1757. The barge as a fountain is an interesting semiosis. The water spout acts as the attribute of its own ultimate destruction. Other popular recipro-destructive images are window dressings of the stuffed fox-disguised-as-hunter and pig-dressed-as-butcher type carrying the tools of their own martyrdom.

18. Anthony Blunt, *Guide to Baroque Rome* (London: Granada, 1982), 232.

grand works of nature reduced to controllable dimensions, for possessing nature was part of the superhuman performance of the movie star. A star of the dimensions of Harold Lloyd had the unspoken obligation to own, apart from his "public"-sized swimming pool, an "800 foot long canoe pond."[16]

Stone Boats Frequently pools and ponds were the stage for yet another confusing display of perversion: stone boats, found in Renaissance garden structures, fountains, and ponds along with other *pièces de milieu* like stone crustaceans, mollusks, and the familiar putti, but rather more bizarre. A well-known example is the *quadrato* in the garden of the Villa Lante at Bagnaia, which accommodates four stone barges spouting water.[17] Stone barges, like lead balloons, bronze birds, and marble angels, are perversions of material integrity. Instead of being in its characteristic delicate state of not sinking, the ship is now weighed down by its ridiculous mass, sitting on the bottom, immovable like an island. These vessels are mysterious things. Why are they spouting water—are they represented in a state of acute sinking? Is it because they are reminders of the fragile balance between floating and sinking, swimming and drowning?

Conservative explanations hint at the repetition of earlier models such as ancient Roman ship fountains or the celebrations at the supposed site of emperor Domitian's *naumachia,* or yet again suggest allusions to the ship of the church. At least this is how they were presented by Anthony Blunt in his description of possibly the most famous of the stone boat families, the barque on the Piazza di Spagna, Rome, erected from 1627 to 1629.[18] Yet none of these explanations is ultimately convincing.

The stone Venetian barge (fig. 6.17) in the bay of James Deering's Vizcaya is another puzzling case. It is most likely that Deering conceived his island-boat as a mnemonic device to remind him and his guests of the discovery of Florida by the Spaniards in 1513. Dumping the mythical trireme in front of his house—not unlike the steel and plaster yacht that was supposed to have delivered Columbus to the Chicago fairgrounds in 1893—he realized his dream of reversing the course of fate. Instead of founding his estate where Ponce de Leon had landed, he had Ponce de Leon land at his estate! Deering's barge and Sir Clough Williams-Ellis's 70-ton two-master in Portmeirion, Wales (see chapter 4), are Western varieties of the cargo cult worship, urgently begging the spirit to settle on the selected spot. The house would certainly gain in value if Ponce de Leon, or maybe even Columbus, were to return to paradise on earth. The most drastic of all ecological estrangements is Gabriele D'Annunzio's installation of the cruiser *Puglia* high up in the park of his villa at Gardone (fig. 6.18).

6.16. *Naumachia* from J. B. Fischer von Erlach,
Entwurff einer historischen Architectur (1721).

6.17. *Below:* Vizcaya, stone boat.
6.18. *Right:* Gardone, Italy: the cruiser *Puglia* at
D'Annunzio's villa.

Rubber Things Almost from the date of the reinvention of swimming, extension pieces such as webbed feet made of oilcloth, dry suits, and inflatable things of all kinds were launched into the swimming pool. Simon Schama notes that a certain Jean-François Pilâtre de Rozier, inventor of hot air balloons and expert on subaquatic activities, offered demonstrations of a "watertight robe" in 1782 in his Musée des Sciences in Paris. "Over seven hundred subscribers signed on from all ranks and conditions and heard Pilâtre himself lecture on the art of swimming as well as demonstrate a watertight robe by emerging dry from a bath filled to a depth of six feet."[19]

Such contraptions, often outrageously dangerous (figs. 6.19, 6.20), form the material ingredients of the cultural history of swimming. Inflatable mattresses and plastic objects in the shapes of dolphins, crocodiles, ducks, and dinosaurs have become familiar pool paraphernalia (fig. 6.21). Amazingly, creatures that normally are held responsible for the depopulation of vast stretches of water are, in their inflatable personas, considered to be saviors of mankind. A commercial message features a girl in a white bikini floating on the back of an inflatable alligator, giving an ironic turn to the trope of Innocence Saved by Her Aggressor (fig. 6.22).

Even movie stars have appeared as inflatable effigies in the wet landscape. Jayne Mansfield once posed on a mattress in her own swimming pool surrounded by a multitude of floating rubber versions of herself (fig. 6.23). Sometimes swimming pools are so completely covered with floating objects that the water is invisible and impenetrable. As the visualization of unsinkable reliability, a swimming pool filled with life preservers illustrated the campaign of mutual investment company Robeco most convincingly.

Few photographs are better able to demonstrate the ambiguities of the swimming pool than society photographer Slim Aarons's picture of a relaxed get-together at the pool on the George Newhall estate at Burlingame near San Francisco. The picture is a study in social discomfort (fig. 6.24). Draped on the lawn are seven ladies of indeterminable age dressed in the garb of a lost era. Lost also is the girl in a bathing suit floating on a rubber mattress in the center of the pool. On the opposite bank sits a witch dressed in black, intensely observing the girl's eventual metamorphosis into a swan. How do we know all this? Because the swimming pool was originally a swan pond, and the girl on the float and the feathery creatures on the lawn are emancipated versions of Lohengrin's enchanted knights. The Newhall house and gardens were designed in 1914 by Walter Hobart and, like many other bourgeois castles, were modeled after the Petit Trianon. Aarons recalled: "Mrs. Newhall personally designed the gardens, and these also reflect Versailles [more or less standard procedure, as we now know]. Originally the swimming pool was a lake with swans, but Dorothy Spreckles, who bought the house, converted the lake into a pool and gave the swans to Golden Gate Park."[20]

As a logical consequence it would be entirely plausible that swimming pool owners, having no desire to get wet themselves, would leave the swimming entirely to their

19. Simon Schama, *Citizens: A Chronicle of the French Revolution* (New York: Knopf, 1989), 126. See also chapter 1, note 22, above.
20. Slim Aarons, *A Wonderful Time: An Intimate Portrait of the Good Life* (New York: Harper and Row, [1974?]), "San Francisco," n.p. The picture was taken in the 1950s. See also Kelly Klein, *Pools* (New York: Knopf, 1992), 136–137, inserts 4–5. Ms. Klein dates the pool "in the late 1920's."

Perverse Hydrophobia

6.19. Poolaris. (Shivers and Hjelte, *Planning Recreational Places*, 1971.)
6.20. *Below:* Rollaris. (Shivers and Hjelte, *Planning Recreational Places*, 1971.)

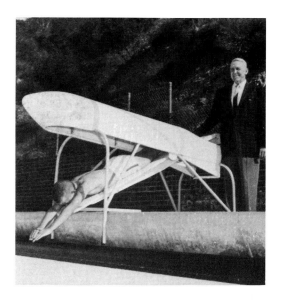
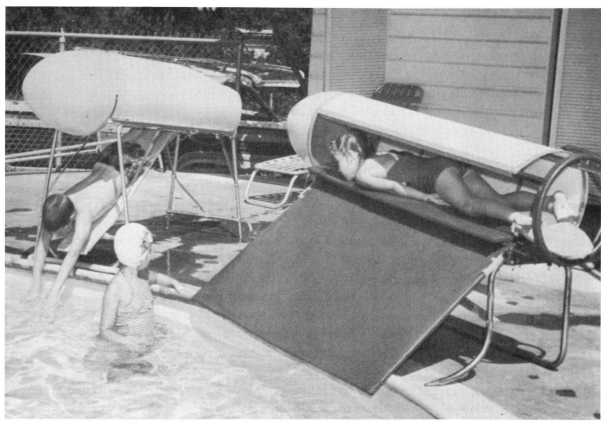

248

6.21. Jacques-Henri Lartigue, photo of Zissou.
(Postcard.)

6.22. *Below:* The girl on the alligator: innocence
saved by her aggressor. (*TWA Ambassador,* June
1987.)

6.23. *Opposite:* Jayne Mansfield in her pool.
(Postcard.)

6.24. Burlingame, California: Newhall estate, photo
of pool by Slim Aarons. (Aarons, *A Wonderful
Time,* 1974.)

21. Quoted in Lockwood, *Dream Palaces*, 70.
22. See Julie Baumgold, "A Robert Evans Production: The Good Life at the Top in Hollywood," *New West,* September 13, 1976, 22.
23. Peter Adam, *Eileen Gray: Architect/ Designer* (London: Thames and Hudson, 1987), 237.

waterfowl. Such was the case with the "King of Comedy" Mack Sennett, producer of innumerable Keystone Kops and Bathing Beauties shorts. Owning a house with a swimming pool in the Hollywood Hills, Sennett found no other use for the pool than to keep a large flock of ducks. "Mother was partial to ducks," Sennett recalled in his autobiography, "and the studio kept my tennis courts and swimming pool overstocked."[21]

Pièce de Milieu Pools like the Newhall/Spreckles one were never intended to be the scenes of aquatic frolicking. Their function was monumental and allegorical. They separated the house from the garden and the dry from the wet. The fact that they were swimmable did not necessarily turn them into pools for human athletic recreation. Even after monumental water had been transformed into recreational water, and ponds had become pools, the original character continued to dominate. The Newhall pool was never able to shed its origin; the best the owners could do was to keep it as a social *pièce de milieu,* exactly what most pools still aspire to. It has often been noted that potential bathers keep a respectful distance from the wet; the nearest they can come to showing their original goodwill is to sit on or near the edge.

Diving boards could also offer civilized sitting space, until the 1950s when most boards were removed, leaving their mountings as the silent witnesses of a happier period. A good example of the transformation into *pièce de milieu* was the former Pendleton pool in Beverly Hills. (Later it was owned by Robert Evans, who kept the pool in its original state, retaining even the dated wrought-iron furniture, which he often used as backdrop for photographic portraits of himself.)[22] The best picture remains the one Aarons made of an informal gathering in 1953 (fig. 6.25), carefully arranged around a central axis. At the far end of the axis, a fireplace heats the pool house, suggesting a cold day, yet the parasols are out and deck chairs and cushions have been arranged in sunbathing positions. Along the lateral axis, their backs turned toward the pool, host and guests entertain each other with all the relaxed look of a group of pyramids along the banks of the Nile. At the far right, partly covered by a parasol, are the stilts of the dismantled springboard.

The dry use of the pool is, in fact, the normal one. A pool containing water presents more dangers than merely drowning. For example, modernist architect and designer Eileen Gray refrained from filling the pool of her house at Cap-Martin because the stagnant water might attract unfriendly bugs.[23] We often find photographs of family members and guests around a pool, flung away from the middle as if by centrifugal force. If it so happens that there are people in the pool, they usually are hydraulic performers or musicians (fig. 6.26). The archetype of half-submerged music-making was of course the Wagnerian soprano Josephine Scheffsky, who waded through the swan pond on the roof of the Residenz in Munich to bring herself within courtship distance of her idol, King Ludwig II (see chapter 2). It may be some

6.25. Beverly Hills, California: Pendleton estate, photo of pool by Slim Aarons. (Aarons, *A Wonderful Time*, 1974.) *Also plate 21.*

6.26. "Jazzy Waters," Paris in the 1930s (?). (Sygma-Keystone, 1979.)

time yet before large-scale opera productions take to the pool, although the performance in 1991 of the Bordeaux version of Mozart's *Così fan tutte* against a backdrop of the Roman Pool at San Simeon is a modest beginning.[24]

The Bathing Beauty and the Lit de Parade Once one is aware of the amazing variety of improper applications of the swimming pool, the interesting genre of promotional photography opens new perspectives. In the 1930s, concurrent with the emergence of the private swimming pool, the film industry began to annex its appealing properties, while movie stars would use their pools as a fitting backdrop for off-studio activities and their semipublic social lives. With promotional photography employed to register these activities, stars increasingly were posed in, around, in front of, or in the near vicinity of their pools.

The connotations are endless. In the beginning the pools acted as unworldly, shining halls of mirrors, cut out of the soft turf of the traditional garden, radiating the pale blue hues of the sky. Pool and star acted in constant mutual support; whatever messages were emitted by the one were immediately reinforced by the other. Usually the star was pictured not so much *in* as *near* the pool, or rather, against the *background* of the pool, wearing a swimsuit, although few stars had actually been in the water. Instructive in its clinical serenity is a picture of Jean Harlow posing on the stepladder of her newly installed pool (fig. 6.27). Here the pool functions as a *lit de parade;* the star receives her guests in the modern version of the king's nightgown: a satin bathing suit. Intimacy has become part of the public domain, in the process becoming hard and inaccessible. Another star, Ava Gardner, also poses on the steps of her pool (fig. 6.28). In this case public intimacy has been given a touch of all too human clumsiness. The apparently everyday scene includes a carpenter, oblivious to the presence of star and photographer, cutting boards in the upper left corner of the picture. Why was he left in? Was it to enhance the ordinary character of the spectacle? With one leg halfway in the water and the other treading the upper rung, the star seems to explain the use of the pool to a lay public, smiling, no effort involved.

This instructional scene of the 1950s is not altogether without relevance. It shows the transition from the traditional bathing beauty to what became known as the pinup.[25] Whereas in the earlier publicity stills the pool had served as a reinforcement of stardom, in the later variety it provided an excuse for undressing. During the ruthless neopuritanism of the postwar years, posing in partial nudity could only escape the censor by suggesting an athletic rationale. In the pinup genre, parts of the swimming pool were inserted into the picture in order to secure legal respectabilty. Understandably, springboards offered the maximum associational power. A glimpse of one was enough to defuse even the lewdest pose. Under studio lights a glamorous Esther Williams was seductively respectable, in a daring proto-wet-look swimsuit, balancing on the tip of a diving board (see fig. 5.3). Marilyn Monroe in the 1950s was

24. The sets were by Hans Schavernoch. See *Opéra International,* July/August 1991.
25. See Richard Martin and Harold Koda, *Splash! A History of Swimwear* (New York: Rizzoli, 1990), 49ff.

6.27. Jean Harlow at the ladder of her newly installed
pool. (Marc Wanamaker/Bison Archives.)
6.28. *Opposite:* Ava Gardner on the steps of her new
pool. (Marc Wanamaker/Bison Archives.)

Epigraph: From a newspaper advertisement, quoted in *Spa and Pool News*, November 17, 1986, 94.

26. The Byzantine emperor Romanos III Argyros was forcibly drowned while bathing in his tub in the bathroom of his palace in Constantinople, whereas Charlotte Corday relied on the use of a knife to stab Marat in the back, while the poor man was sitting and writing letters in the mobile bath in his own living room. Romanos III Argyros ruled from 1028 to 1034. See W. Schleyer, *Bäder und Badeanstaltan* (Leipzig: Carl Scholtze, 1909), 169.

27. V. K. Jarvinen, "Risk Factors in Dental Erosion," *Journal of Dental Research* 70, no. 6 (1991), 942–947. Retold by M. A. J. Eykman, *NRC Handelsblad*, December 12, 1991, 2 of Science Section.

able to evoke the most daring tableaux vivants so long as she stayed in the vicinity of a swimming pool. Hundreds of starlets and pinup girls could expose a maximum of skin as long as a handrail or the mere sliver of a springboard could be glimpsed.

This testifies to an increasing resistance to the wet. An example of this evolution can be observed in a frightening case of synthetic domestication: Virginia Mayo and Ronald Reagan posing for a promotional still for *The Girl from Jones Beach* of 1949. The picture was intended to show the two in a flirtatious pose balanced on the end of a makeshift diving board. Harsh shadows from different directions emphatically reveal the presence of studio lamps. The artificiality of the light, the quaintness of the props, and the dryness of the bodies have transposed the scene from its original wet surroundings to a thoroughly dehydrated environment. The lovers from Jones Beach have turned into an alarmingly middle-aged couple, sitting partly undressed on the bare frame of their living room settee.

The Killer Pool *The only safe pool is a pool filled with sand.*

Water is a lethal element and swimming a dangerous business, as it always has been. Assassins and murderers have felt attracted to the idea of combining the inherent dangers of bathing with other deadly means.[26] Countless murder movies have situated the ultimate crime in pools, tubs, and showers. Although strictly nonviolent, Mike Nichols's cult movie *The Graduate* (1967) is full of references to the swimming pool as a potential threat to life. Significant is the scene in which the graduate (Dustin Hoffman) sets out to explore the home swimming pool in a watertight rubber suit. Outside, his movements are slow and clumsy, accompanied by heavy breathing. Inside, entirely closed off from the world, where neither sound nor smell are allowed and where vision is limited to inarticulate blueness, he finds no other incentive than to lie down in silence like a dead frog. The lifeless environment of the bottom of the pool looks like the site of a nuclear disaster, and its toxicity has driven swimmers to the use of a frogman's suit. Swimming without proper protection belongs to a period of romantic naivete. Today, even swimming without a protective mask could pose serious health problems. The latest of the minor pool-related disasters is erosion of the incisors and frontal molars, resulting from frequent exposure to water with too much chlorination and too high a pH, as is often the case with competition pools.[27]

The microenvironment of the pool is a complex system of very dangerous chemicals that act as clarifiers, sterilizers, disinfectants, colorants, and purifiers. The immediate goal of these disinfectants is to fight the pool's major pollutant: the swimmer. With the first plunge the average bather introduces 600 million microbes, while a class of children pollutes a basically clean pool in a couple of seconds. Fast-acting killers are necessary, but the toxic agents must be balanced in such a way that they destroy bacteria without fatally poisoning

28. Richard Alleman, *The Movie Lover's Guide to Hollywood* (New York: Harper and Row, 1985), 113.

29. *Saturday Evening Post,* August 11, 1951.

30. Robert Burton, *The Anatomy of Melancholy* (1621; London: Dent, 1972). See introduction, note 8, above.

31. Carrie McLean, "Child Drownings Stir Controversy," *Pool and Spa News,* November 17, 1986, 94. Far more dangerous than the fairly innocent small private pools are the contemporary aquaparks with their water slides, water jets, and other lethal equipment. With alarming regularity bathers (swimming is hardly possible in these shallow entertainment pools) are killed or seriously injured by hitting hard objects on their way from the launching point to the water, or by other bathers catapulted from the slides and chutes by powerful waterjets. (*De Telegraaf* [Amsterdam], June 17, 1996.)

the swimmer. Evidently a certain level of poisoning is considered acceptable, on the grounds that it is better to leave the pool with irritated eyes, throat, and skin than with cholera or veteran's disease. Thus taking a dip is a calculated risk.

The folklore of liability suits and the consequent legal, environmental, and social anxiety has reduced enthusiasm for pools considerably. Springboards and other diving equipment have long since been removed from poolside. Fences and electronic warning systems have been installed to keep people, especially drunkards and children, away from the water. Children in particular are at risk. Movie director Cecil B. De Mille owned a circular pool at his estate on Laughlin Park Drive, Hollywood Hills, which he had drastically fenced in for fear of precisely such an accident (fig. 6.29). But fate had it that one of De Mille's grandchildren had to meet death in paradise, despite all precautions. In the summer of 1942, the two-year-old son of De Mille's daughter Katherine and actor Anthony Quinn ventured into the neighboring garden of actor-comedian and legendary mysopaedist W. C. Fields, and drowned.[28]

Fearsome fictions could keep toddlers out of the family swimming pool. Jack Benny—the same who had preferred tweeds to swimming trunks—had a giant octopus with bloodthirsty red eyes set in mosaic on the bottom of his pool (fig. 6.30). Children didn't dare to come near it. Later, when the children had grown up and he wanted some youthful company, he had the eyes removed from the octopus.[29] The octopus in the pool reminds us of Robert Burton's comment in *The Anatomy of Melancholy* (1621) that hydrophobia is "so called because the parties affected cannot endure the sight of water, or any liquor, supposing still they see a mad dog in it."[30]

Since pools have proved a serious danger, ultrasensitive security systems and improbably solid palisades have transformed the once-friendly family pool into a real menace, especially in the angst-ridden southwestern states. "With more than 300,000 pools and spas in the countywide area south of Los Angeles, drowning is the largest single cause of death for Orange County children," the Orange County Trauma Center reported in 1986. Understandably, residents are sharing an increasing concern that death is in their midst and that Arcadia would be less dangerous if it were less lush.[31] As a consequence many pools have been filled in and made into tennis courts or Japanese rock gardens. Another method would be to transform the tennis court back into a decorative pool, with this difference: the swimming would be left to those who are best equipped, namely frogs, waterfowl, and fishes. This is the latest development, and a very fashionable one at that, as the following chapter will develop.

6.29. *Page 259:* Hollywood Hills, California: Cecil B. De Mille estate, fenced-in pool. (Marc Wanamaker/Bison Archives.)

6.30. Jack Benny's pool with its octopus guardian. (*Saturday Evening Post,* 1951.) *Also plate 22.*

seven

The Zoo in the Pool

Modern architecture has selected the penguin as its hydrodynamic experimental pet.
SALLY DARWIN RAND

1. W. Schleyer, *Bäder und Badeanstalten* (Leipzig: Carl Scholtze, 1909), 738. See also Felix Genzmer, *Bade- und Schwimmanstalten*, in Josef Durm et al., eds., *Handbuch der Architektur*, 4:5:3 (Stuttgart: Arnold Bergsträsses Verlagsbuchhandlung, 1899), 271–275: "Anhang Bäder für Thiere." These two sources are the only ones featuring examples of this particular kind of pool. Scattered information may be found in publications on horse care and maintenance, such as Tim Hawcroft, *An Illustrated Handbook of Horse and Pony Care* (London and New York, 1986), 76–77. Hawcroft writes:

Swimming is an excellent form of exercise, serving as a change of routine to alleviate boredom, to help maintain fitness that has been developed, to provide hydrotherapy for horses with leg injuries and as an alternative to the morning exercise when conditions are not suitable for it.

Swimming has very little effect on the horse's cardio-vascular or respiratory system and furthermore is not a total substitute for canter work. Horses can swim in the ocean, in a river or in specially designed pools. . . . The horse can be held from the back of a small boat when swimming and taken into water deep enough for its feet to be just off the bottom. The first time the boat moves in a small semicircle, back to shallow water, where the horse can stand. Most horses are natural swimmers, but a few panic. When you are happy with the horse's confidence in the water, gradually increase the actual swimming time or the distance of each visit.

2. John Hinds, *Veterinary Surgery, and Practice of Medecine* [sic] (London, 1829), 476. He cites the case of stableman Denis Lawler, who would ride his horse to a convenient depth in the Bay of Dublin, jump forward suddenly on the animal's neck, and "souse it head-foremost to the bottom." One day the animal struck back and that was the last of Lawler.
3. J. H. Walsh, *The Horse in the Stable and the Field: The Varieties; Management; in Health and Disease; Anatomy; Physiology* (London, 1883), 266–269, gives drawings and plans of "The Turkish Bath" for horses, and the May 2, 1884, issue of *Building News* (London) reminds its readers that "the Turkish Bath has become an established institution in this country; men of all classes now use it for sanitary as well

It has been said that most land animals swim by instinct, but to assume that all do so instinctively is misleading. Although it may be true that an animal, after it has been thrown or forced into the water, is able to stay afloat for a while, to define such an action as swimming is bound to be an overstatement. The dogpaddle struggle for a safe haven requires unexpected quantities of energy and quickly exhausts the animal. A bit of instruction in the art of swimming would certainly help, and most animals need that bit as much as their human relatives.

"Numerous animals like to take a dip as often as they can," wrote Schleyer in his monumental study on the bathhouses of nineteenth-century Germany, "but an equally large number take to the water only if there is no other means of escape. Dogs and horses are among the most frequent swimmers. Canines often express an inexplicable craving for water; even bitter cold does not prevent a dip. Indeed, fear of water in dogs is so unnatural that it is commonly taken as a sign of illness."[1] The enthusiasm of the horse for bathing seems more commonly related to therapy than to sheer delight. "Swimming the horse 'for strains in the shoulder joint' was a favourite remedy," John Hinds told his early nineteenth-century readers. "Some people submit their horses to 'bathing' by entire submersion."[2] For as long as professional horse care has existed, swimming and bathing horses has been a theme in equestrian theory and practice, and quadrupeds have experienced aqueous pleasures that many humans have never enjoyed: it was not uncommon to have a horse take a sweat in a Turkish bath. Books on horse management as well as handbooks on the architecture of bathhouses illustrate with earnest sincerity plans and sections of luxurious conveniences.[3]

Vegetius, the classical military historian, reported that teaching a horse to swim was quite normal practice in Roman times. Military horses received the same specific training as the soldiers, having to carry armaments, stay in line with the rest of the column, and perform their military task without panic. "Not only the common soldier," he wrote, "but also the horsemen and even their horses . . . must learn to swim to survive hazardous circumstances."[4]

Accustoming horses to water and training them to swim is a task that requires not only professional skill but also specific natural conditions. Wide, fordable rivers, long sloping beaches, and shallow lakes were ideal places for cavalry and mounted artillery to practice. Yet such ideal conditions were not always at hand. "Often," the *Handbuch der Architektur* (1899) informed its readers, "training camps and country homes did not have these facilities, so they had to be built. Pools had to be dug for horses to swim and be washed in."[5] The original *abreuvoirs, Pferdeschwemmen*, or horse ponds (fig. 7.1) were shallow dips in the road or fords in the river, the tender traps of the landscape as horses found their way into the cool by means of gradual seduction; but with advancing urbanism, such formerly natural facilities had to be

7.1. Example of an *abreuvoir* or *Pferdeschwemmen* (horse pond), from an old postcard.

created. In the eighteenth century, man-made pools, often lavishly decorated and situated in the most attractive locations, became a common sight. Well known and still in good condition are the *Pferdeschwemmen* in Salzburg, Eisgrub, Würzburg, and Rudolstadt.[6] The *Hofvijver*—the moat at the castle of the counts of Holland in The Hague—is deeper and larger than the customary horse pond, and contemporary prints show riders swimming their horses there.

At present, swimming pools for horses are an accepted, even fashionable addition to the genre. In 1978, about a dozen pools were in operation at stables throughout the United Kingdom,[7] and therapeutic and exercise pools exist at the equestrian centers of Newmarket and at Windsor House Stables, Lambourn. The shape of an equine swimming pool generally is circular, with an island in the middle where a trainer can walk the horse (fig. 7.2). The pool should be neither too shallow, lest the horse start wading, nor too deep, lest it panic, a reaction triggered when the horse is led into the water too abruptly. Horses do swim naturally and at times seem to enjoy it, but they usually have to overcome fear when entering. Therefore the slope should be gentle, and the sides of the pool, the pool island, and the ramp padded to minimize injuries (fig. 7.3).

Injuries are an inevitable by-product of an anomalous but spectacular technique for equines to enter a swimming pool: tower diving, popular in Atlantic City, New Jersey, during the 1930s. Two horses of a small and fearless breed were trained to dive from a 9-meter-high diving board into a transportable pool shaped like a hatbox. In 1993, newspapers printed an Associated Press photo with the caption "After an absence of fifteen years, the diving horses of Atlantic City are back again" (fig. 7.4).

as remedial purposes. . . . It was thought probable that what was good for the man might also be good for the horse, and that fact has been proved. Messr. Pickford, the eminent carriers, in their hospital for horses at Finchley, have had a Turkish bath in operation over eleven years, and find the horses derive great benefit from its use."

4. The instruction of military swimming must have been an exciting, even salacious spectacle. Or at least that is what we might conclude from the *Codex Theodosianus* of May 27, 391 A.D., by which the emperors Theodosius, Gratianus, and Valentinianus decreed that "soldiers instructing horses to swim should not be riding in the nude and thus cause offense to those civilians who happen to be in the area, nor should they swim their horses upstream of the city and thus pollute the water. They should rather go downstream, where they are free from the looks of the civilians; there they can swim their horses and even expand their training activities." Erwin Mehl, *Antike Schwimmkunst* (Munich: Ernst Heimeran, 1927), 69–70 (Vegetius, *De re militaria*, 3.4).

5. Genzmer, *Bade- und Schwimmanstalten*, 271.

6. See Wolfgang Götz, *Deutsche Marställe des Barock* (Munich and Berlin: Deutscher Kunstverlage, 1964).

7. John Dawes, *Design and Planning of Swimming Pools* (London: Architectural Press; Boston: CBI Press, 1979). "The pro-

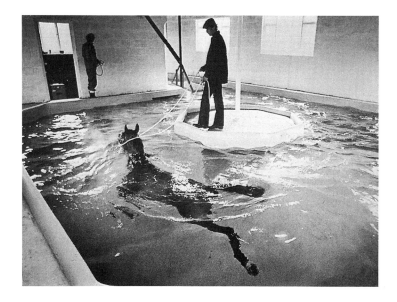

7.2. Equine swimming pool. (Dawes, *Design and Planning of Swimming Pools*, 1979.)

7.3. Plan of lap pool of increasing depth (left) and an island pool (right). (Hawcroft, *An Illustrated Handbook of Horse and Pony Care*, 1986.)

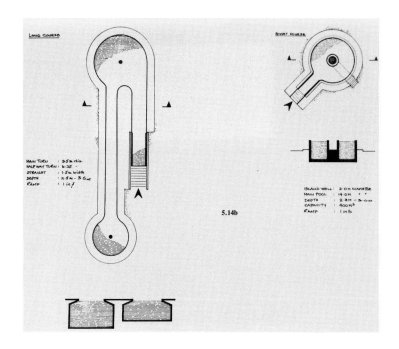

7.4. "The diving horses of Atlantic City." (*NRC Handelsblad*, June 28, 1993; AP photo.)

About water temperature opinions vary, some experts recommending cold, others 18-degree Centigrade (64-degree Fahrenheit) water. It all sounds extravagant, and indeed it is. Recently, some remarkable examples of horse pampering at the five-star beauty farm The Pond House in Somerset, England, were televised, as equines being prepared for the races at Cheltenham were led through a luxurious bridged swimming pool and a solarium with hot lamps.[8] There are also quite a few private establishments of this sort, such as the impressive one near Paris maintained by the French equestrian maecenas Weidenfeld.[9] In the Arab states, known for their racehorses, some spectacular pools can be observed. A hundred-meter-long swimming pool is the pride of the Zabeel stables, property of Dubai's defense minister Sheik Muhammad bin Rashid al-Makhtoum.[10]

In Mexico, where the Andalusian horse was introduced to the American continent, many testaments to indulgent horse care may be encountered, among the most monumental the complex designed in Mexico City by Luis Barragán for Mr. and Mrs. Folke Egerstrom. Barragán, a winner of the prestigious Pritzker Prize, created there, with strikingly empathetic imagination, "a shallow pool where the horses like to swim."[11] Northward, where Jesuit priests drove horses to the Spanish missions, some veritable horse spas are still successfully operating. At Scottsdale, Arizona, Karbo Arabian Farms treats its equine charges to a generous and elegantly curved swimming pool.[12]

Trough Pools The role of the horse in the origin of the lap pool, a type that became popular in the world of the athletically ambitious in the 1960s, is marginal, yet not without interest. In Texas, where everything seems feasible, a couple living on a ranch recycled

vision of equine swimming pools developed in the USA at famous circuits such as Chula Vista and Ocala Stud" (62). Other horse-racing nations have followed this trend.

8. Presented by BBC Television, March 10, 1992. Among U.S. therapeutic centers the New Bolten Center in Pennsylvania stands out in its sophistication.

9. Information from M. Dieudonné, Equestrian Center and Museum, Chantilly, 1992. The Deurne Centrum voor Hippische Opleidingen has a pool unique in the Netherlands, which dates from the early seventies. Thanks to Micheline Tasseron. See also Dawes, *Design and Planning of Swimming Pools*, 61–63, fig. 5.

10. Michael Freitag, "Das Pferdeparadies hat einen Namen: Dubai," *Boulevard Magazine* 7 (1996), 24–30.

11. Barbara Goldstein and Allen Carter, "Architecture: Luis Barragan," *Architectural Digest*, March 1979, 100–107; see also *Domus* 468 (November 1968), n.p.

12. Joan Baeza, "Horses of Arizona," *Arizona Highways*, February 1988, 10.

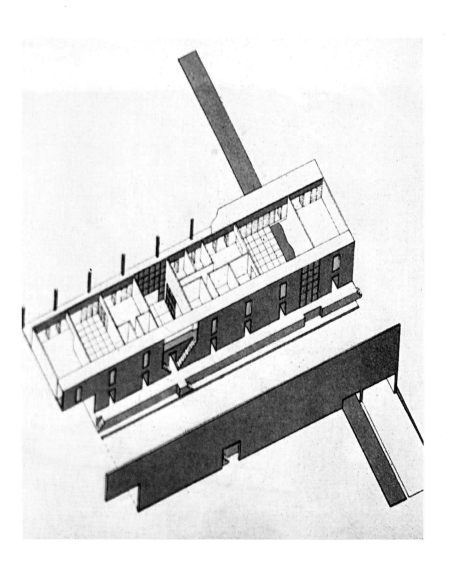

7.5. *Opposite:* Miami: Spear house, 1974 (first project). Laurinda Spear and Rem Koolhaas. (*Progressive Architecture*, January 1975.)

7.6. Majorca: Neuendorf pool, 1989. John Pawson. (Chatwin and Sudjic, *John Pawson*, 1992.)

13. Georgia Dullea, "Sunset for the Old Style Pool," *New York Times,* June 27, 1991, Home Section, C1.

14. *Progressive Architecture,* January 1975, 22nd Annual Awards Program issue, 46–47. The original design was later transformed into a less radical one, the pool measuring 60 by 12 feet (18.3 by 3.7 meters) and turned 45 degrees to fit between the frontal screen wall and the living quarters (see *Life,* March 1981, 62–65).

15. Rob Steiner defined lap pools as "long, shallow, and narrow for maximum swimming length" ("Laps of Luxury," *Angeles,* March 1990, 95). Islamic overtones of the lap pool's layout have been recognized in the southern California pool world. In the same article, Los Angeles landscape architect Emmet Wemple claimed he "drew inspiration from the famed Moorish pool in the Alhambra's Court of the Lions in Granada" (99). Interesting suggestions about the origin of the lap pool came from landscape architect Cleo Baldon of Venice, California, who claimed that she had found inspiration in watching children swim in irrigation ditches: "The ditches were about eight feet wide and they extended for miles. It seemed like a wonderful way to swim" (95).

16. Kelly Klein, *Pools* (New York: Knopf, 1992), 169; Bruce Chatwin and Deyan Sudjic, *John Pawson* (Barcelona: Gustavo Gili, 1992). And thanks to Mr. and Mrs. Hart Woodson, San Francisco.

17. *Sunset* 7 (July 1983), 74–75.

18. The Troy pool was built in 1987 by California Pools and Spas, with engineering by Rowley International.

an unused horse trough for a pool. The wife took to swimming laps in it, and when they moved to San Antonio she wanted the pool inside the new house to be an exact copy of the horse trough—132 by 12 feet (40.2 by 3.7 meters). "She was used to doing laps that length."[13] Although the story may leave us puzzled about the apparent size of a Texas horse trough, it suggests an important element in the lap pool's rationale.

Essentially a lap pool is a strip of water a single lane wide that enables a disciplined swimmer to cover longer distances without having to change direction. The concept, deriving from Austro-Prussian military drill systems, has been revived for modern fitness regimens. The apparent denial of freedom of movement and the infliction of physical stress are compensated for by the fact that the total length of the laps frequently is determined by previous swimming habits.

Such a pool was designed by Laurinda Spear and Rem Koolhaas in 1974 for "The Villa-with-the-Lap-Pool" at Miami Beach (fig. 7.5). Positioned at a 90-degree angle to the house, the pool is excavated over a distance of a hundred yards (close to a hundred meters) straight toward the ocean like a storm flood overflow, only to be stopped a foot or so from the high-water mark of the beach. The owner had suggested the size and layout of the pool, for "she was used to swim into the ocean for about a hundred yards and then return the same way."[14]

Lap pools of this size have become rare for, despite the allure of disciplinary swimming, economic and aesthetic considerations have taken on decisive roles. The lap pool may turn up as a quasi-swimmable garden embellishment that combines energy-saving benefits with Persian/Islamic overtones.[15] Ricardo Ligoretta's 83-by-6-foot (25.3-by-1.8-meter) lap pool at Coyoacán, Mexico, and the lap pool designed in 1989 by minimalist John Pawson, in collaboration with Claudio Silvestrin, for the German art dealer Neuendorf, offer the purest examples of arrangements based on the horse trough/single lane model.[16] Pawson exploited a difficult site, enhancing the sense of precarious equilibrium through the daringly poised, water-filled launching pad that juts out over the slope of a Majorca mountain (fig. 7.6).

The dimensions required for the perfect lap pool depend on place and fashion; a depth of 3½ feet (1.1 meters) will serve, and a ratio of seven lengths to the width is generous. *Sunset* magazine in 1983 cited the sensational 9-by-69.5-foot pool that Peter Heinig had shoehorned between two houses on a San Diego street.[17] Less monomaniacal is the "expanded" lap pool that Joseph Troy of Brentwood, Los Angeles, commissioned for a lush subtropical garden. Provided by architect James G. Pulliam, this consists of a 9-by-75-foot (2.7-by-22.9-meter) double-lane lap pool, a 23-by-35-foot (7.0-by-10.7-meter) family recreational pool, a Jacuzzi bath, and a fountain (fig. 7.7).[18]

Decidedly one-lane, but hardly restricted enough for a proper lap pool, is the monumental strip of water that connects the guest quarters with the main house of the Villa Zapu at Napa, completed in 1988 by Powell-Tuck, Connor & Orefelt for Thomas and Anna Lund-

7.7. *Below:* Brentwood, California: Troy pool, 1987.
James G. Pulliam. *Also plate 23.*

7.8. Pacific Palisades, California: Whitney pool,
1981. Frank Gehry and Mark Mack. (Courtesy
Charles Jencks.) *Also plate 24.*

19. *Arena*, Autumn 1990, 50–55. On lap pools in general see *Sunset* 7 (July 1983), 74–75.

20. Maxime Du Camp, *Paris, ses organes, ses fonctions et sa vie, dans la seconde moitié du XIXe siècle* (Paris: Hachette, 1875), 5:330.

21. Genzmer, *Bade- und Schwimmstalten*, 271, fig. 334.

22. Ibid., 274: "Mit sanfter Neigung in das Wasser gesenkt und entsprechend befestigt."

23. Ibid., 261.

24. Schleyer, *Bäder und Badeanstalten*, 419.

strom. Such a single-lane pool reflects the trends of modern asceticism, which are balanced between radical egotism and total abstinence. The times of the communal, densely populated family pool are over.[19] A lap pool serves only one swimmer at a time; for the rest, it sits there as a contemplative, energy-saving, narrow *pièce d'eau*. The lap pool that Frank Gehry and Mark Mack built in the hillside garden of John Whitney, Jr., in Pacific Palisades (1981) looks more inviting as a decorative element than as a real swimming pool (fig. 7.8).

Pools for Dogs After the horse pool, the dog pool seems to be the inevitable next phase in the evolution of aquatic entertainment for quadrupeds. In Paris, where the first municipal horse pond had been founded in 1293 by the provost of merchants, Jehan Popin, by the later nineteenth century it was considered healthy to allow *chiens* as well as *chevaux* to bathe in the Seine, and therefore no fee was to be paid for these beaches. Bathing facilities for dogs would soon be considered essential.[20]

As we have seen, horse ponds were not a luxury for those whose livelihood depended on their animals. When the free flow of streams and rivers began to be harnessed, banks of stone and brick were erected so steep that, if an animal could get into the water, it was doomed never to get out again. Therefore, embankments were interrupted at specific spots to allow the pavement to slope gradually into the river. These special ramps were officially classified as horse- and/or dog-bathing places. Such conveniences were officially propagated as beneficial to the health and hygiene of a city's animal population.[21] This practice is touchingly commemorated in Hamburg in the Aussenalster: where a steep bank separates the harbor from the boulevard, an opening with a stone ramp slopes gently into the water.[22] At the end of the ramp was placed on a pedestal the statuette of a hunting dog in retrieving stance, reminiscent of Copenhagen's little mermaid (fig. 7.9). This "apportirender Jagdhund," as a plaque at the base identifies him, was sculpted by a Carl Böner.[23]

The first indoor canine pool was built in 1889, in the Städtischen Schwimmbad in Stuttgart (fig. 7.10). Schleyer reported that owners had been taking their dogs to the bathhouse to give them a good weekly scrub, and when some of the other patrons protested, the management decided to provide a canine "bathhouse," consisting of a small (about one by two meters) swimming pool, a bathroom with tubs, and several waiting rooms. It was situated off an L-shaped corridor along the main pool with its own private entrance.[24] Between 1900 and 1909, the Müllersches Volksbad in Munich elaborated on the same idea; next to the main swimming pool there was installed a series of washing tubs and waiting rooms for dogs and their owners. Several novelties—spectator accommodations, a communal hair dryer, and a well-equipped grooming salon—were included (fig. 7.11). With his characteristic regard for detail, Schleyer reported that the dog pool of the Müller baths had to be

7.9. *Top, left:* Carl Böner, *The Little Retriever,* in Hamburg's Aussenalster. (Genzmer, *Bade- und Schwimmanstalten,* 1899.)

7.11. *Bottom, left:* Munich: Müllersches Volksbad, 1900–1909, canine salon. (Schleyer, *Bäder und Badeanstalten,* 1909.)

7.10. Stuttgart: Städtischen Schwimmbad, canine pool, 1889, plan. Wittmann & Stahl. (Genzmer, *Bade- und Schwimmanstalten,* 1899.)

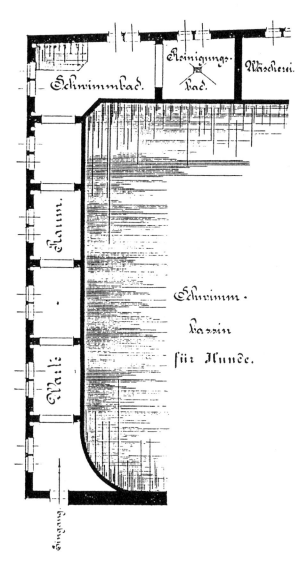

25. Ibid., 420.
26. *Limburgs Dagblad,* March 2, 1992. In the Netherlands, where dogs are sacrosanct and have the same rights as humans, the dog pool has not become common usage. Instead, dogs seem to be sharing the bathing facilities with their masters. On Sunday, September 13, 1992, to celebrate the end of the season, the Montfoort public swimming pool opened its main pool for dogs and their owners for a day of mixed swimming (*NRC Handelsblad,* September 14, 1992: see fig. 7.28). Westcoast Pools, Happisburgh, Norfolk, UK, advertises circular pools for racing dogs to convalesce with "variable current/hydrotherapy/air massage and many other features too numerous to list."
27. *House and Garden,* May 1991, U.S. Edition, 154–159.
28. Salvador Dalí, *The Secret Life of Salvador Dalí* (New York: Dial Press, 1948), 54.

bright and friendly, since it is at the same time a place where owners might want to watch the bathing of their pets. The bathing itself is handled by special attendants who, after having muzzled the animal, soap it in a special hot water tank, measuring 1 by 1.5 meters with a maximum depth of 0.6 meters, sunk into the floor and faced with smooth stone tiles. So that it causes the least trouble, the dog is strapped into a harness and lowered into the water. From there, it is led to another tank, to be rinsed, or it might take a swim in a modestly sized pool. The tanks are refilled at regular intervals with water from the neighboring swimming pool [for humans], perhaps not the most hygienic operation but a sensible measure on grounds of costs. . . . After the bathing comes the drying. The dogs are now led into a room which has two tiers of wooden cages, one for the small and one for the larger dogs. The heating, at the proper temperature, is distributed by a system of tubes that runs behind the cages. . . . There is a table for dogs to receive a haircut from qualified personnel. A constant supply of clean drinking water is required.[25]

The sophistication of the Elisabethstrasse municipal swimming pool and bathhouse (1911) at the ancient bathing resort of Aachen (Aix-la-Chapelle), which accommodated not only a splendid swimming pool but several steam baths of both the Finnish and Turkish types, was signaled by the provision of a specially appointed "dog bath."[26] Perhaps the ultimate step in the continual process of upgrading pet care is the swimming pool for two Bengal tigers owned by Las Vegas magicians Siegfried Fischbacher and Roy Horn, who possess "three swimming pools: one for humans, one for the commoner animals and one for the royal white tigers, though," adds the reporter with conspiratorial jest, "a certain amount of mixed bathing goes on."[27]

Our excursus into the canine pool may be concluded by another reference to the *Little Retriever* in Hamburg, for the sculpture symbolizes the transition from free to regulated swimming. The provision of the ramp is sensible, yet outrageously bureaucratic at the same time. The ramp is rational, the monument hilarious, its justification lying in the increased awareness of the owners that their pets should be entitled to the same level of hygiene, and subjected to the same standard of civic obedience, as they maintained for themselves. This resulted in the curious notion that a dog swimming in the Aussenalster reserve was not merely taking a plunge in the harbor but was having a dip in an open-air swimming pool for dogs. Of course, not every hound would have been able to read the various intentions correctly, but one element would have been instantly and justly interpreted: the ramp. Ramps are the universal signs for animal infrastructure and, more specifically, for animal bathing facilities (fig. 7.12).

7.12. London: elephant tortoises from the Galapagos Islands at their pool in the zoo. (*The Living Animals of the World*, 1902.)

Ramps for All Stairs without steps, ironed-out ascents inclining gradually and curving gently, ideal for dragging up heavy things like blocks of stone or pieces of artillery, ramps in representational architecture serve as lengthy and solemn processional approaches, whereas in industrial architecture they should be crisp, light, and more precipitous. In the Middle Ages, a ramp might be a spiraling path in the heart of a castle, where a mounted horseman—local guides love to ascribe such exploits to the Duke of Mantua—could clatter upstairs to the top-floor bridal (bridle!) suite. In modern times similar inclines are mandated for those who involuntarily, or perhaps by choice, move on wheels. Finally, they prove great fun to those who enjoy a bit of vertigo now and then. Otters, seals, penguins, polar bears, small boys, and Salvador Dalí have in common a love of sliding down ramps or railings. Dalí found great satisfaction in tumbling down the staircase of his local school, or thundering down the ramp in his home town's park on a scooter at life-endangering speed. "From the place where we [Dalí and Galushka, his future wife Gala] were seated rose a rather steep ramp which communicated with an upper walk. Children carrying scooters would walk up this ramp, and then come down with dizzy speed on their grinding and horrible contraptions. . . . Each sudden new interruption of our romance by the clattering onrush . . . would only increase the purity and the passion of our ecstatic contemplation and redouble its agonizing peril."[28] The diagonal direction of the ramp challenges both the vertical and the horizontal as a line of dynamism. A ride down a ramp heightens the awareness of weightlessness and speed, and leads to a state of ecstasy.

The potential of the ramp has been exploited in a widespread family of euphoric architectural concoctions, beginning with the *montagnes russes* of the early nineteenth

29. Gary Kyriazi, *The Great American Amusement Parks* (Secaucus, N. J.: Castle Books, 1978), 38.

30. O. Pilat and J. Ranson, *Sodom by the Sea: An Affectionate History of Coney Island* (New York: Doubleday, 1941), and Rem Koolhaas, *Delirious New York* (New York: Oxford University Press, 1978).

31. Glenwood Springs, Colorado, was, together with Hot Springs, Arkansas, the most popular bathing resort and health spa of nineteenth-century America. The resort lies on an island in the junction of the Colorado and Roaring Fork rivers, where the largest of the springs, the Yampa, throws out 4,000 gallons of spring water a minute at a temperature of 125 degrees Fahrenheit. The springs have been made serviceable by creating large pools (one 600 feet in length) and several immense bathhouses. See George Cromwell, ed., *Scenic Marvels of the New World* (New York, 1894), n.p., courtesy of the Society for the Preservation of Long Island Antiquities (SPLIA), Setauket, N.Y.

32. Jeannot Simmen, *Vertigo; Schwindel der modernen Kunst* (Munich: Klinkhardt & Biermann, 1990); and Simmen, *Schwerelos; der Traum vom Fliegen in der Kunst der Moderne* (Berlin: Grosse Orangerie Schloss Charlottenburg, 1991).

33. A cultural history of the ramp should include the works and theory of Frederick Kiesler and of Meyerhold. See "Frederick Kiesler 1890–1965—A. A. Exhibition Gallery, 1989," *AA Files* 20 (1991), 86, and Edward Braun, ed., *Meyerhold on Theatre* (London: Methuen, 1969).

century, which eventually metamorphosed into the roller coaster, the toboggan ride, and the water chute. Aquachutes became extremely popular in the United States, where they were introduced and developed by Captain Paul Boyton, the inventor of the inflated rubber suit who became famous as the the world's first frogman. In this biomorphic-protective garment he had crossed the English Channel and made a 450-mile voyage down the Rhine. "In 1896 he began travelling around the world," Gary Kyriazi explains, "presenting his aquatic circus, in which he starred, [along with] his trained juggling sea lions. . . . Boyton and his forty sea lions were the top billed attraction of Sea Lion Park [on Coney Island], the forerunner of the several marine-life parks which are so successful today."[29]

It is a curious phenomenon that, from the very beginning, the central attractions of the amusement and aquaparks were chutes and slides of all possible configurations. The human Toboggan and the Helter Skelter, introduced in Coney Island's Luna Park in 1907, were but raw reiterations of the Russian mountains, while Boyton's Shoot-the-Chute was a magnified penguin slide of colossal sophistication. After the sea lions' natural fun on the chutes of Sea Lion Park came the heart-stopping anxiety of elephants apprehensively sliding down the slippery ramps of Coney Island's Luna Park. The Shoot-the-Chute was a big water slide on which flat-bottomed boats raced down to an accelerated quasi-submersion. Boyton's invention, the result of the adaptation to humans of his experiments with sea lions, was carried further at Coney Island's Luna Park and later Dreamland by even larger variations on the theme, and from there dispersed throughout the world.[30]

Water slides had from the early nineteenth century been part of swimming instruction; public pools counted at least one as part of their water adaptation technique for reluctant swimmers. Keeping pace with the evolution of the amusement park, pool slides developed into ever larger and more formidable apparatuses. The Sutro Baths on San Francisco's coastline had a grandly imposing slide, whereas the primitive structure in the extravagantly large swimming pool of Glenwood Springs, Colorado (fig. 7.13), must have resembled to its bucolic visitors a hastily built county fair attraction.[31] The sophisticated water slide was introduced into the most rarefied circles in the 1920s, when Douglas Fairbanks and Mary Pickford had one installed in Pickfair.

The importance of the ramp in modern architecture is partly based on the experiences of eighteenth-century ecstatic progressivists, and partly on the more recent concept that machines and machine-derived artifacts are instrumental in the general improvement of life.[32] Technophilia was, and still is, a sign of forward-looking sophistication. With the introduction of the horseless carriage, ramps and their mechanized counterparts, the conveyor belts, provided the paths for motor-driven traffic. When the automobile became part of everyday life, the diagonal line of the ramp became a sign of messianic fulfillment. This has been modernism's power—to draw the future within the present—and now the line of the future had become the diagonal, as the horizontal had been the line of classicism and the vertical the line of the Gothic. The ramp is thus to modern what the column was to classical architecture.[33]

7.13. Glenwood Springs, Colorado: swimming pool.
(Setauket, Society for the Preservation of Long
Island Antiquities.)

7.14. El Lissitzky, projected set for Meyerhold's production of *I Want a Child*, 1926–1930. (Braun, ed., *Meyerhold on Theatre*, 1969.)

34. Ulrich Conrads, *Programs and Manifestoes on 20th-Century Architecture* (Cambridge: MIT Press, 1975), 36–37. See also Bruno Zevi, "Lines of Futurism," *Architectural Design* 51, nos. 1–2 (1981), 24–25.

35. See *Paris-Moscou: 1990–1930* (Paris: Centre Pompidou, 1979), 184–185.

36. Parisian *passerelles* and small railroad inclines such as Zurich's Polybahn of 1889 could have acted as models, according to Jos Bosman ("Mart Stam's Stadtbild," *Mart Stam; Reise in die Schweiz, 1923–1925* [Zurich: GTA/Ammans Verlag, 1991], 117–135). For a revealing photograph of the Van Nelle ramps, see the picture Giedion took for *Bauwelt*, 1931, reproduced in Jos Bosman and Sokratis Georgiadas, eds., *Sigfried Giedion; der Entwurf einer modernen Tradition* (Zurich: GTA/Ammans Verlag, 1989), 61.

37. *L'Esprit Nouveau* 2 (1920). See also Jürgen Joedicke, "Die Rampe als architektonische Promenade im Werke Le Corbusiers," *Daidalos* 12 (1984), 104–126.

38. Sigfried Giedion, *Space, Time and Architecture* (1941; Cambridge: Harvard University Press, 1946), 556. Currently diagonals are the bread and butter of every progressive architectural practice, such as Coop Himmelblau, Rem Koolhaas, Zaha Hadid, and many others.

39. For a pioneering article on industrial streamlining, see Sigfried Giedion, *Mechanization Takes Command* (1948; New York: Oxford University Press, 1969), 609–611. An enchanting contemporary history

One or more ramps and diagonal lines sufficed cartoonists, illustrators, and stage and film designers for conveying those meanings of flight, speed, and automatization that connoted the future, as demonstrated by the sets for Fritz Lang's *Metropolis* (1926). In the world of Krypton, the archetypal gravitarian-ecstatic *Superman* (1938) used to impress his opponents by taking a diagonal dive, rather than marching horizontally or dropping down vertically. A futurist manifesto of 1914 declared: "I oppose and despise perpendicular, cubic and pyramidal forms that are static, heavy, oppressive and absolutely alien to our new sensibility . . . oblique and elliptical lines are dynamic by their very nature and have an emotive power a thousand times greater than that of perpendicular and horizontal lines . . . a dynamically integrated architecture is impossible without them."[34]

The modern movement made ample use of the medium. The Babylonian spiral of Tatlin's monument and Michael Mantiouchin's rainbow-colored lazy diagonals in *Movement in Space* from the same revolutionary years of 1917–1918, as well as the set designs of the mid-1920s by El Lissitzky (fig. 7.14) and V. E. Meyerhold, all offer eloquent examples.[35] Industrial ramps and stepless inclines, such as the connecting skyways in the Van Nelle Factory in Rotterdam by Brinkman & Van der Vlugt, of 1927–1930, carried unmistakable messages of industrial progressivism.[36] Le Corbusier entertained a never-to-be-relinquished passion for ramps and sang their praises in early publications such as *L'Esprit Nouveau*.[37] Finally, for Sigfried Giedion, exceptionally sensitive to the technical signs of his age, the ramp represented the new line of modernity, which he found "expressive of the space-time conception both in structure and handling of movement."[38]

Streamlining Our discussion of the ramp is not alien to another prominent preoccupation
Man: The of the period—streamlining. The art and science of streamlining had found
Swimmer its origin in hydrodynamics,[39] where a body was moved through water in
order to get a graphic representation of the flow of water particles around it,
the objective being to design objects in such a way that they would meet the least possible
resistance. That water tanks were used for this and not wind tunnels is a fact that surprises
many. It provokes less surprise to discover that the final product of hydrodynamic streamlining
will in appearance be much closer to a whale than to a bird. "The porpoise, small fish, and
falling teardrops were subjected to prolonged study . . . after they had been determined upon
as the most triumphant specimens of gliding forms in nature," wrote streamline ideologist
Sheldon Cheney in 1936. "The British admiralty isolated the Newfoundland shark as represent-
ing the swiftest and most efficient swimmer, and developed seaplane models patterned on its
form."[40] Whales and fishes became models for every sort of streamlined object, whether destined for land, water, or the air.

This insight, although later obscured, nevertheless survives. When commissioned to design two ships for the Los Angeles-based Princess Cruises, Renzo Piano decided
that instead of mimicking the current trend for designing ships "like shoe boxes, like hotels
put on barges," he would turn for inspiration to the dolphin, recognizing that a ship "is a magic
object . . . very important in the collective memory of people." The dolphin-shaped bow and
forehead-shaped dome, described by the architect as having "round corners, soft shapes, belonging to the water," were thus essentially biomorphic in design. According to Piano, the interior of the dome resembles "the inside of a whale."[41]

It might be expected that the human body, too, would be included in the
design process of dynamic modification and streamlining, and thus it has been subjected to
many hydrodynamic tests and experiments. In *Delirious New York*, Rem Koolhaas reminds us of
two features of the 1939 New York World's Fair that are significant for our topic. One was
Salvador Dalí's *tableaux vivants* in glass water tanks; the other was the display of Count Alexis
Sakhnoffsky, an experienced streamliner who had been practicing his craft on automobiles,
watches, and clothes, so that logically next in line would be the human body. "Now let us
streamline men and women," Sakhnoffsky suggested (fig. 7.15). "Improvement is in the air, let
us apply it to ourselves. The scientists would tell us what the body lacks for the things it is
called on to do today. They would point out what it has that it no longer needs. The artist
would then design the perfect human being for the life of today and tomorrow. The toes would
be eliminated. They were given to us to climb trees, and we do not climb trees anymore. This
would permit interchangeable shoes, beautifully streamlined. The ears would be turned
around, slotted and streamlined to the head. Hair would be used only for accent and decoration. The nose would be streamlined. Certain changes would be made in the contours of both
men and women to make them more graceful."[42]

of streamlining as design method was
given by Sheldon Cheney and Martha
Chandler Cheney in *Art and the Machine:
An Account of Industrial Design in 20th-
Century America* (New York and London:
Whittlesey House, 1936).
40. Cheney and Cheney, *Art and the Ma-
chine*, 99–100.
41. Shirley Slater and Harry Basch, "Two
Ships Inspired by the Dolphin," *Los Angeles
Times*, May 6, 1990, L16.
42. Koolhaas, *Delirious New York*, 196.
The orginal text is taken from "Now Let Us
Streamline Men and Women," *Rockefeller
Center Weekly*, September 5, 1935.

7.15. Alexis Sakhnoffsky, proposal to streamline the human head. (Koolhaas, *Delirious New York*, 1978.)

43. See Desmond Morris, *Manwatching: A Field Guide to Human Behavior* (New York: Abrams, 1982), 298. The illustration there was originally taken from Hardy.

44. Stanley Appelbaum, *The New York World's Fair 1939/1940 in 155 Photographs by Richard Wurts and Others* (New York: Dover, 1977), 134–135; Larry Zim, Mel Lerner, and Herbert Rolfes, *The World of Tomorrow: The 1939 New York World's Fair* (New York: Main Street Press, 1988), 172. The 1939 Aquacade was preceded by a similar swim show at the 1933 Chicago Century of Progress Exhibition given by a group of swimming women called "The Mermaids."

45. In order of publication: Lena Lencek and Giedion Bosker, *Making Waves: Swimsuits and the Undressing of America* (San Francisco: Chronicle Books, 1989); Richard Martin and Harold Koda, *Splash! A History of Swimwear* (New York: Rizzali 1990). For the history of nude swimming, see Charles Sprawson, *Haunts of the Black Masseur: The Swimmer as Hero* (London: Jonathan Cape, 1992).

46. Lencek and Bosker, *Making Waves*, 36.

47. Ibid., 47.

48. Donald Albrecht, *Designing Dreams: Modern Architecture in the Movies* (London: Thames and Hudson, 1986), effectively explores the relation between streamlining and film sets, especially the involvement of modernistic designers.

49. Juan Antonio Ramirez, *La arquitectura en el cine: Hollywood, la Edad de Oro* (Madrid: Hermann Blume, 1986).

50. "Fred Astaire among Machines," *California Arts and Architecture*, February 1938, 39.

The count's prescriptions are strikingly in sympathy with Alister Hardy's yet unpublished theory of the aquatic ape (see chapter 1), in which he described the way man's tresses follow the flow of water during forward swimming. The protruding nose shield, when drawn the way Sakhnoffsky suggested it, conforms to the aquatic ape theory in the sense that the nostrils face downward, to reduce the risk of taking in water.[43]

Demonstrations of the streamlined swimmer were given at the New York fairgrounds in Billy Rose's Aquacade, a giant extravaganza of music and dance rendered as aquatic movement, with activities normally done dry cunningly transplanted into the wet. Chorus line dancing was transformed into synchronized swimming, lounging into floating, jumping into diving, with actors recruited from beaches and swimming pools. Olympic medalists Johnny Weissmuller (Tarzan) and Eleanor Holm, and Channel-crosser Gertrude Ederle, attracted enthusiastic audiences. Esther Williams joined the spectacle later, in 1940, when it moved to San Francisco for the Pan-Pacific Exhibition.[44]

It was perfectly reasonable that the first efforts in human streamlining should be applied to swimming. The first thing to be changed was the traditional bathing costume, a topic that has recently attracted keen interest.[45] The revolution had been initiated by champion swimmer Annette Kellerman (see fig. 1.16), who had made it quite clear to the public that the body had to be stripped of all obstacles with her admirably succinct statement of 1907: "I want to swim. And I can't swim wearing more stuff than you hang on a clothes line."[46] The knitwear manufacturer Jantzen carried the idea further and started to commercialize the so-called "one-piece bathing suit," a term used to distinguish their product from the ubiquitous combination of knickerbockers with long blouse or short dress of the pre-Kellerman period. Jantzen's choice of the slogan "the suit that changed bathing into swimming" proved to be a brilliant market maneuver.[47]

The evolution of the bathing suit could be succinctly described as the transition from immobility to mobility. Bathing became swimming, and the costume changed accordingly. The principles of streamlined automobiles could be equally applied to humans and vice versa, as is evidenced by the image of a designer modeling the masthead figures of forties and fifties cars after bathing beauties (fig. 7.16). Next the location of the activity came under scrutiny, as free bathing changed into pool swimming and the swimming pool turned into a hydrodynamic laboratory. Swimming pools in the 1930s changed from picturesque ponds into clinical places of research, developed to optimize human movement against resistance.

A powerful communicator of the message of streamlining was the movie industry,[48] where ample use was made of ramps, slides, pools, and smooth swimmers no less than fast dancers. Films such as Edward Sutherland's musical comedy *Palmy Days* (1931; see fig. 5.1), for which a rooftop gymnasium and high-tech swimming pool, in the spirit of Le Corbusier, were installed to provide the employees with sufficient opportunities for exercise during working hours, Busby Berkeley's synchronized wet and dry spectaculars like *Gold Diggers of 1933* and *Footlight Parade* (1929/1933), and William Cameron Menzies's *Things to Come* (1936), in which Norman Bel Geddes gave the theme its proper application,[49] offer conspicuous examples of this trend. Then there were the numerous Fred Astaire films, of which *Shall We Dance* (1937) may be the most dynamic in its convergence of ocean liner aesthetics and tap dancing. *California Arts and Architecture* had noted in 1938 that America, lacking great representatives of the serious art forms, excelled in those media in which a physical coordination was sought between man and the machinelike pace of his time, and that it had been Astaire who was the "first to express perfectly the *Zeitgeist* of the American machine age in an art form. . . . In *Shall We Dance,* Mr. Astaire creates . . . an American apotheosis of our time. The setting for the dance is the engine room of an ocean liner. . . . He dances from machine to machine, translating into dance rhythms and gestures the mechanical movements of the machines."[50]

The same aesthetics were applied to swimming itself, as illustrated by the mechanized movements in Busby Berkeley's extravaganzas, as well as by such occasional elegant individual interruptions as that in the original 1942 *Cat People,* where the heroine takes an after-office plunge in the hypermodern swimming pool of her apartment building, or the swimming pool scene in *Dancing Lady* (1933; see fig. 5.20). It should be noted that scenes like this one will be repeated in forties and fifties films like *Dangerous When Wet* and, interestingly enough, in the design of the Minoletti pool in Monza, Italy, of 1951 (see figs. 5.19 and 7.21).

During the 1930s, Hollywood was busy experimenting with a multitude of different spatial and temporal situations as protagonists flew, floated, jumped, and dived through air and into water. The movie director who could resist having the actors move in at least three elements would be difficult to find, a trend that can be observed in the other arts.

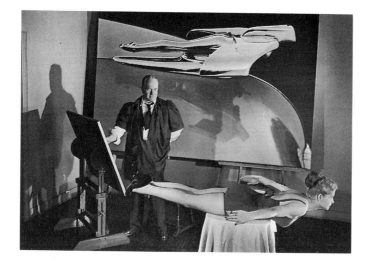

7.16. Gordon Coster, hood ornament designer, c. 1945. (Keith de Lellis Gallery, New York.)

51. Andrew Saint, "Some Thoughts about the Architectural Use of Concrete," *AA Files* 22 (Autumn 1991), 8, and *Thirties: British Art and Design before the War* (London: Arts Council of Great Britain, 1979).

52. John Allan of Avanti Architects, with the collaboration of Lubetkin himself and the original engineers, Ove Arup and Partners, took up the restoration of the penguin pool in 1987. Allan is the author of the monumental study *Berthold Lubetkin: Architecture and the Tradition of Progress* (London: RIBA Publications, 1992), where he wrote that the pool was "destined to become possibly the best-known Modernist artefact of the 1930's" (208). See also Hugh Pearman, "Redoing It in Style," *The Sunday Times*, February 23, 1992, 6–13. My study of swimming pools has perhaps led me to be more than normally focused on the presence of water in architecture, but we must nevertheless recognize that the other single great monument of modernism, Mies van der Rohe's 1929 Barcelona Pavilion, is also centered around (two) pools, one "inside," one out.

If there is one common feature that links the various versions of modern architecture, it is this sense of experiment. The traditional product is analyzed, put under stress, subjected to new criteria of functionality, rejected, and replaced by the new. But the new also is tested, observed, and developed. Reinforced concrete, for example, was by nature in compliance with the capriciousness of the new forms. In Europe, beginning in the 1910s, constructors had experimented with the ferroconcrete parabolic arch, which became the darling of the era, finding welcome application in market and exhibition halls, churches, and, not seldom, in swimming baths.[51] It would not find ready application in the land of the swimming pool, however, until well after World War II.

Man the Penguin If one were to synthesize in a single work of architecture the elements analyzed above—ramps and diagonals, smoothly curving reinforced concrete, hydrodynamic forms, empathic design, the entertaining use of water, and the streamlining of bodies—one would end up with Berthold Lubetkin's penguin pool of 1933–1934 in London (fig. 7.17). It could be regarded as a modernist laboratory for a future hydrodynamic society of men, since the new architectural configuration is here tested on penguins, long known for their abilities to simulate human bipedal propulsion and to excite sympathetic responses in their human observers. The penguin pool's location in one of the world's best-known zoological gardens meant, moreover, that humans interested in the experiment could have ready access to this desirable model home. The good taste of those who expressed a sincere interest in the modest structure was rewarded generously, for it has since become universally acclaimed as one of the key monuments of the modern movement.[52]

7.17. London: penguin pool, 1933–1934. Lubetkin,
Drake and Tecton. View after the 1987
restoration. *Also plate 25.*

53. Allan, *Berthold Lubetkin,* 199.
54. Braun, *Meyerhold on Theatre,* 237. In that publication, see also El Lissitzky's project for *I Want a Child, 1926–1930,* with circus and fireworks, 240; the plan for the New Meyerhold Theater (second variant, 1932) by Mikhail Barkhin and Sergei Vakhtankov, 288; and *The Bath House,* 1930, "Meyerhold's best performance of Mayakovsky," 273.
55. Allan, *Berthold Lubetkin,* 201.
56. Ibid., 208.
57. William Curtis, *Le Corbusier* (Milton Keynes: Open University Press, 1975), 52.
58. Manfredo Tafuri and Francesco Dal Co, *Modern Architecture* (New York: Rizzoli, 1976), 259.

The elliptical plan of the penguin house and pool incorporates a shallow basin and a deep diving tank, surrounded by a thin wall which has been opened up selectively to permit optimal viewing. In the center, two ramps, taking off from opposite ends, curve down into the pool to form an interlocking pattern. Lubetkin explained this pattern as a means to create "an atmosphere comparable to that of the circus," which might be understood in both meanings of the term, the circular form as well as the spectacle (fig. 7.18). It is not known whether Lubetkin got his inspiration directly from Meyerhold, but his insistence on "designing architectural settings for the animals in such a way as to present them dramatically to the public" brings him close to the theatrical reformer.[53] One thinks especially of Meyerhold's staging of *The Commander of the Second Army,* by Ilya Selvinsky (fig. 7.19), where he created reciprocal reinforcement of the various communicative media. "The acting area was enclosed by a lofty wooden screen which functioned as a sounding board. . . . Against it a flight of steps descended in a gradual spiral. At one point the Battle of Beloyarsk was described whilst a refrain in mazurka time was chanted by the entire company. Both commentator and chorus used megaphones . . . which magnified their voices to awesome power."[54]

John Allan, who restored the penguin pool and wrote a masterful biography of Lubetkin, explained that "the relationship between animals and public should not be one of dispassionate mutual inspection [but] more like that between performers and audience."[55] Lubetkin obviously was fascinated—who is not?—by the antics of the penguins for whom he had to design such a glamorous and showy home. Very much inspired by their "speed and grace when swimming and their agility and buoyancy in diving," Lubetkin succeeded in transposing their movements into a building that was at once "a zoological exhibit, an aquatic sculpture and an engineering capriccio."[56]

A number of scholars have linked Lubetkin's masterwork to sculpture and to theater design. Thus William Curtis: "The constructivist influence is obvious . . . the ramps recall Soviet stage sets of the twenties. The taut, sculptural image of the whole comes extremely close to Naum Gabo's constructions."[57] The late Manfredo Tafuri recognized the sculptural beauty of "the staggered ramps rising from the pool in a helix recalling the scenery by El Lissitzky for the Meyerhold Theatre" (see fig. 7.14) but could not hide his doubts about the ideological correctness of the building. "As a veritable dictionary of the motifs that had become the stock-in-trade of radical architecture," it was deliberately and unsettlingly paradoxical. The penguin pool, Tafuri concluded in Benjaminian terms, "definitively canceled out the aura and expectations on which radical architecture had nourished itself. Carried to its maximum purity, architecture becomes mere spectacle."[58]

Isn't that precisely the point? With all of its technical bravura and architectural explicitness, Lubetkin's achievement was above all a playhouse for the creature that is probably best equipped for theatrical entertainment. At the same time the penguin, because of its streamlined appearance, could convincingly pose as a being with futuristic aspirations.

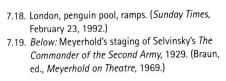

7.18. London, penguin pool, ramps. (*Sunday Times,* February 23, 1992.)

7.19. *Below:* Meyerhold's staging of Selvinsky's *The Commander of the Second Army,* 1929. (Braun, ed., *Meyerhold on Theatre,* 1969.)

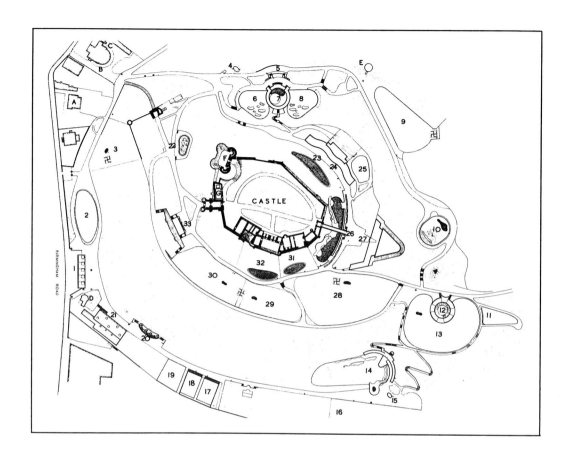

7.20. Castle Hill, Dudley: zoo, 1935–1937, site plan.
Lubetkin and Tecton. (Allan, *Berthold Lubetkin*,
1992.)

Other streamlined water animals are often used in science fiction to perform as metahumans, as in the movie *The Day of the Dolphin* (Mike Nichols, 1973). The idea of animals being trained as nuclear combat units doubtless derived from the 1946 Dutch comic book action drama, *Het Penguinland van Professor Lupardi*.[59]

Dynamic Pools Lubetkin's virtuosity in designing playhouses for animals was partly due to his capacity to empathize with the ambitions and passions of his prospective clients. The transition from human to animal client is not so large a step, for every brief requires a certain amount of migrant imagination. Animals vary, however, in their capacity to excite a human response. Having spent a great deal of his evolutionary existence in the company of his fellow amphibians, man has developed a distinct capacity to project himself into their social and emotional life. Sea mammals excite massive feelings of sympathy, as do penguins. Lubetkin, who was a fervent believer in Wilhelm Worringer's theory of *Einfühlung* (empathy), naturally inserted himself into the minds of his clients. Apparently he could imagine himself sailing down the ramps, diving into the pool, swiftly turning and rolling, picking up a herring, and finally, propped against the curved wall, spreading wings to dry in the reflected warmth of the low winter sun. With infallible understanding of its idea of having fun, Lubetkin realized the penguin's dream.[60]

Another characteristic of Lubetkin's work for the zoological community was its unmitigated modernity. This is logical. Apart from acting unhappy at the finished product, animals have no real say in the design process, and so inherit in one way or another the role of the guinea pig: doing things for which humans are not yet prepared. And so it is that London penguins and Birmingham seals came to live in houses that only the rich and fashionable could afford, and a few years ahead of them, at that.

In the Dudley Zoo in Birmingham, designed by Lubetkin and the firm of Tecton in 1937, the lines of empathic pleasure were made even more evident. The zoo was intended to transform the grounds of Dudley Castle into a park of educational entertainment. A ring of organically shaped centers in ovals and semicircles was laid out around the derelict castle and moat, interconnected with ramps and walkways and scattered with pools (fig. 7.20). Each of the habitats was to be an individual study in architectural amusement. The bear ravine, for example, looked like an exercise in southern Californian thirties moderne, with extensive terracing and a medium-sized kidney-shaped swimming pool. A quick stroll through the zoological garden evokes the mood of an international architectural exposition of experimental bungalows, demonstrating Lubetkin's tasteful balance between advanced modernity and practical usability. A harmonious relation between indoors and out has been established and the contrast between the clinical crispness of the athletic facilities and the softer lines of the dwellings has been minimized, so that everything ultimately exudes the same degree of coziness. It

59. Pieter Kuhn, *Het Penguinland van Professor Lupardi*, 1971 reprint of the 1946 original. Penguins became popular through Antarctic expeditions of the beginning of the twentieth century; see, for example, Cherry Kearton, *The Island of Penguins* (New York: R. M. McBride, 1930).
Belgian penguinomaniac Monsieur David has a huge collection of penguiniana. Occasionally he can be seen wearing a penguin suit. A reporter from the English *Observer Life* (July 18, 1995) asked him whether he collected anything else. "Silence. 'Stamps?' I ventured lamely. 'Yes. Stamps. . . . All with penguins on them.'"
60. See Paul Smith Suits, advertisement in *Elle*, April 1992, illustrating our automatic comparison to penguins as the overdressed, hyperbourgeois upstarts of the animal world.

7.21. Monza, Italy: free-form pool, 1951. Giulio
Minoletti. (Ortner, *Sportbauten,* 1953.)
7.22. *Below:* Monza pool, porthole peep show.
(Ortner, *Sportbauten,* 1953.)

derives from the same spirit that granted the California Case Study Houses their demeanor as self-evident experimental kindergartens for grown-ups.[61]

The various constructions at the Dudley Zoo have elegantly curved white concrete walls, smoothly faced ramps, spacious gardens, and artistically shaped ponds. The polar bears, penguins, and sea lions enjoy generously proportioned swimming pools. The penguins are housed in a two-story banana-shaped villa, the roof doubling as a promenade, from which ramps and walkways lead to a lower level with a 60-foot pool and diving tank. The upper level, connected with the shelter by ramps, is cut out in undulating patterns and intended to allow some spectacular diving. This feature comes closest to the equivalent of a diving tower, so characteristic of human pools yet so conspicuously absent from zoos.

Fittingly, Lubetkin's transcendent explorations not only borrowed from sympathetic human solutions but repaid the favor to the source. Thus the cookie-cutter pattern would soon be echoed in public and private pools, such as that of the resort hotel of 1940 at Arrowhead Springs by Gordon Kaufmann and Paul R. Williams, executed by free-form pioneers Paddock Pools. There is also a strong similarity between the amenities for the bears and tigers at the Dudley Zoo and the shallow, elliptical moat pool for fishes of Richard Neutra's house for Josef von Sternberg of 1927 in the San Fernando Valley.[62] After the war, Italian architect Giulio Minoletti borrowed from another type of zoo pool, the aquarium, for such elements as the subterranean display windows of his pool at Monza (figs. 7.21, 7.22). Here Minoletti gave his patrons the opportunity to transform themselves into fishes exploring in elegant movements the coral arches on the bottom, witnessed by other guests through the portholes of the lower level (see fig. 5.19). What these aquatic monuments have in common is their evident educational exhibitionism; whereas the average screened-off pool is an exercise in privacy, these zoo-related ones have made swimming into a public display.

By far the most striking continuation of Lubetkin's concept of zoological empathy is found in the work of California architect John Lautner. The Villa Marbrisa or Arango house of 1973, situated on a steep hill overlooking Acapulco Bay in Mexico (figs. 7.23, 7.24), is a child's dream of "If I were a penguin."[63] Like Lubetkin's enterprises, the villa is a study in free-flying reinforced concrete, composed of generously cantilevered slabs and saucers connected by stairs, ramps, and the small concrete bridges that span a miniature beltway of water. From the exterior the house is not unlike the Guggenheim Museum, an unsurprising affinity since Lautner served an apprenticeship with the master in Taliesin, Wisconsin. Nevertheless it is striking how the original rationale of Wright's ramps—an aestheticized reworking of a parking garage—has found its just application in the infrastructure of the house. Instead of the customary round-the-fireplace coziness, the interior—or rather the space allotted to residential use—has been inspired by various forms of mechanized traffic. The concrete screens and roof slabs, carried by hefty concrete pylons, project the light and shade of an interstate overpass, allowing about the same degree of domesticity as a tramp must feel pitching his tent under a freeway

61. See Elizabeth Smith, ed., *Blueprints for Modern Living: History and Legacy of the Case Study Houses* (Los Angeles: Museum of Contemporary Art; Cambridge: MIT Press, 1989).

62. Cheney and Cheney, *Art and the Machine,* 163, and Thomas S. Hines, *Richard Neutra and the Search for Modern Architecture* (New York: Oxford University Press, 1982), 132–137.

63. The Arango house is generously illustrated in the new compendium edited by Frank Escher: *John Lautner, Architect* (London, Zurich, and Munich: Artemis, 1994), 180–189. See also *Architecture d'Aujourd'hui* 250 (April 1987), 91; *Architectural Digest* 104 (May 1978), 104–107, 111, 114.

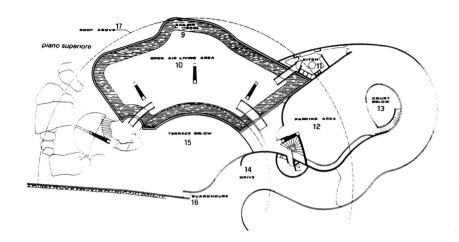

7.23. Acapulco: Villa Marbrisa (Arango house), 1973, plan. John Lautner. (*Architecture d'Aujourd'hui,* 1987.)

7.24. *Opposite:* Arango house pool. (Escher, *John Lautner, Architect,* 1994.)

64. Escher, *John Lautner,* 181.
65. Joseph Rosa, *Albert Frey, Architect* (New York: Rizzoli, 1990), 71–72. For Church's comment, see Thomas D. Church, *Gardens Are for People* (1955; New York: McGraw-Hill, 1983).

flyover. The connections that are forged by ramps and loosely arranged steps are strongly suggestive of intersections on highways and in parking garages. Most of the house is an open-air theater of fixed concrete furniture and curved concrete bands demarcating the space.

Around the terrace runs a "moated pool" measuring about 350 square feet. The "vanishing edge" technique of concealing the outer rim of the pool by a continuous overflow of water spilling into a gutter, already tested in Silver Top House, Silver Lake, Los Angeles, of 1957, has become Lautner's trademark. The recent monograph edited by Frank Escher has targeted some thrilling if equivocal merits of this specific type of pool, "wide enough to allow uninterrupted swimming and also [to act] as a moat to keep crawling animals and insects out of the house." Out of the house, perhaps, but not out of the pool,[64] making "uninterrupted swimming" an act more of compulsion than of free will.

The Villa Marbrisa is a dramatic demonstration of the integrated pool concept, in which house and swimming pool have become a single unitary whole, neither claiming dominance over the other. Unlike the simpler concept of juxtaposition, in which the pool remains separated, here water runs through the house in the form of fluent corridors and hallways. The indoor-outdoor pools of the prewar period (see chapter 3) and the London penguin pool were the models on which the postwar free-form integrated pools were based. When pool builder/landscape architect Thomas Church observed in 1955 that "the pool is a place to gather around, much as a fire place is in a room," he must have been aware of the projects of Philip Ilsley and other southern California architects who, inspired by the cooling properties of its contents, extended the swimming pool to the cozy inglenook around the fireplace, as in designer Raymond Loewy's house by Albert Frey (1947; fig. 7.25), situated in the hot desert climate of Palm Springs.[65]

7.25. Palm Springs, California: Raymond Loewy
house, 1947. Albert Frey. (Rosa, *Albert Frey,
Architect,* 1990; photo: Julius Shulman.)

Pools of the aquachute-aquapark period of the early twentieth century relied for their effect on the public's inability to provide its own interpretation of water, and its resistance to high-energy outputs where rewards in terms of excitement are low. In present-day aquaparks, swimming has become secondary to playing and watching. Lubetkin was right on the mark when he said that his zoo pool had to be a union of the swimming pool and the circus, of active and passive entertainment.

66. Thomas D. Church, *Your Private World: A Study of Intimate Gardens* (San Francisco: McGraw-Hill, 1969), 130; Church, *Gardens Are for People*, 186. I am grateful to Daniel Gregory of *Sunset* (Menlo Park, Calif.: Lane Publishing Co.) for his wise counsel.
67. Church, *Gardens Are for People*, 182–186.

A Dog in a Kidney-Shaped Pool The design that brought Church fame as the consummate designer of the free-form pool was the 60-foot kidney-shaped pool of 1949 for Mr. and Mrs. Dewey Donnell, in Sonoma, California (fig. 7.26).[66] To publicize his "invention," Church had recourse to a characteristic set of photographs by Carolyn Caddes showing the pool's most appropriate uses, at least three of which were selected to illustrate Church's books on garden design. The photograph shown here (fig. 7.27) is of a slightly deviant nature, and perhaps especially powerful in its *modus explicandi*. It has been taken from an elevated standpoint, probably from one of two live oaks to the left of the springboard, a position required to articulate clearly the pool's undulating circumference. To assist the viewer in drawing the correct conclusions, several objects of analogous organicity are randomly arranged within the picture's frame. A quartet of butterfly chairs from 1938 (one pair dressed, the other without their covering garment) may be glimpsed on the far deck, while an arbitrarily shaped plaything floating on the pool's surface demonstrates careless capriciousness. But the most penetrating demonstration is given by the owner, shown encouraging his dog to make free use of the master's pool by flinging into it some compelling lure. The photographer has taken great pains to freeze the splash, so that the pet's eventual dive should not escape the observer. A dog in the pool (fig. 7.28) suggests total social emancipation, the sort of freedom California has always symbolized. In this context, freedom of use serves as the index of freedom of form.[67]

Still, in following organic shapes like kidneys or hearts, or the biomorphic forms of Picasso's ceramics and Calder's mobiles, free-form pools were actually following preset patterns. Really free the free-form pool rarely was. Apart from this episode, in which the form was only as free as the silent norms of associative naturalism allowed it to be, the contours of domestic pools remained uniform. On offer were the rectangle, the oval, the rectangle combined with the oval to produce the "Roman" or "Pompeian" pool, the circle, and finally the kidney shape, no more than an oval with two eccentric circles—at least that was the rule of thumb by which they were constructed.

Church distinguished various kinds of swimming pools. The first, "for swimming," was not the sort of commission Church considered fulfilling, and he recommended merely that the design be of "the old-familiar rectangular" type. Then there was the theatrical type, in which "we can sacrifice the convenience of the swimmer in order to enhance the view

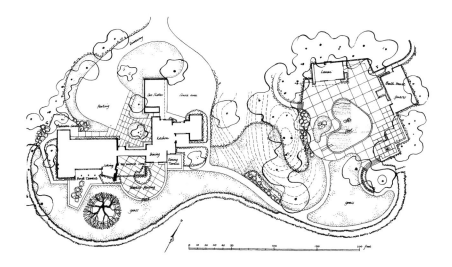

7.26. *Top:* Sonoma, California: Dewey Donnell pool, 1949, site plan. Thomas Church. (Church, *Your Private World*, 1969.)

7.27. Donnell pool, photo by Carolyn Caddes. (Church, *Your Private World*, 1969.) *Also plate 26.*

7.28. On a sunny Saturday afternoon, the public swimming pool of Montfoort, the Netherlands, was reserved for dogs and their owners. (*NRC Handelsblad,* September 14, 1992; photo: Roel Rozenburg.)

of the observer." The pool was stage, the swimmer actor. "One step further away from strict functionalism gets us to the European-style villa pool"; next is the "Garden Pool . . . obviously never intended to be swum in, but to add highlight and emphasis to the garden." And finally we arrive at the "High Formalist pool," which need not be "at all useful," argued Church with the conviction of the landscape architect, "but very handsome."[68]

68. Church, *Your Private World,* 127ff.
69. Dawes, *Design and Planning of Swimming Pools,* 61.
70. Cocteau explained his technique in a documentary film made by Edgardo Cozarinsky (1983). Thanks to Teri Damisch, Paris.

Swimming Pools for Fishes "Within the next decade," predicted swimming pool builder and writer John Dawes in 1969, "it is quite on the cards that many people will want to keep water animals as pets outside zoos. Some families already have grey seals and freshwater otters in their own swimming pools, and there is even a successful trout fishery in one self-sufficient enthusiast's converted back-garden swimming pool."[69]

The idea of a seal pool for human use was certainly not unprecedented. In making *Sang d'un poète,* in which the protagonist rolls over into a small swimming basin and subsequently breaks through a mirror into a world beyond, Jean Cocteau employed an actual seal pool for better effect. "You cannot begin to imagine what it was like," Cocteau later explained. "I got the seal pool from the Zoo. And I shot the sequence from the roof [accomplished by the perpendicular rigging of the camera]. . . . When the man steps into the mirror he is really stepping into the seal pool."[70]

The ordinary outdoor swimming pool is falling out of favor as people become disgusted by the foul air and unhealthful water, or just get bored. It is now fashionable to fill in the pool and make a Japanese rock garden instead. The private tennis court is preferred, but

7.29. Santa Barbara, California: Nishiki-Koi nursery, Montecito Street, mural. *Also plate 27.*
7.30. *Opposite:* Narbonne, France: church of St.-Paul, font with frog that was petrified because it had sung in the church. (Postcard.)

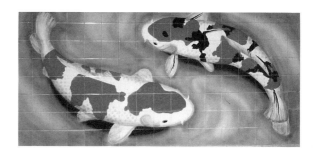

71. Maggie Valentine, *The Show Starts on the Sidewalk: An Architectural History of the Movie Theatre* (New Haven: Yale University Press, 1994), 181. Lee died in January 1990, having completed the work on his pool/pond during the time koi collecting was at its peak.
72. Robert Smaus, "Fish Fanciers in the Swim with 'Living Jewels,'" *Los Angeles Times,* February 25, 1990, K16. The article provides a list of addresses of koi clubs.

its fate is equally uncertain; pollution affects the tennis player as much as the swimmer. And the biggest problem with the private tennis court is that in an increasingly autistic society, there are too many owners and not enough players.

One diversion that is quietly gaining popularity is the fish pond. Fish are indubitably back in the garden, but which kind should one choose? The status seeker would seem unlikely to settle for a pair of quaint, reliable, and modestly priced goldfish. What the smart set currently craves is the Japanese *nishiki-koi*. Like the goldfish, the koi belongs to the carp family, but it has two obvious advantages for the fashion-conscious: it is far more expensive than the goldfish—koi cost several hundred dollars each—and it is too fragile to survive in an ordinary garden pond. For the rest, the very attractive color patterns that run over its back are best viewed from above, and it is a friendly and docile pet. What the koi needs is clear water that is constantly kept to a strict standard of purity by sophisticated filtration systems.

The quality of the water should approach that of good drinking water and contain no harmful chemicals, unlike most swimming pools. As for what a koi pond should look like, no stringent prescriptions have been given. Japanese-style garden ponds provide excellent models, as do traditional free-form pools from the 1930–1950 period. To convert an organically shaped swimming pool into a koi pond is not difficult, as long as the fish have sufficient water, some 300 gallons per fish being needed when the koi is maturing. The larger the pond, the bigger it grows. Maggie Valentine, biographer of movie theater architect S. Charles Lee, reported that Lee had the swimming pool of his Beverly Hills house converted into an emphatically hydrophobic ensemble: "The swimming pool in the backyard was converted into a lake engineered with electric boats and a pier for his grandchildren and later became home of his koi collection."[71]

West Coast koi nurseries are prestigious enterprises (fig. 7.29), requiring as they do considerable capital. In 1990, an article devoted to the new fad reported the theft of 400 fish from the Philip Ishizu nursery of San Gabriel.[72] What makes the koi phenomenon so interesting is the alarmingly brief amount of time in which man has evolved from a devoted outdoor creature to a frightened indoor one, leaving his carefully recreated similacrum of the great wilderness/garden cum pool to a couple of carp and turning his costly investment into an expensive aquarium. Where man used to do battle with the elements, fortifying his body by early morning laps or playing the frontiersman at his weekend poolside cookout, he is now content to watch a fleet of Japanese replacements braving the lethal toxins of his former Robinsonian paradise.

Humans dug holes in the ground, filled them with water, fitted ladders, and installed springboards. Then they added disinfectants and coloring agents but eventually, apprehensive of what they had wrought, came to shun the family pool, influenced by environmental superstition, fear of litigation, and, perhaps most of all, boredom. First they banned the springboard, then they banned their children, and finally they banned themselves. Now the road is free for a new generation of social swimmers: goldfish, koi, even sharks begin to populate the family pool. The circle is complete. The *piscine* has been restored to its original state (fig. 7.30).

Aarons, Slim. *A Wonderful Time: An Intimate Portrait of the Good Life.* New York: Harper and Row, 1974.

Adam, Peter. *Eileen Gray: Architect/Designer.* London: Thames and Hudson, 1987.

Adamson, Simon. *Seaside Piers.* London: Batsford, 1977.

Albrecht, Donald. *Designing Dreams: Modern Architecture in the Movies.* London: Thames and Hudson, 1986.

Allan, John. *Berthold Lubetkin: Architecture and the Tradition of Progress.* London: RIBA Publications, 1992.

Alleman, Richard. *The Movie Lover's Guide to Hollywood.* New York: Harper and Row, 1985.

Anderson, Timothy, Eudorah Moore, and Robert Winter. *California Design 1910.* Salt Lake City: Gibbs and Smith, 1980.

Andree, Herb, and Noel Young. *Santa Barbara Architecture: From Spanish Colonial to Modern.* Santa Barbara: Capra Press, 1980.

Appelbaum, Stanley. *The New York World's Fair, 1939/40 in 155 Photographs by Richard Wurts and Others.* New York: Dover, 1977.

Architectural Digest. "Academy Awards Collectors Item." April 1990.

Architectural Digest. "Academy Awards Collectors Item." April 1992.

Argy, d'. *Instruction für den Schwimmunterricht in der französischen Armee.* 4th ed. [Berlin], 1877.

Armbruster, D. A., Robert Allen, and Bruce Harlan. *Swimming and Diving.* St. Louis: Mosby, 1958.

Armitage, John. *Man at Play: Nine Centuries of Pleasure Making.* London: F. Warne, 1977.

Astor, Mary. *A Life on Film.* New York: Delacorte Press, 1971.

Bàccolo, Luigi. "Una donna che si sfoglia; storia dello strip-tease." *Ciga Hotels Magazine* 47: 24–35.

Bachelard, Gaston. *L'eau et les rêves; essai sur l'imagination de la matière.* 1942; Paris: José Corti, 1989.

Bachstrom, Jean F. *L'art de nager, ou l'invention à l'aide de laquelle on peut toujours se sauver du naufrage, etc.* Amsterdam, 1741.

Bachstrom, Jean F. *De konst van zwemmen of Nieuwe Uitvinding door behulp van welke men zich by Schipbreuk altyd kan redden, en in tyd van nood geheele Legers de grootste Rivieren kan doen passeren. Seer Nu en noodzakelyk voor Officieren, Matroozen, Soldaaten en andere Varende lieden; So te water als te Land.* Haarlem: J. van Lee, 1742.

Bacon, Mardges. *Ernest Flagg: Beaux-Arts Architect and Urban Reformer.* Cambridge: MIT Press; New York: Architectural History Foundation, 1986.

Baker, Paul. *Stanny: The Gilded Life of Stanford White.* London and New York: Macmillan, 1989.

Balint, Michael. *Thrills and Regressions.* New York: International Universities Press, 1959.

Banham, Reyner. *Los Angeles: The Architecture of Four Ecologies.* New York: Harper and Row, 1971.

Banner, Lois W. *American Beauty: A Social History.* New York: Knopf, 1983.

Bates, Karen Grigsby. *Paul R. Williams, Architect: A Legend of Style.* New York: Rizzoli, 1993.

Battisti, Eugenio. *L'antirinascimento.* Milan: Feltrinelli, 1962.

Bazin, Germain. *Théodore Géricault; étude critique.* Paris: Bibliothèque des Arts, 1987.

Beaumont-Maillet, Laure. *Histoire de l'eau à Paris.* Paris: Hazan, 1991.

Berger, Albrecht. *Das Bad in de byzantinischen Zeit.* Munich: Institut für Byzantinistik und neugriechische Philologie der Universität, 1982.

Bernink, Mieke. "Een brekingsindex van 1.3.: De filmische aantrekkingskracht van zwembaden." *Film op waterbasis.* Amsterdam, 1990.

Biehn, Heinz, and Johanna, Baronin Herzogenberg. *Grosse Welt reist ins Bad, nach Briefen, Erinnerungen und anderen Quellen zur Darstellung gebracht.* Munich: Prestel, 1960.

Blaisdell, Marilyn. *San Francisciana: Photographs of Sutro Baths.* San Francisco: Blaisdell Publisher, 1987.

Blume, Bernhard. *Existenz und Dichtung.* Frankfort: Insel, 1980.

Blunt, Anthony. *Guide to Baroque Rome.* London: Granada Publishing, 1982.

Blunt, Wilfrid. *The Ark in the Park: The Zoo in the Nineteenth Century.* London: Hamilton, 1961.

Blunt, Wilfrid. *The Dream King: Ludwig II of Bavaria.* Harmondsworth: Penguin, 1973.

Böhme, Hartmut, ed. *Kulturgeschichte des Wassers.* Frankfurt: Suhrkamp, 1988.

Böhme, Hartmut, and Gernot Böhme. *Feuer, Wasser, Erde, Luft: Eine Kulturgeschichte der Elemente.* Munich: Beck, 1996.

Bongaardt, Jos van den. *Elke Week een goed Bad; Geschiedenis en Architectuur van de Badhuizen van Amsterdam.* Amsterdam: Stadsuitgeverij, 1990.

Bonta, Juan Pablo. *Architecture and Its Interpretation.* New York: Rizzoli, 1979.

Borchmeyer, Dieter, ed. *Wege des Mythos in der Moderne: Richard Wagner: Der Ring des Nibelungen.* Munich: Deutscher Taschenbuch Verlag, 1987.

Bosman, Jos. *Mart Stam; Reise in die Schweiz, 1923–1925.* Zurich: GTA/Ammans Verlag, 1991.

Bosman, Jos, and Sokratis Georgiadas, eds. *Sigfried Giedion; der Entwurf einer modernen Tradition.* Zurich: GTA/Ammans Verlag, 1989.

Bothe, Rolf, ed. *Kurstädte in Deutschland.* Berlin: Frölich & Kaufmann, 1984.

Bourke, Captain John G. *Scatologic Rites of All Nations.* Washington, D.C.: W. H. Loudermilk, 1891.

Boutelle, Sara Holmes. *Julia Morgan, Architect.* New York: Abbeville Press, 1988.

Boyle, Robert H. *Sport—Mirror of American Life.* Boston: Little, Brown, 1963.

Braun, Edward, ed. *Meyerhold on Theatre.* London: Methuen, 1969.

Briffault, Eugène. "Une journée à l'école de natation." In *Le diable à Paris,* vol. 2, 124–146. Paris: J. Hetzel, 1844.

Buddensieg, Tilmann. *Villa Hugal; das Wohnhaus Krupp in Essen.* Berlin: Siedler, 1984.

California Arts and Architecture. "A monthly magazine covering the field of architecture and the allied arts and crafts. Combining the *Pacific Coast Architect,* established 1911, and *California Southland,* established 1918, with which has been merged *California Home Owner,* established 1922." On the staff were Thomas D. Church and Mark Daniels; Gordon Kaufmann was on the editorial advisory board.

"California Pools." *California Arts and Architecture* 57 (April 1940), 32–33. Article with photos of pools by Paddock Pools, Inc.

Canter Cremers-Van der Does, Eline. *Het Bad.* Bussum: Van Dishoeck, n.d. [1950s].

Carasso-Kok, Marijke. *Amsterdam Historisch; een stadsgeschiedenis aan de hand van de collectie van het Amsterdams Historisch Museum.* Bussum: Fibula-Van Dishoeck, 1975.

Chatwin, Bruce, and Deyan Sudjic. *John Pawson.* Barcelona: Gustavo Gili, 1992.

Cheney, Sheldon. *The New World Architecture.* London and New York: Longmans, Green, 1930.

Cheney, Sheldon, and Martha Cheney. *Art and the Machine.* New York and London: Whittlesey House, 1936.

Cheyne, George. *The English Malady, or a Treatise of Nervous Diseases of All Kinds.* Tavistock: Routledge, 1990.

Church, Thomas D. *Your Private World: A Study of Intimate Gardens.* San Francisco: McGraw-Hill, 1969.

Clark, Alson. "The California Architecture of Gordon B. Kaufmann." *Society of Architectural Historians, Southern California Chapter* 1, no. 3 (Summer 1982), 1–7.

Coffman, Taylor. *Hearst Castle: The Story of William Randolph Hearst and San Simeon.* Santa Barbara: Sequoia Books, 1989.

Collins, Peter. *Changing Ideals in Modern Architecture.* Montreal: McGill-Queen's University Press, 1967.

Collins, Peter. *Concrete, the Vision of a New Architecture: A Study of Auguste Perret and His Precursors.* London: Faber and Faber, 1959.

Cople Jaher, F., ed. *The Rich, the Well-Born and the Powerful.* Urbana: University of Illinois Press, 1973.

Corbin, Alain. *The Lure of the Sea: The Discovery of the Seaside in the Western World, 1750–1840.* Berkeley: University of California Press, 1994. (Originally *La territoire du vide,* 1988.)

Corbin, Alain. *Le miasme et la jonquille; l'odorat et l'imaginaire social, XVIIIe–XIXe siècles.* Paris: Aubier Montaigne, 1982.

Coupe, Fay. "Pool History: A History of the Pool and Spa Industry." *Pool and Spa News,* 15 installments numbered I–XV, from November 17, 1986, to October 23, 1989.

Cross, Alfred W. S. *Public Baths and Wash Houses.* London: Batsford, 1906.

Cross, Alfred W. S., and K. B. M. Cross. *Modern Public Baths.* London, 1938.

Cross, Rick, ed. *The ASA Guide to Better Swimming.* London: Pan Books, 1987.

Croutier, Alev Lytle. *Taking the Waters: Spirit, Art, Sensuality.* New York: Abbeville, 1992.

Curl, Donald W. *Mizner's Florida.* Cambridge: MIT Press, 1984.

Czigens, Ilse, Franziska Schmitt, and Detlev Zinke, eds. *Naturbetrachtung/Naturverfremdung.* Stuttgart: Württembergischer Kunstverein, 1977.

Dalí, Salvador. *The Secret Life of Salvador Dali*. New York: Dial Press, 1942.

Davies, Marion. *The Times We Had: Life with William Randolph Hearst*. New York: Ballantine, 1975.

Dawes, John. *Design and Planning of Swimming Pools*. London: Architectural Press; Boston: CBI Press, 1979.

Dekkers, Midas. *Lief Dier; over Bestialiteit*. Amsterdam: Contact, 1992. Trans. as *Dearest Pet: On Bestiality*; London and New York: Verso, 1994.

Delevoy, Robert, and Maurice Culot. *Henri Sauvage, 1873–1932*. Brussels: Archives d'Architecture Moderne, 1977.

Delong, David, et al. *Design in America: The Cranbrook Vision*. New York: Abrams, 1983.

Deux siècles d'architecture sportive à Paris: piscines, gymnases . . . Paris: Délégation à l'action artistique de la ville de Paris, Mairie du XXe arrondissement, 1984.

Digby, Edward. *De arte natandi. Libri duo*. London, 1587.

Dix-Huitième Siècle: revue annuelle publiée par la société française d'étude du 18e siècle 9 (1977), special issue: *Le sain et le malsain*.

Dobyns, Winifred Starr. *California Gardens*. New York: Macmillan, 1931.

Du Camp, Maxime. *Paris, ses organes, ses fonctions et sa vie, dans la seconde moitié du XIXe siècle*. 6 vols. Paris: Hachette, 1875. Rpt. in one volume, 1993.

Dulles, Foster Rhea. *A History of Recreation: America Learns to Play*. New York: Appleton-Century-Crofts, 1965.

Dunaway, David King. *Huxley in Hollywood*. 1989; New York: Doubleday, 1991.

Dunning, E. *The Sociology of Sport*. London: F. Cass, 1968.

Eco, Umberto. *Travels in Hyperreality*. London: Picador, 1986.

Edgell, G. H. *The American Architecture of To-day*. New York: Charles Scribner's Sons, 1928.

Eleb-Vidal, Monique, with Anne Debarre-Blanchard. *Architectures de la vie privée: maisons et mentalités XVIIe et XIXe siècles*. Brussels: Archives d'Architecture Moderne, 1989.

Eliade, Mircea. *Mythes, rêves, et mystères*. Paris: Gallimard, 1957.

Elias, Norbert. *Der hofische Gesellschaft: Über den Prozess der Zivilisation*. 2 vols. Frankfurt: Suhrkamp, 1990.

Elias, Norbert, and Eric Dunning. *Quest for Excitement: Sport and Leisure in the Civilizing Process*. Oxford: Basil Blackwell, 1968.

Escher, Frank, ed. *John Lautner, Architect*. London and Zurich: Artemis, 1994.

Fagiolo dell'Arco, Marcello. *Villa Aldobrandina Tusculana*. Rome, 1986.

Failing, P. "William Randolph Hearst's Enchanted Hill." *Art News* 78, no. 1 (January 1979), 53–59.

Fitzgerald, F. Scott. *The Great Gatsby*. 1925; New York: Charles Scribner's Sons, 1953.

Forest de Belidor, Bernard. *Architecture hydraulique ou l'art de conduire, d'élever et de ménager les eaux*. Paris, 1739.

Frank, Manfred. *Die unendliche Fahrt; die Geschichte des Fliegenden Holländers und verwandter Motive*. Leipzig: Reclam, 1995.

Franklin, B. *The Art of Swimming Made Safe, Easy, Pleasant and Healthful, to which are added cautions to learners and advice to bathers.* London, n.d. (1850?).

Garbrecht, Günther, et al. *Geschichte der Wasserversorgung.* Mainz: Philip von Zabern Verlag, 1987.

Gebhard, David, ed. *George Washington Smith, 1876–1930: The Spanish Colonial Revival in California.* Santa Barbara: Art Gallery of the University of California at Santa Barbara, 1964.

Geis, Christine. *Georgian Court.* 1982; Philadelphia: Art Alliance Press, 1991.

Genzmer, Felix. *Bade- und Schwimmanstalten.* In Josef Durm, *Handbuch der Architektur,* 4:5:3. Stuttgart: Arnold Bergsträsser Verlagsbuchhandlung, 1899.

Gerhard, W. P. *Modern Baths and Bath Houses.* Boston: Stanhope Press, 1908.

Giedion, Sigfried. *Das Bad im Kulturganzen.* Zurich: Kunstgewerbemuseum, 1935.

Giedion, Sigfried. "Das Bad als Kulturmass." *Schweizerische Bauzeitung,* July 1935.

Giedion, Sigfried. *Mechanization Takes Command: A Contribution to Anonymous History.* 1948; New York: Oxford University Press, 1969.

Giedion, Sigfried. *Space, Time and Architecture.* Cambridge: Harvard University Press, 1941.

Gill, Brendan. *The Dream Come True: Great Houses of Los Angeles.* New York: Lippincott and Crowell, 1980.

Ginouvès, René. *Balaneutikè, recherches sur le bain dans l'antiquité grècque.* Paris: E. de Boccard, 1962.

Gleye, Paul. *The Architecture of Los Angeles.* Los Angeles: Rosebud Books, 1981.

Götz, Wolfgang. *Deutsche Marställe des Barock.* Munich and Berlin: Deutscher Kunstverlag, 1964.

Goubert, Jean-Pierre. *The Conquest of Water: The Advent of Health in the Industrial Age.* Oxford: Polity Press, 1989. (Originally *La conquète d'eau,* 1986.)

Gowans, Alan. *Images of American Living: Four Centuries of Architecture and Furniture as Cultural Expression.* New York: Harper and Row, 1976.

Graham, Sheilah. *The Garden of Allah.* New York: Crown, 1970.

Granick, Harry. *Underneath New York.* New York and Toronto, 1947.

Grenier, Lise, ed. *Villes d'eaux en France.* Paris: Institut Français d'Architecture, 1989.

Guillerme, André. *Les temps de l'eau; la cité, l'eau et les techniques.* Champ Vallon: Seyssel, 1983.

Hamst, Olphar [Ralph Thomas]. *A List of Works on Swimming from the Invention of Printing to the Present Time Bound Together with R. Harrington, A Few Words on Swimming.* London, 1876.

Handlin, David. *The American Home: Architecture and Society 1815–1915.* Boston and Toronto: Little, Brown, 1979.

Hansen, Gladys, and Emmet Condon. *Denial of Disaster: The Untold Story and Photographs of the San Francisco Earthquake and Fire of 1906.* San Francisco: Cameron, 1990.

Hardy, Alister. *The Biology of God: A Scientist's Study of Man the Religious Animal.* London: J. Cape, 1984.

Hardy, Alister. *Darwin and the Spirit of Man*. London: Collins, 1984.

Hardy, Alister. *Great Waters: A Voyage of Natural History to Study Whales, Plankton and the Waters of the Southern Ocean in the Old Royal Research Ship "Discovery."* London: Collins, 1967.

Hardy, Alister. *The Open Sea: Its Natural History*. Boston: Houghton Mifflin, 1956–1959.

Harwood, Kathryn Chapman. *The Lives of Vizcaya: Annals of a Great House*. Miami, 1985.

Hatton, Hap. *Tropical Splendor: An Architectural History of Florida*. New York: Knopf, 1987.

Haver, Ronald. *David O. Selznick's Hollywood*. London: Secker and Warburg, 1980.

Hawcroft, Tim. *Horse and Pony Care: An Illustrated Handbook*. London and New York, 1986.

Hepburn, Andrew. *Great Resorts of North America*. Garden City, N.Y.: Doubleday, 1965.

Hess, Thomas B., and Linda Nochlin, eds. *Woman as Sex Object: Studies in Erotic Art, 1730–1970*. London: Allan Lane, 1972.

Hine, Robert V. *California's Utopian Colonies*. 1953; Berkeley: University of California Press, 1966.

Hine, Thomas. *Populuxe*. New York: Knopf, 1986.

Hines, Thomas S. "Los Angeles Architecture: The Issue of Tradition in a Twentieth Century City." In David De Long, Helen Searing, and R. A. M. Stern, eds., *American Architecture: Innovation and Tradition*. New York: Rizzoli, 1986, 112–129.

Hines, Thomas S. *Richard Neutra and the Search for Modern Architecture*. New York: Oxford University Press, 1982.

Hovorka, Hans. *Republik "Konge": ein Schwimmbad erzählt seine Geschichte*. Vienna: Verlag der Österreichischen Staatsdruckerei, 1988.

Hudson, Karen E. *Paul R. Williams, Architect: A Legacy of Style*. New York: Rizzoli, 1993.

Humphreys, Phoebe Westcott. *The Practical Book of Garden Architecture*. Philadelphia: J. B. Lippincott, 1914.

Hunt, A. Lowell. *Florida Today*. New York, 1950.

Huret, Jules. *L'Amérique moderne*. 2 vols. Paris: Pierre Lafitte & Cie, 1911.

Huxley, Aldous. *After Many a Summer Dies the Swan*. London: Tauchshnitz, 1939.

Illich, Ivan. *H_2O and the Waters of Forgetfulness*. London: Boyars, 1986.

Ingle, Marjorie. *The Mayan Revival Style*. Albuquerque: University of New Mexico Press, 1984.

Jarry, Alfred. *Gestes et opinions du docteur Faustroll, Pataphysicien, hors commerce*. 1898; Paris: Gallimard, 1980.

Jervis, Simon, and Gerhard Hojer. *Designs for the Dream King: The Castles and Palaces of Ludwig II of Bavaria*. Exh. cat. London: Debrett's Peerage in association with the Victoria and Albert Museum, London, and Cooper-Hewitt Museum, New York, 1978.

Kahrl, William L., ed. *The California Water Atlas*. Sacramento: State of California, 1978, 1979, etc.

Kantorowitz, Ernst Hartwig. *The King's Two Bodies*. 1957; Princeton: Princeton University Press, 1966.

Kiby, Ulrika. *Bäder und Badekultur in Orient und Okzident, Antike bis Spätbarock.* Cologne: DuMont, 1995.

Kiby, Ulrika, and Erich Küthe. *Badewonnen: Gestern, Heute, Morgen.* Cologne: Hansgrohe & DuMont, 1993.

Kiby, Ulrika, and Erich Küthe. *Bad und Badevergnügen von der Antike bis zur Gegenwart.* Cologne: DuMont, 1993.

King, Robert B., with Charles O. MacLean. *The Vanderbilt Homes.* New York: Rizzoli, 1989.

Kingsley, Charles. *The Water-Babies: A Fairy Tale for a Land-Baby.* 1863; London: Macmillan, 1889.

Kinney, Abbot. *Tasks by Twilight.* Los Angeles: B. R. Baumgardt, 1893.

Klein, Kelly. *Pools.* New York: Knopf, 1992.

Klingensmith, Samuel John. *The Utility of Splendor: Ceremony, Social Life, and Architecture at the Court of Bavaria, 1600–1800.* Chicago: University of Chicago Press, 1993.

Koch, Hugo. *Gartenkunst im Städtebau.* Berlin: Wasmuth, 1914.

Koolhaas, Rem. *Delirious New York.* New York: Oxford University Press, 1978.

Kopilchack, Madeline. *The New American Garden.* New York: Prentice-Hall, 1988.

Krieg, Joann P., ed. *Robert Moses: Single Minded Genius.* Interlaken, N.Y.: Heart of the Lakes Publishing, 1989.

Kyriazi, Gary. *The Great American Amusement Parks.* Secaucus, N.J.: Castle Books, 1978.

Lachmayer, Herbert, Sylvia Mattl-Wurm, and Christian Gargerle, eds. *Das Bad; eine Geschichte der Badekultur im 19. und 20. Jahrhundert.* Salzburg: Residenz Verlag, 1991.

Lambton, Lucinda. *Temples of Convenience.* London: Pavilion, 1995.

Landmann, Robert. *Ascona–Monte Verità; auf der Suche nach dem Paradies.* Zurich and Cologne: Benzinger, 1973.

Leakey, L. S. B., and Vanne Morris Goodall. *Unveiling Man's Origins: Ten Decades of Thought about Human Evolution.* London: Methuen, 1969.

Leeuwen, Thomas A. P. van. *The Skyward Trend of Thought.* Cambridge: MIT Press, 1988.

Lefevre, Dorothy Jane. "Geographic Aspects of the Private Swimming Pool Industry in Los Angeles." M.A. thesis, University of California at Los Angeles, 1961.

Leistner, Dieter, Hans-Eberhard Hess, and Dirk Meyerhöfer. *The Water Temple: Gründerzeit and Jugendstil Public Baths.* London: Academy Editions, 1994.

Lemmen, Hans van. *Tiles in Architecture.* London: Laurence King, 1993.

Lencek, Lena, and Gideon Bosker. *Making Waves: Swimsuits and the Undressing of America.* San Francisco: Chronicle Books, 1989.

Lincoln, Bruce. "The Waters of Remembrance and Forgetfulness." *Fabula* 23, 19–34.

Lockwood, Charles. *Dream Palaces: Hollywood at Home.* New York: Viking Press, 1981.

Lockwood, Charles, and Jeff Hyland. *The Estates of Beverly Hills.* Beverly Hills, Calif.: Lockwood and Hyland, 1989.

Loyer, François. *Paris: Nineteenth Century.* New York: Abbeville Press, 1988.

Lurie, Alson. "The Pool People." *Vogue,* August 1991, 251–317.

Macfadden, Bernarr. *Macfadden's Encyclopedia of Physical Culture.* 5 vols. New York: Physical Culture Publishing Company, 1911. 10th ed., 1928.

MacPherson, R. *A Dissertation on the Preservative from Drowning, etc.* 1783.

Mandelbaum, Howard, and Eric Meyers. *Screen Deco: A Celebration of High Style in Hollywood.* Bromley, Kent: Columbus Books, 1985.

Manderscheid, Hubertus. *Bibliographie zum roemischen Badewesen.* Munich, 1988.

Mantzneff, Gabriel. *L'archimandrite.* Paris, 1966.

Marin, Louis. *Utopics: Spatial Play.* Atlantic Highlands, N.J.: Humanities Press, 1984.

Martin, Alfred. *Deutsches Badewesen in vergangenen Tagen; nebst einem Beitrage zur Geschichte der Deutschen Wasserheilkunde.* Jena: Diederichs, 1906.

Martin, Richard, and Harold Koda. *Splash! A History of Swimwear.* New York: Rizzoli, 1990.

Mattl-Wurm, Sylvia, and Ursula Storch, eds. *Das Bad; Körperkultur und Hygiene im 19. und 20. Jahrhundert.* Exh. cat. Vienna: Eigenverlag der Museen der Stadt Wien, 1991.

Mayo, Morrow. *Los Angeles.* New York: Knopf, 1933.

Mehl, Erwin. *Antike Schwimmkunst.* Munich: Ernst Heimeran, 1927.

Meyers, Gifford. *Multiple Listings, Real Estate.* Exh. cat. Santa Barbara: University Art Museum, 1985.

Miller, Naomi. *Heavenly Caves: Reflections on the Garden Grotto.* New York: Braziller, 1982.

Millington, Barry, and Stewart Spencer. *Wagner in Performance.* New Haven: Yale University Press, 1992.

Moore, Charles. *Los Angeles: The City Observed.* New York: Vintage, 1984.

Moore, Charles W. "Water and Architecture." Thesis, Princeton University, 1957.

Morgan, Elaine. *The Scars of Evolution: What Our Bodies Tell Us about Human Origins.* Harmondsworth: Pelican, 1990.

Morgan, Keith. *Charles A. Platt: The Artist as Architect.* Cambridge: MIT Press; New York: Architectural History Foundation, 1985.

Morris, Desmond. *Manwatching: A Field Guide to Human Behavior.* New York: Abrams, 1982.

Murphy, Emmet. *The Great Bordellos of the World.* London: Quartet Books, 1983.

Murray, K. *The Golden Days of San Simeon.* Garden City, N.Y.: Doubleday, 1971.

Nadeau, Remi. *Los Angeles from Mission to Modern City.* London and New York: Longmans, Green, 1960.

Odent, Michel. *Genèse de l'homme écologique, l'instinct retrouvé.* Paris: Epi, 1979.

Oliver, Richard. *Bertram Grosvenor Goodhue.* Cambridge: MIT Press, 1983.

Orme, Nicholas. *Early British Swimming, 55 BC–AD 1719.* Exeter: University of Exeter Press, 1983.

Ortner, Rudolf. *Sportbauten: Anlage, Bau, Gestaltung.* Munich: Callwey, 1953.

Patterson, Augusta Owen. *American Homes of To-day: Their Architectural Style—Their Environment—Their Characteristics.* New York: Macmillan, 1924.

Patterson, Jerry F. *The Vanderbilts*. New York: Abrams, 1989.

Pautrat, Daniel. *Zwemmen*. Antwerp and Amsterdam: Standard, 1977.

Pérez-Gómez, Alberto. *Architecture and the Crisis of Modern Science*. Cambridge: MIT Press, 1984.

Perrin, Gerald A. *Sports Halls and Swimming Pools: A Design and Briefing Guide*. London and New York: E. & F. N. Spon, 1980.

Petzet, Michael, ed. *König Ludwig II und die Kunst*. Exh. cat. Munich: Münchener Residenz, 1968.

Petzet, Michael. *Ludwig II und seine Schlösser; die Welt des Bayerischen Märchenkönigs*. 1985; Munich: Prestel, 1995.

Pilat, Oliver, and Jo Ranson. *Sodom by the Sea*. New York: Doubleday, 1941.

Platt, Charles A. With an overview by Keith N. Morgan. *Italian Gardens*. 1894; London: Thames and Hudson, 1993.

Pliny. *The Letters of the Younger Pliny*. Trans. Betty Radice. Harmondsworth: Penguin, 1969.

Pozzi, G., and L. A. Pozzi. "La cultura figurativa di Francesco Colonna e l'arte veneta." In V. Branca, ed., *Umanesimo europeo e umanesimo veneziano*. Florence: Sansoni, 1963.

Rader, Benjamin G. *American Sports: From the Age of Folk Games to the Age of Spectators*. Englewood Cliffs, N.J.: Prentice Hall, 1983.

Ramirez, Juan Antonio. *La arquitectura en el cine; Hollywood, la Edad de Oro*. Madrid: Hermann Blume, 1986.

Randall, Monica. *The Mansions of Long Island's Gold Coast*. New York: Rizzoli, 1979.

Rasmussen, Steen Eiler. *Experiencing Architecture*. Cambridge: MIT Press, 1962.

Rindge, Ronald, and Thomas W. Doyle. *Ceramic Art of the Malibu Potteries: 1926–1932*. Malibu: Malibu Lagoon Museum, 1988.

Roché-Soulié, Sophie, and Sophie Roulet. *Piscines; équipements nautiques*. Paris: Le Moniteur, 1992.

Roding, Juliette. *Schoon en net: Hygiene in Woning en Stad*. The Hague: Staatsuitgeverij, 1986.

Roede, Machteld, et al., eds. *The Aquatic Ape: Fact or Fiction? The First Scientific Evaluation of a Controversial Theory of Human Evolution*. London: Souvenir Press, 1991.

Rosa, Joseph. *Albert Frey, Architect*. New York: Rizzoli, 1990.

Ross, Ishbel. *Taste in America: An Illustrated History of the Evolution of Architecture, Furnishings, Fashions and Customs of the American People*. New York: Crowell, 1967.

Rudolph, Jean. *Psychoanalysis and Synchronized Swimming*. Toronto: XYZ, 1991.

Rykwert, Joseph. *The First Moderns*. Cambridge: MIT Press, 1980.

Sarnitz, August. *R. M. Schindler, Architekt*. Vienna and Munich: Christian Brandstätter, 1986.

Schama, Simon. *Citizen: A Chronicle of the French Revolution*. New York: Knopf, 1989.

Schimmel, Annemarie, et al. *Water and Architecture*. Special issue of A.A.R.P. *Environmental Design Journal of the Islamic Environmental Design Research Centre* 2 (1985).

Schleyer, W. *Bäder und Badeanstalten*. Leipzig: Carl Scholtze, 1909.

Schmidt, Ulrich. *Inseln; Streifzüge von Geschichte und Gegenwart einer zauberhaften Welt. Von Atlantis bis Mallorca.* Lucerne and Frankfurt: E. J. Bücher, 1972.

Schnabels, J. G. "Wunderliche Fata Aufklärung: Romantik oder Biedermeier." *Nerthus* 2 (1969).

Schneider, Michel. *Un rêve de pierre; le Radeau de la Méduse, Géricault.* Paris: Gallimard, 1991.

Sclare, Liisa, and Donald Sclare. *Beaux-Arts Estates: A Guide to the Architecture of Long Island.* New York: Viking Press, 1980.

Scott, George Ripley. *The Story of Baths and Bathing.* London: Werner Laurie, 1939.

Seale, William. *The President's House: A History.* 2 vols. Washington, D.C.: White House Historical Association, 1986.

Seledec, Wilhelm, Helmut Kretschmer, and Herbert Lauscha, eds. *Baden und Bäder der Stadt Wien.* Vienna: Europa Verlag, 1987.

Sennett, Richard. *The Fall of Public Man.* 1977; New York: Norton, 1992.

Sexton, R. W. Intro. Arthur C. Holden. *The American Country Houses of Today.* New York: Architectural Book Publishing Co., 1930.

Sheridan, Mike. "Dive In!" *Sky* magazine (Delta Airlines), September 1989, 40–49.

Simmen, Jeannot. *Schwerelos; der Traum vom Fliegen in der Kunst der Moderne.* Berlin and Stuttgart: Schloss Charlottenburg/Edition Cantz, 1991.

Simmen, Jeannot. *Vertigo; Schwindel der modernen Kunst.* Munich: Klinkhardt & Biermann, 1990.

Simmen, Jeannot, and Uwe Drepper. *Der Fahrstuhl; die Geschichte der vertikalen Eroberung.* Munich: Prestel, 1983.

Simond, Charles. *Paris de 1800 à 1900; la vie parisienne au XIXe siècle.* 4 vols. Paris: Plon, 1900.

Sinclair, Archibald, and William Henry. *Swimming.* 1893; London: Longmans & Green (The Badminton Library), 1903.

Sklar, Robert. *Movie-Made America.* New York: Vintage Books, 1976.

Sky, Alison, and Michelle Stone. *Unbuilt New York.* New York: McGraw-Hill, 1976.

Smith, James Revel. *Springs and Wells of Manhattan and the Bronx: New York City at the End of the Nineteenth Century.* New York: New-York Historical Society, 1938.

Spaander, P. *Zweminrichtingen; hygienische Wenken voor Bouw en Exploitatie.* Amsterdam: Kosmos, 1944.

Spinzia, Raymond. *A Guide to New York: Suffolk and Nassau Counties.* New York: Hyppocrene Book, 1988.

Sprawson, Charles. *Haunts of the Black Masseur: The Swimmer as Hero.* London: Jonathan Cape, 1992.

Stafford, Barbara Maria. *Body Criticism: Imagining the Unseen in Enlightenment Art and Medicine.* Cambridge: MIT Press, 1991.

Starr, Kevin. *Material Dreams: Southern California through the 1920s.* New York: Oxford University Press, 1990.

Stein, Susan, ed. *The Architecture of R. M. Hunt.* Chicago: University of Chicago Press, 1986.

Strong, Roy. *Art and Power: Renaissance Festivals, 1450–1650*. Berkeley: University of California Press, 1984.

Strutt, Joseph. *The Sports and Pastimes of the People of England*. London: Chatto and Windus, 1876.

Swanberg, W. A. *Citizen Hearst: A Biography of William Randolph Hearst*. New York: Charles Scribner's Sons, 1961.

Szeemann, Harald, ed. *Der Hang zum Gesamtkunstwerk*. Aarau and Frankfurt: Sauerländer, 1983.

Szeemann, Harald, and Jean Clair. *Le macchine celibi/The Bachelor Machines*. Venice: Alfieri, 1975.

Tabaa, Yasser. "Towards an Interpretation of the Use of Water in Islamic Courtyards and Courtyard Gardens." *Journal of Garden History* 7, no. 3 (July/September 1987), 197–220.

Tafuri, Manfredo, and Francesco Dal Co. *Modern Architecture*. New York: Rizzoli, 1986.

Tebbel, John. *The Life and Good Times of William Randolph Hearst*. New York: Dutton, 1952.

Thévenot. *L'art de nager, démonstré par figures, avec des avis pour se baigner utilement*. Paris: T. Moette, 1696.

Thompson, Rudy. *A History of the Southern California Swimming Pool and Spa Industry*. Los Angeles: National Spa & Pool Institute, 1988.

Thümen. *Instruktion für den militärischen Schwimmunterricht nach der Pfuelschen Methode*. Berlin, 1861. (Source: Brockhaus 1903.)

Tissandier, Albert. *Six mois aux Etats-Unis; voyage d'un touriste dans l'Amérique du Nord suivi d'une excursion à Panama*. Paris: G. Masson, 1886 (?).

Touny, A. D., and Stefan Wenig. *Sport in Ancient Egypt*. Leipzig: Edition Leipzig, 1969.

Tunnard, Christopher. "The Adventure of Water." *Architectural Record* 86 (September 1939), 101.

Urry, J. *The Tourist Gaze*. London: Sage Press, 1991.

Vanderbilt, Cornelius, Jr. *Farewell to Fifth Avenue*. New York: Simon and Schuster, 1935.

Veblen, Thorstein. *The Theory of the Leisure Class*. 1899; Harmondsworth: Pelican Books, 1979.

Vigarello, Georges. *Le propre et le sale: hygiène du corps depuis le moyen âge*. Paris: Seuil, 1985.

Virilio, Paul. *L'art du moteur*. Paris: Galilée, 1993.

Vogt, Matthias. "Taking the Waters at Bayreuth." In Barry Millington and Stewart Spencer, eds., *Wagner in Performance*. New Haven: Yale University Press, 1993.

Ward, Susan. *Biltmore Estate*. Asheville, N.C.: Biltmore Estate, 1989.

Wasserman, Françoise. *Des hommes et des grenouilles*. Fresnes: Ecomusée, 1982.

Wasserman, Françoise. *La grenouille dans tous ses états*. Paris: Gallimard, 1990.

Webb, Michael. *Hollywood: Legend and Reality*. New York: Little, Brown, 1986.

Werner, Harold, and August P. Windolph. "The Public Bath." In five installments. *The Brickbuilder* 17, nos. 2–6 (February-May 1908).

Willemin, Véronique, and Gilles-Antoine Langlois. *Les 7 folies capitales*. Paris: Editions Alternatives, 1986.

Wilson, W. *Swimming, Diving, and How to Save Life*. Glasgow, 1876.

Wittfogel, Karl. *Oriental Despotism*. New Haven: Yale University Press, 1957.

Wynman, Nikolaus. *Colymbetes sive de Arte Natandi, dialogus & festivus & iucundus lectu per . . .* Ingolstadt: Augustae Vindelicorum, 1583.

Yegül, Fikret. *Baths and Bathing in Classical Antiquity.* Cambridge: MIT Press, 1992.

Yoch, James J. *Landscaping the American Dream: The Gardens and Film Sets of Florence Yoch, 1890–1972.* New York: Abrams/Sagapress, 1989.

Zettler, Curt Wilhelm. "Die Entwicklung der Hallenschwimmbäder im Deutschen Reich." *Deutsche Bauzeitung* 43/44 (1914), 414–424.

Zim, Larry, Mel Lerner, and Herbert Rolfes. *The World of Tomorrow.* New York: Main Street Press, 1988.

Zimmer, Dieter E. "Der Garten Eden." *Zeitmagazin* 45 (October 8, 1991), 56–66.